The St William Window at York Minster

Rediscovering a Miraculous Narrative

First published in Great Britain in 2026 by
Profile Editions, an imprint of Profile Books Ltd

29 Cloth Fair
London
EC1A 7JQ
www.profileeditions.com

10 9 8 7 6 5 4 3 2 1

Design: Eleanor Ridsdale Colussi
Project Management: Kim Harris
Art Direction: Caroline Clark

Printed and bound in Italy by L.E.G.O. S.p.A.

A CIP catalogue record for this book is available from the British Library.

ISBN 978 1 805225 607 HB
978 1 805225 614 PB

MIX
Paper | Supporting responsible forestry
FSC® C023419

Acknowledgements

Our greatest debt is to the conservators of the York Glaziers Trust, past and present, for sharing their insights into technical aspects of the St William Window, for their extraordinary skill and talent and for the pleasure of their continuing collaboration. It has been a great privilege to work with you on both the St William Window and the Great East Window, John Thornton's two great masterpieces.

Thanks are also due to fellow members of the St William Window Advisory Group, and in particular to the late Tom French and Professor Richard Marks for many stimulating discussions. In the 1990s we also benefitted greatly from conversations with research students at the University of York Ben Nilson and Janice Smith.

For their support and encouragement of this publication project, we thank Dr Helen Rawson, Director of Collections, Cultural Heritage and Learning at York Minster, and Neil Sanderson, until recently director of the York Minster Fund.

We also thank those friends and colleagues who have lent particular assistance in the preparation of this publication: Gillian Galloway, Dr Marie Groll, Sophie Gwynn, Dr Katie Harrison, Dr Stuart Harrison, Anna Milsom, Lydia Walter, Dr Christine Williamson, Susanna Wyse Jackson and Peter Young.

At Profile Books we acknowledge the enthusiastic support of Joel Burden, Caroline Clark, Kim Harris, Peter Jones and designer Eleanor Ridsdale Colussi, who have seen the book through to publication on the Feast of St William 2026, the 800th anniversary year of his papal canonisation.

We offer this book to our friend and colleague Richard Marks, Emeritus Professor of Stained Glass Studies at the University of York.

Professor Christopher Norton and Professor Sarah Brown, the Centre for Medieval Studies, University of York

Unless otherwise stated, all images and artwork are by the York Glaziers Trust, reproduced courtesy of the Chapter of York,.

5.3, 5.15 © Borthwick Institute for Archives, University of York
4.7, 4.9, 7.1 © British Library Board
3.14 © Christopher Norton
4.10, 7.10 © CRBMC Centre de Restauració de Béns Mobles de Catalunya
2.4 © Durham Cathedral
2.5, 3.2, 3.6 © Historic England Archive
4.11 © National Galleries of Scotland, D595A
4.3 © Oxford, Bodleian Library, Ms. Top. Yorks. C14, fol. 28r
2.2, 3.3, 3.5, 3.7. 3.8 © Stuart Harrison
5.7, 5.8, 5.10, 5.12 © Victoria and Albert Museum, London
2.7 © York Minster Archive
3.4, 3.20, 3.21, 7.9 © York Museums Trust

YORK MINSTER

THE YORK GLAZIERS TRUST
Over 50 Years of Excellence in Stained Glass Craft and Conservation

The St William Window at York Minster

Rediscovering a Miraculous Narrative

Christopher Norton
and Sarah Brown

PROFILE
EDITIONS

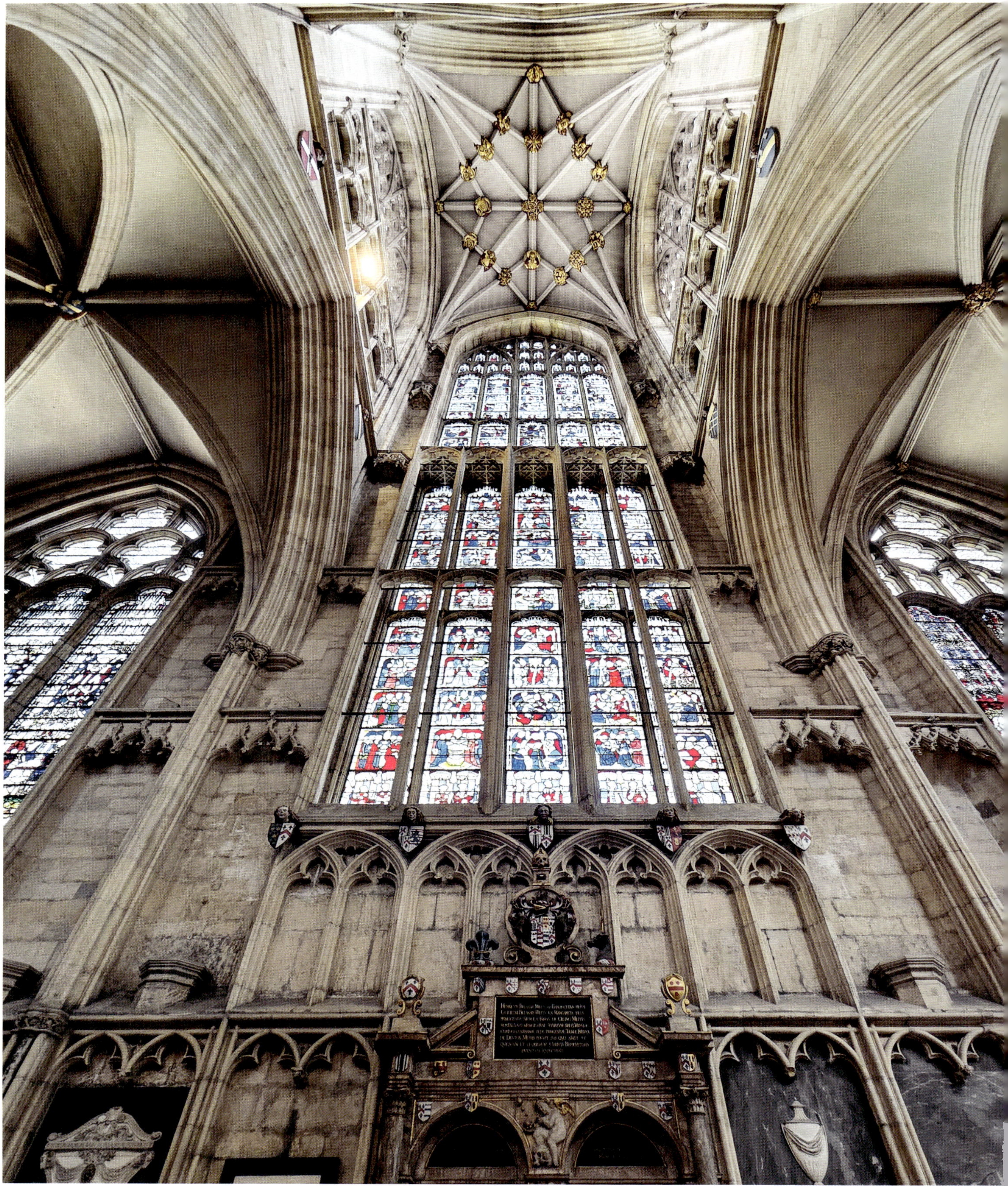

Contents

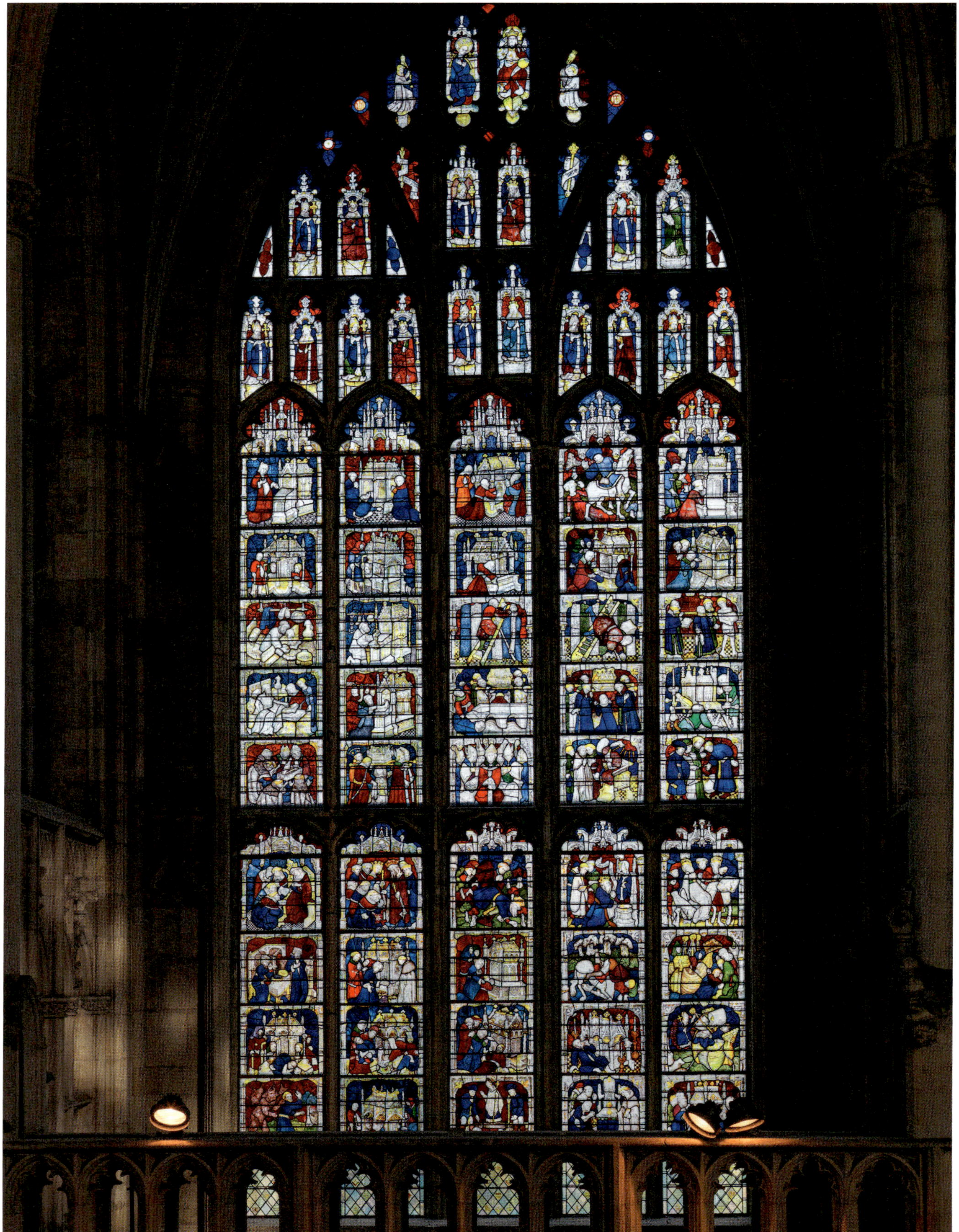

Chapter 1

Introducing the St William Window

The Great East Window of York Minster is an undisputed masterpiece of medieval stained glass. Created between 1405 and 1408 by John Thornton of Coventry, it is the largest, most ambitious and theologically most sophisticated window in existence. Its subject matter depicts nothing less than the entire history of the world, from the Creation to the Last Judgement, with the church in York in the bottom row, taking its place in the divine plan, while the tracery lights contain a vast assembly of the blessed in heaven. The brilliance of the designs is matched by the quality of their execution, placing Thornton in the top rank of stained-glass artists anywhere in Europe. The restoration of the window by the York Glaziers Trust between 2011 and 2017 attracted widespread interest, and the window is a highlight of a tour of York Minster for hundreds of thousands of tourists from around the world each year. What is not generally appreciated, however, is that the Minster possesses a second great masterpiece from the workshop of John Thornton, namely the St William Window; and that the restoration of the Great East Window would not have been possible without the restoration of the St William Window, which preceded it.

The St William Window was completed in about 1415. It was the gift of the Roos family of Helmsley, who are depicted in five donor panels in the bottom row (Fig. 4.6), and it contains 95 scenes of the life and miracles of St William, by some margin the largest cycle of the life and miracles of any saint. The window occupies a prominent position on the north side of the choir (Fig. 1.1), overlooking the site of the medieval high altar, where the principal relics of St William were housed. The equivalent window on the south side, devoted to the life of St Cuthbert (s7), dates from around 1440, but was almost certainly planned at an earlier date. The St William Window and the St Cuthbert Window are, as it were, the wings of a stained-glass triptych for the high altar (Fig. 1.2), whose centre-piece is formed by the Great East Window

Fig 1.1
The upper part of the St William Window, showing rows 14–25 and the tracery lights.

(Fig. 1.3), a unique arrangement in an English cathedral and a fitting climax to the centuries-old tradition of stained glass at the Minster.

By the 1990s, the St William Window was in a parlous condition. Centuries of exposure to the elements had left the glass cracked and corroded and it has also been disfigured by unsympathetic repairs and heavy leading. The lead matrix was failing and required total replacement. Furthermore, as a result of piecemeal repairs and well-meaning but misconceived interventions, the majority of the panels were no longer in their correct positions. The original narrative order had been lost, and the subject matter of many of the scenes was uncertain. In fact, in many respects the St William Window presented an even greater challenge than the Great East Window.

The window was restored by the York Glaziers Trust between 1997 and 2007. In view of the scale of the project, the Dean and Chapter set up the St William Window Advisory Group (SWWAG) to advise on the appropriate principles and techniques for restoring the window and offer support throughout the project. The membership of SWAGG included art historians specialising in medieval stained glass, and a key element of the restoration was the collaboration between the conservators of the York Glaziers Trust and the art historians, each bringing their own skills and perspectives to the decision-making process. Every panel was discussed by the group, and this collaborative process ensured a consistency of approach over what turned out to be a lengthy project. New techniques of repair were adopted, and the panels were releaded with a much lighter gauge of lead, resulting in the greatly increased legibility of each scene. Research carried out during the project revealed the original narrative order, and the panels were replaced in their correct sequence. The window was reinstalled with a system of internally ventilated environmental protective glazing (EPG), the first of the Minster's windows to be protected in this way, ensuring its preservation for generations to come.

The overall results were transformative, enabling the window to be seen more or less as John Thornton intended for the first time in centuries. And its impact did not end with the completion of the restoration. The success of the St William Window project gave the Chapter, the York Glaziers Trust and the art historians the confidence to embark on the even greater task of restoring the Great East Window. Some of the most important decisions of that project were based on the experience gained on the St William Window. Firstly, a new East Window Advisory Group (EWAG) was set up along the lines of SWAGG to embed the collaboration between the conservators and the art historians in the new project. Secondly, it was decided to relead the entire

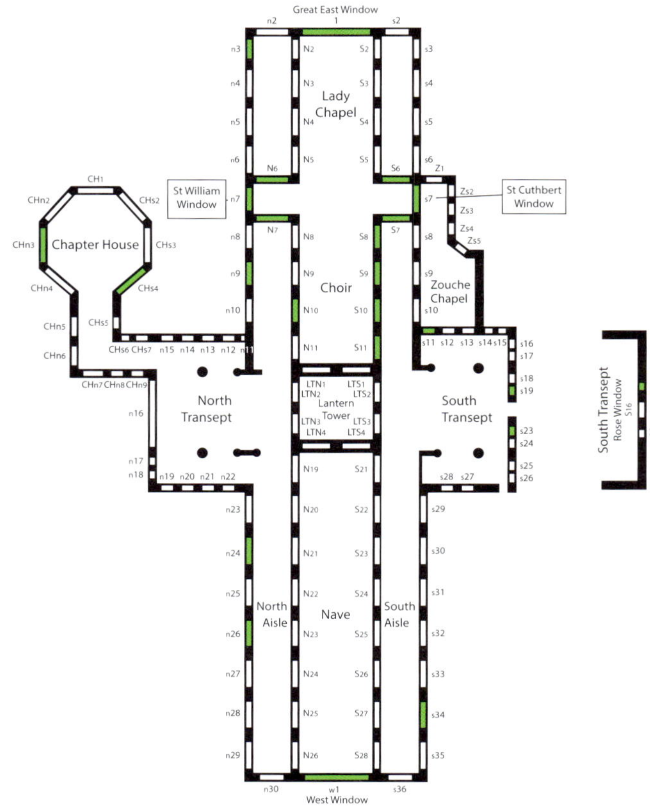

Fig 1.2
Location plan of the windows of York Minster. Those discussed in this book are highlighted.

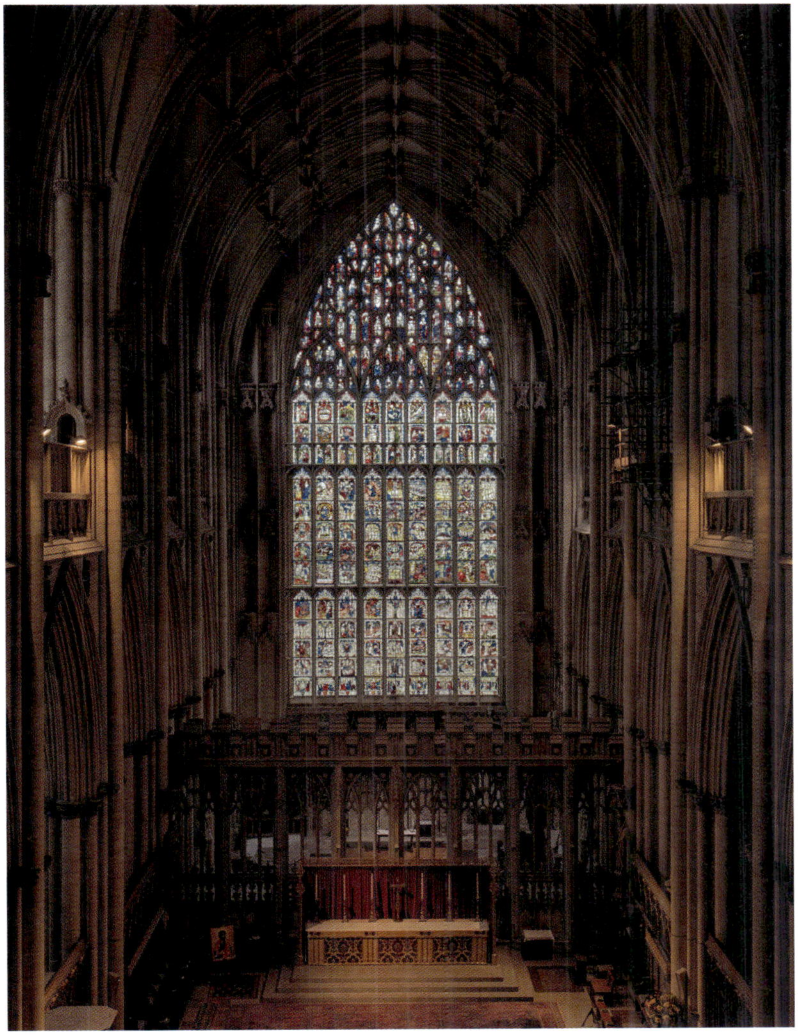

Fig 1.3
The view into the choir towards the Great East Window and the High Altar. This was pushed one bay east against the stone screen in the eighteenth century. The last shrine of St William once occupied this space.

window in order to restore as far as possible John Thornton's vision. Thirdly the experience of the St William Window had underlined the importance of preliminary research to inform the decision-making process. And crucially, the St William Window was reinstalled with EPG. This has now become standard for the Minster windows, and a long-term programme was launched after the completion of the Great East Window to provide EPG for all of the Minster's unprotected medieval windows. This has become all the more important in view of the increasingly strong winds and heavy rains consequent upon climate change. The restoration of the St William Window was therefore a key moment in the continuing story of the care of the Minster's glass.

The restoration was also a catalyst for historical and art historical research, which has been continued into the present. The initial research prompted by the work on the window has been deepened and broadened, and new avenues of investigation have opened up. The list of further reading is testament to the volume of work that has emerged over the last thirty years. Indeed, it is no exaggeration to say that the St William Window has been the spur to the recovery of the memory of York's long-neglected saint. The present book is therefore more than merely a record of the restoration. It is a distillation of recent work both on the window itself and on the wider context of William's life and cult in so far as they illuminate or are illuminated by Thornton's window.

The next chapter considers William's life, which occupies nearly half of the window, and it examines the long-running dispute over his archiepiscopate against the background of the often-violent dissensions that tore apart church and society during the civil war between King Stephen and the Empress Matilda. It concludes with his dramatic return to York and his death on 8 June 1154. Chapter 3 discusses the posthumous miracles that led to William being revered as a saint, and which occupy more than half of the window. We trace the development of his cult within the Minster, from the initial focus on his tomb at the east end of the nave, to the Translation of his relics in 1284, and the subsequent division of his bones between the tomb and the high altar. We consider the place of the window within the sacred topography of the Minster, its relationship to other images of St William, and the continuation of the cult until its suppression at the Reformation.

In Chapter 4 we turn our attention to the creation of the St William Window itself and the two individuals to whom we owe this great work. Beatrice de Roos, the matriarch of the Roos family, who appears by herself at the head of her family in panel 1e, has only recently emerged from the shadows. Not only was she the principal patron of the window and one of the most munificent lay donors to the Minster, but she was also one of the most important female patrons of the arts in this country during the Middle Ages. She deserves to stand alongside John Thornton.

The restoration of the Great East Window immediately after the St William Window provided an unrepeatable opportunity to examine the panels from his two great masterpieces in the studio – and the high-resolution digital colour photographs that are now available online mean we can continue their study in ways that were previously impossible. Comparison of the two highlights the similarities between the St William Window and the Great East Window, in spite of the difference in subject matter. It also helps define the essential qualities of John Thornton's artistic achievement, above all as a designer and supervisor of a workshop capable of conceiving and delivering projects of unparalleled scale and ambition.

The post-Reformation history of the window, the subject of Chapter 5, is largely a story of the loss of coherence of Thornton's vision as panels were damaged and displaced, and the loss of understanding as the story

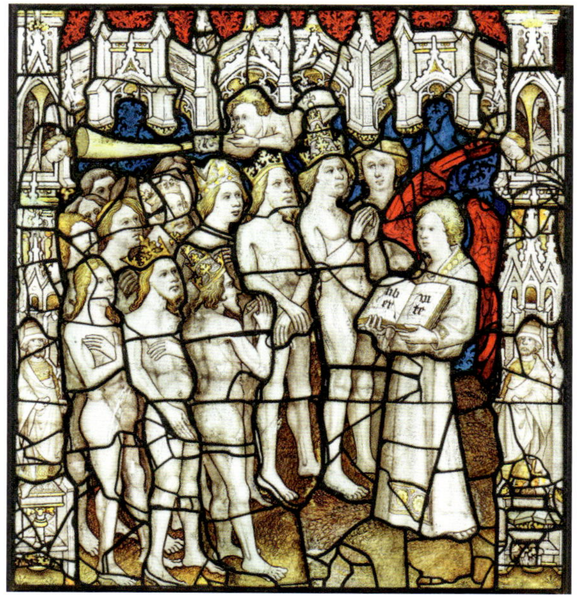

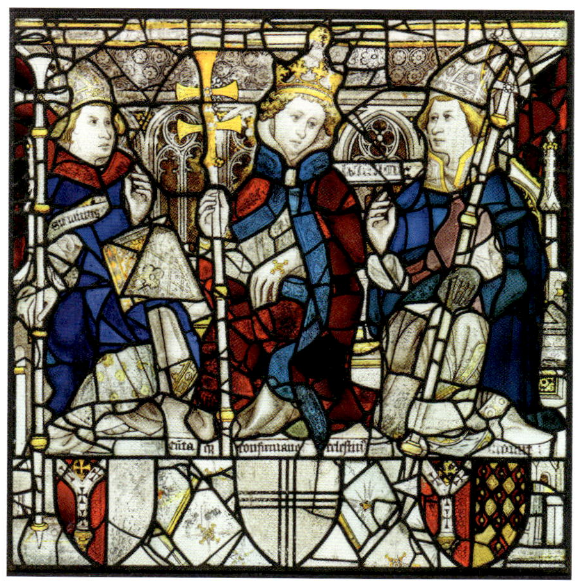

Fig. 1.4
The Great East Window, panel 2d, the Saved.

Fig 1.5
The Great East Window, panel 1j. St William is enthroned on the right-hand side, accompanied by an unidentified archbishop and Pope Celestine III.

Fig. 1.6
Diagram showing the St William Window panel numbering used throughout this book.

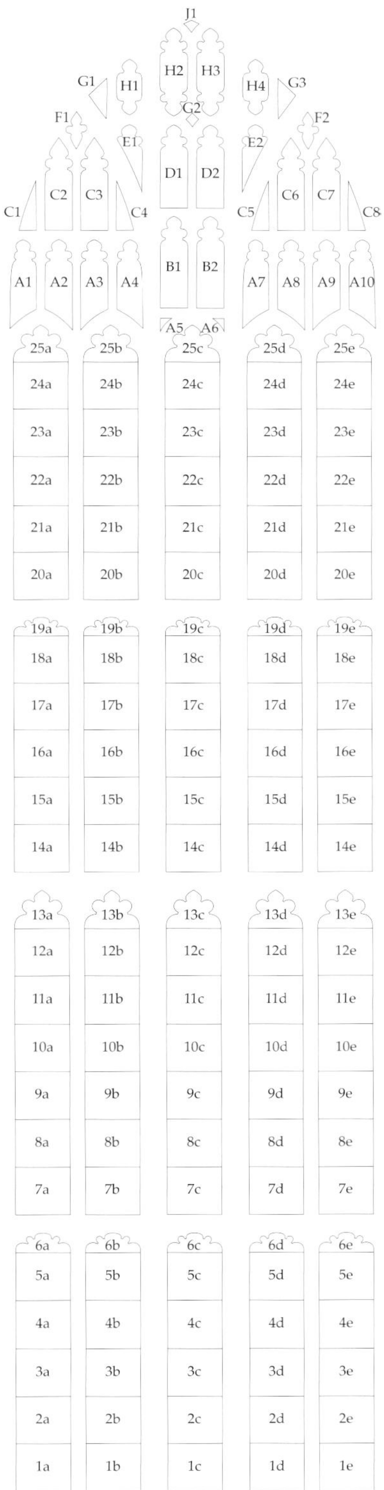

was forgotten. In the seventeenth-century antiquarians recorded precious heraldic evidence, which was subsequently destroyed, and the York antiquary James Torre has left us an extraordinary description of the window (printed in Appendix One) which testifies both to his obsessive eye for detail and his apparent total ignorance of the subject matter of the scenes he was looking at. Attempts to recover the meaning and order of the window began in the nineteenth century, notably through the work of Dr James Fowler, and the 1895 restoration by J. W. Knowles was crucial in preventing further decay and loss to the glass. At the same time, however, his well-meaning reordering of the panels (on the best evidence available at the time) left the window in a state of utter confusion, which lasted until the 1990s.

Chapter 6 describes the recent restoration carried out by the York Glaziers Trust, the challenges faced therein, and the solutions adopted. It discusses the system of EPG, and it summarises the evidence that led to the rediscovery of the original order of the panels and their reinstallation in their correct positions.

The recovery of the original narrative order, the identification of all the scenes and the dramatic increase in legibility of the entire window make it possible to assess John Thornton's achievement in the St William Window with greater clarity. The final chapter presents some of the insights into his creative process: collecting enough scenes of St William's life and miracles to fill a vast window; structuring the overall narrative; designing the individual scenes, and creating the panels with his team in the workshop. These achievements are testament to Thornton's brilliance.

All of the panels are illustrated and described in the Catalogue, and the Latin sources on which they are based are listed in Appendix Two. The scenes are populated with a multitude of people, of all ranks, clerical and lay, from popes and archbishops to acolytes and virgers, from kings and nobles to York citizens and disabled people: a broad conspectus of medieval society. In complete contrast, the Great East Window presents us with important biblical figures and dramatic Apocalypse scenes in a cosmic world-view of the place of mankind in the divine plan for creation. Yet different though they are, Thornton's two great masterpieces complement each other in providing us with windows into medieval life and medieval thought respectively. And there are thematic and visual connections between the two. In the Last Judgement panels at the end of the Apocalypse, the souls of the dead rise at the last trump to be judged by Christ. As well as ordinary souls, popes, kings and archbishops are among the saved (Fig. 1.4), while other kings and popes (but not archbishops!) are sent down to hell. Beneath the Last Judgement is a line of kings, popes and archbishops from the early history of the Minster, and the last figure in the row, at the bottom right-hand corner of the Great East Window, is St William himself (Fig. 1.5).

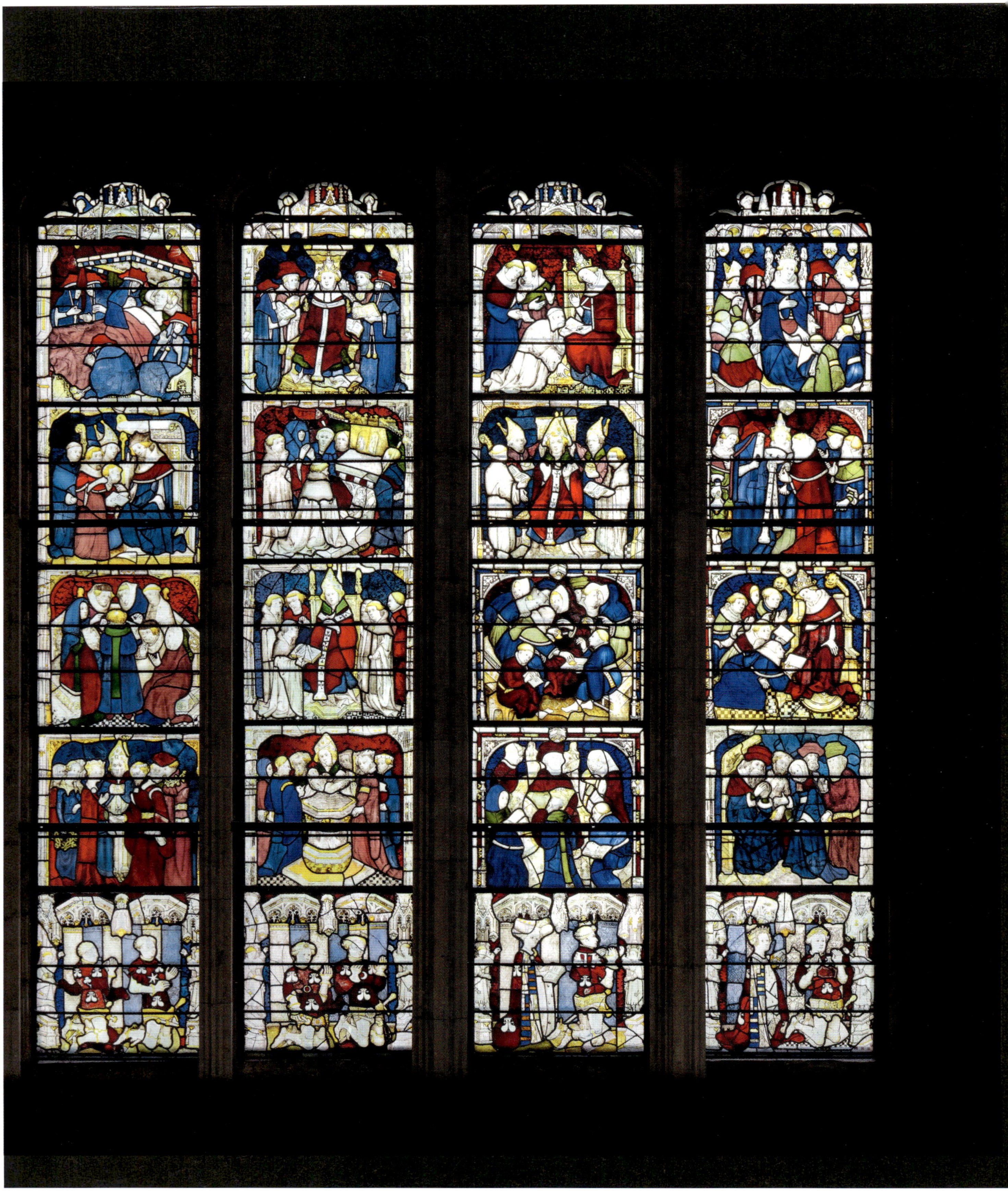

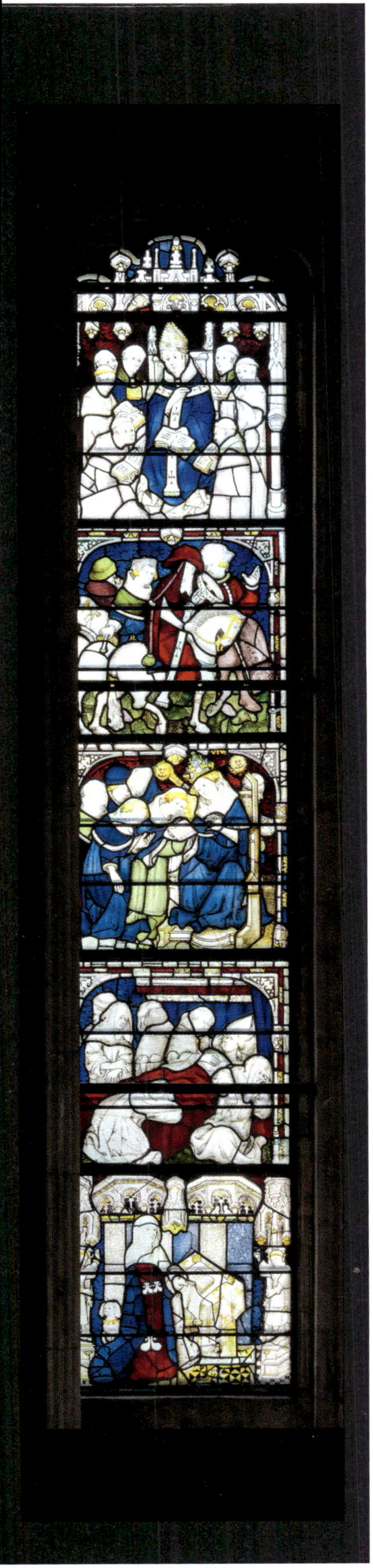

Chapter 2

The Life of William FitzHerbert

By the time John Thornton came to design the St William Window, practically nothing was known about William's early life and career prior to becoming archbishop (Fig. 2.1). The only available information came from the early thirteenth-century Latin *Life of St William*, which covered the first five decades of William's life in just a page and a half. As a result, Thornton devoted a mere five scenes (panels 2a-2e) to this whole period. We, however, are better informed, thanks to the resources of modern scholarship, and knowing more of William's earlier life helps us understand the turbulent story of his archiepiscopate, which occupies nearly half of the window.

Early Years

William FitzHerbert, born sometime in the 1080s, was the son of a senior royal official called Herbert the Chamberlain and his wife Emma (panels 2a–2b). The Latin *Life*, which was written about a century after they died, says that Herbert was a count, and that Emma was a sister of King Stephen. This is incorrect, but it does preserve a confused reminiscence of some genuine family connections. Herbert was not a count, but he is thought to have been the illegitimate son of Count Herbert, the last independent ruler of the county of Maine in France. When Count Herbert died young and without male heir in the early 1060s, the county of Maine passed into the hands of William the Conqueror, and so too, it seems, did the infant boy Herbert. In due course he entered royal service in England and rose to the top of the treasury of the Norman kings at Winchester. Emma was not the sister of King Stephen, but she was apparently the half-sister of King Stephen's father, Count Stephen of Blois, being the

Fig 2.1
The St William Window with the donor panels in row 1 and the life of St William rows 2–6.

illegitimate daughter of Count Stephen's father, Count Theobald of Blois. Emma was therefore an aunt of King Stephen, and William a cousin. This family connection was to prove extremely important for William after King Stephen came to the throne in 1135. Herbert the Chamberlain had the reputation of driving a hard bargain at the royal treasury during negotiations with impecunious churchmen, often to his own advantage. It was one such transaction that saw the young William appointed to a senior position in the church at York. His upbringing at Winchester (panel 2c, page 12) gave him early experience of court and church circles, and as a younger son he was destined for a career in the church. In 1108 the new archbishop of York, Archbishop Thomas II, found himself in urgent need of funds. It is no coincidence that, shortly afterwards, extensive archiepiscopal estates in the East Riding were made over to Herbert the Chamberlain and William took up office as treasurer of York Minster and archdeacon of the East Riding. Thus, the young southerner was parachuted into one of the most lucrative benefices in the English church, from which he could keep an eye on the newly acquired family estates in Yorkshire.

William held the combined office of Minster treasurer and archdeacon of the East Riding for more than thirty years. The *Life* gives no details, contenting itself with some conventional phrases about his character and his concern for the poor; Thornton passed over it with just a single panel in the window (2d, page 12). Other early sources, however, give us glimpses of William's activities – activities that anticipate and help make sense of the disputes concerning his archiepiscopate.

The early years of Archbishop Thurstan (1114–40) were dominated by a long-drawn-out dispute over the archbishop of Canterbury's claim to primacy over York – a claim that Thurstan doggedly resisted. Both Henry I and the pope were drawn into the affair, and William, with his contacts at court, was well placed to promote York's cause. He can be traced on missions to the king in Normandy and to the pope in Rome, and he probably accompanied Thurstan into exile in France in 1119–20, part of which was spent in the company of the pope who was in France at the time. In the end, York was vindicated, and William was probably a prime source for the account of the affair in Hugh the Chanter's *History of the Church of York*, written in 1127–8. The primacy dispute gave him experience of international ecclesiastical politics, which must have stood him in good stead during the dispute that engulfed his own archiepiscopacy many years later.

In the midst of this public dispute, William was hit by private tragedy. In 1119 Herbert the Chamberlain was implicated in a plot to assassinate Henry I. The plot failed, and Herbert suffered the consequences: he was blinded and castrated. By the standards of the day, this was lenient treatment; execution and forfeiture of estates would have been the norm, resulting in the disgrace and impoverishment of the whole family. If they escaped this fate, retaining their estates in Yorkshire and elsewhere, it was perhaps because Herbert the Chamberlain's daughter-in-law (the wife of William's elder brother) was Henry I's resident mistress at Winchester. She was also the mother of several of Henry's illegitimate children, one of whom was married to the king of Scotland. The personal and the political were closely intertwined. The effect on William himself can only be imagined, but it is a curious irony that his father's punishment anticipated the fate of an unjustly accused man called Ralph who was the beneficiary of St William's most famous posthumous miracle a century later (panels 12a–12e).

His father's disgrace put paid to any hopes William may have entertained of a bishopric, since the choice of bishops was controlled by the king. For the rest of the 1120s and 1130s, so far as we know, William withdrew

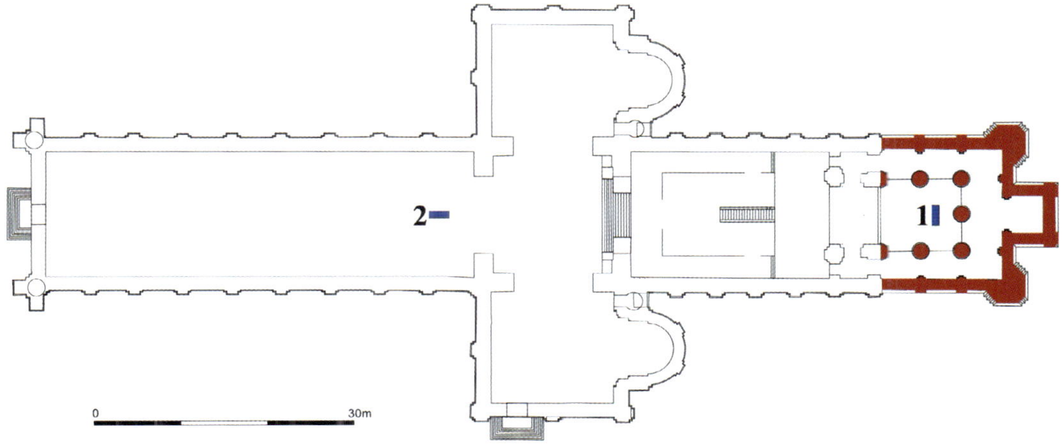

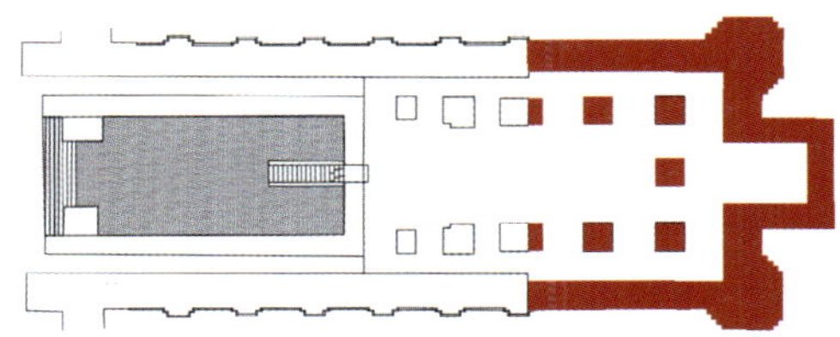

Fig. 2.2
Plan of York Minster in 1155 showing the eleventh-century cathedral of Archbishop Thomas of Bayeux and (in brown) the *c.*1130 extension of Archbishop Thurstan, with the location of the High Altar (1) and the tomb of St William (2).

from the national and international stage and focused on the Minster and the diocese. He was involved in two of Archbishop Thurstan's major initiatives. As treasurer, William was responsible for the Minster's finances, including work on the building. Thomas of Bayeux, the first Norman archbishop (1070–1100), had replaced the old Anglo-Saxon cathedral with a new building. In typical Norman fashion, it was conceived on a huge scale, but its design was unique. It had an exceptionally wide, aisleless nave, square transepts to match, and an enormous central tower. The east end was unusually long, and on two levels: a crypt below, and an upper level containing the choir stalls and the high altar, which stood at the entrance to a large eastern apse and was flanked by towers. Recent research has revealed a long-forgotten extension dating to the time of Archbishop Thurstan. The eastern apse was demolished and a new two-storey, aisled extension constructed (Fig. 2.2). This had space for a number of altars, including a central Lady Chapel at crypt level. This would have housed the exquisite, though sadly mutilated, sculpture of the Virgin and Child (Fig. 2.3), which dates to this period. The new extension, which went up just across the way from the Treasurer's House, was probably consecrated during the week of Pentecost, 1137, near the end of Thurstan's archiepiscopate. The week between Pentecost and Trinity Sunday was traditionally a time when parishioners from around the diocese came to the Minster. It was therefore an appropriate time for a public celebration, as William himself recognised when he was archbishop. As Minster treasurer William was responsible for the finances of work on the building. To what extent he was also personally involved in the design of Thurstan's extension and the commissioning of the works of art that adorned it can never be known, but he certainly had the opportunity, if he had the inclination. Thurstan's extension did not long outlast William himself, but its destruction was part of William's story, as we shall see, and its design influenced the later east end, which replaced it.

In 1132 William was involved in a notorious incident that was to have profound repercussions for him when he became archbishop. In 1131 some monks were sent by Bernard of Clairvaux (St Bernard) to found a Cistercian monastery at Rievaulx. The Cistercians were a reformed order of Benedictine monks who sought remote locations where they could live out a strict interpretation of the Rule of St Benedict in poverty and austerity, away from the cares and distractions of the outside world. The arrival of the Rievaulx monks caused some soul-searching among the monks of St Mary's Abbey, York, who followed a traditional Benedictine way of life just outside the city walls. A group of them put forward wide-ranging proposals for reform, but these were rejected by the majority of the monks and by the abbot, who also refused to let the reformers go, as they included some of the most able members of the community. The reformers, for their part, had sworn obedience to the abbot, yet they could no longer accept his views. With no resolution in sight, in October 1132 Archbishop Thurstan went to St Mary's Abbey for a formal visitation, accompanied by William and other senior clergy and monks from the diocese. However, when he and his retinue entered the Chapter House, they were first heckled and then assaulted by some of the traditionalist monks, and they were forced to retreat, taking with them thirteen of the reformist monks. A letter to the archbishop of Canterbury written by Thurstan immediately afterwards gives a remarkable first-hand account of the incident. The affair was a national scandal and took on an international aspect as Bernard of Clairvaux

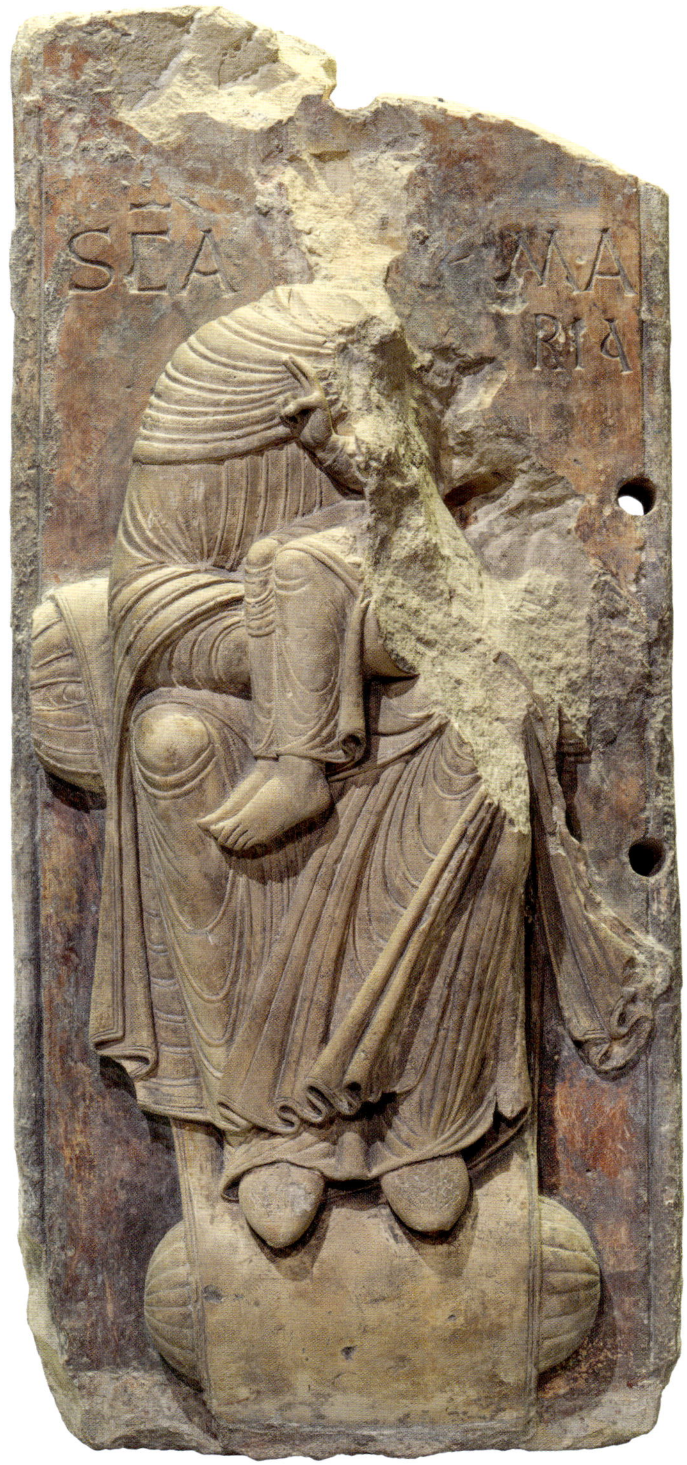

weighed in with characteristic forcefulness on behalf of the reformers. At the end of December, since compromise was impossible, Thurstan settled the thirteen reformist monks in the valley of the Skell near Ripon, and a few months later Fountains Abbey was accepted into the Cistercian Order as a daughter house of Clairvaux. William's views on the episode are not recorded, though it seems likely that his sympathies lay with the traditionalist party. What is clear is that the profound differences of opinion and the deep passions overflowing into violence were a premonition of much worse things to come. A decade later, during the dispute over the archbishopric, William's most implacable opponents were to be Bernard of Clairvaux and the monks of Fountains, some of whom had been present with William on the fateful day at St Mary's Abbey in October 1132.

Archbishop William

The death of Archbishop Thurstan in February 1140 (panel 2e) plunged the church of York into the bitterest and most protracted dispute in its long history. William's election as archbishop split the cathedral Chapter and the wider church in the diocese into irreconcilable factions. The dispute was played out in an atmosphere of hostility and violence fostered by the civil war between King Stephen and the Empress Matilda, which was convulsing the country at the time. And it rapidly acquired an international element through the involvement of Bernard of Clairvaux and a succession of popes in Rome, whose unusually rapid turnover introduced an element of unpredictability beyond the control of the protagonists in England. The complicated sequence of events was documented in the mid twelfth-century *Chronicle* of John of Hexham, which was Thornton's primary source in the design of rows 3–5 of the window.

After nearly a year of uncertainty, William was elected archbishop by a majority of the Chapter in January 1141 (panels 3a–3b). He immediately took himself off to Lincoln to get his election ratified by his cousin, King Stephen. His opponents, however, refused to accept the result and appealed against it on the grounds of interference in the election on behalf of the king by the earl of York, William of Aumale, who was King Stephen's most powerful ally in Yorkshire (panel 3c). William's opponents included two of his fellow archdeacons, Osbert of Bayeux and Walter of London, and the heads of several Yorkshire monasteries, including the abbots of Rievaulx and Fountains. The papal legate in England at the time was the bishop of Winchester, Henry of Blois, who was the brother of the king and thus also a cousin of William's. He referred the matter to Pope Innocent II. So, William and a delegation of his opponents (including Aelred, abbot of Rievaulx) travelled to Rome to put their respective cases to the pope. Unwilling to make an immediate decision, Innocent ordered both parties to return the following spring, at which point he announced his decision (panels 3d–3e, conflating the

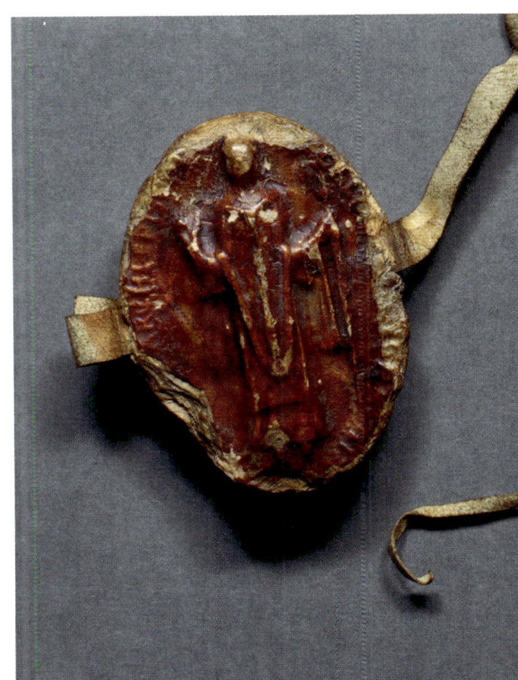

Fig. 2.3
The damaged twelfth-century statue of the Virgin and Child, made to adorn the Lady Chapel in the central bay of the crypt.

Fig. 2.4
The seal of Archbishop William FitzHerbert, Durham Cathedral Muniments 4.1 Archiep. 7. This is the only example of the seal of St William to have survived.

two visits). He referred the matter back to Henry of Blois, instructing him to consecrate William, on condition that the dean of York, or other suitable persons, should swear on oath that the election had not been swayed by interference from the king. In the interim, the dean of York had himself been elected bishop of Durham, and he did not appear, but Henry of Blois accepted oaths from three other senior Yorkshire clerics, and he consecrated William archbishop (Fig. 2.4) at Winchester on 26 September 1143 (panels 4a–4c). On the very same day in Rome, a new pope was elected to succeed Innocent II, who had died two days earlier. But the new pope only lived for a few months, to be succeeded in his turn by Lucius II. Pope Lucius sent Cardinal Hincmar to England with a pallium for William (panels 4d–4e). The pallium was a thin band of white cloth, which went round the shoulders (Fig. 2.5), with long strips hanging vertically down in front and behind. It was worn by archbishops over their other vestments, to which it was fastened by cross-headed pins, as can be seen in some of the scenes in the window, such as panels 5e and 9e. The grant of the pallium was the final seal of approval by the pope. Once vested with it, William would have been immune from further appeals. This should have been the end of the matter, but a chance event at Rome, which no one could possibly have foreseen, changed the course of affairs at York. Pope Lucius was in dispute with the citizens of Rome about papal rule of the city. One day, he was hit on the head by a rock while attempting to deal with some protestors ensconced on the Capitol, and he died in February 1145 (panel 5a). The new pope, hurriedly elected on the day that Lucius died, was Eugenius III, a Cistercian abbot who had been a monk at Clairvaux under Bernard (panel 5b). When Cardinal Hincmar heard the news, he returned to Rome without handing over the pallium to William. Bernard, meanwhile, had sent another Clairvaux monk, the Englishman Henry

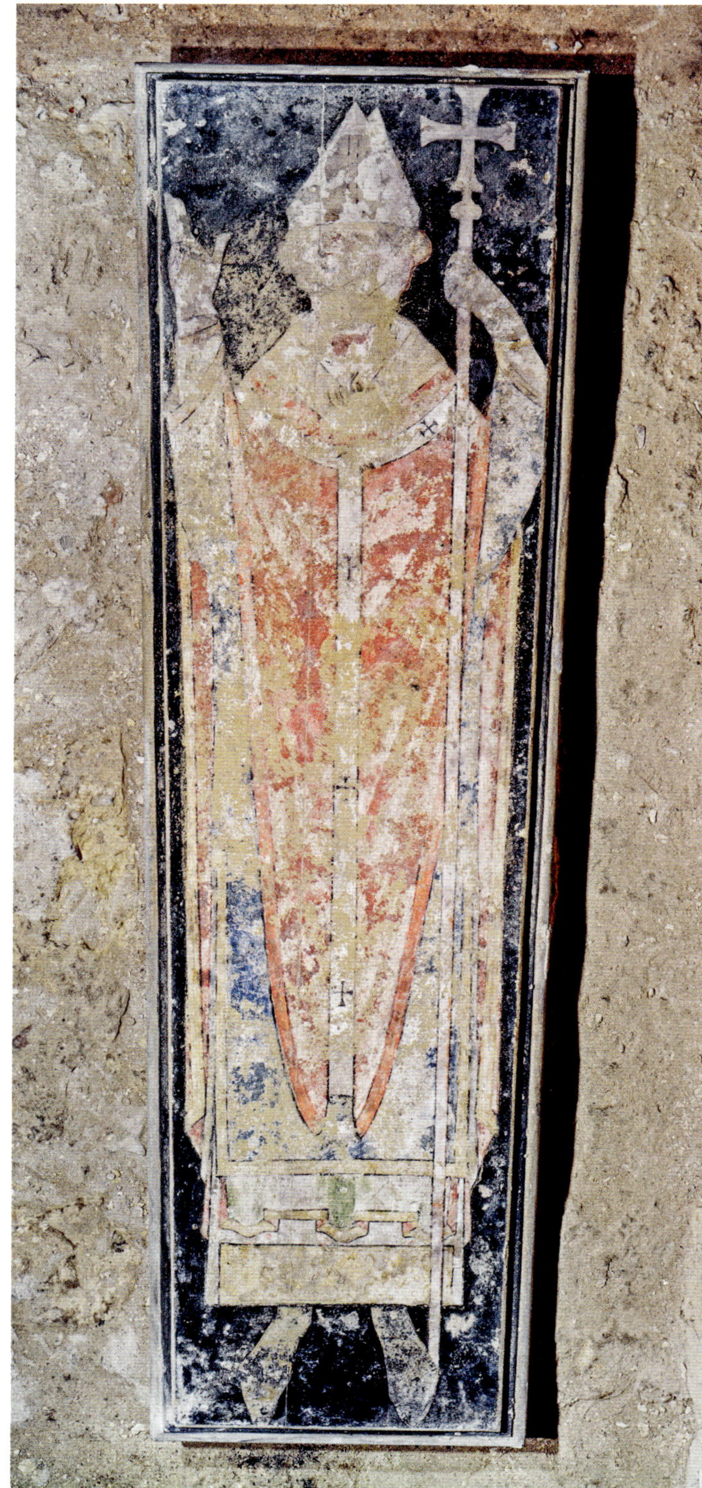

Fig. 2.5
The pallium, the strip of linen worn around the shoulders, as shown on the painted coffin lid of Archbishop Walter de Grey (d.1255).

Murdac, to be abbot of Fountains. William was now faced with a formidable trio of Cistercian opponents. Bernard persuaded Pope Eugenius to re-open the case; Eugenius summoned William back to Rome and then deposed him (panels 5c–5d), and in 1147 none other than Henry Murdac was elected to the vacant see at York. The Cistercian triumph was complete. Thornton concluded the bottom section of the window with a scene of Murdac as archbishop teaching his Cistercian monks (panel 5e).

Rows 3–5 of the window are populated by a cast of monks and canons, bishops and archbishops, cardinals and popes. They give the impression that the dispute was a purely ecclesiastical one, fought out in church circles with due decorum. In reality, however, powerful secular interests were involved, and the fighting was sometimes physical, even intensely violent. Previous archbishops had been chosen by William the Conqueror and his successors, but by 1140 an increasingly assertive reformist papacy was promoting the ideal of election by the cathedral Chapter, free of any secular interference, an ideal that chimed with the reforming instincts of the Cistercians. Yet the archbishop was a prominent member of the court and a senior royal counsellor; he held extensive estates from the king, and he had duties and responsibilities in the temporal sphere that he was expected to carry out in support of royal policy. Archbishop Thurstan, for instance, had gone out in his old age to support the English forces against the Scots at the Battle of the Standard in 1138. The choice of archbishop therefore could not fail to be of interest to the king. The matter was further complicated by the fact that there were two claimants to the throne. Henry I had died in 1135 leaving numerous illegitimate children but no male heir. He had tried to arrange the succession in favour of his daughter, the Empress Matilda. In the event it was King Stephen who succeeded to the throne, but Matilda and her supporters refused to recognise him, and a bitter civil war broke out. A compliant archbishop of York was a key prize for both sides. Furthermore, with the breakdown of royal authority, and with Stephen and Matilda engaged further south, the Yorkshire barons on both sides took every opportunity to advance their own interests, not hesitating to fight over estates and on occasion attacking monasteries. They too had their own interests in securing a sympathetic archbishop, and they expected the monasteries of which they were founders or patrons to rally to their cause. A broad geographical division became apparent. York and the East Riding were largely held by William's supporters, notably William of Aumale, the earl of York, as well as William's own family with their East Riding estates. By contrast, William's and King Stephen's opponents were stronger in the north and west of the county. It is no coincidence that Henry Murdac's election as archbishop, after William had been deposed, was held, uniquely, at Richmond, well away from York and the East Riding, in an area controlled by Matilda's supporters.

So, although ecclesiastical channels and procedures were the route taken by William's opponents to unseat him, there were powerful secular forces behind the affair. And in a period of civil unrest and a breakdown of law and order, when, it was said, God and his angels slept, it is perhaps not surprising to learn of violent incidents in the course of the dispute. In 1141, when William went to Lincoln to gain the assent of King Stephen to his election, his opponents despatched their own representative to the king, but he was waylaid en route and kidnapped to stop him presenting his case. In 1143, after his consecration, William himself was assaulted inside Ripon Minster by Alan, earl of Richmond, and took refuge at the shrine of St Wilfrid. After William had left for Rome, in the winter of 1146–7, a gang of his supporters attacked Fountains Abbey, set fire to the buildings and hunted for Henry Murdac, who hid in the church. Layers of ash, which have turned up in excavation, bear witness to the extent of the fire. Sometime later, Archdeacon Walter of London was beaten up and mutilated by some of William's family and he then passes out of the historical record.

These assaults cannot be laid at William's door. Indeed, the whole affair was not really about William personally – though there clearly were personal animosities involved, possibly going back to the affair of St Mary's Abbey in 1132. Rather, it was about what William represented, in the eyes of churchmen of reformist views and political opponents of King Stephen in the civil war – a toxic combination of ecclesiastical and secular motives all focused on the office of archbishop. It was not just William: whoever had been elected, from either party, would have been engulfed in the maelstrom. That this was so is evident from the fact that bitter disagreements continued through the years of Henry Murdac's archiepiscopate (1147–53), after William had withdrawn from the fray. But that is not part of William's story and is not depicted in the window.

When he had concluded his business with Pope Eugenius in Rome, William travelled on down to the Norman kingdom of Sicily, where a Yorkshireman, Robert of Selby, was chancellor to King Roger. An ivory casket of Siculo-Arabic manufacture preserved at the Minster (Fig. 2.6) may have been acquired by William at this time. On his return to England, he withdrew to Winchester, the city of his youth, where he was welcomed by Henry of Blois (panel 7a). He spent the next six years in retirement at Winchester (panel 7b), taking no further part in the disputes at York until another unexpected turn of fate thrust him once more into the limelight.

The last year of William's life is more fully documented in the thirteenth-century *Life* and other sources than any previous period, and it occupies eighteen panels in the window, almost as many as the whole of the rest of his life (panels 7c–10e). In the early autumn of 1153, William's three Cistercian opponents – Pope Eugenius, Bernard of Clairvaux and Archbishop Henry Murdac – all died within a few weeks of each other (panel 7c). News of Murdac's death reached Winchester at a critical juncture. Under the auspices of Henry of Blois and the archbishop of Canterbury, negotiations were under way to put an end to the civil war. A settlement was agreed at Winchester in November, whereby King Stephen would remain on the throne until he died and would then be succeeded by the Empress Matilda's son, the future Henry II. The country was weary of war, and there was no appetite for further dissension at York. William was brought out of retirement to fill the vacancy and was packed off to Rome to secure papal approval (panels 7d–8a) – a gruelling winter journey for a man of about seventy. The new pope, Anastasius IV, approved the arrangement and gave William, at last, his pallium (panel 8b). William returned to England (panel 8c) and reached Winchester again in time for Easter,

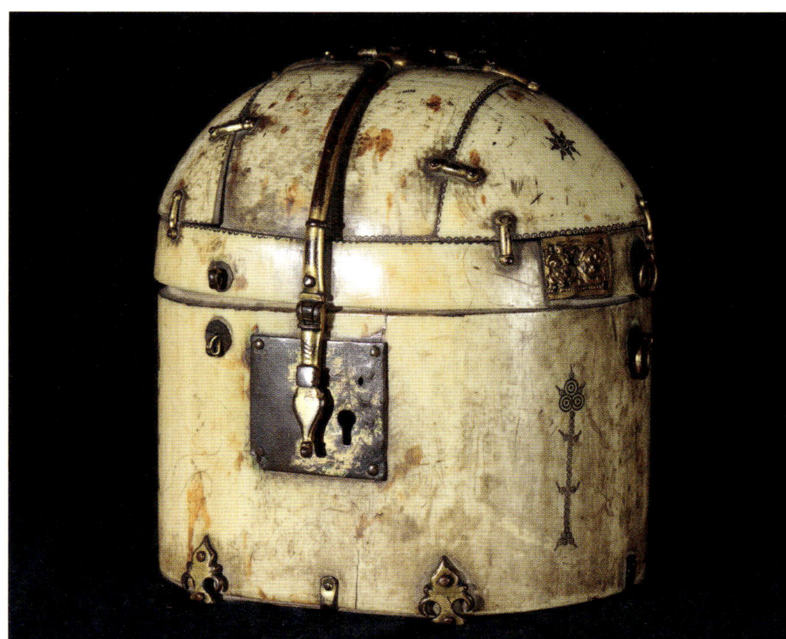

Fig. 2.6
Siculo-Arabic casket at York Minster.

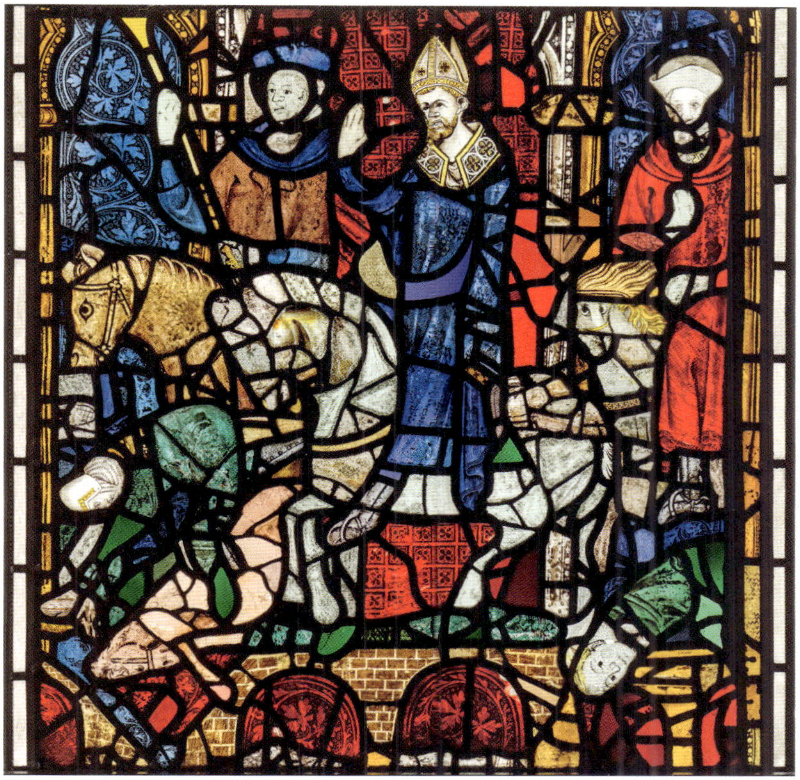

Fig. 2.7
The Ouse Bridge Miracle, window s34. The original nave location of this scene is uncertain.

stopping off en route at Canterbury, where he announced that his successor would be Roger of Pont l'Evêque, a rising star in the household of the archbishop of Canterbury alongside Thomas Becket (panels 8d–8e).

After just a few days' rest at Winchester, William headed north again. He did a tour of the diocese (panel 9a), including a visit to Fountains Abbey to make peace with the Cistercian community there. He arrived back at York on Sunday, 9 May, having been on the road almost continuously for five months or more. He was greeted at Micklegate Bar by civic dignitaries (panel 9b). Processing down Micklegate, he crossed Ouse Bridge. The bridge gave way behind him beneath the press of people; William turned and gave a blessing, and no one was hurt (panel 9c). This was the incident subsequently celebrated as the miracle of Ouse Bridge (Fig. 2.7). He was greeted at the entrance to the Minster by the Minster clergy and then proceeded to take his place once more in his cathedral (panels 9d–9e).

The next few weeks were spent preparing for a great celebration, which took place on Trinity Sunday, 30 May, to take advantage of the crowds of people who would be in York during the week of Pentecost. William celebrated mass at the high altar of the Minster, for the first time wearing his pallium (panel 10a). He and his guests then went across to the archbishop's palace for a celebratory feast. William gave orders for the guests to be served (panel 10b) but felt too ill to join them. He retired to his chamber and took to his bed (panel 10c). Feeling his end approaching, he bade farewell to his household, and he died on 8 June 1154 (panels 10d–10e).

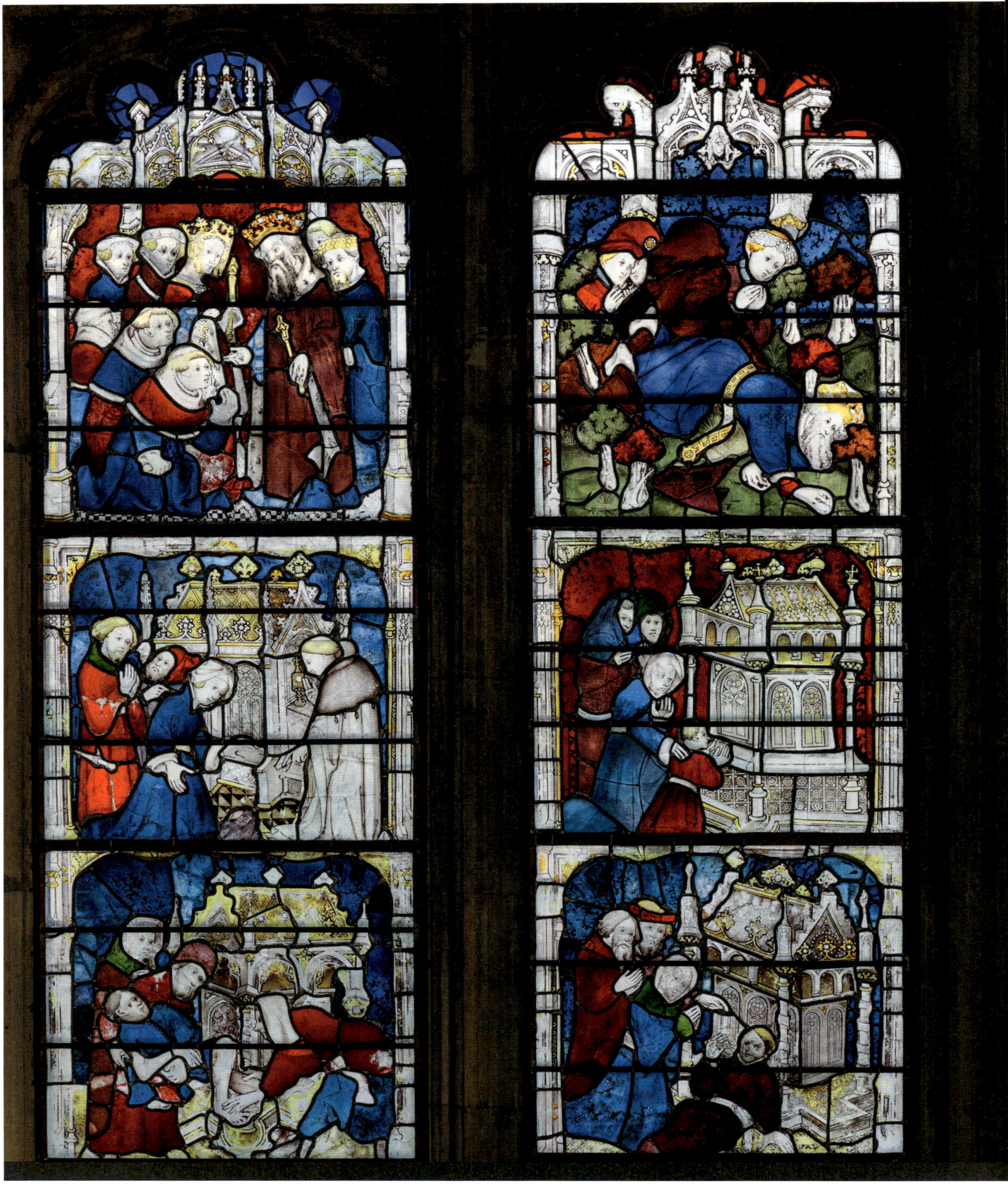

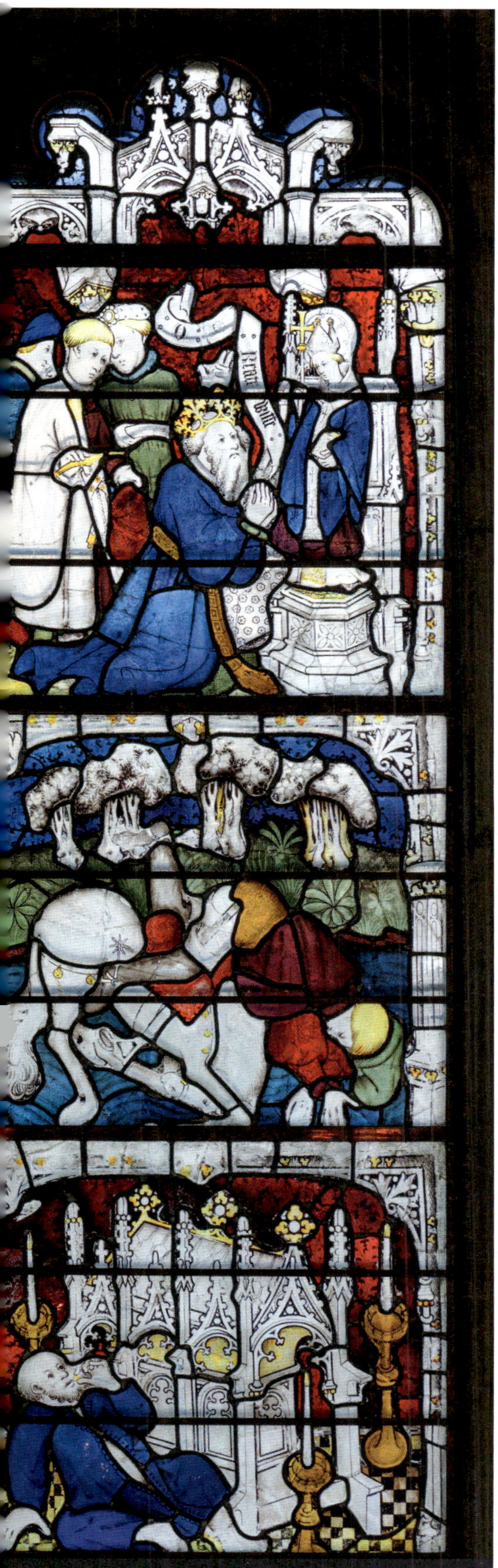

Chapter 3

The Cult of Saint William

To the modern mind, and perhaps many of his contemporaries as well, there was little in the external course of William's life to qualify him for sainthood. And unlike his fellow saint (and persistent opponent) Bernard of Clairvaux, William left no letters or other writings to reveal something of the inner man. We do not even know what he thought of the archbishopric – whether as a prize to be grasped, or a burden to be endured. In fact, it was not his life, but rather events that took place after his death, that led to him being revered as a saint.

In the immediate aftermath of his death, rumours circulated that William had been poisoned. His long-time rival, Archdeacon Osbert of Bayeux, was suspected of putting poison in the chalice during the Mass on Trinity Sunday. Formal proceedings were begun against him, and they dragged on for some years without, it seems, reaching any conclusion. Suspicions remained, and some twelfth-century writers reported the poisoning as fact – though others were less certain. A surviving Latin hymn (of uncertain date) states that William was poisoned and describes him as a martyr. This was not, however, part of the official cult. The alleged poisoning is not mentioned in the thirteenth-century *Life*, or in the canonisation documents, or in the authorised liturgical texts in honour of St William. Nor does it feature in the St William Window. Instead, the focus in all these sources is on the tomb.

William was laid to rest in a monolithic Roman sarcophagus (Fig. 3.2), presumably salvaged from one of the Roman cemeteries around York (panel 11a). It was placed in a position of honour at the east end of the nave on the central axis of the Minster, one bay west of the crossing. An altar of the Holy Cross probably stood just to the east. The bottom 25cm or so were set into the ground, but the greater part of it stood proud of

Fig. 3.1
The St William Window, panels 15–19 b–d, depicting miracles of the saint.

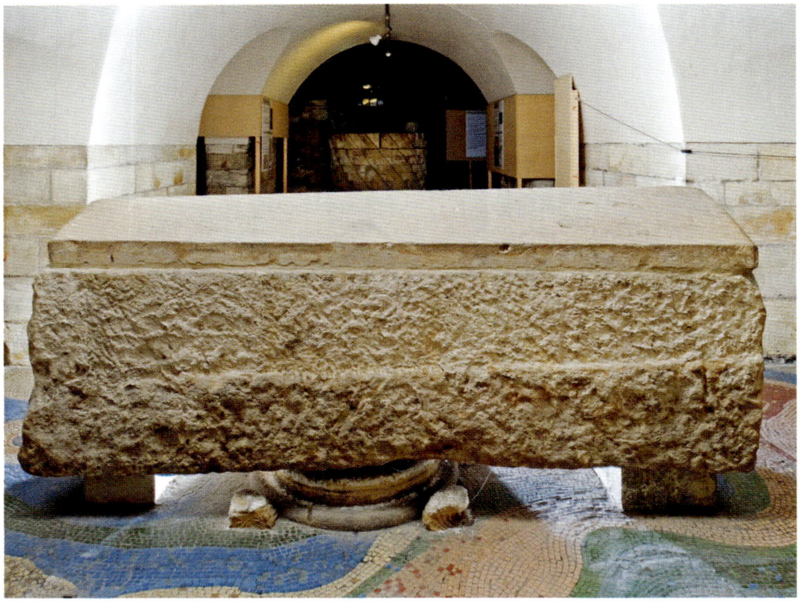

Fig. 3.2
The Roman sarcophagus in which St William was buried in 1154 at the east end of the nave. The lid needed to be replaced after the fire depicted in panel 11b.

the floor. The roughly tooled sides were finished with a layer of plaster, and it was covered with a stone lid. The position and form of the tomb were key factors in the development of the cult.

Saint William

Sometime in the 1150s – the exact date is uncertain – a devastating fire broke out in the Minster. Burning timbers from the roof crashed down onto William's tomb. The lid was broken, but the body and the vestments inside were not harmed (panel 11b). This largely forgotten fire is recorded only in the thirteenth-century *Life*, but fire-reddened stones in a strip of *in situ* masonry from the north-west corner of the eleventh-century crossing tower attest to the severity of the blaze. As was the case with the 1984 south transept fire, the roof was destroyed without the masonry beneath being seriously damaged. The nave, transepts and crossing tower were repaired and brought back into use, but Archbishop Roger of Pont l'Evêque (1154–81) decided to rebuild the eastern arm (Fig. 3.3). The eleventh-century choir and Archbishop Thurstan's eastern extension were demolished and replaced by a magnificent aisled eastern arm raised above a large, ornate crypt. When William's sarcophagus was rediscovered in about 1970 during work on the foundations of the central tower, it was

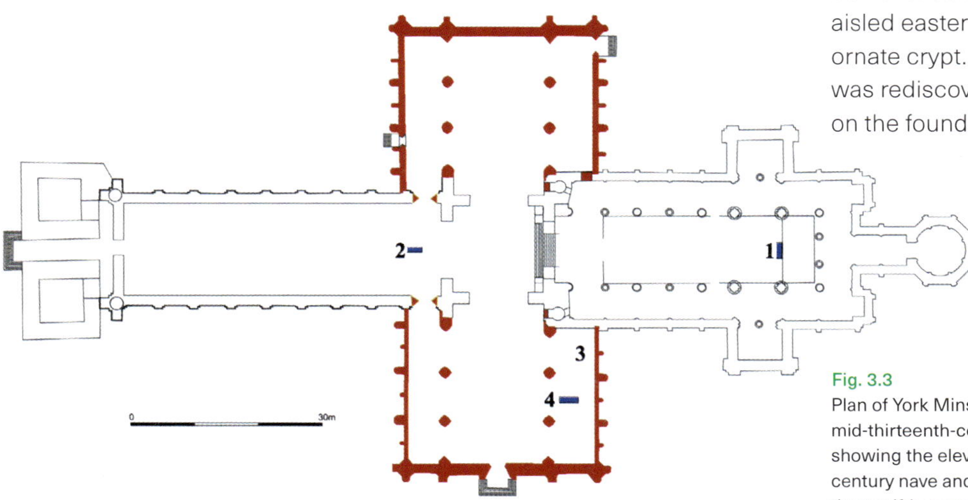

Fig. 3.3
Plan of York Minster in the mid-thirteenth-century, showing the eleventh-century nave and crossing, the twelfth-century choir of Archbishop Roger, the late-twelfth-century western towers and (in brown) the early-thirteenth-century transepts.

1. The High Altar
2. The tomb of St William
3. St William's chapel
4. St Michael's chapel and tomb of Archbishop Walter de Grey.

decided to relocate it to the crypt, where it now lies, appropriately enough, next to the massive columns of Archbishop Roger's crypt. The monolithic lid is presumably the replacement for the one destroyed in the 1150s fire.

Archbishop Roger lived to see the completion of the new choir in the 1170s and the start of the cult of St William. During the week of Pentecost 1177, when the city was once again crowded with visitors, there was an outbreak of healing miracles at William's tomb. In the course of one week, more than thirty miracles were recorded. Miracles were a sign of sanctity, and from then on William was revered as a saint. In 1170 Thomas Becket had been murdered in Canterbury Cathedral, and he had been recognised as a saint almost immediately. Now York had a new archiepiscopal saint of its own.

The 1177 miracles were recorded in a Latin text known as the *Miracula*, which was displayed on a board in the Minster as evidence of William's healing power. The board is lost, but fortunately the text was transcribed in the seventeenth century before the board disappeared. The text lists the 1177 miracles in order, stating briefly the nature of the illness or affliction that was healed and, in many cases, the name and/or place of origin of the person healed. Other miracles were added to the text in subsequent decades. In the 1220s many of these early miracle stories were incorporated into the Latin *Life*, where they are recounted in a more florid, literary style, without the names or origins of the individuals concerned. Thornton drew on these early miracles for most of the scenes in rows 11–17. They all concern lay people, so the cast of characters here is very different from the predominantly ecclesiastical line-up in the lower section of the window. Blindness, hydropsy, leprosy and other skin complaints, curvature of the spine, limb injuries – these are some of the ailments cured. Most of the miracles occupy just one or two panels, but the story of Ralph and Besing occupies a whole row (panels

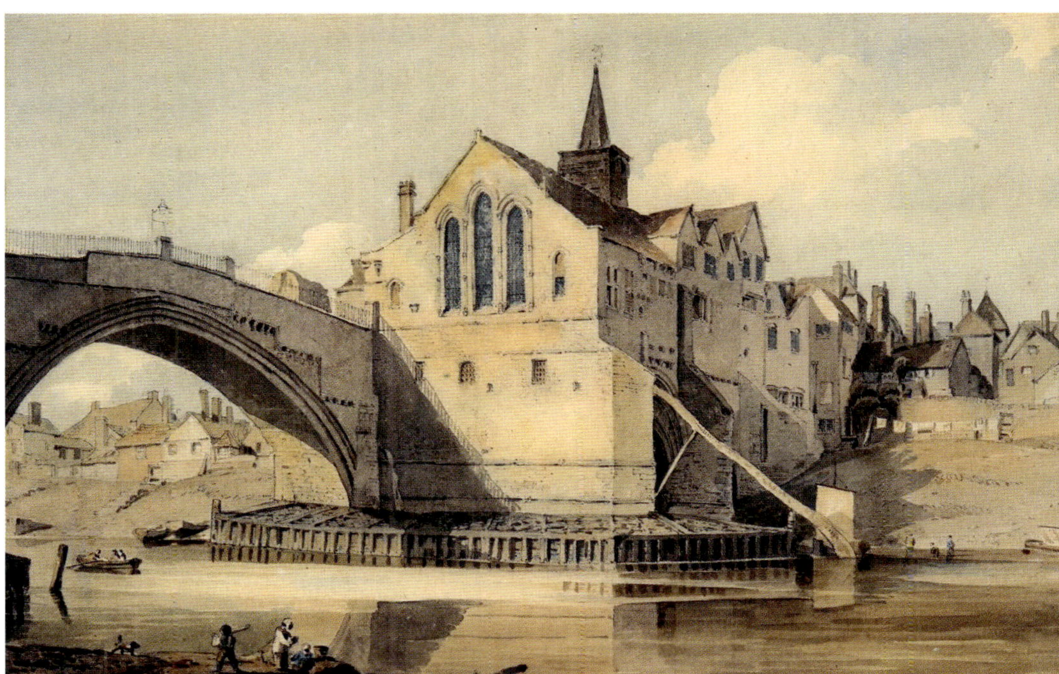

Fig. 3.4
Old Ouse Bridge and St William's chapel, pencil and watercolour, John Varley, 1803–05.

12a–12e). Ralph was an innocent man falsely accused by Besing. The case was decided by a judicial duel (trial by combat), which got out of hand and resulted in Ralph being blinded by Besing. Knowing himself to be innocent, Ralph prayed at the tomb of St William, where he received new eyes. Thus, William could be both a healer and a corrector of injustice. The incident can probably be dated from a prosaic entry in the royal archives for the year 1210–11, which records a man called Besing of Ripon being fined for a wrongly fought duel.

St William could also protect against threatened assault. In 1192, during a dispute between Archbishop Geoffrey Plantagenet (1189–1212) and members of the Chapter, the dean and the treasurer were set upon by some enraged supporters of the archbishop during a service in the choir. They ran down the steps from Archbishop Roger's choir into the crossing, and the dean fled through the south transept door and back to the deanery (at that time situated near the south transept). The treasurer, however, sensing that he would be caught before he could reach the treasurer's house on the north side of the Minster, ran to William's tomb and entrusted himself to the protection of his sainted predecessor. Although the tomb was the focus of his cult, a chapel in St William's honour was built about this time on Ouse Bridge, commemorating the Ouse Bridge miracle of 1154. The bridge was also the location for another of the early posthumous healing miracles.

In 1226 St William was formally canonised by Pope Honorius IV (panel 18a). This was in effect the second time that William was canonised – that is to say, enrolled in the list or canon of the saints. Traditionally, canonisation was an informal process carried out at the local level. In recognition of the merits of an individual's life and/or miracles, a cult might grow up, which, if tolerated or promoted by the local ecclesiastical authorities, would result in recognition as a saint, without any formal proclamation being necessary. This was what happened in William's case following the miracles of 1177. However, in the second half of the twelfth century the papacy, in line with its centralising and bureaucratising agenda, was increasingly asserting control over the canonisation process. One of the first to be canonised in this way was Thomas Becket. The scandal of the archbishop murdered in his own cathedral in 1170, followed by papal canonisation just three years later, resulted in the rapid dissemination of his cult across western Europe. St William never received comparable recognition; by the early 1220s – prompted perhaps by the Translation of Becket's relics into a magnificent new shrine in Canterbury Cathedral in 1220 – the authorities at York seem to have decided that William's status would be enhanced by a formal papal canonisation. An official process was launched, evidence of miracles submitted (including the Ralph and Besing story), and the bull of canonisation was issued by the pope on 18 March 1226. To help promote the cult, the Latin *Life of St William* was written about this time. Extensive extracts were incorporated into the York *Breviary* as readings for the Feast of St William on 8 June and other commemorations of the saint. The *Breviary* continued to be used by the clergy across the diocese until the Reformation, and it helped popularise St William's story among the wider community.

It was probably around this time – if it had not been done earlier – that William's tomb was transformed into a shrine worthy of a saint. Not one stone survives of this early tomb-shrine, but its basic form can be reconstructed from traces on the sarcophagus. The sides and the ends of the sarcophagus were encased in masonry cladding. The lid remained visible, and a stonework canopy was erected above it, supported on ten slender circular columns (Fig. 3.5). The bases of the columns rested partly on the new stone cladding, partly on the edges of the lid. This design combined

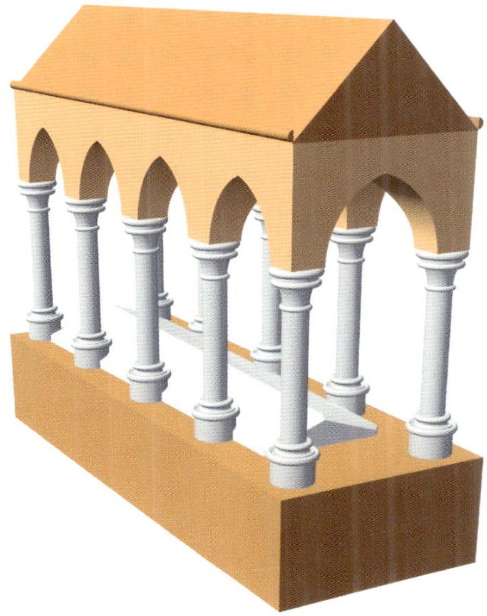

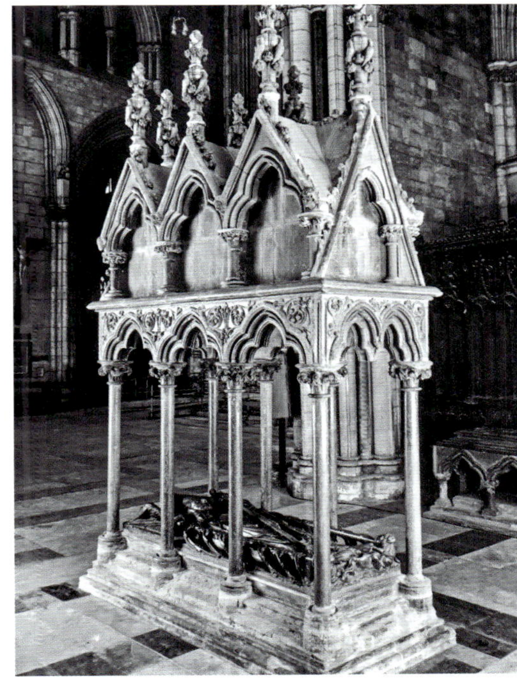

Fig. 3.5
St William's early tomb-shrine at the east end of the nave, as reconstructed by Stuart Harrison.

Fig. 3.6
The tomb of Archbishop Walter de Grey, d.1255, chapel of St Michael in the south transept.

accessibility with security. It allowed pilgrims kneeling at the shrine to run their hands over the lid, while preventing anyone from prising it open and tampering with the relics within. The new masonry was probably of Purbeck marble or some other fine stone, richly ornamented and probably enhanced with polychromy and gilding. The magnificent Purbeck marble tomb of Archbishop Walter de Grey (1215–55) in the south transept (Fig. 3.6) gives some idea of the possible scale and quality of William's tomb-shrine, which was enclosed within a screen for security.

Walter de Grey was one of the most energetic and influential of archbishops, and he was probably the driving force behind the promotion of the cult of St William. He was certainly responsible for rebuilding the south transept, while the north transept was rebuilt by William's successor as Minster treasurer, John le Romeyn. The central tower and spire were also enlarged at this time. The new transepts were more than twice the size of their eleventh-century predecessors, and were conceived on a vast scale, with the cult of St William in mind. They have aisles on the west side – by no means a standard feature of transepts, even in high-status cathedrals – and these were connected to the nave by openings pierced through the easternmost bay of the eleventh-century nave on either side. They therefore provided a means of circulation around the shrine, alleviating the pressure of two-way traffic under the western crossing arch. Visitors entering through the south transept doorway (which was the main entrance on a day-to-day basis from the top of Stonegate) would have been able to see through to the shrine on their left from near the entrance, while on their right the northernmost chapel on the east side, next to the crossing, was dedicated to St William. The central chapel on the east side was chosen by Walter de Grey as his own burial place, while his successors were laid to rest in the southernmost chapel nearest to the entrance. Thus, the eastern aisle became

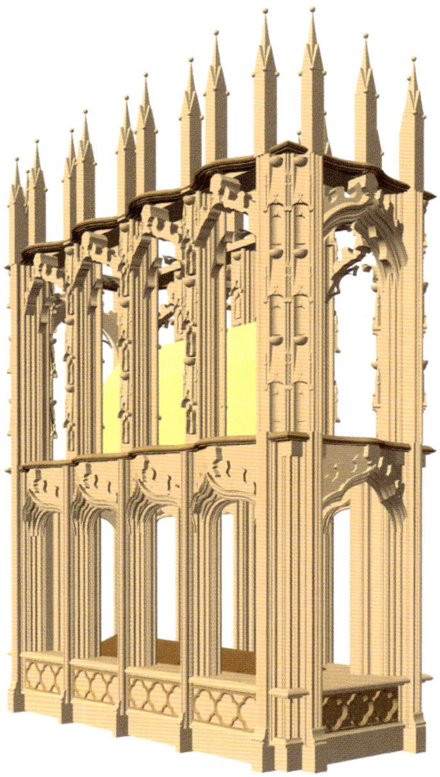

Fig. 3.7
The nave shrine commissioned *c.*1330 by Archbishop William Melton, as reconstructed by Stuart Harrison.

a mausoleum for the archbishops next to the chapel of their sainted predecessor.

In the decades following the papal canonisation, there is little record of activity at the tomb. Access may have been restricted during the building campaign, but Henry III made a generous offering of wax for candles to burn round the tomb during a visit in July 1244, followed by a gift of two gold brooches at Christmas 1251. The royal connection continued when the bones of St William were removed from the sarcophagus and translated into a reliquary in January 1284 in the presence of Edward I and Queen Eleanor of Castile. The events surrounding the Translation were recorded in a Latin text, which was incorporated into the York *Breviary* as readings for the new Feast of the Translation of St William on 8 January. This text was used by John Thornton when designing rows 18 and 20–21 of the St William Window. Edward I was campaigning in Wales when he received an invitation to the Translation (panel 18b). Shortly afterwards, he had a fall on a mountain in Wales but escaped unharmed, a deliverance he attributed to St William's protection (panels 18c–18d). He and the queen then hastened to York for the Translation (panel 18e). The ceremony was presided over by Archbishop William Wickwane (1279–85), accompanied by Anthony Bek, the newly elected bishop of Durham. Bek paid for the ceremony and was consecrated bishop on the same day. Thornton depicted the bones being removed from the sarcophagus, the reliquary being processed round the Minster and Archbishop Wickwane accompanied by six bishops (panels 20a–20c). At one point, a servant of one of the canons fell asleep beneath the pulpit and was hit on the head by a falling stone. His hat was damaged, but he was unharmed, thanks to the intervention of the saint (panels 20d–20e). The account of the Translation also recounts some miracles that took place in the years immediately following, and which Thornton included in row 21 of the window.

During the Translation ceremony, Edward I made offerings to St William, and was given a finger bone of the saint. He took it with him during his Scottish campaigns, and it turned up later in the royal relic collection at St George's Chapel, Windsor. This was the only one of the saint's bones to leave York. The others were carefully preserved at the Minster, but as was often the case with saints' relics, they were divided up. It is not clear whether this took place immediately after the Translation, or some years later, but from the fourteenth century there were three separate reliquaries. One containing the principal bones was enshrined in a position of honour at the high altar. A separate head-reliquary containing the skull was kept nearby, and errant clergy were sometimes required to make monetary offerings

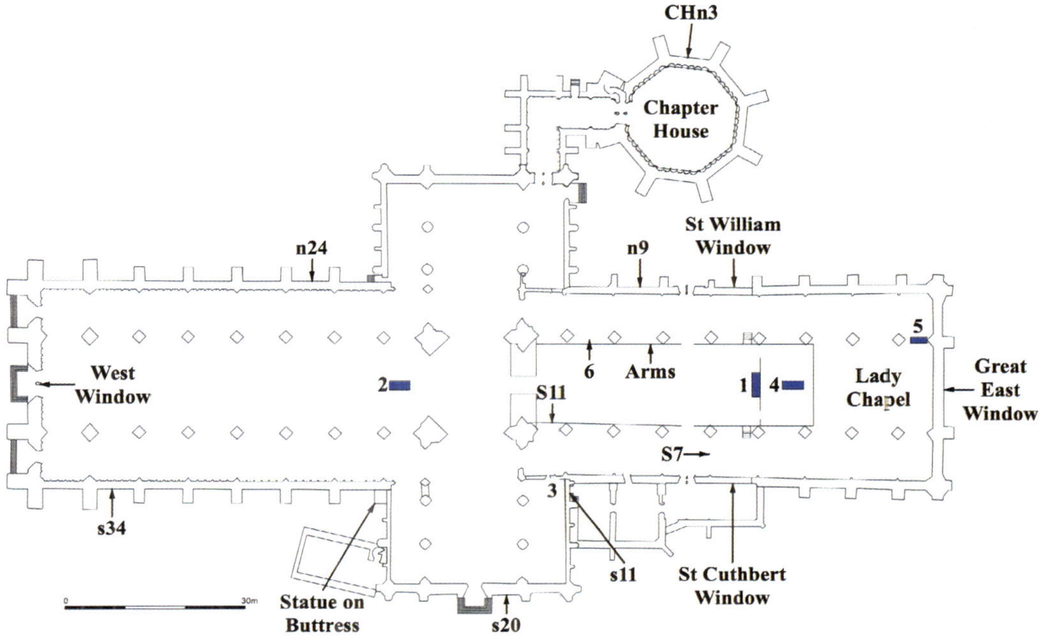

Fig. 3.8
Plan of York Minster showing the locations of St William sites and imagery.
1. The High Altar
2. The nave tomb-shrine
3. The truncated chapel of St William
4. The High Altar shrine
5. The chapel of St Stephen and the tomb of Archbishop Richard Scrope
6. The arms of Beatrice de Roos in window N10.

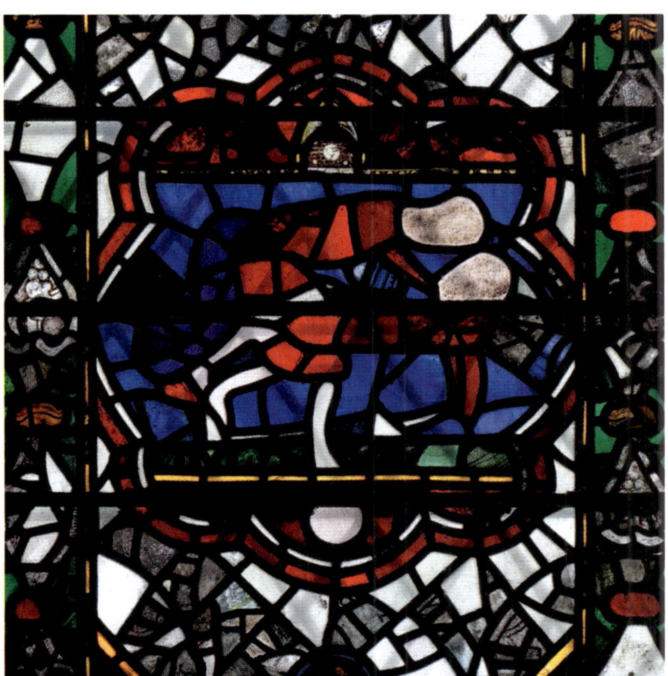

Fig. 3.9
Ralph and Besing fight, in Chapter House n3, *c.*1290. The panel is heavily restored.

there as part of their penance for faults committed. A third reliquary containing the lesser bones was kept at the tomb in the nave. One of the reliquaries would be processed around on special occasions, notably an annual procession around the city at the season of Pentecost, as can be seen in some of the panels in the window (panels 21c, 21e and 22e).

At the time of the Translation, in order for the lid of the sarcophagus to be removed, the shrine structure – or at least the canopy and its supporting columns – must have been dismantled. The sarcophagus was now empty, but it retained a numinous power as the saint's first resting place; since access to the choir and high altar was largely confined to the clergy, the tomb (with its lid replaced) remained the main focus of popular devotion. A miraculous cure was recorded there on St William's Day 1290. In 1291 the foundation stone of the present Gothic

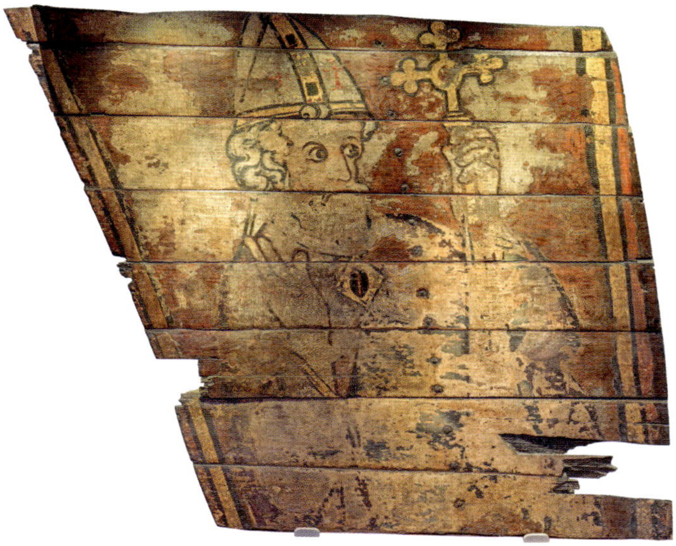

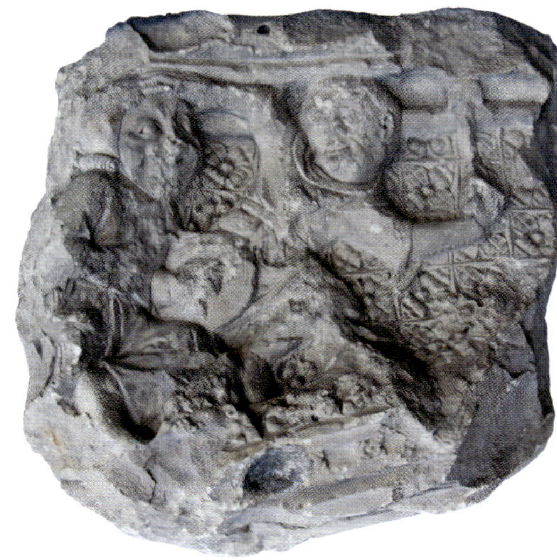

nave was laid, and work continued right through to the 1350s. There must have been periods when access to the tomb was restricted, if not impossible. However, miraculous cures were recorded there in 1308 and 1325, and in about 1330 a new tomb-shrine was constructed at the expense of Archbishop Melton (1316–40).

Melton's shrine has been reconstructed from fragments by Stuart Harrison (Fig. 3.7). Its basic conception was similar to the earlier tomb-shrine, but grander. Once again, the sarcophagus was enclosed in masonry, leaving the lid visible. Sturdy shafts supported a substantial two-stage superstructure. This incorporated a platform on which the nave reliquary was placed. Thus, pilgrims could see the reliquary of the saint elevated above them, and (as before) they could touch the lid of the sarcophagus. The whole structure was covered in elaborate architectural detailing and rich sculptural ornament, all exquisitely carved in a bravura display of masoncraft. The altar of the Holy Cross had been moved by this date, and a small altar was placed against the west end of the tomb-shrine, as can be seen in some of the scenes in the window (e.g. panels 12a, 15d and 24a). Dominating the vast spaces of the new aisled nave, the tomb-shrine cannot have failed to impress. It remained in place until the Reformation, and although there is little documentary evidence of pilgrims at the tomb, the lid of the sarcophagus provides a mute testimony to St William's continuing popularity. It has been worn smooth by the touch of countless pilgrims.

St William Imagery and the St William Window

The earliest surviving images of St William date to shortly after the Translation. The Chapter House, which was completed around 1290, has one whole window (CHn3) devoted to scenes from the life and miracles of St William. Unfortunately, the glass has suffered badly over the centuries. There were originally twenty scenes, but some have been lost, and the remainder are in poor condition and have been moved around. They include the story of Ralph and Besing and miracles at the tomb. Becket features in another of the

Fig. 3.10
Painted panel from the vault of the Chapter House, depicting an image of an archbishop (St William?), *c.*1290.

Fig. 3.11
The Ralph and Besing battle scene carved on the interior of the canopy of Melton's nave shrine, *c.*1330, where only a pilgrim crouching under the structure to get close to the exposed coffin lid would see it.

Chapter House windows (CHs4) but was given only four scenes. The Chapter House vault contained large painted figures on wooden panels in the cells between the ribs. These included two archbishops, no doubt William and Becket. Part of one of the panels survives, its surface much abraded but nonetheless an exceptionally rare survival of a thirteenth-century panel painting (Fig. 3.10). St William may also have featured in the long-lost wall paintings over the doorway into the Chapter House, directly opposite the seats of the dean and the other Minster dignitaries.

The new nave provided further opportunities. The so-called Bellfounders' Window in the north nave aisle (n24), dating to *c.*1310–20, was given by Richard Tunnoc, who was a goldsmith as well as a bellfounder, and who was buried nearby in 1330. In the centre near the bottom of the window, closest to the viewer, Tunnoc is represented kneeling before St William and offering the window to him (Fig. 3.12). His name is displayed prominently. In the upper register, the miracle of Ouse Bridge is represented, spread across three panels. The choice of subject-matter reflects Tunnoc's own interests. He was prominent in the affairs of the city, rising to be bailiff of the city in 1320–1, and mayor in 1327. The civic authorities had their offices on Ouse Bridge, next to St William's chapel. They administered the chapel and seem to have been promoting it at the time, since no fewer than four chantries were founded there between 1310 and 1320. Tunnoc's window has not only preserved his name for posterity; it has helped fix the miracle of Ouse Bridge in the popular imagination as the most memorable event in William's life. Another

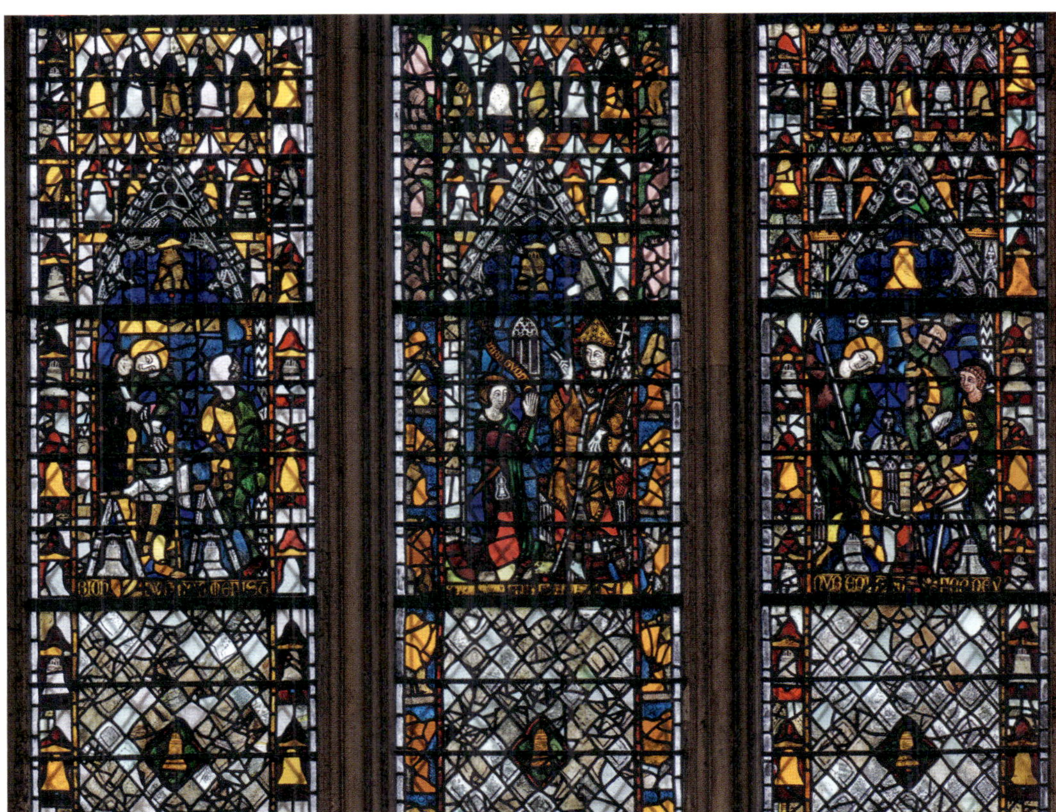

Fig. 3.12
Richard Tunnoc's Bellfounders' Window, n24, *c.*1310–20. Tunnoc kneels before St William, offering a model of his window. He is flanked by scenes of bell-founders at work.

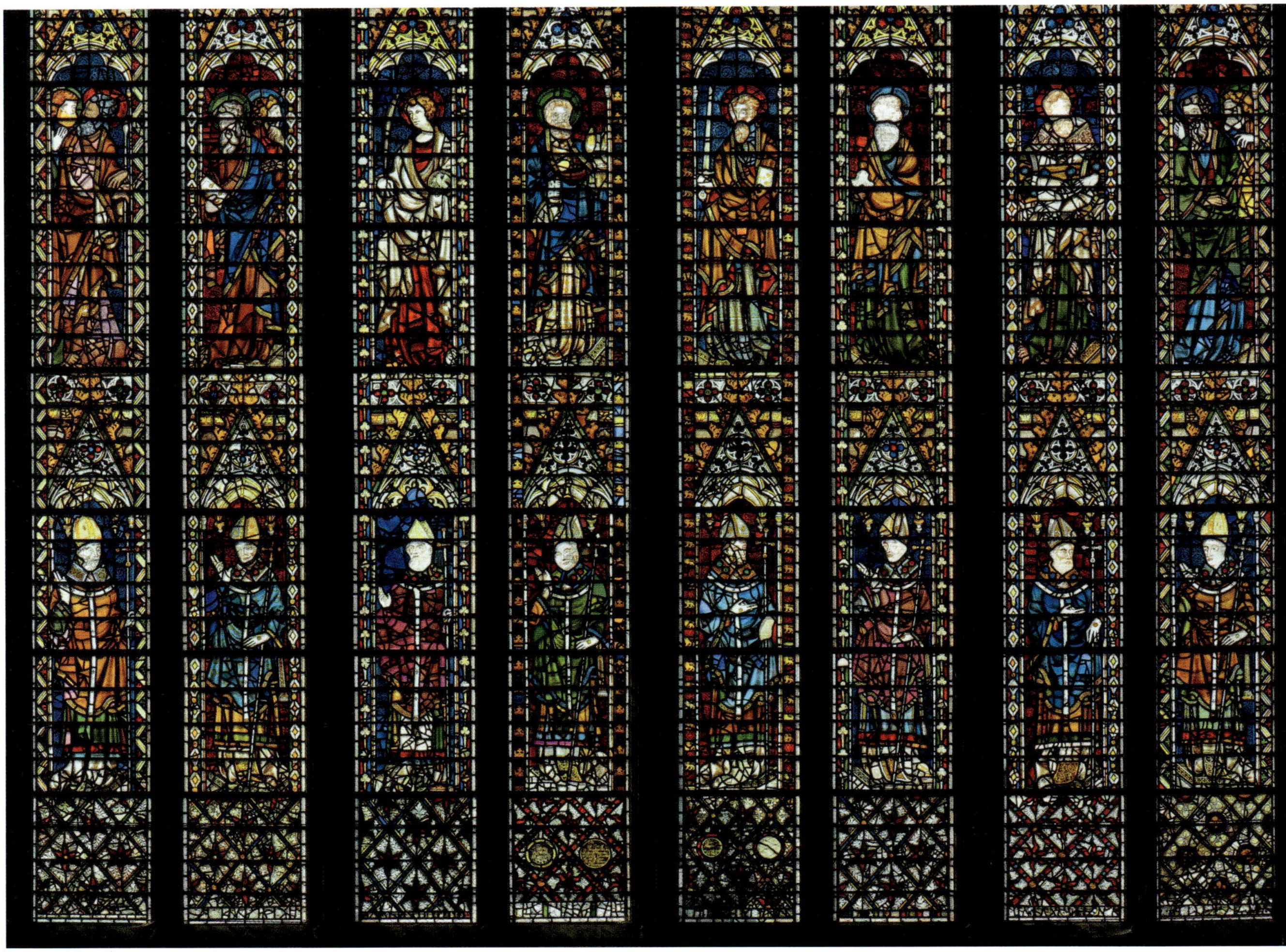

Fig. 3.13
The West Window, commissioned by Archbishop William Melton from glazier Robert Kettlebarn in 1339. St William is depicted in the lower register of panels, second from the right.

panel depicting the miracle, of similar date, survives in a south nave aisle (window s34, Fig. 2.7), though its original position is unknown.

Melton's tomb-shrine incorporates what appears to modern eyes a curious mixture of imagery: small standing figures of saints; Evangelists' symbols; figures of a pilgrim and a mason; a falconer with angel wings and a human-headed creature. On the surviving pieces there is only one scene relating directly to St William, namely the duel of Ralph and Besing (Fig. 3.11). The precious metal reliquary kept at the tomb-shrine (which may perhaps have been looked after or even created by Richard Tunnoc) may well have featured some of his miracles.

As well as the tomb-shrine, Archbishop Melton also paid for the great west window, begun in 1339. St William appears here again in the row of eight standing archbishops at its base (Fig. 3.13). Around the same time, a life-sized statue of an archbishop was placed on the exterior of the Minster on top of the easternmost buttress of the south nave aisle wall. This was a late-twelfth-century statue, one of a large set of figures, mostly of prophets and apostles, which had been carefully taken down from the late-twelfth-century west front

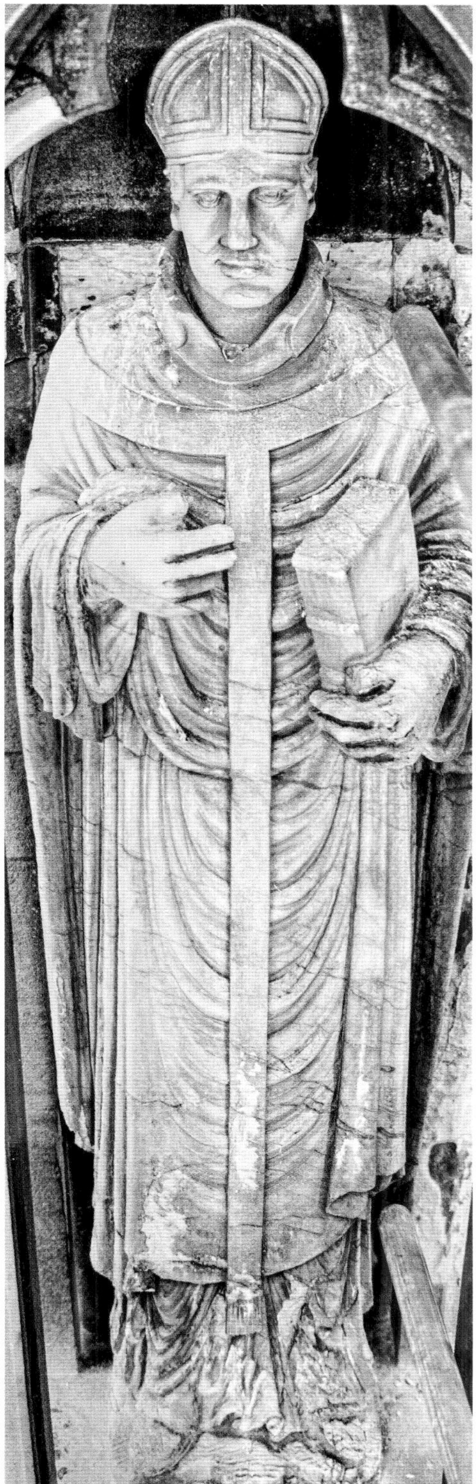

Fig. 3.14
An early-nineteenth-century replacement of a twelfth-century statue of an archbishop, easternmost south buttress of the nave aisle.

of the Minster. It is now known only from an early-nineteenth-century replacement (Fig. 3.14). The choice of this particular statue in this position was not coincidental: it stands immediately above St William's tomb-shrine, and it was clearly intended to represent him and remind passers-by of his shrine within. We cannot be certain whether it was originally carved to represent St William or some other archbishop. If it was him, it is much the earliest image of St William known to us, dating to not long after the 1177 miracles.

After the trauma of the Black Death, work began on a new east end in 1361. The Lady Chapel was constructed first. Then, after something of a hiatus, services were moved out of the old choir into the new vestry in 1394 so that the choir could be rebuilt. The new vestry was what is now known, erroneously, as the Zouche Chapel, and the high altar reliquary and the head reliquary were presumably transferred there for safekeeping. The new choir was brought into use *c.*1420, having no doubt been delayed by the collapse of the central tower in 1407. At the time of the collapse, John Thornton was hard at work on the Great East Window. This contains Thornton's first image of St William, at the bottom right-hand corner. Seated next to another archbishop and a pope, he is the very last of a row of important figures from the early history of the Minster. Beneath him is a shield bearing the heraldic arms that were invented for him long after his death, consisting of red lozenges on a gold ground, combined with a pallium and cross-staff to signify his archiepiscopal rank. At about the same time, St William's arms (without the pallium and cross-staff) were carved in stone and placed on the north side of the choir (Fig. 3.15), above the choir stalls. Here St William was in the most exalted company. He is next in line after four shields of arms representing Christ, the Virgin Mary, St Peter and St Paul.

In the north choir aisle, behind the stone shield of arms, is another image of St William attributed to John Thornton. Window n9 was given by Canon Thomas Parker in the second decade of the fifteenth century. Each of its three lights contains a large standing figure of a saint above three scenes from the saint's life. St Thomas Becket, the donor's name-saint, is in the centre light, flanked by St John of Beverley on the left and St William on the right. Underneath St William are panels depicting the miracle of Ouse Bridge, William's enthronement as archbishop, and a rather damaged scene at the tomb (Fig. 3.16). For the St William Window two bays further east, Thornton needed to create more than thirty times as many scenes!

By any reckoning, the St William Window was a monumental achievement. The commissioning of the window and its place within John Thornton's oeuvre will be discussed in the next chapter. For now, we will focus on the window's spatial and symbolic connections to the new choir.

The window was installed in about 1415, around the time the new choir was being brought into use. The high altar, which currently stands in front of the stone screen overlooking the Lady Chapel, was originally one bay further west. It stood against a wooden screen, with a door on either side, which gave access to the bay beyond. In this enclosed space, supported on the crypt beneath, the high altar reliquary of St William was kept. The head reliquary was also kept at the high altar. The crypt was constructed with columns and vault ribs re-used from the twelfth-century crypt of Roger of Pont l'Evêque; the high altar stood in the same position as in the twelfth-century choir and in the earlier, eleventh-century choir of Thomas of Bayeux. Thus, the whole arrangement deliberately perpetuated the memory of the earlier Minster, and St William's relics were venerated just next to the spot where he himself had celebrated Mass as archbishop (as depicted in panel 10a).

In another respect, too, the new choir harked back to its twelfth-century predecessor. Roger's choir had small, projecting eastern transepts and its high altar stood symbolically at the centre of the cross formed by the eastern transepts and the main east–west axis of the building. The present choir does not have projecting eastern transepts. However, the same symbolism is achieved by extending the high vault of the choir laterally into the adjacent bays of the north and south aisles (Fig. 7.1), creating eastern transepts in elevation if not in plan. Raising the end walls to the full height of the choir creates the space for the St William Window and the St Cuthbert Window opposite. Thus, the two huge windows form the ends of the arms of the cross, which was centred on the high altar. The symbolism was made explicit by the large crucifix that stood high above the wooden screen behind the high altar. The link between the high altar and the two great windows to either side is reinforced by the fact that they can only be seen in their entirety from the original high altar bay at the centre of the eastern crossing. From the aisles, only the bottom sections of the two windows are visible. In fact the St William Window and the St Cuthbert Window can be understood as the wings of a vast high altar triptych in stained glass, the centre of which is formed by the Great East Window. This sense of a triptych is

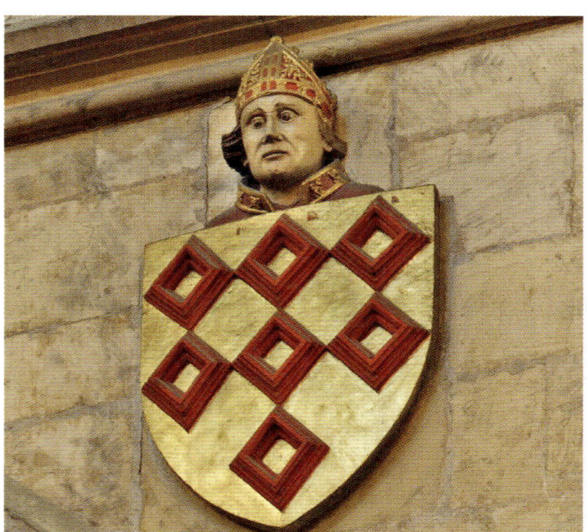

Fig. 3.15
Arms of St William, north arcade spandrel of the choir.

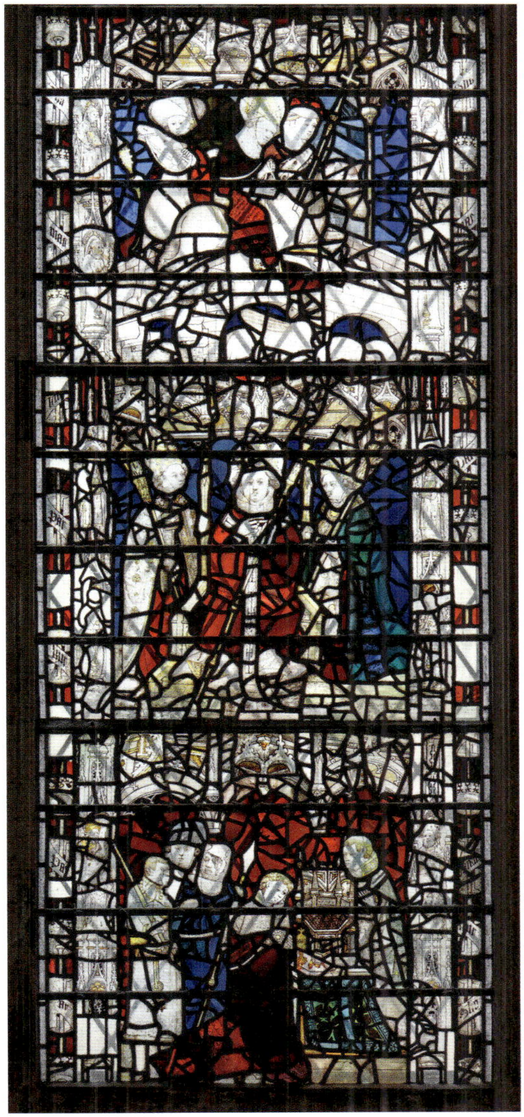

Fig. 3.16
Window n9, scenes from the life of St William. The window was given by Canon Thomas Parker, in the second decade of the fifteenth century.

reinforced by the fact that the members of the Roos family in the bottom row of the window all face to the right, looking out towards the high altar. Thus in various ways the St William Window was symbolically linked to the high altar and the reliquaries of St William kept there. These carefully conceived relationships were lost when the reliquaries were destroyed at the Reformation and the high altar was moved from its original position in the eighteenth century.

St William and Richard Scrope

A different set of relationships, which could not have been envisaged when the new choir was originally planned, had emerged by the time the St William Window was created. In 1405 Archbishop Richard Scrope (1398–1405) was executed for leading a rebellion against Henry IV. He was hastily buried in the chapel of St Stephen at the east end of the north choir aisle, next to the Lady Chapel. Very soon, Scrope was being revered as a saint, and an unofficial cult grew up around his tomb, despite royal attempts to suppress it. Scrope's cult had many local adherents (including some of the York clergy) and numerous offerings were made at his tomb. The Scrope family were a powerful presence within the Minster, and they developed St Stephen's chapel as a family mausoleum, a unique privilege accorded to no other family. Between 1405 and 1475 at least ten other members of the family, both clerical and lay, were buried there, and chantry priests were appointed to serve the chapel. The burials included the archbishop's nephew, Stephen Scrope, archdeacon of Richmond from 1402 until his death in 1418 and a leading promoter of his uncle's memory. Given this enduring Scrope connection, the archbishop's memory could not be erased. Nor could ordinary people be prevented from visiting the tomb, since the daily Mass in honour of the Virgin was celebrated at the Lady Chapel altar immediately adjacent to the tomb.

The Minster authorities were therefore faced with a delicate situation. They could not realistically suppress the cult, even if they wanted to, in the face of huge popular support, but neither could they risk the wrath of Henry IV and his Lancastrian successors by promoting it. A tricky situation was further complicated by the fact that Scrope had been executed on 8 June, the Feast of St William. The two cults were therefore inextricably linked, and not just by their physical proximity. Each year, 8 June was a potential flashpoint as possibly rival groups of devotees were drawn to the tombs of the two archbishops. The nervousness of the Minster clergy around this time is illustrated by the case of Margery Kempe, who came to the Minster on pilgrimage in 1417. Her behaviour attracted the attention of the authorities and she was summoned for questioning. Afraid that she would cause a disturbance, but unable to make any charges stick, they were relieved when she moved on. Margery would have been one of the first pilgrims to see the St William Window.

The fluctuating relationships between the two cults over the decades is not easy to discern, though it is clear that Scrope's popularity in the years following his death threatened to eclipse St William. However, in due course some sort of *modus vivendi* was achieved. Visitors were invited to make offerings to St William rather than Scrope; any monetary offerings that were made at Scrope's tomb were allocated to the fabric fund, and any *ex votos* left there were removed. These measures, it has to be said, were of only limited effectiveness. In 1415–16 for instance, offerings at Scrope's tomb amounted to £78 3*s*, more than John Thornton personally received for his work on the Great East Window. Against this background, the reinstatement of St William's principal reliquary and his head reliquary at the new high altar, and the installation of the St William Window *c*.1415, can be seen as part of the Minster's policy of promoting St William ahead of Scrope. Visitors approaching Scrope's tomb along the north choir aisle would have had to pass beneath the St William Window. Thus, William's cult could be used to contain the devotion to Scrope, but at the same time it also provided a cover for it.

The careful distinction that was made between St William and Scrope is illustrated by two windows that were inserted *c*.1440 at clerestory level in the south-east transept, either side of the St Cuthbert Window. The central light of window S7, on the west side, contains a standing figure of St William in standard archiepiscopal garb beneath an elaborate architectural canopy (Fig. 3.17). Beneath him is a kneeling figure of the donor, Robert Wolveden, canon of York from 1400 and treasurer from 1426 until his death in 1432. The arms of Wolveden and of St William are depicted in the side lights. Window S6 opposite has an almost identical figure of Scrope above the posthumous kneeling figure of his nephew, Archdeacon Stephen Scrope. Scrope arms appear in the side lights. Archbishop Scrope, like St William in S7, has a discrete halo, and the visual equivalence between the two implies an equality of status. However, there are subtle differences of wording. Beneath the figure of William is a label identifying him unequivocally as 'St William', and Wolveden is accompanied by a speech-scroll with the words 'St William, pray for the soul of your servant, Robert'. By contrast, the label beneath Scrope identifies

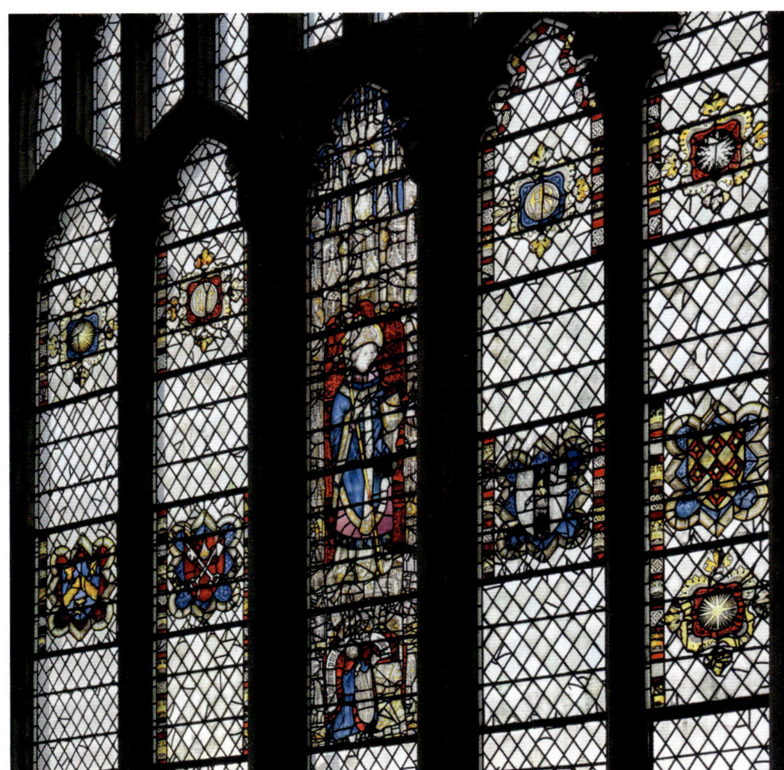

Fig. 3.17
Window S7, given by Treasurer Robert Wolveden, *c*.1430.

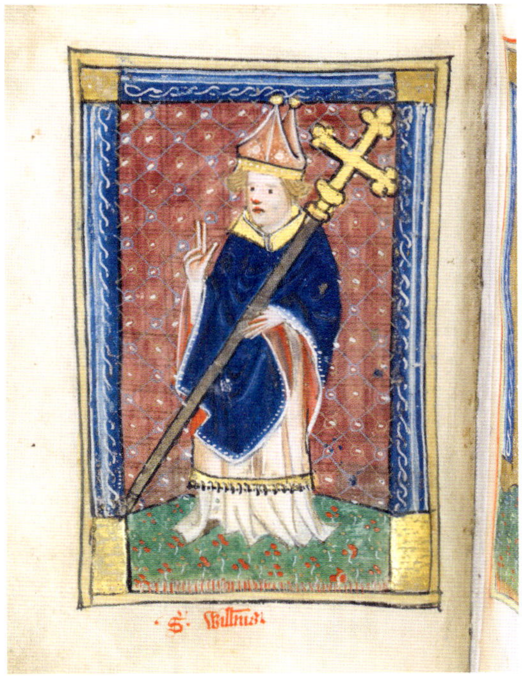

Fig. 3.18
A miniature of St William in the early-fifteenth-century Bolton *Books of Hours*. York Minster Library Add. Ms. 2 , f. 39v.

him simply as 'Lord Richard Scrope', while Stephen Scrope's speech scroll says, 'O good shepherd Richard, have mercy on your servant, Stephen'. The phrase 'good shepherd' refers back, of course, to Christ the Good Shepherd, and could be used of any faithful pastor. However, the clergy would have been familiar with a prayer in the York *Breviary,* which starts by addressing St William as a good shepherd. Thus, the window implies Scrope's equivalence with St William, while avoiding actually calling him a saint, in line with official Minster policy. Such fine distinctions enabled the Minster to preserve the delicate balance between St William and Scrope. Among Scrope's devotees outside the Minster, however, such niceties could be dispensed with. The Bolton *Book of Hours*, produced for a wealthy York family around the time that the St William Window was being made, contains images of many different saints, including St William (Fig. 3.18). There are two images of Scrope, who is addressed unambiguously as St Richard Scrope.

Robert Wolveden was also the donor of another window depicting St William, completed after his death in 1434–5. St William's chapel next to the crossing on the east side of the south transept had been reduced to half its width by the construction of the south choir aisle *c.*1400. One of its pair of thirteenth-century lancet windows had been destroyed. The remaining lancet (s11) was given a new stained-glass window by Wolveden. The design is very different from his other window. A large figure of St William is set against lozenge-shaped quarries (Fig. 3.19), with no architectural canopy, and Wolveden's arms appear prominently above his head. Scrope does not appear. Whatever place Scrope held in the hearts of his devotees, he had no place in the official liturgy. It was St William who had his own chapel in the Minster, who had two feast days – the Feast of the Translation in January as well as 8 June – and who had services, readings and prayers in his honour.

In March 1462 the Chapter held a meeting to discuss the possible canonisation and Translation of the relics of Richard Scrope 'of blessed and pious memory'. They had been asked to consider the matter by King Edward IV, who had recently replaced King Henry VI on the throne. During the Wars of the Roses, the Yorkists adopted Scrope as a martyr to their cause, and official canonisation would have bolstered Edward's claim to the throne. While some members of the Chapter were probably sympathetic, others who owed their appointment to the Lancastrian regime were unlikely to support the proposal The meeting dragged on for three days and was then adjourned. When it reconvened in August, nothing more was said of the matter. Instead, the Chapter reiterated the importance of the annual procession of St William's relics round the city. William's pre-eminence was implicitly reaffirmed. Indeed, it may be that the renewed interest in Scrope under the Yorkist regime had the unintended effect of further strengthening

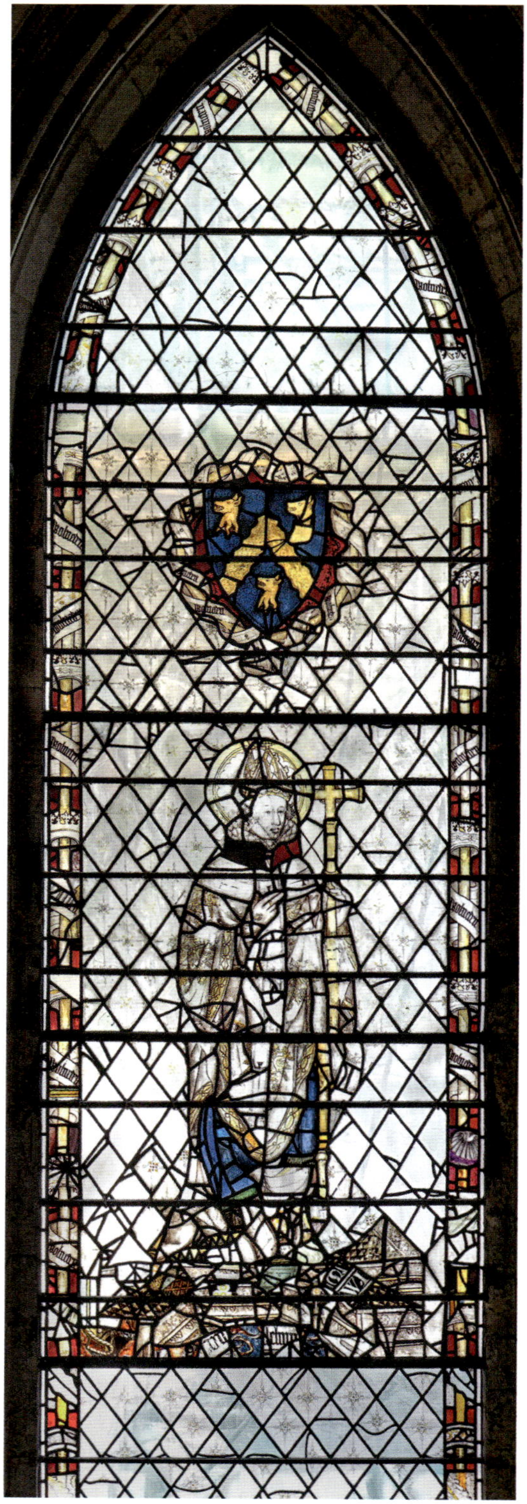

Fig. 3.19
St William in window s11, given by Treasurer Robert Wolveden, *c.*1430.

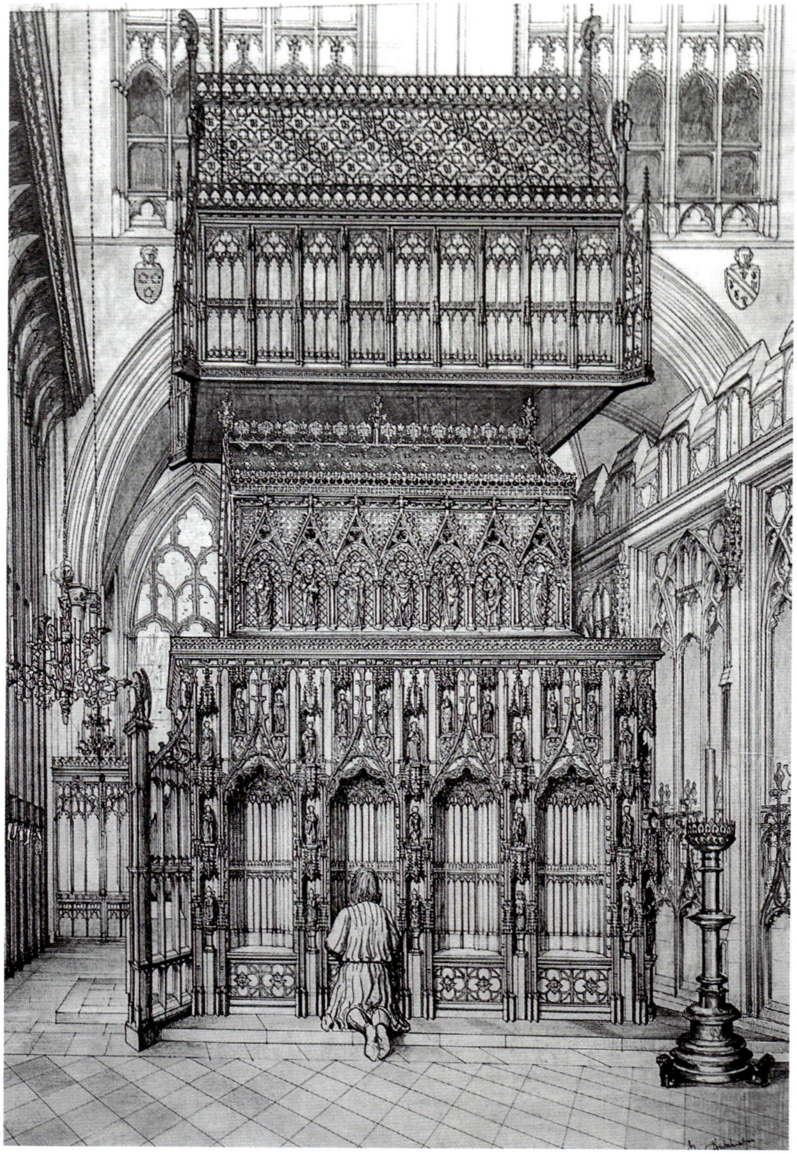

Fig. 3.20
The late-fifteenth-century high altar shrine of St William; reconstruction by Christopher Wilson. Drawing by John Hutchinson.

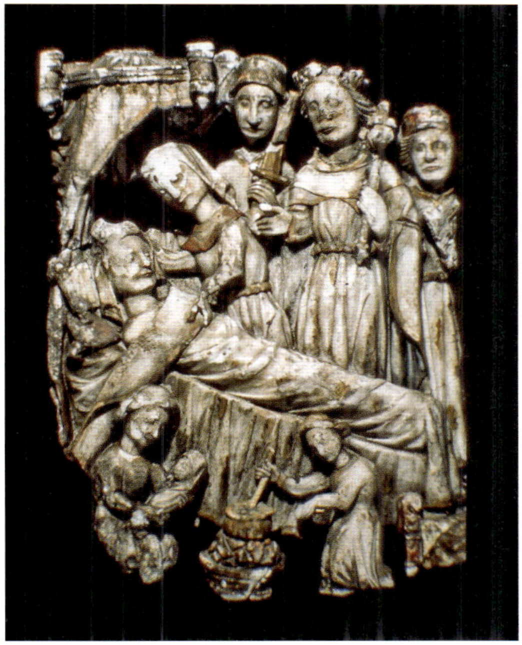

Fig. 3.21
A fifteenth-century alabaster found at Peaseholme Green in 1957, depicting the Birth of St William.

William's position, for a major upgrade of his cult was set in motion at the end of the decade. A grand, exquisitely detailed shrine-base, carved out of Frosterley marble, was commissioned for the high altar reliquary (Fig. 3.20). It was probably completed in time for the reconsecration of the Minster in 1472. Like Archbishop Melton's tomb-shrine in the nave, it had a raised platform on which the precious reliquary was placed. But unlike the nave tomb-shrine, whose open-work structure enabled pilgrims to touch William's sarcophagus, it had a solid base, with niches down the side where the faithful could kneel to offer prayers to the saint. It was the largest shrine-base of its kind, and it was erected in the bay behind the high altar, looking down on Scrope's tomb in St Stephen's chapel. With both the tomb-shrine in the nave, and the marble shrine-base behind the high altar, St William's relics were housed as magnificently as any in England.

It was probably sometime later that some of the St William alabasters were made, which were discovered in 1957 on the site of a house of parish chantry priests at Peaseholme Green. They had been deliberately buried face down, very likely at the Reformation. Four panels in varying degrees of completeness depict the birth of St William (which is not in the St William Window, Fig. 3.21), the Miracle of Ouse Bridge, King Edward I falling down a mountain in Wales (Fig. 7.9) and a very fragmentary Translation of the relics. In iconography and style, they make an interesting contrast to the St William Window.

An inventory of Minster possessions drawn up in the first decade of the sixteenth century gives us glimpses of the offerings that had been made to St William over the centuries. The objects displayed with the portable shrine, the head reliquary and the main reliquary included prayer beads of coral and precious metal, little crucifixes, belts, buckles and brooches, and miniature body parts including a golden nose, silver-gilt hearts and silver-gilt women's breasts. The inventory only lists valuable items, and there would have been numerous *ex votos* in wax and other cheaper materials as well. Some of these items are said to have been transferred from the tomb of Lord Richard Scrope (the same title as in window S6), in accordance with the instruction that had been issued soon after Scrope's death. But the inventory also lists numerous items that had been allowed to stay at Scrope's tomb. These were similar to the offerings to St William, but they also (for reasons that are not clear) included a number of silver model ships, oars and anchors. Other miniature body parts included hands, legs, feet and teeth. The inventory is clear evidence of Scrope's popularity, though by this date his tomb may not have been attracting as many pilgrims as before, since the generations of people who remembered him had all passed away, and his political relevance had faded with the establishment of the Tudor monarchy. The *ex votos* at Scrope's tomb were attached to rods, which were numbered A–F. Panels 21b and 22b

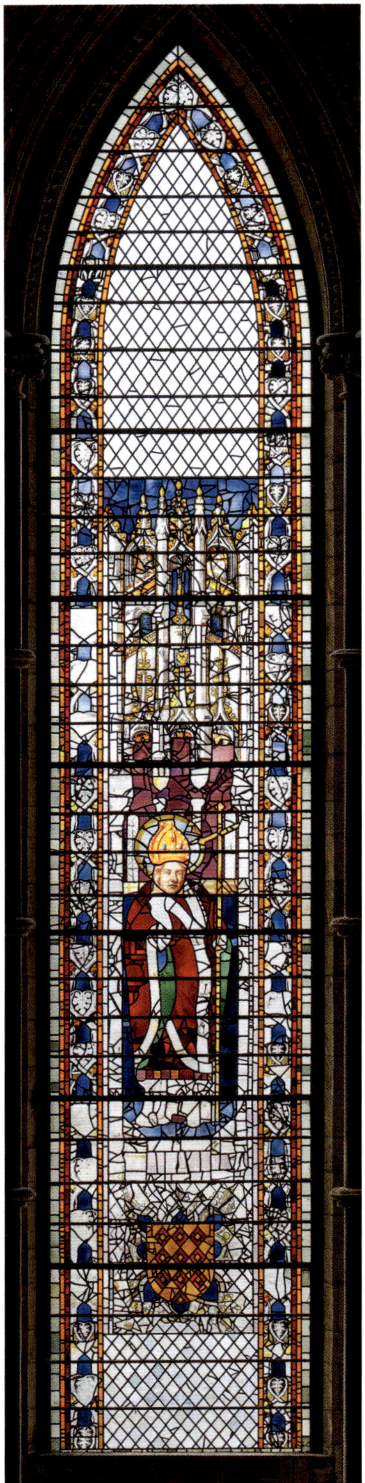

Fig. 3.22
St William in s20, created by Robert Petty, *c.*1500

in the window illustrate a similar arrangement at St William's tomb-shrine in the nave.

Around the time that the inventory was made, a figure of St William accompanied by his coat of arms was installed in one of the windows in the end wall of the south transept, beneath the rose window (s20, Fig. 3.22). Once again, William was in exalted company. The other windows in the set, which was made by the York glazier Robert Petty (d.1528), contain figures of St Peter, St Paul and St Wilfrid. This was the final addition to the iconography of St William in the Minster before the Reformation put an end to saints' cults in England. A York *Breviary* of *c.*1500 bears eloquent testimony to the suppression of the cult of St William. All of the readings in his honour had been crossed out (Fig. 3.23), and not long afterwards the Latin *Breviary* was replaced by the Prayer Book in English.

In 1535, as storm clouds gathered over the English church, an inventory of Minster valuables made on the orders of Henry VIII estimated the value of the main reliquary at £100 and the portable reliquary at £200. These sums were soon to be realised. In September 1541 the Privy Council, during Henry VIII's visit to York, ordered the archbishop to have all the saints' 'shrines and their hovels' in the province of York destroyed. The next month the Dean and Chapter instructed that St William's head reliquary should be broken up and the proceeds allocated to general Minster funds. The skull had apparently already been removed, and it is not heard of again. The other two reliquaries are not mentioned. They may have been previously destroyed. The Frosterley marble shrine-base behind the high altar was demolished, as was Melton's tomb-shrine in the nave. In the latter case, the removal of the shrine structure left William's sarcophagus standing proud of the floor where it had stood since 1154. The sarcophagus with its lid was buried beneath the pavement on the same spot. Thus, all traces of the shrines and the

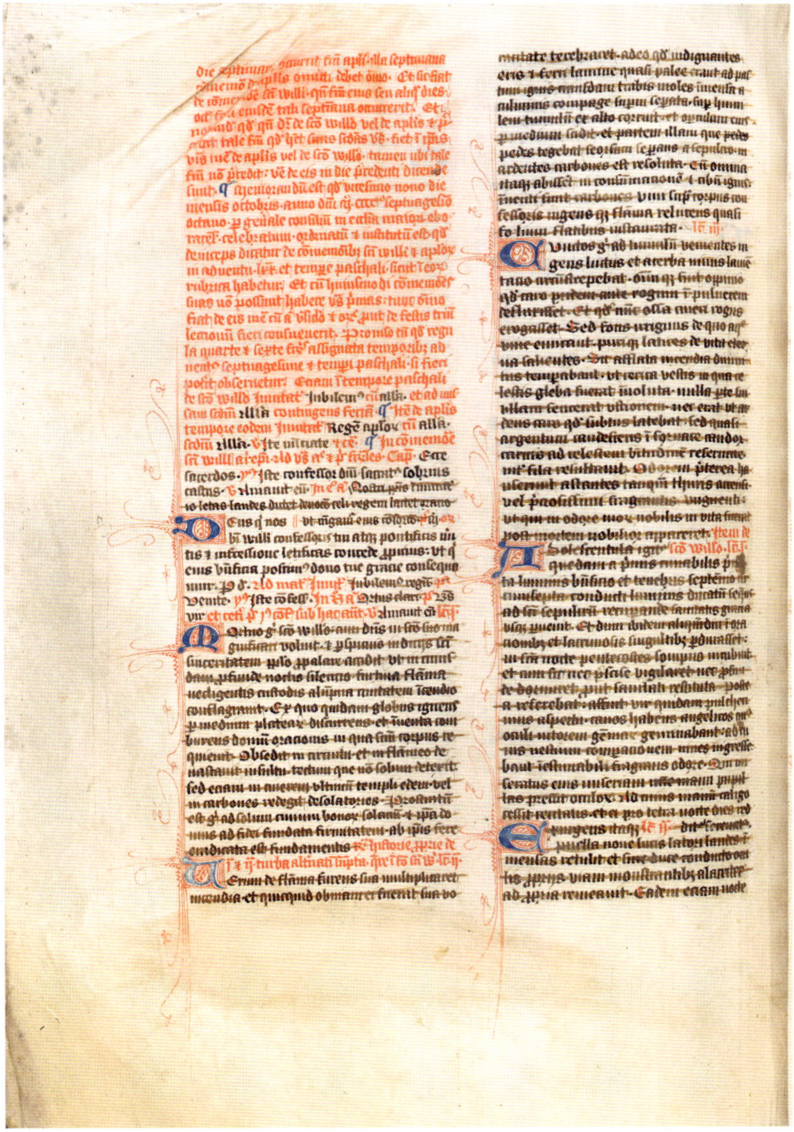

Fig. 3.23
A *c*.1500 York *Breviary* with the readings commemorating St William crossed out. York Minster Library, MS Add. 69, f. 143v.

reliquaries disappeared from the Minster, leaving the St William Window as the principal memorial to York's soon-to-be-forgotten saint.

Yet this was not the end of the story. In the early seventeenth century visitors to the Minster were shown the long bones of St William, which were kept in the vestry. These would have been the bones that had been contained in the reliquary behind the high altar. They subsequently disappeared, very likely during the Civil War. In the 1730s William's sarcophagus was discovered underneath the floor of the nave and then reburied during the laying of the Burlington pavement. When it was rediscovered in about 1970, its contents were examined before it was transferred to its present position within the twelfth-century crypt. It was found to contain the bones of a new-born baby, and the skeleton of a man of advanced years who had lived an energetic life. The latter skeleton, however, was incomplete. It lacked the long bones and the skull, the very bones that had been kept in the high altar reliquary and the head reliquary during the Middle Ages. The surviving bones are almost certainly the mortal remains of William FitzHerbert, which must have been taken from the reliquary at the tomb-shrine in the nave and placed once more in his sarcophagus before it was buried at the Reformation. They still lie in the sarcophagus today.

The nave tomb-shrine and the Frosterley marble shrine-base behind the high altar have also been resurrected. Fragments of both have turned up at No.10, Precentor's Court at various times since the early eighteenth century. This has enabled Christopher Wilson and Stuart Harrison to reconstruct both. Now the St William Window has also been brought back to life.

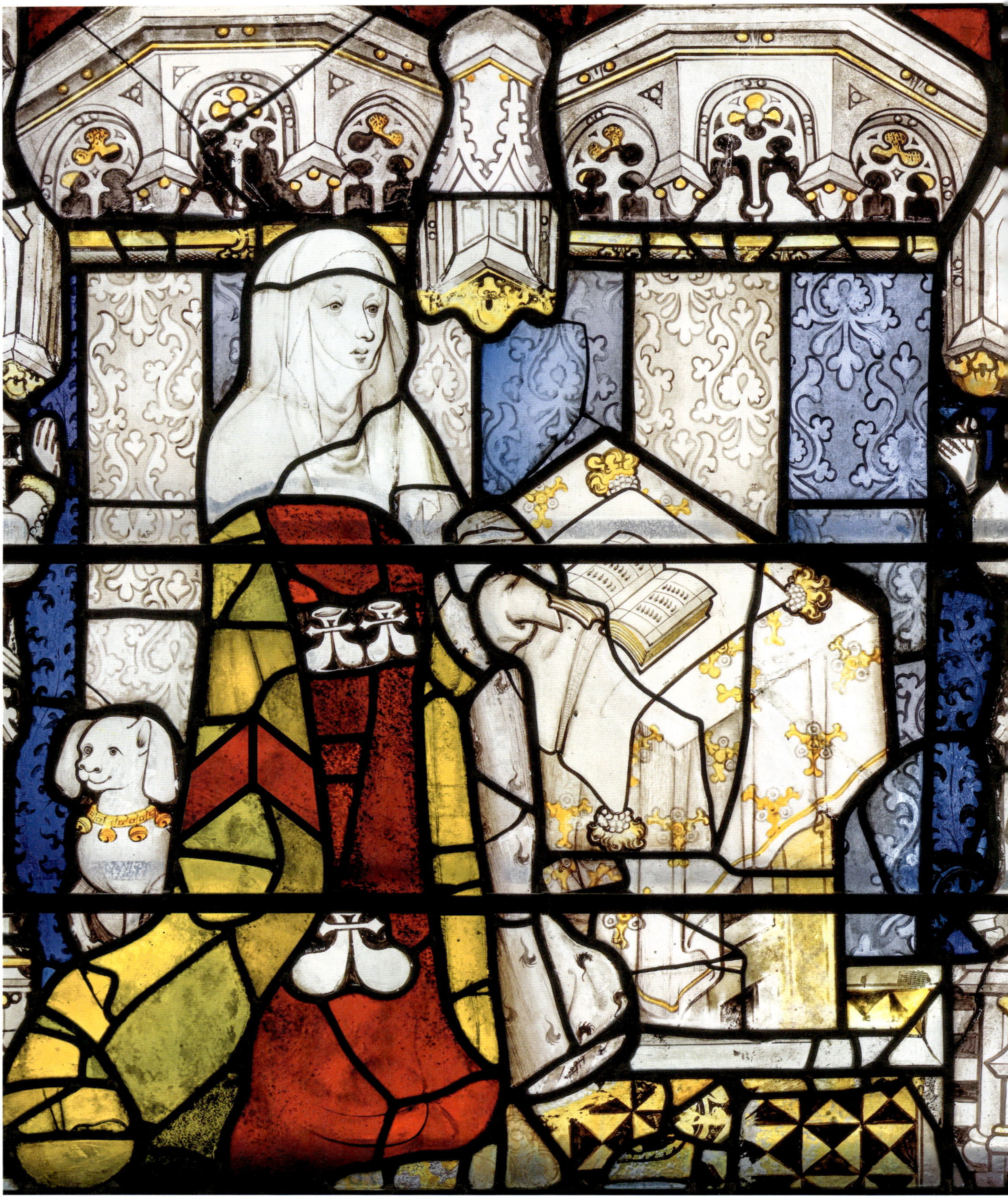

Chapter 4

The Widow and the Glazier

Unlike the Great East Window, for which the record of a contract provides dates and evidence of authorship, the St William Window can only be dated through the careful piecing together of circumstantial evidence derived from its architectural context and its imagery. The two windows are, however, related in a number of ways, not least through the artistic genius of John Thornton, the subject of Chapter 7. The St William Window, together with the Great East Window and the St Cuthbert Window in the equivalent location in the south-east transept, is one of three enormous, glazed narratives lighting the choir, with the windows dedicated to St William (n7) and St Cuthbert (s7), the pre-eminent saints of the North, intended to illuminate the Minster's medieval high altar. The two windows also 'bookend' a series of historical figures at clerestory level that represent the history of the North from the period of the Anglo-Saxon conversion to the twelfth century. As explained in more detail in Chapter 3, the tall eastern transepts, with their cliff-like windows, frequently called the 'lanterns' in the medieval records (frontispiece), must have been envisaged in the earliest stages of architectural planning of the new eastern arm, as they replicated a feature found in the earlier twelfth-century building. The Great East Window, the St William Window and the St Cuthbert Window together form a dazzling triptych of coloured light at the east end of the cathedral (Fig. 1.3), and it is quite possible that thought had been given to the imagery that would eventually fill these huge openings, even as work first began in the early 1360s.

Compelling evidence that the three largest windows in the eastern arm were perceived as a single related entity is contained in the fabric roll surviving for 1399. The inventory compiled in that year, just as work on the western bays of the choir gathered pace, lists a large team of twenty-four masons working under the direction of Master Hugh de Hedon, and importantly for our purposes, records a large stockpile of white glass intended for the 'great windows of the choir', an unmistakable reference to these three windows, which far exceed all other choir windows in

Fig. 4.1
The donor figure of Beatrice de Roos with her heraldic clothing digitally reconstructed, as seen by Henry Johnston in 1670.

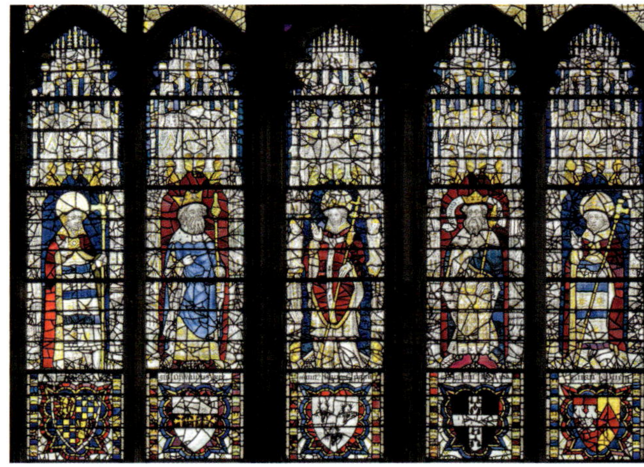

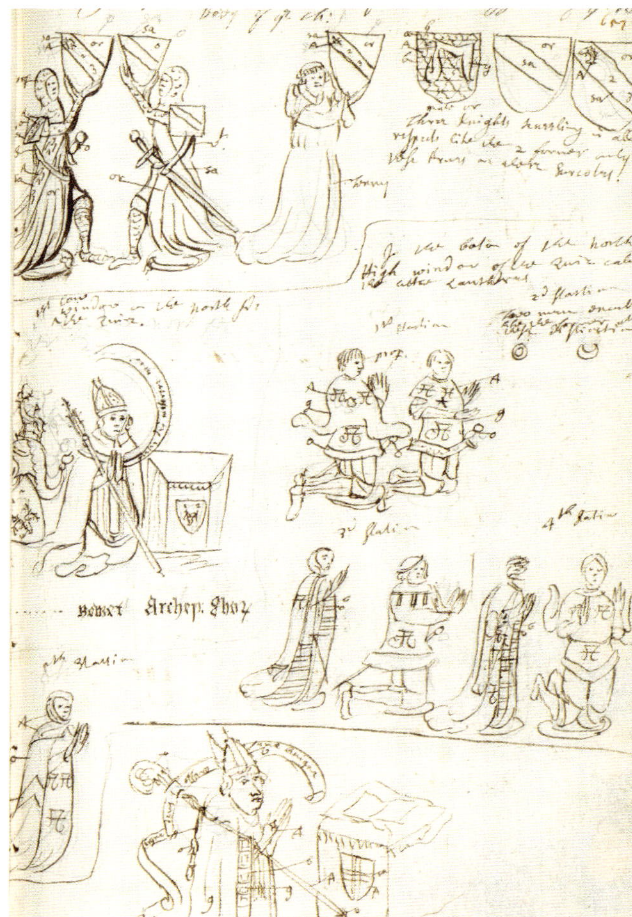

terms of their scale. A step-change in the progress of the choir glazing occurred in the year 1405 with the commissioning of the Great East Window. Copies of the indenture recording the commission reveal that the window was to be complete by 1408 and was made by a team of glaziers (unnamed and unnumbered) led by Master John Thornton of Coventry, a glazier and glass-painter who was also required to cartoon every one of over 300 stained-glass panels. In the bottom row, located in the central panel (1e), is an image of the man who gave the money for the window, Bishop Walter Skirlaw of Durham (d.1406, Fig. 4.4), who did not live to see his great gift to the Minster completed.

The window is hugely ambitious in scope, recounting the Beginning and the End, from Creation to the Second Coming of Christ. It is also a subtle interpretation of the ages of humankind, incorporating historical figures representing key periods in the history of the city and see of York, including St William (1j, Fig. 1.5). John Thornton was a designer of extraordinary talent. His Apocalypse imagery, which occupies the largest section of the Great East Window, was an inspired response to complex biblical sources and a strong visual tradition in English medieval art, as well as being a masterful use of the stained-glass medium on a monumental scale. The case for Thornton's association with the St William Window will be made later in this chapter, but it was the glazing of the Great East Window between 1405 and 1408 that triggered an uninterrupted period of exceptional glazing activity that continued up to the final completion of the choir *c.*1420, a programme that encompassed the windows of the choir aisles and the clerestory, and also included the creation of the St William Window. Only the St Cuthbert Window, created *c.*1440, delayed by structural issues, sits outside this programme of work (Fig. 7.7). Thornton's workshop, active in both York and his native Coventry,

Fig. 4.2
Saints of the North: figures of St Aidan of Lindisfarne, St Oswald, king and martyr, Pope Honorius, St Oswin, King and Martyr, and St Finan of Lindisfarne, with shields of arms beneath them. Window N10.

Fig. 4.3
Henry Johnston's 1670 drawing of glass in the Minster windows. Attracted by their heraldry, Johnston drew Archbishop Henry Bowet in N9 (middle left), the Roos family in the St William Window (middle right) and Bishop Walter Skirlaw, donor of the Great East Window (bottom right). Beatrice is drawn at the bottom on the left.

Fig. 4.4
The Great East Window, panel 1e. The donor, Bishop Walter Skirlaw (d.1406).

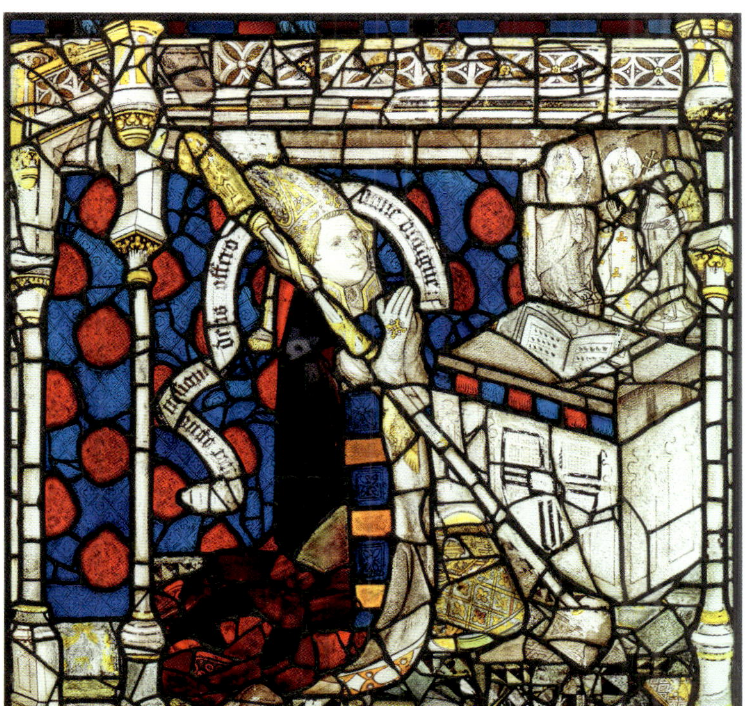

revitalised stained-glass design and creation in York, establishing it as a 'go to' location for anyone interested in the glazier's art and no doubt making it easier for the cathedral Chapter to attract prestigious and wealthy donors for the many windows in the new eastern arm that now required stained glass.

As the making of the Great East Window drew to a close in 1408, attention turned next to the glazing of the high clerestory windows immediately above the choir stalls, at the worshipping heart of the building. Heraldic evidence in glass and stone places this work in the period *c.*1408–14. Logistically, filling these inaccessible high windows before dropping the scaffolding that would have impeded the functioning of the choir also made good sense. The patrons of the clerestory windows, indicated by their coats of arms displayed at the bottom of each light, included the new archbishop of York, Henry Bowet (1408–23), former archbishop of York and archbishop of Canterbury Thomas Arundel (1396–1414), senior members of the cathedral Chapter, including Treasurer John de Neuton (1393–1414), and leading members of the northern nobility (Fig. 4.2). Some shields were included in memory of past members of the Minster community.

In the midst of this scheme at the liturgical epicentre of York Minster is the only shield of arms relating specifically to a female donor (the arms of Roos impaling Stafford), displayed under a figure in the fifth light of clerestory window N10. This is an unequivocal reference to Beatrice, dowager baroness Roos (née Stafford, d.1415), who can now be identified as the donor of the St William Window. The role of Beatrice was almost lost to history as a consequence of damage done to the St William Window in the late seventeenth century. Thankfully, in 1669 eagle-eyed antiquary Henry Johnston recorded her figure prior to the damage, showing her wearing the same heraldry on her clothing, leaving her identity unambiguous (Fig. 4.3). Nonetheless, she remained hiding in plain sight, her identity overlooked and ignored, until recent modern scholarship confirmed beyond doubt Beatrice's role as the window's patron. This establishes her as the most important secular patron of stained glass in the medieval cathedral, on a par with ecclesiastical (male) donors Archbishop William Melton, Bishop Walter Skirlaw and Bishop Thomas Langley, respectively, donors of the West Window, the Great East Window and the St Cuthbert Windows. She is also arguably York Minster's most important lay patron since the Norse nobleman Ulph gave property and a horn of tenure in *c.*1030.

Beatrice de Roos and Her Family

Beatrice was third daughter of the powerful nobleman and courtier Ralph, first earl of Stafford (1301–72) and the widow of Thomas, fourth Lord Roos of Helmsley (1336–84). The latter's arms, suspended under the shoulders

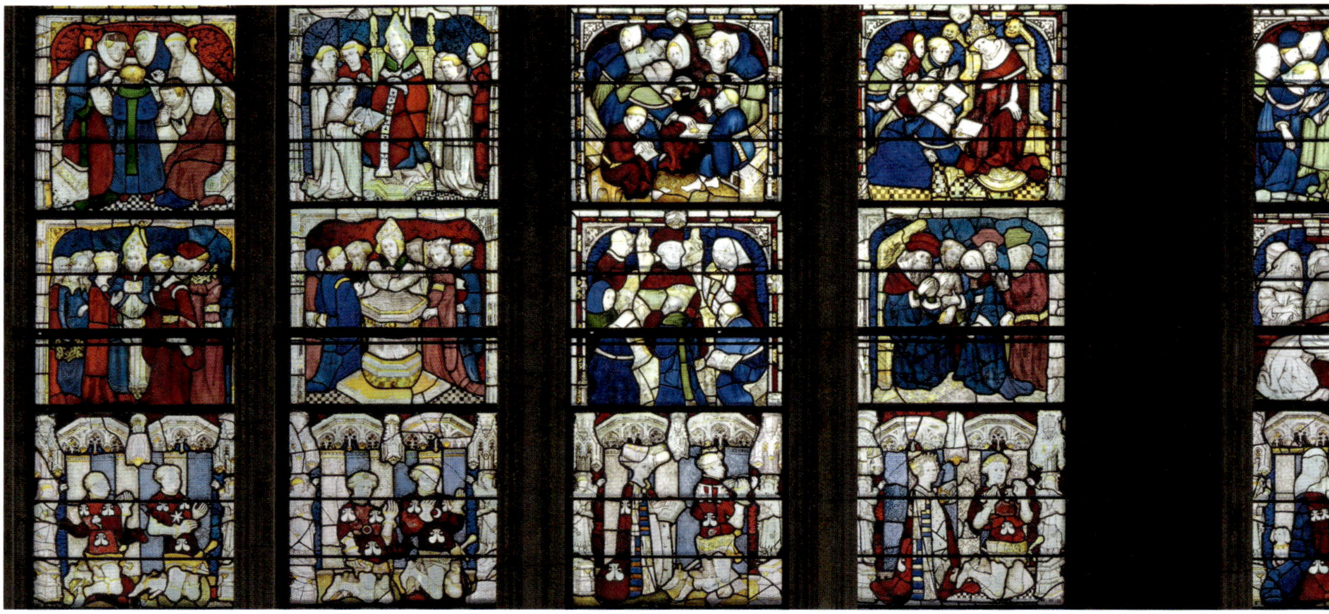

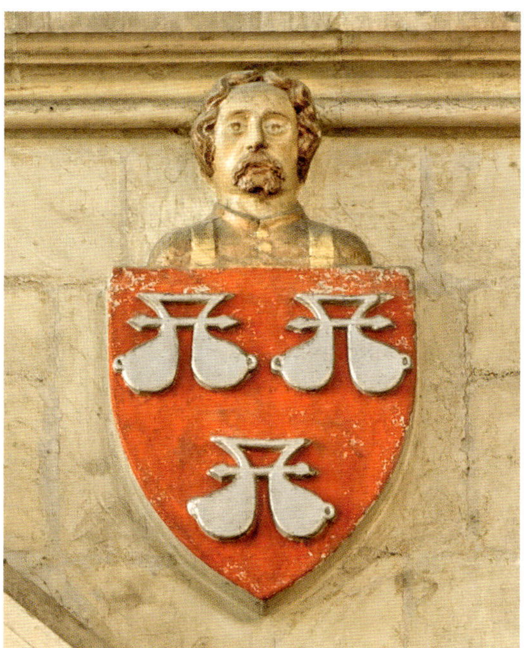

Fig. 4.5
The arms of Thomas, Lord Roos in the south arcade of the Lady Chapel.

Fig.4.6
The bottom section of the St William Window (rows 1–3) with the members of the Roos family ranged in order of seniority from right to left in row 1.

of a man with a goatee beard, are carved in stone in the south-west bay of the Lady Chapel arcade (Fig. 4.5), a reminder of the family's long association with York Minster. Beatrice married Thomas in 1359 very soon after the death of her first husband, and by the time he died she had borne him six children, four boys and two girls. Her two eldest sons, John (d.1393) and William (d.1414), succeeded their father as fifth and sixth Lords Roos respectively. Johnston's drawing recorded her in 'the fifth position' (i.e. panel 1e) of the St William Window, effectively at the head of her family, who accompanied her at the base of the window. All of the figures face east, towards the high altar and the location of the reliquary and shrine of St William (Fig. 4.6). The damage to Beatrice's own clothing and the repetition of the same impaled Despenser arms on the dress of two of the other women in row 1 has, in the past, caused some confusion as to the identity of the figures and thus the date of the window. However, the confirmation of Beatrice's identity, the number of Roos men depicted and the careful differentiation of the heraldry on the surcoats of the men make it clear that the figures accompanying Beatrice are a mother, father and five sons, one of them married, a combination that can only have fitted Beatrice's son William, sixth Lord Roos, his wife Margaret (Arundel) and their five sons.

By the fifteenth century the visual language of heraldry was well developed as a means of identifying members of the aristocracy. Coats of arms were altered and adjusted ('differenced') to a set of increasingly complex rules in order to distinguish between different branches of the same family, to identify the familial connections of married women and the younger male members of the same family. This is what we see at the base of the St William Window, in the distinctive marks carefully added to the basic arms of Roos that decorate the surcoats worn over the armour by William's sons. The four youngest boys, Robert and Richard (in panel 1a), and William and Thomas (1b), were probably only children at the time of the window's making, and John (1c), although married, was still only sixteen or seventeen. However, according to convention, all are shown attired as soldiers, albeit rather boyish ones. The inclusion of John's wife Margery (Despenser) in 1c means that the base of the window could not have been conceived in this form before 1404 when she married him. As John is shown with the differenced arms of the eldest son, the figure with undifferenced arms in 1d must represent his father William, Beatrice's eldest surviving son, accompanied by his own wife Margaret (Arundel) albeit with the wrong heraldry on her cloak. This means that the window must have been planned before William's death on 1 September 1414, and probably even earlier, as no mention of any funds for the window are mentioned in Beatrice's will made in June of that year. In fact, it is likely that the window was still unfinished at the time of William's death, and that the confusing double depiction of the Despenser arms on the heraldic clothing of the two wives in 1c and 1d was an attempt to update the imagery in the bottom row of panels, presumably still in store awaiting installation, in order to show Beatrice's grandson and heir John, only just legally of age, as the new head of the family. Beatrice herself died less than a year later, on 14 April 1415.

This is a highly contrived family portrait. Beatrice is not only the oldest person representing the Roos family in the St William Window, she is also located in a position that places her at the head of her family. Unlike the rest of her family, she kneels alone, before a prayer desk, singled out by her solitude and the sobriety of her widow's clothing, in contrast to the modish dress of the younger women depicted behind her. Her isolation actually underlines her importance and might be compared to the donor panel in the Great East Window, where Bishop Walter Skirlaw also kneels alone (Fig. 4.4). Beatrice is accompanied only by her pet dog. She is depicted as a Roos widow and dowager. Neither her husband nor her eldest son, John, who had died in 1393, are represented in the window at all. Indeed, by the time the window was created, Beatrice had actually married again and been widowed for the third time by the death in 1387 of her last husband, Sir Richard Burley KG. Nor does the window include any of Beatrice's still-living daughters or grand-daughters, although her will

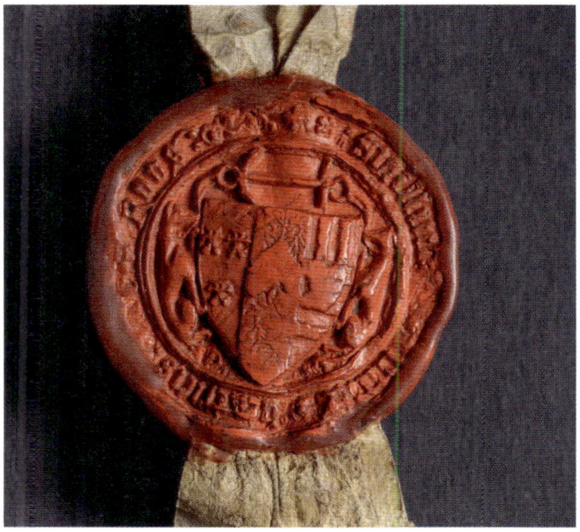

Fig. 4.7
The seal of Beatrice de Roos, inscribed '*Sigillum domine beatricis de Roos*', used to seal documents between 1388 and 1414. British Library Add. Ch. 22, 391.

suggests close and loving attachments. The window is therefore not a memorial to Beatrice's immediate family, nor a commemoration of the Roos's succession. Rather, it presents a precise snapshot of Beatrice as progenitrice of a secure Roos dynasty, represented by her eldest surviving son at the time the window was commissioned, William, the sixth lord Roos, replete with his plentiful male heirs. And her own experience underlined the fragility of familial succession and the importance of this achievement. Both her first and second husbands had succeeded to their titles due to the deaths of their own elder brothers, and Beatrice and Thomas's own eldest son, John, had died young and childless. In the event, Beatrice's grandson and her own designated heir, also named John (panel 1c), also died young and without children. However, as the father of five sons, William's line was secure and it was Beatrice's younger grandson Thomas (depicted in 1b), originally destined for a career in the church, who carried on the family line.

As a widowed woman in possession of the dower assigned to her from three marriages, Beatrice would have accumulated very substantial wealth, and the survival of documents sealed in the years of her widowhood with her very distinctive and unusual heraldic seal, shows her to have been proactive in the management of her property as well as the manipulation of her heraldic identity. The impression of a seal acted as the owner's proxy and gave force to the wishes and instructions of its owner. Beatrice's seal (Fig. 4.7) is an atypical form that fused the centrally positioned arms of her father with those of her Roos and Burley husbands, thereby creating a new heraldic persona that is unique to her. Johnston's drawing shows that a similar flouting of heraldic convention was adopted in the portrait image of Beatrice in the St William Window. A woman's arms would normally place those of her husband on the more honorific right-hand side of the shield (viewer's left) and those of her family on the left (viewer's right), as is the case in window N10 (Fig. 4.8). In the St William Window the wives in 1d and 1c are conventionally attired with their gowns decorated with their natal arms (heraldically on the left) and the Roos arms on their cloaks (heraldically on the right), in the more senior position. In Beatrice's case, as Johnston's drawing shows, the order was deliberately reversed, with the Roos gown overlaid with a Stafford cloak, making her original appearance all the more distinctive (Fig. 4.1). The subtle inversion of heraldic convention is a process normally only associated with men, particularly men at the highest echelons of feudal society, including King Richard II, who impaled his arms with those of St Edward the Confessor, and John of Gaunt, Duke of Lancaster, who impaled his arms with those of his wife Blanche of Castile, heir to the throne of Spain. Modern scholarship establishes Beatrice as a woman equally prepared to manipulate heraldic conventions to construct her own visual identity.

Not only was Beatrice wealthy; in the years around 1408 she was also very active in the commissioning of art, and was in negotiation with the leading ecclesiastical artists and craftsmen of the day. In that year she established a chantry at St Paul's Cathedral in London in memory of her third husband, a prominent retainer of John of Gaunt, Duke of Lancaster (and father of King Henry IV). In fulfilment of the requirements of Sir Richard Burley's will, she had also commissioned a large and expensive tomb close to the Duke of Lancaster's own sumptuous double monument in the choir of Old St Paul's. Although she chose not to be buried with Sir Richard, whose effigy reclined alone on his monument, her distinctive personal heraldry, as seen on her seal, decorated the monument's canopy (Fig. 4.9). This project was almost certainly commissioned from the London workshop of the leading architect of the day, the king's mason Henry Yevele.

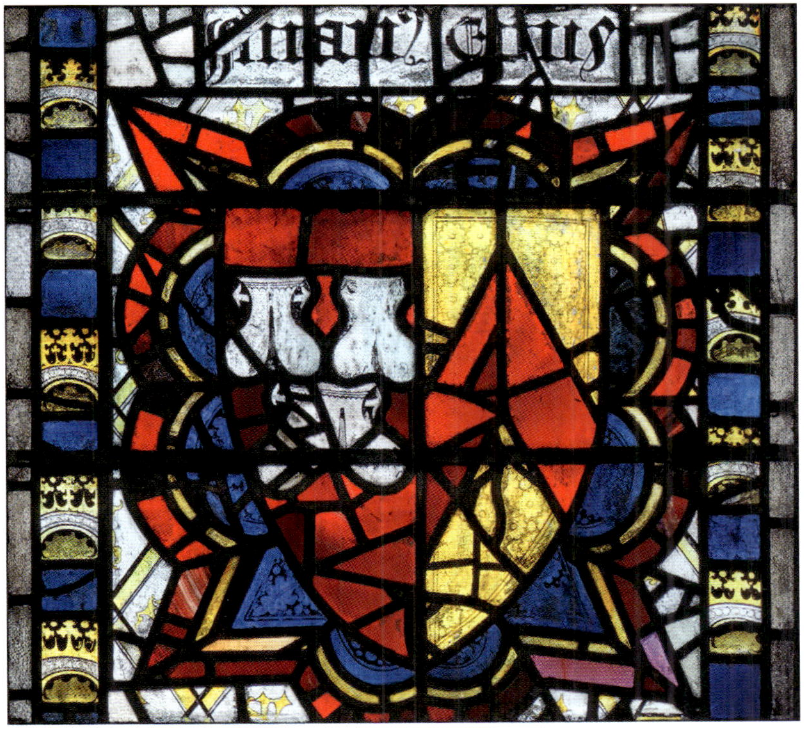

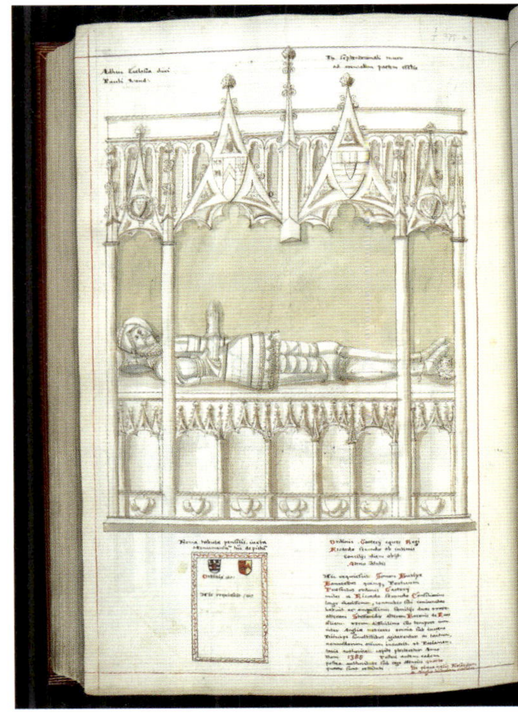

Fig. 4.8
The arms of Beatrice de Roos (Roos impaling Stafford) in window N10, panel 2e (detail).

Fig. 4.9
The tomb of Sir Richard Burley KG in Old St Paul's Cathedral, recorded for William Dugdale's *Book of Monuments*. Watercolour by William Sedgwick, June 1641. British Library, Add. MS 71474, fol. 181v.

Her outstanding credentials as a patron would hardly have been missed by those in charge of the fabric of the Minster, themselves well connected in Lancastrian circles. The years around 1408 therefore stand out as likely to have been a crucial period in the process of commissioning the St William Window and securing Beatrice's interest in it. The Great East Window was complete, freeing an outstanding designer and project manager in the person of John Thornton. The glazing of the choir clerestory was getting under way, a scheme which also includes the unmistakable heraldry of Beatrice de Roos. Someone associated with the work at York, perhaps the Treasurer John de Neuton (d.1414), himself a prominent donor to the Minster, had obviously spotted a potential patron of the next great glazing project in need of financial support, the St William Window.

If a large window dedicated to the life of St William had been a long time in the planning, its physical realisation came at a particularly advantageous moment, boosting the prestige of the Minster's officially enshrined saint. As discussed in Chapter 3, William's cult had lost some ground during a long construction period in which the choir shrine would have been relatively inaccessible, and in the face of the popular appeal of the new, unofficial cult of Archbishop Richard Scrope (d. 1405). Through their saintly relative Archbishop Richard, the Scopes of Masham had rapidly achieved prominence in the Minster, and the chapel of St Stephen at the east end of the north choir aisle had been appropriated as a Scope mausoleum, as discussed in the previous chapter. Archbishop Richard's nephew, Stephen Scrope, archdeacon of Richmond between 1402 and his death in 1418, was probably the patron of one of the north choir clerestory windows (N9), next to the window including Beatrice's arms, and gave another window in the south-east transept clerestory (S6). In his will, the archbishop's other nephew,

Henry Lord Scrope of Masham, whose arms are prominently featured in window N9, outlined two options for his own burial, one of which was in St Stephen's chapel, close to his family members. His first preference, should his royal bride consent to be buried with him, was to be buried in the Minster choir, immediately north of the shrine of St William and thereby directly in sight of Beatrice's window. This would have made him the only layman to be buried in such a prestigious location, a plan confounded by his execution for treason in 1415.

In contrast to the Scropes, the Roos family's associations with the Minster were very long-standing, going back to at least the late thirteenth century. The Roos arms feature in the glass of the Chapter House and carved shields of the family appear four times in the north nave arcade. The creation of the St William Window was therefore an opportunity to reassert the credentials of the Roos family as leading Minster benefactors. It is also easy to see how the Chapter could make the patronage of the window into an especially attractive project for a wealthy Roos matriarch. An advantageous marriage in the distant past meant that the Roos family could legitimately claim St William as a family member, through the union of Lucy FitzHerbert, daughter of St William's great-nephew Peter FitzHerbert (d. 1235) to William de Roos (d. 1264). The name William was also favoured in the family. The predominance of imagery relating to female beneficiaries of St William's miracle-working – twelve episodes – would probably have exerted a particular appeal for a female donor, and the very first of St William's healing miracles (panel 11c), given particular visual prominence in the window's centre light, involved a young blind girl. Four of the stories involving St William's protection of women are afforded a pair of panels, including panels 24d and 24e.

Panels 24d and 24e are of particular importance in relation to Beatrice's patronage of the window. They are the final two panels at the very top of the narrative and immediately above the figure of Beatrice herself. They depict an accident taking place in a landscape. An aristocratic woman dressed in red and wearing an ermine and bejewelled hat, the only elite woman depicted in the window other than the female members of the royal family represented in panels 18b and 18e, is first apparently trampled by a horse, and then gives thanks for her deliverance at the shrine of St William. These panels conclude the sequence, which in broad terms follows a temporal chronology. Unlike some of the other panels in the last two rows, these two scenes are unique designs and owe nothing to visual elements elsewhere in the window. They have no parallel in the written sources known to have informed the design process. They evidently depict a specific and recent incident, and have clearly been specially chosen to fill the last two places in the narrative, in such a way that the lady kneeling in front of the shrine in panel 24e is located immediately above the figure of Beatrice de Roos kneeling at her prie-dieu. It is tempting to identify this sumptuously dressed noblewoman as Beatrice herself, the personal beneficiary of some unrecorded saintly intercession that she asked to have woven into the window's narrative. We know that Beatrice engaged in potentially dangerous leisure pursuits, for in 1372, when she was about twenty-seven, John of Gaunt, the duke of Lancaster, gave permission for her to conduct a hunting expedition on his lands. We can speculate that in her old age she attributed a lucky escape from death or injury to the intercession of St William!

Beatrice's portrait in the St William Window survives as the only monument to her memory. She chose to be buried alone in the church of the small Augustinian house at Warter, to the east of York, close to the house where she spent her final years. The church has disappeared without a trace, and along with it Beatrice's tomb.

John Thornton and the St William Window

The Minster's Great East Window, the largest single window ever glazed in medieval England, is the only documented work of master glazier John Thornton of Coventry. However, Thornton is known to have remained in York for at least twenty-five years after the window's completion. He was therefore free to accept another major commission at exactly the right moment in the history of the St William Window. He became a freeman of the city in 1410 and was still living in York in 1433, in a property owned by the Dean and Chapter, although he was also running a business in Coventry. Many commentators, including the authors of this work, believe that Thornton was also the designer of the St William Window, as well as having a pervasive influence on much of the glazing of the Minster's eastern arm in the period 1408–20. On what is this opinion founded?

The conservation of the Great East Window between 2011 and 2017 provided an unparalleled opportunity for art historians and conservators to re-examine the physical evidence for the role John Thornton played, especially in light of the 1405 indenture, which laid out his responsibilities and rewards. The 1405 contract provides invaluable insights into the portfolio of competencies and responsibilities required of a master glazier. Thornton was expected to paint some of the window himself, to recruit and organise the necessary workforce and to procure all the materials, but above all, to create with his own hand every one of over 300 full-scale 'cartoons' from which the window was made, accurate 1:1 outlines of all the essential design data laid out on a whitened glazier's table, such as survives in Girona in Catalonia, an extraordinarily rare survival (Fig. 4.10). It was this aspect of the window, entrusted to Thornton alone, that was placed first in the list of his responsibilities. When read alongside the detailed glazing accounts for another elite project, for the royal chapel of St Stephen at the Palace of Westminster, dating from the middle of the fourteenth century, we can see that the painting of glass was by no means the most highly rewarded skill expected of the master.

The contract for the creation of a window, the document that confirmed financial terms and conditions and set a time-scale for the project's delivery, would only be signed once essential preparatory work was complete. This would have included the sourcing and ordering of materials and tools, and the recruiting of a workforce sufficient to make a prompt start on the work, as well as liaising with the master mason concerning the templating of stone openings and perhaps even discussions with the master blacksmith who would forge the iron support system for the glass. Above all, the background research that informed the window's overall narrative, and which was critical to the design of individual panels, needed to be complete. This was especially important if the subject matter was unprecedented, as was the case with the St William Window. This process required an intimate knowledge of the Latin sources, and so must have included a theologically trained Chapter representative, and perhaps even an agent representing the patron. It is known that most contracts were complemented by a visual 'attachment', a small-scale drawing of the overall appearance of the window known as a 'vidimus' (meaning 'we have seen'). Very few vidimuses have survived. Some are annotated with notes that can, in some instances, be attributed to the hand of the master glazier, suggesting an early dialogue between glazier and patron. Even the largest and most detailed, such as the early-sixteenth-century one for an apparently unrealised thirteen-light project for Cardinal Wolsey (Fig. 4.11), which includes a figure of St William, reveals the huge gulf between the preliminary design and the degree of detail needed by the glaziers entrusted with the making of the window. This was the gap that the master glazier was required to fill in the creation of the full-size cartoon. It was this task that transformed the small, lightly coloured sketch into a viable stained-glass panel, accurately dimensioned to the window opening and achievable as a work of art in richly coloured glass and lead.

While no vidimus for the Great East Window or St William Window survives, some of the illuminated manuscripts that informed the iconography of the Apocalypse cycle in the Great East Window have recently been identified. A comparison of the tiny manuscript images with the monumental metre-square stained-glass panels, each weighing in the region of 25kg, makes the sheer audacity of Thornton's transformation of his models into the medium of stained glass immediately apparent.

It is therefore easy to see why the Chapter of York insisted that Thornton take personal responsibility for every one of the full-size 'cartoons' of the Great East Window, and that it was his ability as a designer of outstanding talent, not to mention a craftsman and project manager of exceptional skill, that defined his attraction to the Dean and Chapter. This is in marked contrast to the workshop practices at the royal chapel of St Stephen at Westminster, where several draughtsmen assisted in the preparation of the full-scale cartoons, working under the direction of the overall master, John of Chester. These differences may indicate the time pressures under which the Westminster glaziers were working, but may also reflect the greater creative challenges posed by the creation of narrative panels as opposed to standing figures under canopies.

And if his genius as a designer was essential to the success of the Great East Window, how much more critical was his ability to the creation of the St William Window? The St William Window is only marginally smaller than the Great East Window – 100 versus 117 main light panels. Only the tracery of the Great East Window exceeds that of the St William Window to an appreciable degree.

The narratives in the Great East Window were all derived from pre-existing textual sources – the Old Testament (rows 13–15), the Book of Revelation (the Apocalypse, rows 2–11) and a late-fourteenth-century, locally composed chronicle (row 1). This is in no way to diminish Thornton's outstanding achievement in creating a unique version of this complex subject in stained glass, but there was absolutely no precedent for a stained-glass life of St William of York on such a scale. There were Latin texts to inform a St William narrative but these

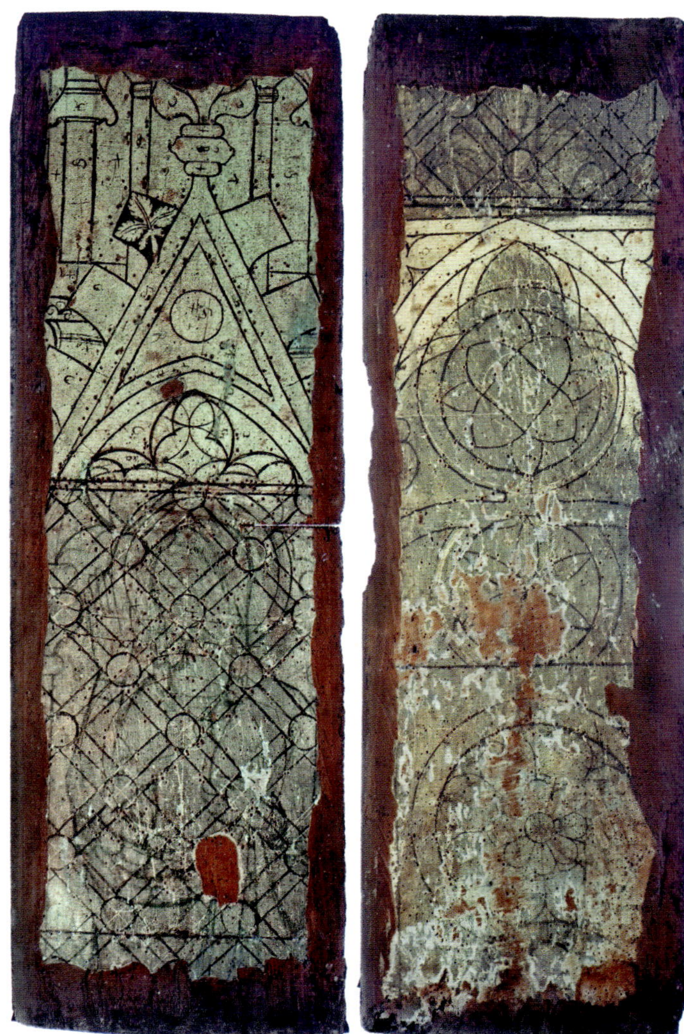

Fig. 4.10
The Girona glaziers' table, cut into two sections, was used *c.*1340 to manufacture panels for the glazing of the choir clerestory of Girona cathedral. UV examination of the surfaces reveals evidence of washing and reuse of the table, as described in the twelfth century by the writer known as Theophilus. Museu d'Art, Girona.

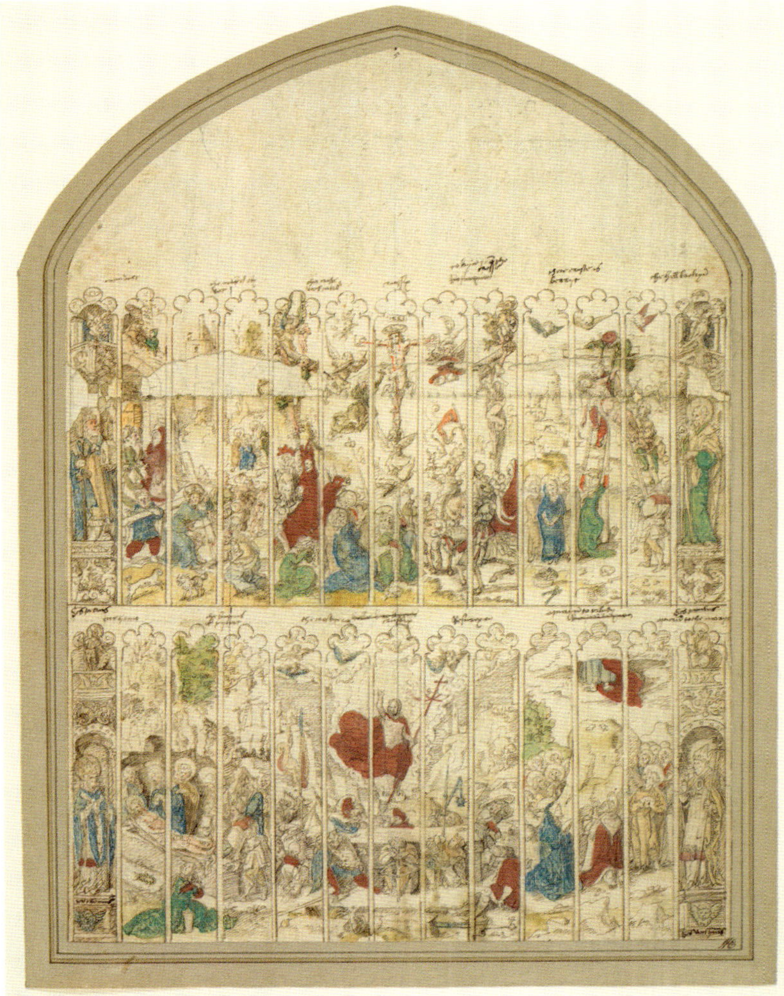

Fig. 4.11
Vidimus for an unrealised thirteen-light glazing project for Cardinal Thomas Wolsey. St William is depicted in the bottom-right corner of the design, which has been attributed to the designer Erhard Schön. National Gallery of Scotland, Nuremberg School, D959A.

sources needed to be carefully sifted and collated to create a strong story and there was no pre-existing extended illustrated cycle of the life and miracles of St William to which the designer could turn for inspiration. As discussed in Chapter 3, the earlier imagery featuring aspects of William's life provided no model capable of informing a window comprising ninety-five narrative panels. Certain iconographic tropes were a mainstay of all windows devoted to saints – a blameless life, martyrdom and miracle-working, especially after death. However, in comparison to Thomas Becket of Canterbury or Cuthbert of Durham, St William of York was far from being the most exciting of saints, with a life overshadowed by ecclesiastical bureaucracy and legal dispute. If anyone could turn this material into a narrative fit for a location next to the high altar of the mother church of the Northern Province of the Church in England, a window that told the story of the saint enshrined behind that altar, it was John Thornton. Thornton's achievements as the designer of the St William Window are a subject to which we will return in Chapter 7.

If we cannot document Thornton's association with the St William Window in the historical record, neither can we substantiate an association between the St William Window, John Thornton and the Great East Window based on glass-painting style, though to lay undue stress on this aspect of the window is, as we have seen, to misunderstand what contemporaries valued most about John Thornton. If his role as a glass-painter has attracted modern interest, it was certainly not what mattered most to Thornton's medieval patrons. In fact, the Great East Window indenture does not make it clear exactly what Thornton would be expected to paint, although it was something that we were anxious to examine more carefully during the window's recent restoration. Reluctantly, however, we were forced to conclude that while the glass-painting was executed to a consistent and exceptionally high standard, probably by four or five different painters, who sometimes worked together across a single panel, it was impossible to define what was meant by the expectation that Thornton himself should 'paynt the same where need required according to the Ordination of the Dean & Chapter', as worded in the indenture. Consequently, we cannot even identify Thornton the glass-painter in the painting of the one window documented as containing his work. It is clear, however, that some of the painters who worked on the Great East Window were also involved in painting the St William Window, as well as some of the glass in the windows of the western choir aisles.

The style in which the painters of the Great East Window worked has been described as the hallmark of a 'Thornton workshop', and these characteristics are clearly present in the St William Window too. The characterful faces with long noses with bulbous ends and the wide-eyed faces with carefully delineated pupils are common to both windows (Fig. 4.12). Numerous details in the St William Window show that the glass-painters entrusted with the execution of Thornton's designs had access to the same repertoire of visual sources – head types, gestures, decorative details – as those who painted the Great East Window. The rocky landscapes frequently depicted in the Great East Window (e.g. panels 11b (Fig. 4.13), 11d, 10g, 9a, 9j, 8c, 4a, 4j, 3h, 3j) have their counterparts in the St William Window (notably 8c). The verdant foliage of trees and bushes in the Great East Window (e.g. 15a, 14a) have grown even more luxurious in the St William Window (7b, 7d, 17d), where they are also better preserved. The ships in the St William Window (8c, 16e, 17e) are closely related to their counterparts in the Great East Window (11b), and the eager little dog on the forecastle of Noah's ark (Great East Window 14b, Fig 4.14) has his equivalent in the scene of St William at sea in 8c. These playful details are not determined by any iconographic requirement. Both little dogs are also closely related to Beatrice de Roos's pet. Likewise, many of the horses depicted in both windows have clearly been bred from the same stables! The figure with crutches and bandaged legs in the Great East Window scene of Moses and the serpent of brass (13f) is a forerunner to many of the afflicted supplicants in the St William Window. Gestures, especially those used to express grief or consternation, and a repertoire of head types (for example, the man with dark, close-cropped hair with a widow's peak), not always executed by the same painter, can be tracked across both windows .

Most instructive is the evidence of a comparable approach to the construction of figure groups. The designer of both windows could position figure groups within three-

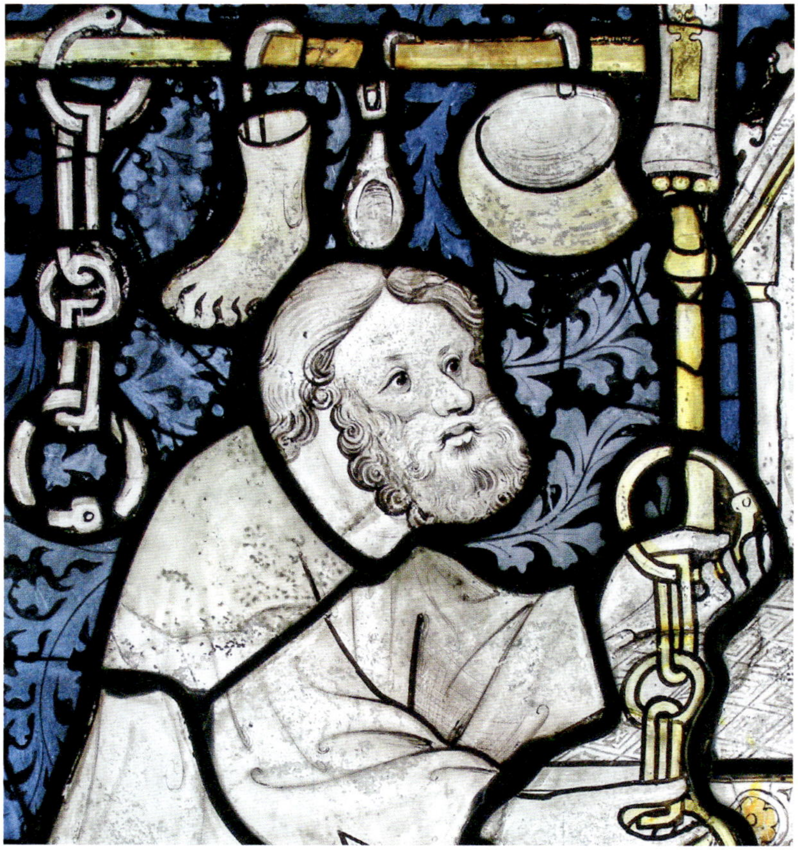

Fig. 4.12
The 'Thornton style'. The head of a liberated prisoner, the St William Window, panel 22b (detail).

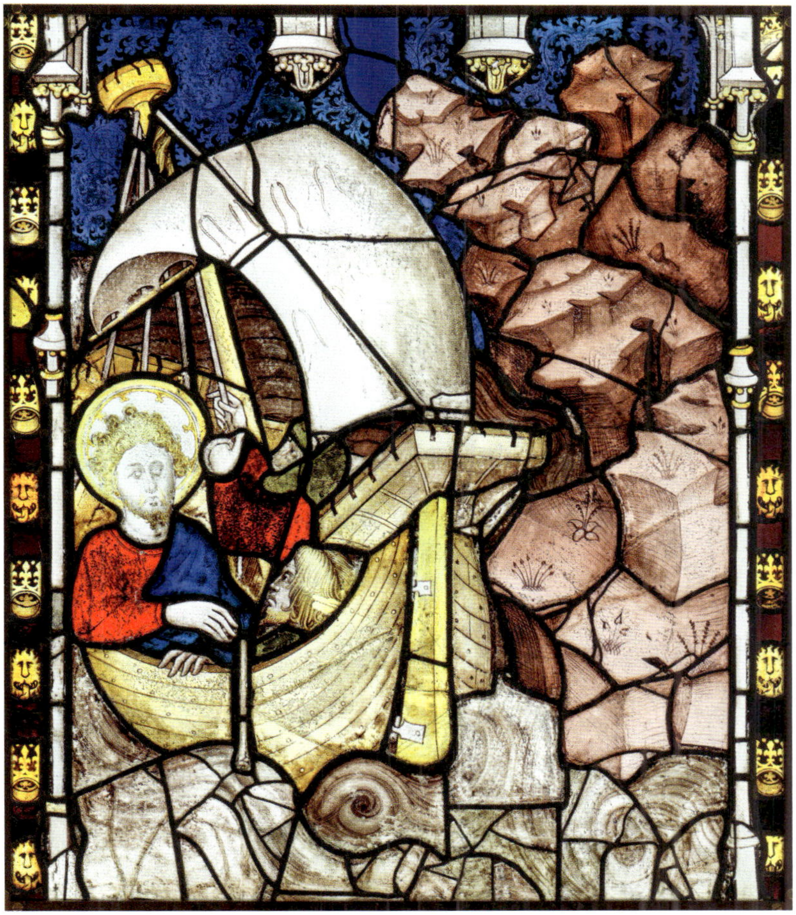

Fig. 4.13
The Great East Window, panel 11b. St John sails to the island of Patmos.

dimensional architectural structures (Great East Window 8j, Fig. 4.15; St William Window 7b, 7d) and frequently uses micro-architectural forms to indicate the switch between rural and urban settings. The device of overlapping 'whispering' heads, a frequent detail in the St William Window (see, for example, 3a, 3c, 4d, 5c, 8n, 8d,18a, 19d, 20d, 20e), where those witnessing the narrative are often shown in a conspiratorial huddle, their bent heads balanced by pointing fingers that define the focus of the panel's narrative interest, can also be found in embryo in the Great East Window. Good examples include the men amazed at the sight of the serpent of brass (13f) and in the cowled and whispering heads gathered to hear the preaching of St John in panel 17c (Fig. 4.16). This last scene also highlights a shared taste across both windows for circular groupings of figures, something that is exploited even more in the later St William Window (2c, 3a, 3c, 5d).

Above all, the design of the St William Window shares with Thornton's work in the Great East Window the capacity to manage a story on a huge scale, requiring the expansion and contraction of narrative components across a large window. The compression of elements in the account of St John writing to the Seven Churches into a single panel (Great East Window, 11f), might be compared to the triple deathbed scene of St William's three Cistercian opponents in 1153, ingeniously accommodated in a single panel (St William Window, 7c). The effect of a 'timelapse' in the action in a single panel is also shared across the two windows. The circle of arms in the temptation of Adam (Great East Window, 15h), in which the devil points to a fruit that is plucked and offered by Eve, to be grasped and bitten by Adam, might be compared to the frog-poisoning episode in panel 17a of the St William Window. A woman seated at a table stretches out to take a slice of bread with one hand, bringing another slice to her mouth, while the frog sits balefully at the top of the sliced loaf, ready to be eaten in her next mouthful. Next to the table the same woman, now standing and in great discomfort, has unfastened her girdle and opened her gown to ease her pain. The choice of costume and colour palette ensures that the viewer recognises that the scene is depicting the same person in two episodes of the same story, albeit presented in single pictorial space. This device is also used in panel 2j of the Great East Window, although the loss of the original head of the left-hand figure of St John obscures the fact that the saint appears twice in the same scene. These story-telling devices are employed deliberately and with editorial intent, because elsewhere in the two windows several panels can be made available for those

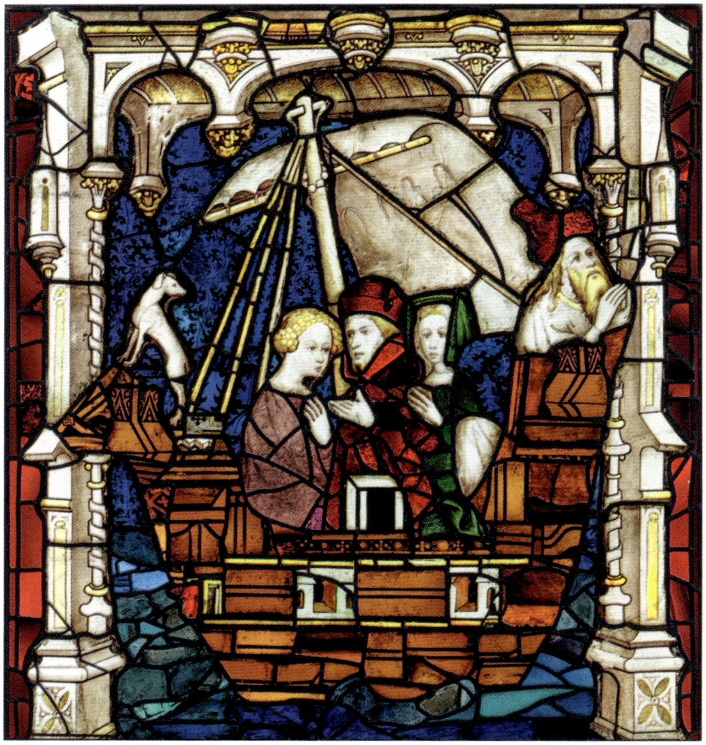

Fig. 4.14
The Great East Window, panel 14b. Noah's ark. While the ship has been badly damaged, the little dog on the forecastle is original.

sequences to be accorded greater emphasis – such as the five horsemen of the Apocalypse and the sounding of the Seven Trumpets (Great East Window, 10e–10h, 9h, 9j, 8a–8d), the Ralph and Besing story (St William Window, 12a–12e), and King Edward I and the Translation of St William's relics (St William Window, 18a–18e).

Past writers have suggested that some of the same cartoons were used in the two windows. This is very unlikely given the passage of time between them (probably a decade between their respective design stages) and the inherently unwieldy nature of medieval 'cartoons', which did not lend themselves to easy replication and adaptation except within the orbit of the same project. While paper became more affordable and accessible in the post-medieval period, the functionality of the wooden glaziers' table, which combined cartoon, cut-line and workbench, prevailed for many centuries. The table was washed, in whole or in part, to allow the adaptation of a design between panels or rows, but its size and rigidity meant that it could not be easily stored over long periods like the Victorian workshop method of rolled-up paper cartoons. The difference in panel size and shape between one window and another would also have made retention of a cartoon with the intention of adaptive reuse of limited value. Any close similarities between the two windows are above all indicative of the shared authorship at the highest level of design, reinforced by the workshop members' access to a 'library' of design ideas, figure and head types, gestures and decorative and architectural motifs, potentially over long periods of time. Like vidimuses, medieval sketch books are rare, but we can almost imagine the contents of John Thornton's from these two windows.

Above all, it is a shared capacity for the expression of the humanity of its subjects – joy,

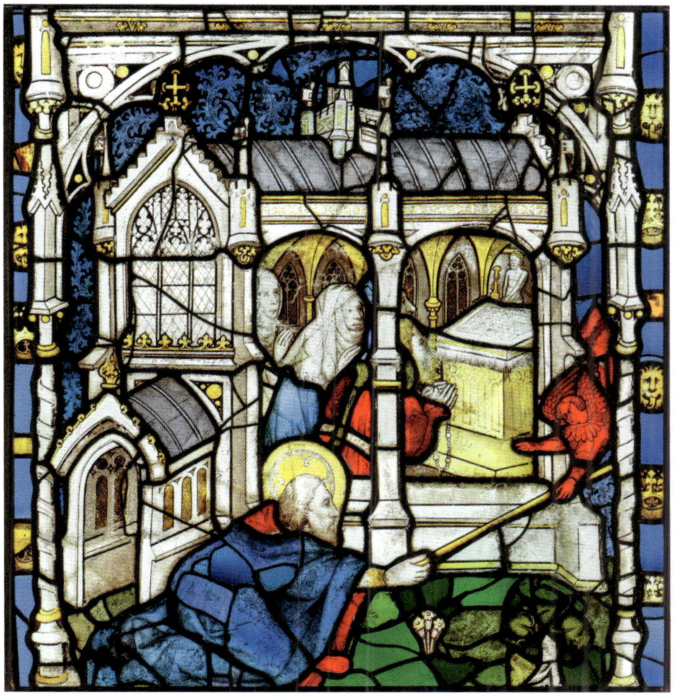

Fig. 4.15
The Great East Window, panel 8j. St John measures the Temple.

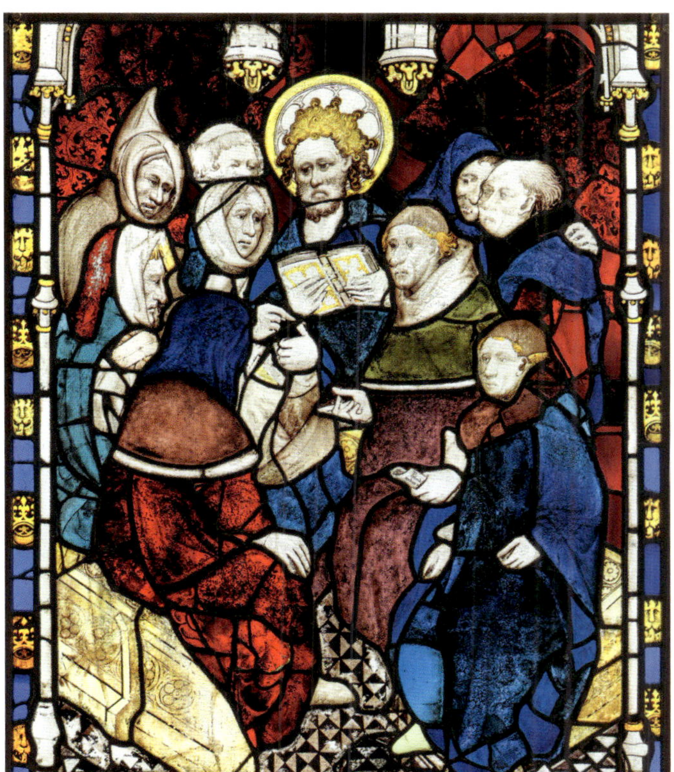

Fig. 4.16
The Great East Window, panel 11c. St John teaching.

sorrow, consternation, amazement, fear, pain, resignation, mental anguish and quiet devotion – that marks these two windows as being the product of the same outstanding storyteller. Thornton's people are not wooden or doll-like. They exude energy and vitality. In Thornton's windows the narrative is actually experienced by those depicted. Their gestures, their faces and even their body language tell us what they see and feel, and invite us to enter into their space and to listen to their conversations. And it was the St William Window, in particular, that gave this creative genius free rein, as we shall explore further in Chapter 7.

5t Quire Windows

Moreover it is to be observed that this 3d Window (as the first) hath about the borders of each Light this Inscription viz Robtus Waldon/

Arms in stone in the Roof over agst this Window viz

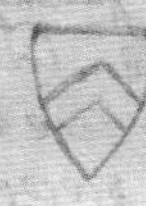

A a chev. inter 3 heads O

4th The Cross Window

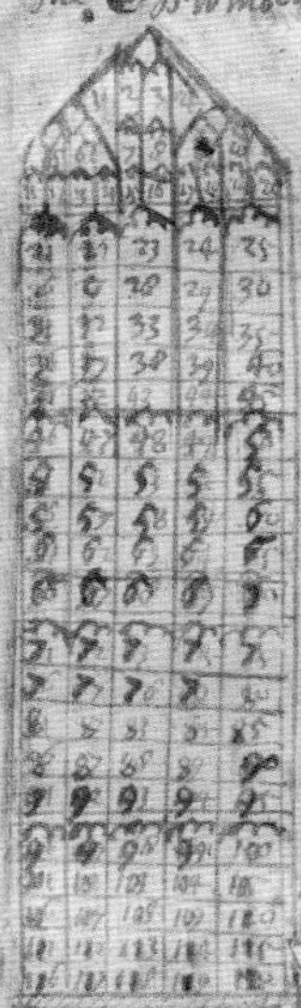

The 4th Window may be called the Cross or Lanthorn Window for that it gives Light both to this & the midle quire in wch respect a whole Arch does here want its Roof

It is of double stone work as far as the turn of the top & contains 5 Lights wch are divided by 4 Transoms

At top of all are 4 in a Row whereof in the midle sitt enthroned

2 a Queen robed B. Crowned O holding her hand Cross upon her breast & a litle elevated

3/ Also a King by her Robed A & gu. Globe & Crown O.

1/ 2/ On each side them kneels a man in white Rayment wth a golden bird upon their heads

2d Top Row/ In a lower Row stand 6 other persons

5/ One is an Abp. Robed B. pall A. Myter & Cross staff O.

6/ A King robed gu. mantle Erm. Scepter & Crown O

7 An Abp. habited B pall & Myter A Cross staff O.

8/ A King robed Sanguine. Mantle Erm. Crowned O

9/ An Abp habited B. pall & Cross staff A Myter O.

10 A King Robed Vt. Crowned A. Scepter O.

3d Top Row. Below the last stand 10 persons in a Row wthin as many apartments viz

11/ An Abp. habited B & Sanguine pall A. Myter & Cross staff O

12/ a King robed gu. Mantle A. Crown & Scepter O.

13/ An Abp. habited B. pall A Myter & Cross O

14 A King robed gu. Mantle A. Scepter & Crown O

15/ An Abp. habited B. pall & Myter A Cross staff O

16. A King Robed B & Murry. Mantle A. Crown & Scepter O

17/ An Abp habited B pall & Myter A. Cross staff O.

18/ A King Robed gu. Mantle Erm Crown & Scepter O

19/ An Abp. habited gu. pall A. Cross staff & Myter O

20/ A King robed gu. & A. mantle Vt. Crown & Scepter O.

In the partitions under the Window top are 5 Rows of Imagry/ 1st R

In the first Row viz In the

21/ first Light is the picture of a Church & an Alter wth a bare-bellyed Woman habited gu. standing before them

22/ In 2d Light sitts a pope Inthroned robed gu. tripple Crowned O giving a book (or Charter) to two Monks yt submissively kneel before him the one habited B hooded gu. the other hooded B/

23/ In the 3d Light is another Church & Altar A & O. wth a Checky pavement before it upon wch kneels a Nun habited gu vayled A. holding out a golden Coronet or Wreath to an old Man who kneles over agst her wth hands Conjoyned at prayer. he being habited gu & B/

24/ In 4th Light a man habited B leans backwards upon a White Horse, wth hands spread respecting a Woman habited gu lying under the horse. as

Chapter 5

A Vision Obscured

The post-Reformation history of the window is the story of the progressive loss of John Thornton's vision. The suppression of the cult of St William and the abandonment of the medieval Latin *Breviary* brought to an end the annual cycle of liturgical commemorations that had kept his memory alive. Having lost its cultural and liturgical significance, the story of St William was gradually forgotten. Meanwhile, as the decades passed into centuries, damage to the glass, disfiguring repairs and the movement of panels disturbed the window so badly that it descended into visual confusion and indecipherability. Serious attempts to make sense of the window began in the mid-nineteenth century, but it has taken the best part of two centuries of scholarly endeavour and successive restorations to recover the story and return the window to a state where its vision shines through once again

Despite the common assumption that medieval religious imagery was the subject of wholesale attack by Protestant reformers, there is no evidence that the St William Window suffered from significant iconoclasm in the sixteenth century.The work of maintaining and repairing the fabric of the Minster continued almost unabated, and its windows were critical in maintaining its weatherproof outer skin. In 1577 Minster glazier Robert Thompson and his man were paid for forty-six days of work in the 'north cross aisle on the north side'. This might have included work on the St William Window as well as the adjoining clerestory windows (N6 and N7), by this point denuded of most of their medieval glass. The installation in 1624 of Nicolas Stone's large monument to Sir Henry Bellasis and his wife at the base of the window must have posed a risk to the glass. However, in the event, it was the sculpted shields, supported by beautifully carved angels at the window's sill, that suffered in order to accommodate the monument's pediment (Fig. 5.2). The Roos arms that must once have decorated the carved shields were repainted to show Bellasis connections instead.

Fig. 5.1
James Torre's description of the St William Window, described as 'The Cross Window'. York Minster Archive, YMA/ZC/L/1/7, f. 35r).

The heraldry and the Roos figures in the window's bottom row escaped unscathed, and were described by antiquaries Robert Glover (1584–5), Roger Dodsworth (*c.*1620) and Henry Johnston (1669), for all of whom heraldry and genealogy were the focus of their interest. As we have seen, Johnston also roughly sketched the Roos family members. It is therefore thanks to Johnston's testimony that we can date with some precision the first major disturbance of the window, for by 1690 when the window is described panel by panel by James Torre, not only had the Stafford arms on Beatrice de Roos's cloak been lost, but the donor figures had been moved from row 1 into row 2, with panels from row 2 occupying the bottom row in their place.

It is not known exactly when the Lincolnshire-born antiquary and genealogist James Torre (1649–99) settled in York, but he devoted his career in his adopted city to the meticulous and systematic compilation of five volumes on the ecclesiastical antiquities of York and Yorkshire. His manuscripts combine acute personal observations of windows, monuments, images and furnishings, all described in minute objective detail, with careful transcriptions of documents and wills derived from the registers of the medieval archbishops and deans. His panel-by-panel descriptions of every window in the Minster are an astonishing achievement, unparalleled at any other cathedral. The result represents a source of information that remains the bedrock of all modern research into the history and decoration of the Minster. Torre clearly intended to publish his work, which attracted the attention of Archbishop John Sharpe (1691–1714), to whom his fair copies, dated 1691, passed at his unexpected death in 1699. Sharpe eventually donated the books to the Minster library where they have recently been photographed at high resolution and can now be consulted online (Fig. 5.1).

Torre's account of the St William Window is the first one to provide a comprehensive description of the whole window, and its importance cannot therefore be over-emphasised. He is the first observer to display an interest in the window's narrative content, although he did not mention, or perhaps did not recognise, the window's association with the life and miracles of St William. While this may have reflected his ignorance of the subject matter he was describing with such care, a certain delicacy in acknowledging recognition of the lives of medieval saints might be understandable in the years immediately after the 'Glorious

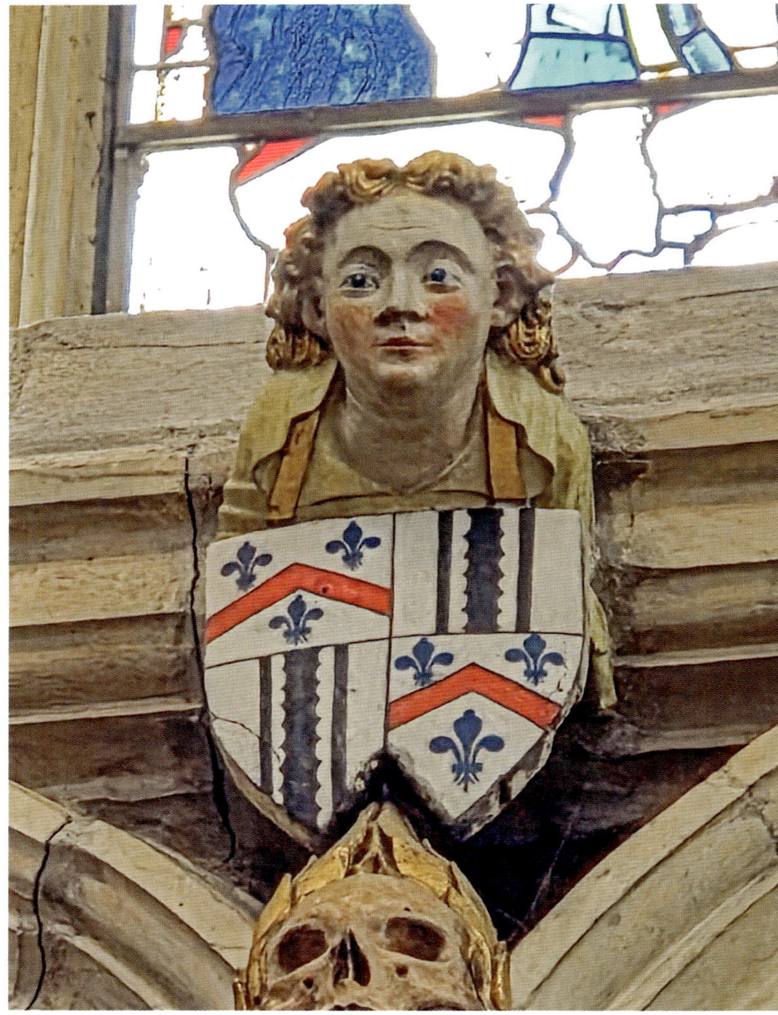

Fig. 5.2
Damage to a shield-bearing angel at the sill of the St William Window. Roos heraldry has been replaced by a Bellasis shield.

Revolution' of 1688, in which Catholic King James II had been forced to relinquish his throne to Protestant William and Mary.

Torre's panel descriptions, which are printed in Appendix One, are fascinating. Whether or not he knew that the window related to St William, he can have had little or no understanding of what was represented in the individual narrative panels. He often misidentified figures. Women are often described as nuns; men are often monks; and not infrequently he got the sex of the figures wrong. Likewise, he misinterpreted both major features and minor details. In the miracle scenes, the shrine is consistently described as a church. In panel 12b, Ralph and Besing's wooden shields are described as great or broad stones. And so on. But his descriptions of colours are generally reliable and help to distinguish panels with very similar designs. In fact, every panel in the window can be identified from Torre, including the two panels that are now lost, 2d and 10d. The most memorable and unexpected of his panel descriptions is that for panel 10e, William's deathbed scene, which he describes thus: 'a monk habited *blue*, mantled *argent*, sitts upon the knee of a lady abbess, habited and mytred *argent*, to salute her.' The only panel in the entire window where Torre offers an interpretation of the scene is panel 17d, the man falling from his horse in front of some trees, which he describes as St Paul's conversion, the tree-trunks being interpreted as rays of silver light issuing out of a cloud!

Torre's description also provides crucial evidence about the number of panels that had been moved from their original position by this date. Apart from the complete transposition of row 1 and row 2, fifteen other panels had been displaced. The three out-of-position panels in rows 3 and 4 could have been displaced at the same time as rows 1 and 2. The other displaced panels consisted of three in the second section of the window, and nine in the top half, right up to row 24. Closer inspection shows that these panels fall into four sub-groups of two or four (shown in different colours in Fig. 6.18), which could have been swapped over among themselves at different times. However, any work at these higher levels would have required scaffolding of some sort, perhaps suggesting a single, large-scale intervention. What is not in doubt is that by about 1690 a quarter of the main light panels were no longer in their correct position.

Thomas Gent's idiosyncratic description of 1730 confirms that few if any changes had occurred since Torre's day. Francis Drake's ambitious history of the city, *Eboracum*, published in 1736, made extensive use of Torre's manuscripts. He displayed an interest in the history of St William and he was aware of a list of St William's miracles in 1177, known from a transcription of the lost original in the Dodsworth manuscripts in the Bodleian Library in Oxford. His interest in stained glass was limited, however, and although he included a large plate of the Great East Window and thanks to Torre was able to attribute it to John Thornton, of the St William Window, he makes no mention.

Possibly the greatest threat to the window occurred on the night of 1–2 February 1829, when the choir was catastrophically damaged by fire. The windows of the south-west choir clerestory (S8–S11), directly above the seat of the blaze, display considerable physical evidence of thermal shock and micro-cracking. The glazier John Barnett was paid for miscellaneous glazing work throughout the choir as a whole, and glaziers' graffiti on the choir clerestory windows dated to the years 1830–2 are numerous. In April 1830 Minster architect Robert Smirke described unspecified work 'in the two small transepts' as being in hand. The suspicion that some remedial work to the relatively sheltered St William Window was required can now be substantiated. During the most recent conservation programme, graffiti of 1830 was found on panels 11b and 16c, the latter reading 'This window was restored in the year of Our Lord 1830 when it will be again God knows'. That these repairs had also involved further panel movements cannot therefore be discounted. The names of other glaziers and plumbers, and the date 1838, were scratched on panels in row 1. The subsequent removal of any post-medieval glass introduced into the window during the restoration of 1895 by John Ward Knowles (1838–1931) discussed later in the chapter makes the full extent and character of earlier work difficult to evaluate, although some of Knowles's pre-restoration photographs reveal areas of streaky patching typical of eighteenth- and early-nineteenth-century glazing work in York Minster (Fig. 5.3).

John Browne's interest in the history, the shrines and the cult of St William first surfaces in his important history of the Minster published in 1847 with engravings made by his son based on his own expert drawings. Unlike Torre, Browne had no university education and had begun his career as a house painter. The fires of 1829 and 1840 and their aftermath provided him with opportunities to investigate the Minster from scaffolding, and he secured permission to use the Minster's extensive archives. He was also familiar with Dodsworth's list of the 1177 miracles and referred to the York *Breviary*. At this time, however, he made no mention of the St William Window. It is only in his 1859 work *A Description Representations and Arms on the Glass in the Windows of York Minster also the Arms on the Stone,* unpublished until 1915, that he looked in depth at the window, the first historian of the Minster to identify it as being dedicated to the life and miracles of St William. Recognising that many of the scenes were physically out of order, Browne discussed them in what he thought to be their correct narrative order, although he began at the top of the window and worked his way down, contrary to what we know to be the correct reading order of the window. He relied heavily on Dodsworth for his identification of the miracles, and while not always correct, he shows himself to be a careful and astute observer. He recognised the correct sequence of the Ralph and Besing narrative in row 12, for example, but mistook the scene in 21c (of a woman falling into the river as the portable reliquary is carried over Ouse Bridge) as the more famous Ouse Bridge miracle (depicted in 9c). Browne's description, despite the importance of his insights, was only published posthumously and so was to have no influence on the most important study of the nineteenth century, an account that was to have a momentous impact on modern perceptions of the window and was to remain unchallenged for over 100 years.

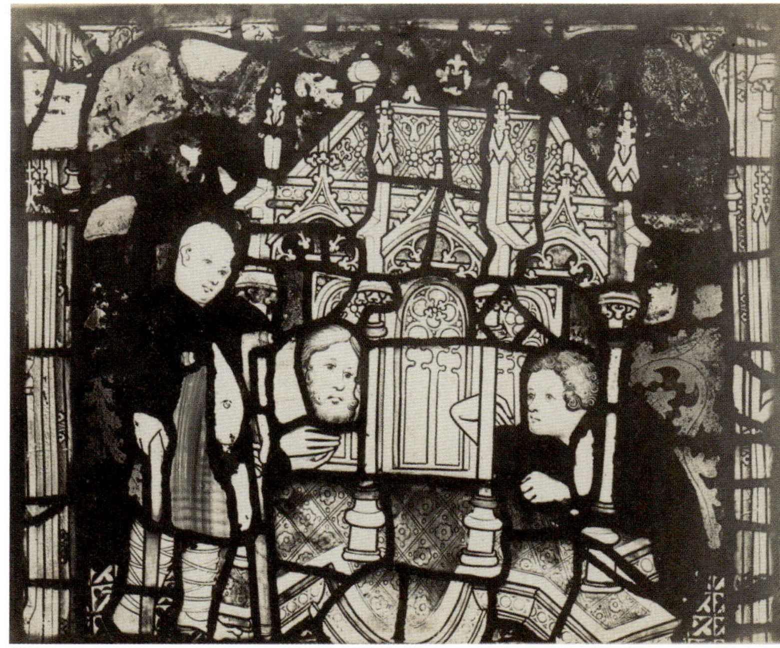

Fig. 5.3
Panel 23a before restoration in 1895, as photographed by J. W. Knowles. The clothing of the man on the left has been patched with a streaky glass (probably red), typical of the eighteenth century.

Dr James Fowler (1839–80) was born in Winterton in Lincolnshire, the grandson of antiquary William Fowler (b.1761), admired for his accurate watercolours of Roman mosaics and stained glass (including of the Minster's Great East Window). James was a physician and member of the Royal College of Surgeons, but during a busy professional life found time to lecture and publish fifteen articles on medieval art and architecture, six of them devoted to stained glass. He was elected Fellow of the Society of Antiquaries in 1867. In 1874 he published a long, scholarly article on the window in the *Yorkshire Archaeological Journal*. He made extensive use of Torre's description, which he actually published alongside his own panel descriptions. He recognised that Torre's description provided an invaluable glimpse of a window little altered since its creation, although he disregarded Torre's evidence when it did not accord with his own theories. Like Browne, he was conversant with Dodsworth's list of the 1177 miracles and he consulted all of the Latin sources that were available to him at the time, using them to identify as many of the scenes as he could. Importantly, he examined the evidence of the window's heraldry to suggest the identity of the donors at its base, concluding that the window depicted John Roos, his wife Margery Despenser, four of his brothers and 'one or more of his sisters'. Fowler saw the death of John and his younger brother in 1421 as a pivotal moment in the window's creation and, rather remarkably for his day, was prepared to attribute its creation to the agency of a woman, John's widow Margery (Despenser), prior to her remarriage *c.*1423–4.

Aware that a number of the panels were not in their correct position, Fowler proposed a theoretical reconstruction of what he believed to be their original order. He realised that the window was intended to be read from the bottom to the top, and in his summary of the main themes explored in each section of the window, he was essentially correct, although he did not appreciate that row 14, invisible from the ground, had always been left plain glazed. This error was to have more serious implications when his younger brother, Joseph Thomas Fowler (1833–1924), antiquary, historian, lecturer in Hebrew at Durham University, Canon of Durham Cathedral and author of the later study of the St Cuthbert Window, came to influence the restoration of that window in the 1880s.

James Fowler did make some basic and somewhat baffling misidentifications, for example describing the baptism of St William (2b), readily recognised by Torre and Browne, as the miracle of the boy drowned in the well (15c). In fairness to Fowler, it is clear that many panels were already out of order and some were in an extremely misleading state of confusion (Fig. 5.4). Perhaps his most serious misconception in terms of its implications for the ordering of panels was his theory that the background fields of the narrative panels had always been arranged in alternating blue and red rows, with blue the dominating colour, maintaining that this was a common phenomenon in medieval stained glass. Fowler had observed that red backgrounds outnumbered blue ones, but explained this to his own satisfaction as being the result of panel losses from row 14. He even suggested that some backgrounds had been tampered with. This erroneous conclusion was to cast a long shadow in terms of later attempts to reorder the narrative satisfactorily. Nonetheless, Fowler's article was an impressive piece of work, all the more so considering that, as far as we know, he had to study the panels from ground level.

Fowler received the cooperation and assistance of the Minster stoneyard in his studies. Measurements were provided by the master mason Mr Bradley, and his article was illustrated with three coloured plates derived from tracings made directly from the glass by former master mason Mr R. Cane (Figs 5.5 and 5.6). There is no evidence that James Fowler was writing in anticipation of major restoration of the window, so to him and many of the readers of the *Yorkshire Archaeological Journal*, his scholarly hypotheses were not seen as an agenda for rearrangement of the glass, but rather an attempt to improve public understanding and appreciation of an overlooked medieval monument of great significance, quality and interest. Indeed, in his closing remarks, he deplores the 'deluge' of modern restoration that he held accountable for the loss of historical value, citing the views of John Ruskin with approbation and describing admiringly the recent cautious restoration of the east window of Gloucester Cathedral, a project conducted under the influence of stained-glass historian Charles Winston (1814–64). He also advocated the use of external protective glazing, a trend begun in York as early as 1861. Fowler's was the first dedicated study of the St William Window to appear in print, and its length and detail meant that it has cast a long shadow over all other studies of the glass. It might be wondered, however, whether its author would have altogether approved of the restoration of the window that was soon to be conducted, with his vision of its narrative as its guiding light.

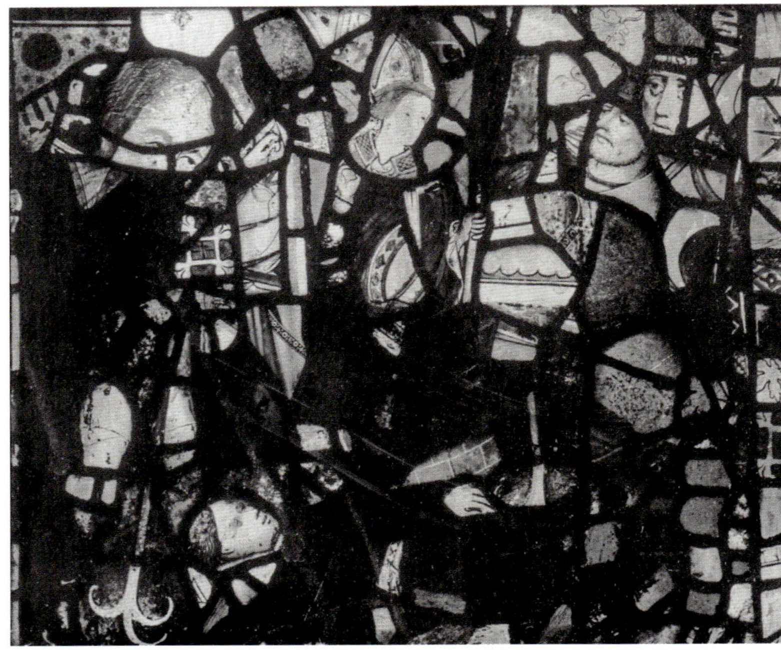

Fig. 5.4
The exceptionally jumbled and damaged state of panel 15c, photographed in 1895 by J. W. Knowles.

Restoration 1895

In 1894, local glazier J. W. Knowles, who had already been entrusted with the restoration of the St Cuthbert Window in the south-east transept (1886–88), was instructed to examine the St William Window with a view to restoration. Alarmed at the state of the stone, Knowles urged the Dean and Chapter to seek the advice of the cathedral architect George Frederick Bodley (1827–1907). Bodley reported in July 1894 on the extremely perilous condition of the stonework, riven by the expansion of the rusting ferramenta, and called for its urgent repair. He also observed the poor state of the glass, and especially the deformation of its leadwork, which he believed to be the cause of much damage: 'It is at present twisted and bent in a manner so remarkable that we hardly think it would be possible, without reglazing it, to fix it into the grooves of the mullions.' <transpose> The glass was probably removed from the window to Knowles's Stonegate studio in May and June 1895, when Knowles, assisted by his three children, John, Jane and Kathleen, began to make carefully coloured watercolour drawings of the panels, recording all glass believed to be original, and leaving blank any areas of intrusion or patching (Figs 5.7 and 5.8). His watercolours are now in the Victoria and Albert Museum. Knowles was also a pioneer in the use of record photographs, so that the combination of his black-and-white photos and coloured drawings provide an unprecedented record of the window at this time. His pre-restoration photographs assembled into a large photo-montage preserved in the York Glaziers Trust show that the window was in extremely poor condition, with broken glass throughout the window and glass at risk of loss, for example in panel 10b (Fig. 5.9), where jagged holes can be seen.

A contract for the restoration of the window was signed on 30 July 1895. This document, a copy of which is preserved in the National Art Library in the Victoria and Albert Museum, prescribed a very conservative approach:

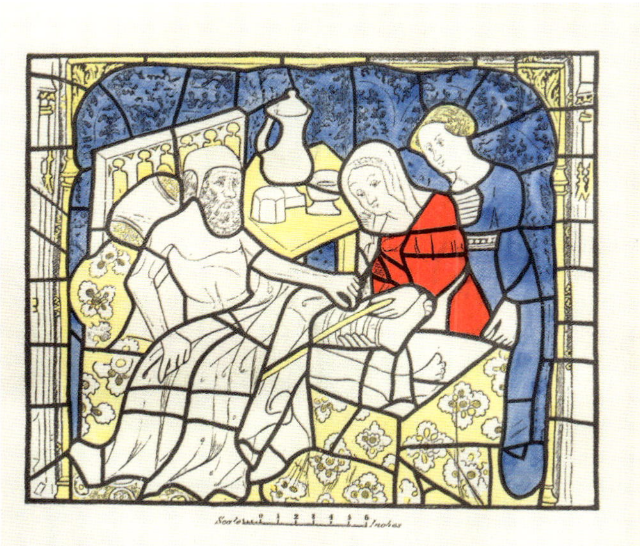

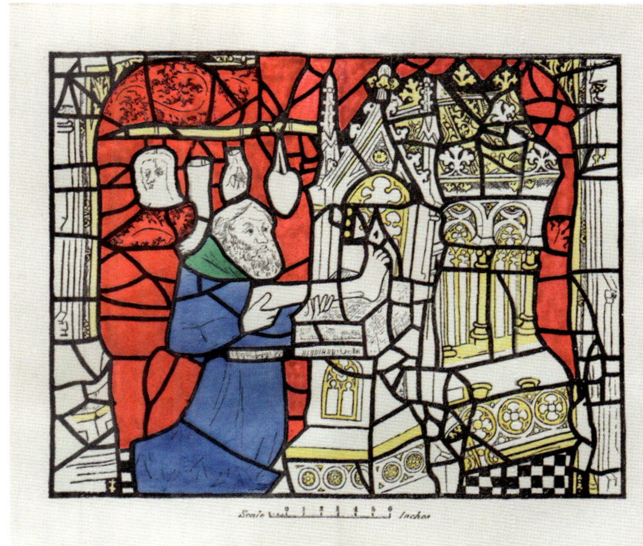

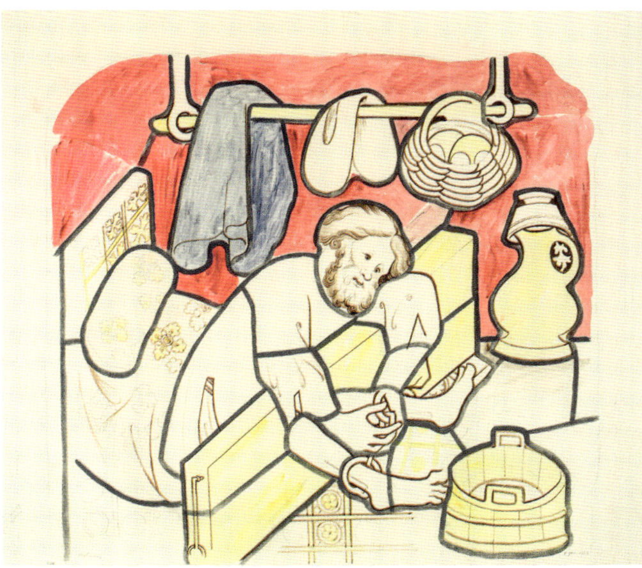

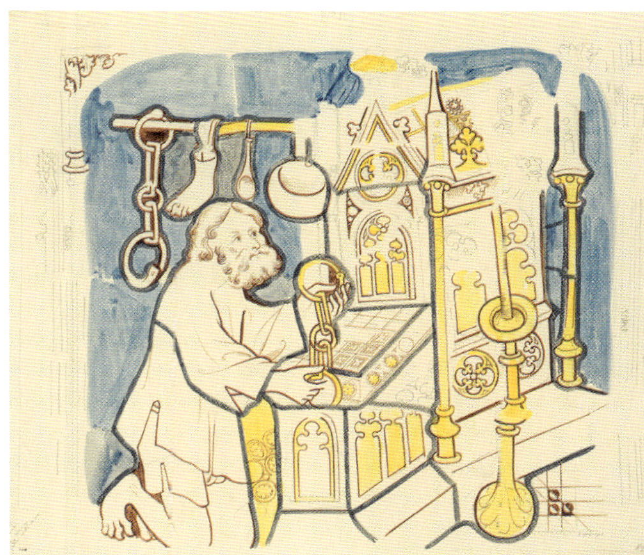

Fig. 5.5
Panel 21a as drawn by Minster mason Mr Cane, for publication by Dr James Fowler in 1874.

Fig. 5.6
Panel 21b as drawn by Minster mason Mr Cane, for publication by Dr James Fowler in 1874.

Fig. 5.7
J. W. Knowles's 1895 watercolour of panel 22a.

Fig. 5.8
J. W. Knowles's 1895 watercolour of panel 22b.

> *Mr Knowles is to repair the lead work of the window and renew it as required. As regards the glass the present condition of the window is to be maintained as far as possible: no attempt is to be made to supply details which no longer exist or to develop those that still remain. In the event of any portions of drapery or moulding being irretrievably broken so that the piece of glass cannot be mended Mr Knowles is at liberty to replace it with a piece of glass as similar as possible but in all other cases any deficiency is to be filled up with a piece of plain glass of such a tincture as will best harmonise with the surrounding glass.*

It must be acknowledged that the techniques of conservation and repair available to Knowles were far more limited than today, although he was working in a period in which concepts of ethical restoration were quickly evolving. Broken glass could only be secured through the introduction of additional mending leads, a process that tended to impede the transmission of light, undermine the legibility of an original design and adversely alter the balance of glass to lead within the window. He was urged to retain as much as he could, but holes needed to be filled in order to maintain the weathertight integrity of the window. Under the influence of Winston, painted 'restorations', especially anything that speculated about lost detail, were increasingly frowned upon and the contract seems to imply the extensive use of unpainted glass of appropriate colour as he advocated. As we have seen, James Fowler strongly approved of Winston's cautious approach to restoration. Cathedral architect Bodley was also an advocate of conservative restoration, having written critically of the excesses of restoration and replacement that he observed in government-sponsored restoration of the great French cathedrals. It is perhaps ironic, therefore, that in the official Chapter records of this period, it tends to be Bodley to whom the credit for the conservation of the north-east transept, including the St William Window, is accorded. In fact, research into the impact of the 1895 restoration programme conducted from 1997 to 2002 by Janice Smith, to which our understanding of the window's restoration history is indebted, has revealed the degree to which it was Knowles who moulded the agenda and made flesh James Fowler's interpretation of the window's narrative. In so doing he took the restoration far beyond the limits set out in his contract.

The watercolours give a first hint of what was in Knowles's thoughts as he approached the task. The drawings focus attention on the medieval glass and the central action of each scene. What he perceived to be later additions, even in the form of stop-gaps of medieval glass, are generally omitted and even mending leads are left out. A comparison of the illustration

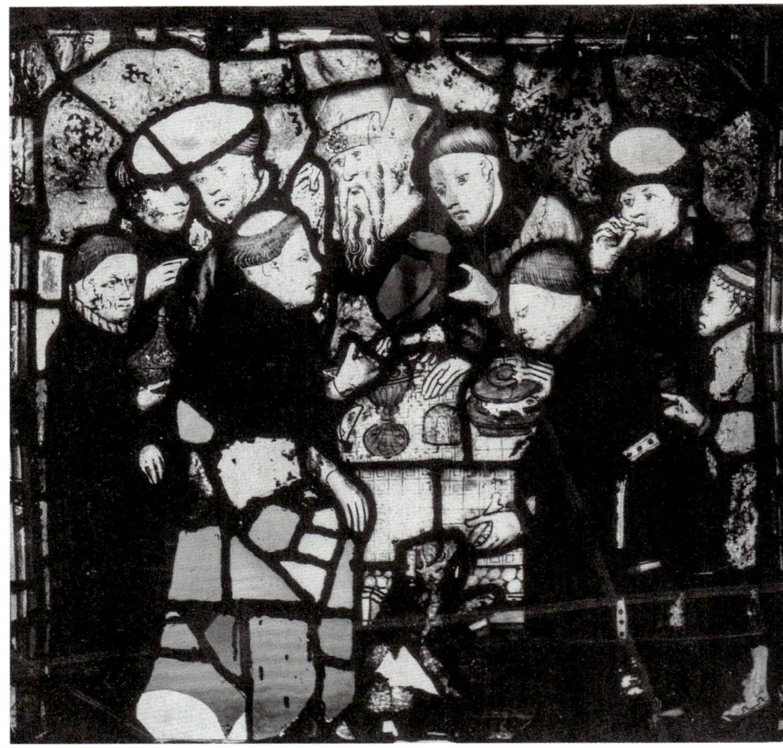

Fig. 5.9
J. W. Knowles's pre-restoration photograph of panel 10b, showing jagged holes in several pieces of medieval glass.

used by James Fowler with those of Knowles is very revealing. Both men record the scene now in panel 21b in which a man offers a model of his leg at the shrine, in 1895 one of the best-preserved panels in the window. The Fowler illustration (Fig. 5.6), traced by master mason Mr Cane, faithfully records all the leads, original as well as mending leads. In the background a distinction is made between painted seaweed diaper (original) and unpainted red glass (later patch repairs). Cane's drawings are presented with a scale. This is the kind of archaeological detail more characteristic of Winston's watercolours of glass, but actually also a characteristic of James Fowler's grandfather's even earlier records of Roman mosaics and stained glass. By comparison, Knowles's watercolour is less 'archaeological' and more 'artistic' in its character (Fig. 5.10). It lacks a scale, rationalises the figure and the shrine and leaves out numerous lead lines as well as mending leads, thereby emphasising the visual coherence of the scene.

Fig. 5.10
J. W. Knowles's 1895 watercolour of panel 21b.

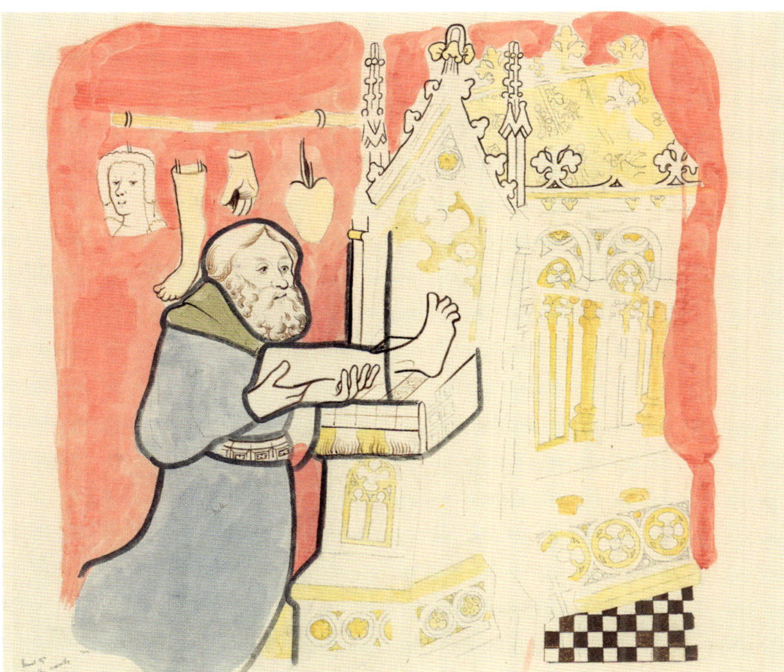

It is also clear that at an early stage, Knowles was considering the issue of panel order, for he took it upon himself to contact his former collaborator in the restoration of the St Cuthbert Window, Canon Joseph Fowler, asking his advice concerning the narrative order of the panels in the absence of his deceased brother. Canon Fowler, who had presided over the reordering of the Cuthbert panels, strongly advocated that the order proposed in his brother's 1874 article should be adopted without alteration, and this is what Knowles did, even rather surprisingly, in cases where he knew James Fowler to have misidentified a scene. For example, Knowles's watercolour of panel 2b is labelled 'baptism of the infant William' and yet even after his interventions that restored its legibility, it was relocated to panel 11b in accordance with James Fowler's misattribution of it as the miracle of the boy drowned in the well. Knowles's initiative in approaching Canon Fowler annoyed Dean Arthur Purey-Cust, who instructed him thereafter to refer any 'difficulties' directly to him. However, Canon Fowler's advice was not specifically countermanded, allowing Knowles to proceed.

The entirely necessary re-leading of the collapsing panels provided Knowles with the welcome opportunity to reorder actual glass pieces within individual panels in ways that reflected his desire to achieve greater narrative legibility. This also took the project another step away from the 'conserve-as-found' principles implied in the contract. Stop-gaps of earlier glass were almost all removed, to be substituted with painted insertions, in defiance of the contract's expectation of plain unpainted glass. In a few cases it is possible that Knowles may even have mistakenly discarded original glass. In numerous instances, however, his new painted pieces were based on sound evidence, notably in the restoration of the architectural frames and canopies. The removal of foliated grisaille and fragments of diamond

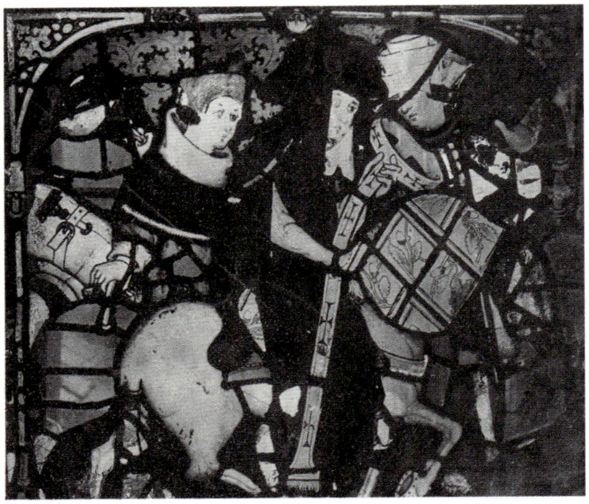

quarries from the bodies of horses in panels 4e and 8a (Fig. 5.11), for example, is also hardly controversial, as gaps could easily be filled with painted detail based on the numerous other figures of horses in the window. The insertion of painted and coloured drapery in the place of distracting plain light-coloured patch glass in panels like 8e also improved the legibility of the narrative. Heads are particularly important to the reading of a scene, so the creation of new heads in place of an inserted fragment of text in panel 3d and an oversized later medieval head in 5b enhances rather than diminishes the window, although the fate of removed stop-gaps remains a mystery. Knowles made numerous drawings of details throughout the window (Fig. 5.12) and his insertions are usually well painted and stylistically sympathetic to the medieval original. However, there are cases where he went beyond the evidence that could be gleaned from the window itself. In the creation of a new papal head for the enthroned figure in 5b, for example, the testimony of Torre was critical, and justified the restoration that rendered the panel legible. The evidence of an additional horse's head and forelegs in 4e is more conjectural, but does not materially affect the iconographic identity of the scene. In one instance, however, the restoration of detail in panel 3a proved to be misleading; the young, tonsured figure standing in the centre of the panel with his back to the viewer was provided with a pallium (Figs 5.13 and 5.14), thereby incorrectly transforming him into an archbishop, a detail that was reversed in the most recent programme of conservation.

Knowles's insertions are usually easy to spot when viewed at close quarters. His glass paint is of a different (pinkish) tone and finish to the trace line of the original glass and his pieces are all painted on machine-rolled glass of consistent thickness. That he intended his own glass to be distinguishable from the original medieval glass is reinforced by the fact that he numbered many of his new pieces, suggesting an awareness of emerging ideas promoted by followers of Ruskin and the Society for the Protection of Ancient Buildings (SPAB). However, the choice of glass may also have reflected economic considerations. Antique mouth-blown glasses were expensive, and although the total restoration cost of £592 was a not inconsiderable sum, it is likely that Knowles did not wish to advertise the amount of new painted glass that he was surreptitiously introducing into the window by increasing the budget even further.

While it is unlikely that James Fowler would have approved of all aspects of

Fig. 5.11
J. W. Knowles's pre-restoration photograph of panel 4e, showing medieval quarries used to patch the neck and Cardinal Hincmar's horse.

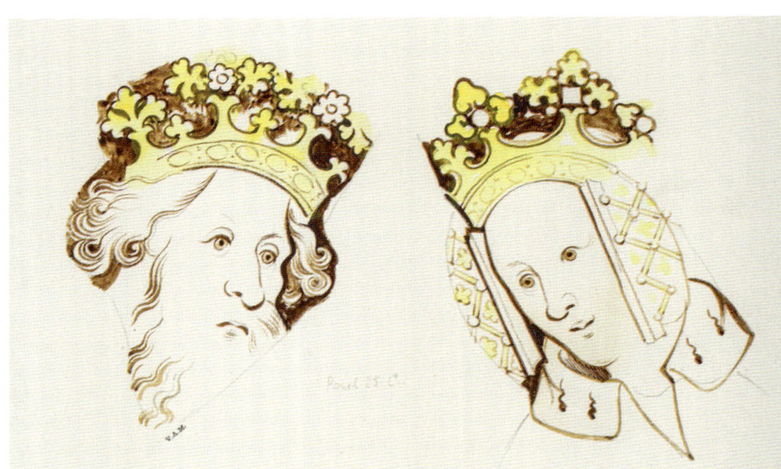

Fig. 5.12
J. W. Knowles's detailed drawings of the heads of King Edward I and Queen Eleanor in panel 18e.

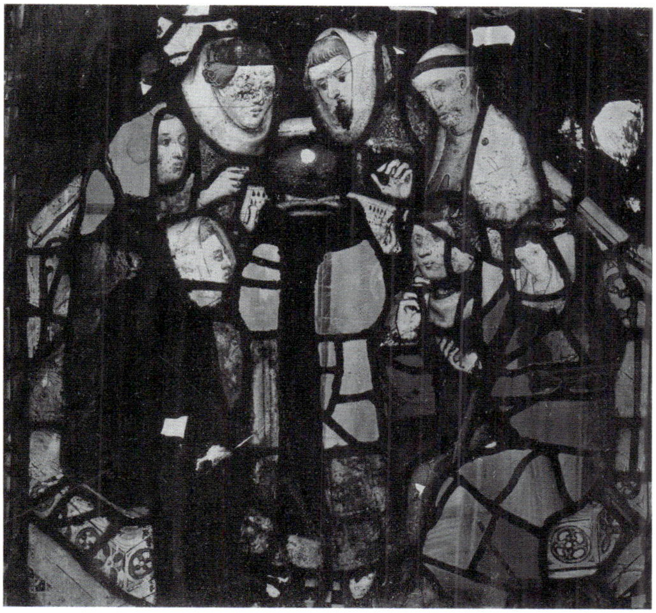

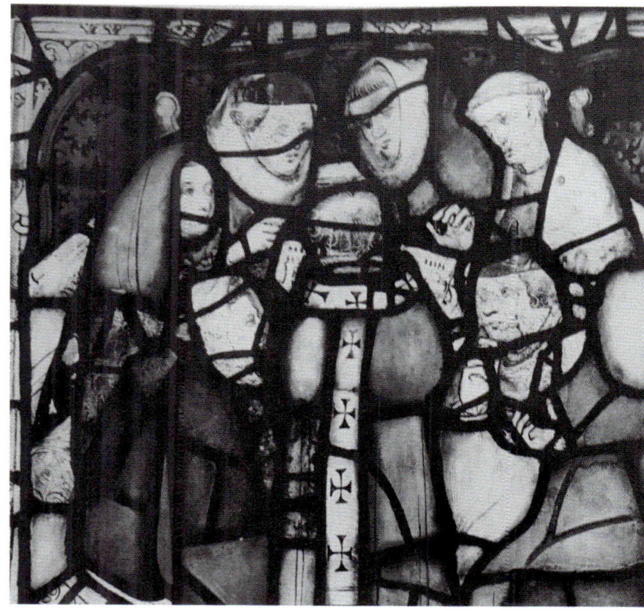

Fig. 5.13
J. W. Knowles's 1895 pre-restoration photograph of panel 3a.

Fig. 5.14
Panel 3a as restored by J. W. Knowles in 1895, with the central figure, viewed from behind, given a misleading pallium.

Knowles's work, which also effectively erased physical evidence of earlier interventions, the restoration of 1895 not only saved the window from collapse and loss, but also massively enhanced its impact on public consciousness. It also ensured that James Fowler's academic and theoretical transformation of the narrative was made into a physical reality, warts and all. It would be another half-century before Knowles's version of Fowler's vision was challenged.

The Twentieth Century

Such was the authority of James Fowler's account of the life and miracles of St William, as expressed in Knowles's 1895 restoration, that neither of the early-twentieth-century descriptions of the glass, by George Benson (1915) and Frederick Harrison (1927), challenged his identifications or his dating of the window, and Harrison did not make use of John Browne's observations, which were available in print from 1917. The scholarly Minster librarian, Canon Chancellor Frederick Harrison, played up the contribution of Canon Joseph Fowler. As a consequence, J. W. Knowles's importance seems to have been continually overlooked, and in 1920, when a major new campaign of window restoration throughout the Minster was launched, Knowles's appeal to Dean William Foxley-Norris to be involved in the work, was ignored.

This neglect of Knowles's work began to be redressed in the writing of his son, John Alder Knowles (1881–1961), who as a teenager had assisted his father in making watercolours of the St William Window. J. A. Knowles combined stained-glass scholarship with practical glazing experience, having worked for nine years in a commercial stained-glass studio in the USA, before returning to England in 1912 to work in his father's business. He served in both World Wars and was a long-standing editor of the *Journal of the British Society of Master Glass Painters*, to which he contributed numerous articles. In 1936 his *Essays in the York School of Glass Painting,* first published as journal articles, was published as a single volume, demonstrating his deep familiarity with both the windows of his native city and its historical archives.

He was elected a Fellow of the Society of Antiquaries in 1926 and awarded an honorary Master of Arts by the University of Hull in 1957.

In his earliest published study of the St William Window, Knowles's stated aim was to share some of the additional insights he had gleaned from Canon Joseph Fowler, which he had failed to persuade him to publish. Knowles made good use of Browne's now-published work, appreciating that he had benefitted from scaffolded access to the glass. He underlined the importance of the window as a document for understanding the history of William's cult in York Minster and contextualised the sources for William's life and miracles by reference to other saints' lives known to him from recent scholarly editions. Although he offered some corrections to Dr James Fowler's identifications as well as numerous observations of his own, he stressed his admiration for Fowler's work, carried out in the face of considerable difficulties of access, to both glass and historical records. He followed his panel order, interleaved with Browne's descriptions. In one fleeting reference to the frame design in panel 8e, he presaged a new approach to the study of the window, based on close observation of its physical properties, explaining that any panel with a flat top to its frame cannot have been intended for the top row of each window section.

He developed these observations significantly in his article 'Technical Notes on the St William Window in York Minster' (1950). This piece also marked a shift into a more interdisciplinary approach to the study of the window. While Knowles continued to refer to the iconographic interpretations of both James Fowler and Browne, he used his own insights as a master craftsman and historian of York stained glass to show how design elements in the glass could have a direct bearing on the location of panels within the window, thereby assisting in the grouping of scenes that were otherwise difficult to identify. He provided drawings of frame designs to substantiate his

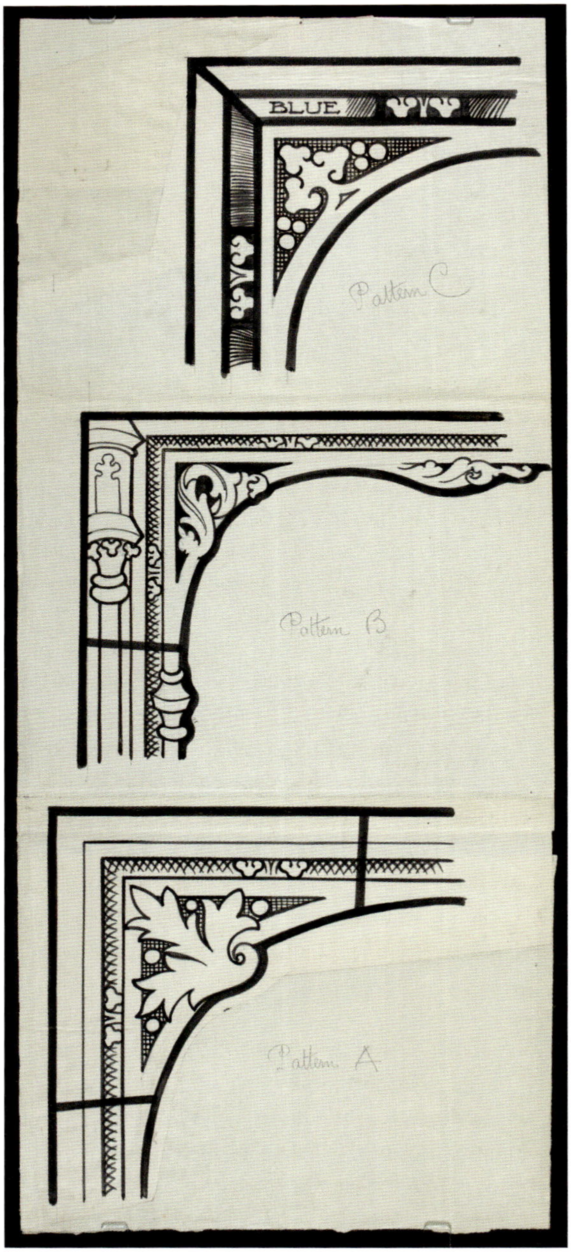

Fig. 5.15
J. A. Knowles's drawings of the St William Window frame designs (Types C, B and F), *c.*1950.

observations (Fig. 5.15) and for the first time considered how the glazing workshop may have been organised. He noted what he believed to be examples of adaptive reuse of cartoons, identified three or four different painters at work, and, for the first time, suggested that the 'guiding hand' in the window's creation was John Thornton of Coventry, author of the Great East Window, a suggestion that has received wide acceptance in modern scholarship. He also put forward the idea that the glass had once been divided between two windows of fifty figurative panels each, a theory that has not been borne out in subsequent studies. Despite this rather eccentric hypothesis, Knowles was highlighting the potential of new ways of looking at the window, which were only to be fully realised nearly half a century later.

The Post-War Years

At the outbreak of the Second World War, eighty Minster windows, including the three great narrative windows of the choir, were removed to places of safety throughout the county. The St William Window, removed in November 1940, spent the war divided between Nun Appleton and Howsham Halls, returning home only on 11 August 1948. In 1941 Eric Milner-White (1884–1963), formerly dean of King's College, Cambridge, and already an acknowledged stained-glass expert, was appointed dean to a cathedral largely denuded of its glass. Milner-White was to make the restoration and reinstallation of the windows one of his highest post-war priorities. In addition to oversight of the restoration of the Great East Window in the years 1943–53, Milner-White became the dominating presence in the Minster glazing studio, providing art-historical, theological and aesthetic direction. The progress of the return of the windows was chronicled by the dean in the pages of the *Annual Reports of the Friends of York Minster*, and the return of the St William Window, 'a landmark as important as that of the East Window', is described in the twenty-seventh annual report (1955). Precise detail is scarce, but in summary all the tracery panels were releaded, together with three canopy heads and eleven of the main narrative panels (although he did not specify which ones). One panel that underwent considerable alteration in 1954 is panel 15c, moved from 18a to 11b by Dean Milner-White and heavily restored as the miracle of the drowned boy (Fig. 5.16). It is clear, however, that less drastic interventions were made in almost every panel, and that fragments entirely alien to the window, derived from miscellaneous gifts of old glass, were introduced with little documentation. The introduction of plated 'sandwiches' of modern plain glass holding medieval fragments in place enabled the restorers to eliminate some of the mending leads. Perhaps most dramatically, three excessively fragmented panels were removed altogether, and three panels judged to be stylistically and aesthetically harmonious to the window were introduced in their stead. Panel 2c (St William's education), identifiable by its architectural frame as original to the window, was retrieved from St Stephen's chapel (n3). The other two panels are not original to the window, but are not dissimilar in style and date. The panel now in 2d (depicting a woman before a judge), was moved from the south transept (s23) to occupy panel 2e. The third new addition, now in 10d, depicting a scene of bloodletting, was brought from window s19 and was placed in 18e, having been formerly in the St Cuthbert Window (s7). While one of these panels (2c) had 'come home', Milner-White's main preoccupation was aesthetic rather than historical. He did not seriously challenge James Fowler's authority (although 'four or five' (unspecified) mistakes were corrected. The dean also acknowledged the value of J. A. Knowles's technical notes of 1950, and took up his attribution of the window to John Thornton.

One aspect of the dean's presentation of the window deserves particular notice. J. A. Knowles had not revisited the question of the window's date and patronage, first examined by Browne and particularly by James Fowler. The 1954 re-leading convinced the Minster glaziers that panel 1e had only ever contained a single female figure (as indeed was shown in Johnston's 1669 drawing, of which Milner-White was unaware). At the same time, glazier Oswald Lazenby's own genealogical research drew the dean's attention to the death in battle in 1421 of both John and William Roos (depicted in panels 1c and 1b respectively), the first and second sons of William (in 1d). Milner-White did not challenge James Fowler's dating of 1421–3, but decided that the donor of the window was not the widowed Margery Despenser, as Fowler had proposed, but Margaret Arundel, widow of the elder William and the grief-strickened mother of two sons killed in battle. It is not hard to see how an explanation of this kind would resonate with someone decorated for his distinguished service as an army chaplain during the First World War, who had created a memorial chapel for the fallen at his alma mater, King's College, Cambridge and who, in 1918, campaigned for a more fitting liturgy for the burial of the dead.

The St William Window and Modern Scholarship

From the 1960s onwards new forces impacted stained-glass studies in York. In 1965 the University of York appointed stained-glass specialist Dr Peter Newton (1935–87) as Paul Mellon Lecturer in British Art at the Centre for Medieval Studies. For the first time stained glass was systematically taught as an academic subject in a British university. Around the same time, former 'monuments man' T. W. French (1917–2001), who had joined the York office of the Royal Commission on Historical Monuments in 1954 to work on its inventory of monuments throughout the city, began taking a particular interest in stained glass. From the late 1960s, as the Minster was filled with scaffolding designed to address the threat of structural collapse, he took advantage of high-level access throughout the building to examine and record the windows, an experience that decisively shifted the direction of his own research. Under the influence of Newton and French, stained glass in the Minster and city was now subjected to the rigours of modern art-historical scrutiny. In 1977 the first modern academic survey of the Minster's glass authored by two Newton students, David O'Connor and Jeremy Haselock, appeared in a new multi-authored history of the Minster, in which the windows were contextualised within a broad art-historical framework. Understandably, little space in such a wide-ranging overview could be devoted to the St William Window, although the excellence of its design and its association with John Thornton was upheld, and his influence identified in all of the fifteenth-century glazing of the eastern arm. Meanwhile, the in-depth research into the rich

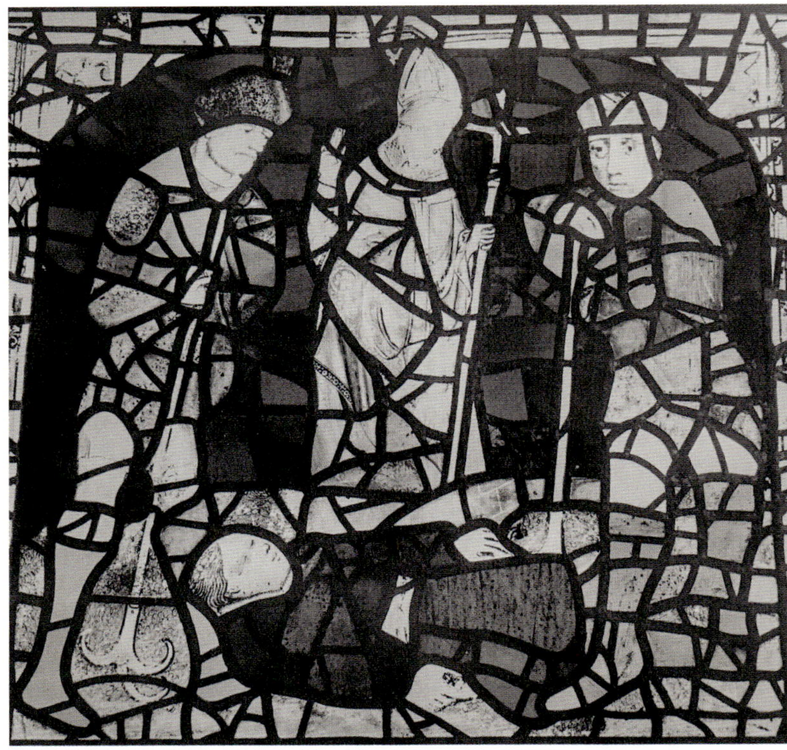

Fig. 5.16
Panel 15c following restoration in 1954 under the direction of Dean Eric Milner-White.

antiquarian sources of the city by the staff of the Royal Commission was bringing to light fresh evidence relevant to stained glass, and in 1987 Tom French published a new interpretation of the patronage and date of the St William Window, identifying the figure in 1e for the first time as Beatrice de Roos, re-dating it to *c.*1414 and locating it within the wider glazing history of the eastern arm. In 1997 a university student and historian of cathedral pilgrimage, Dr Ben Nilson, revisited the iconographic content of the window, suggesting new identifications for some of the scenes and paying serious attention to Torre's evidence of the window's narrative order. Based on this re-reading, he also proposed a more complex chequerboard arrangement of the panels based on their counterchanging background colours, an observation that proved to be very nearly correct. Nilson also observed that some of the window narratives had missing elements, but attributed this not so much to medieval editorial intent as to the persistent idea that row 14 had once been filled with images since lost.

In 1987 under the auspices of the Corpus Vitrearum Medii Aevi and the British Academy and in partnership with David O'Connor, French had published the first volume of a proposed catalogue of the Minster's stained glass, devoted to the West Window and the other windows of the west wall. In 1995 this was followed by a study of the Great East Window. His monograph on the St William Window appeared in 1999. Although his catalogue continued to reflect the 1954 ordering of the glass, by revisiting the antiquarian and hagiographical sources, French not only reiterated his new chronology for the window, but also seriously challenged Fowler's panel ordering and offered a coherent overview of the window's original narrative structure. By the time his book went to press, the first six rows of the window had been removed to the studio of the York Glaziers Trust, the first phase of a restoration programme that was to have an even more transformative effect on the window than Knowles's work of 1895.

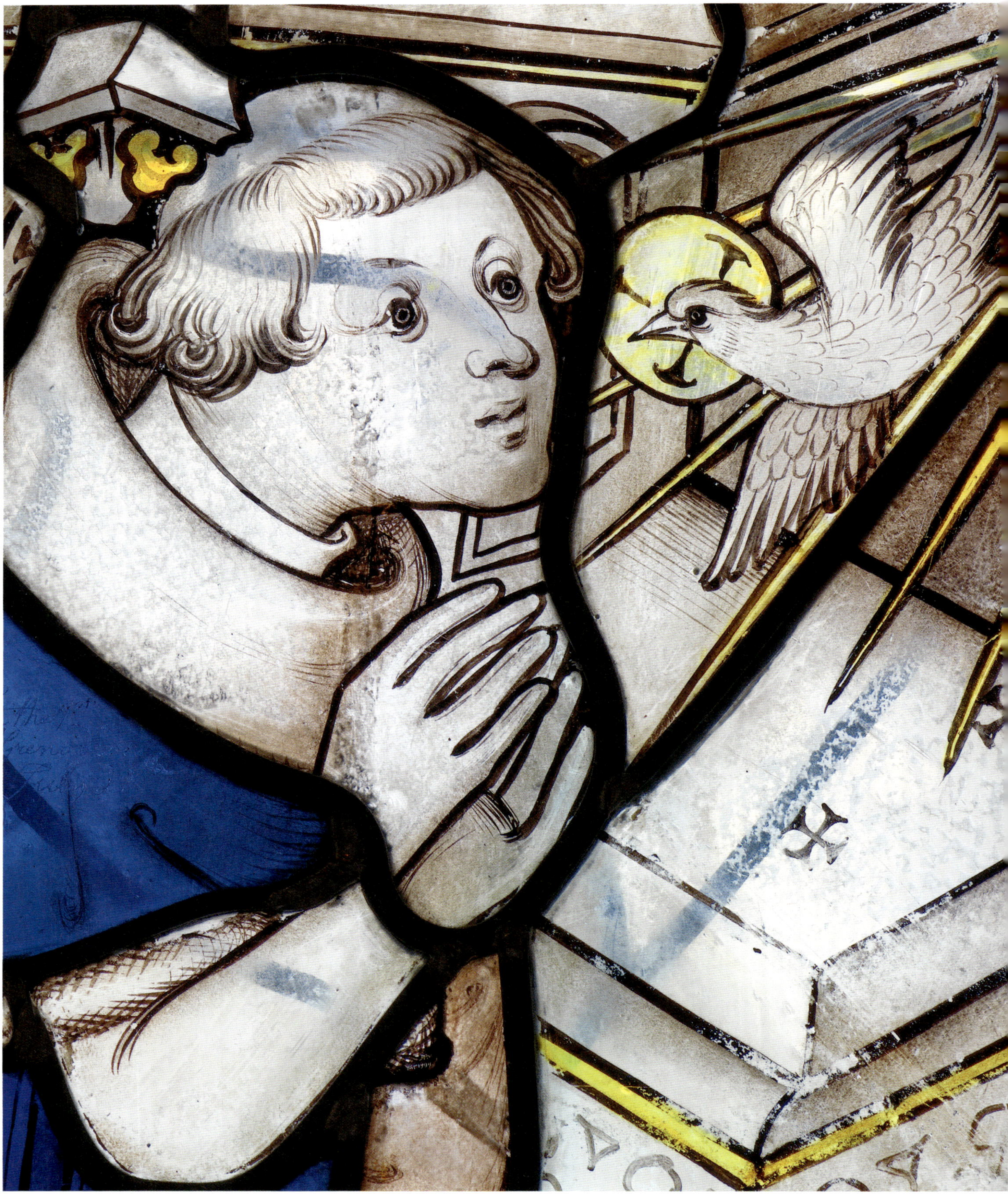

Chapter 6

A Masterpiece Restored

The Birth of the York Glaziers Trust

In the post-war years, under the direction of Dean Eric Milner-White and with extensive funding from the Pilgrim Trust from 1948 onwards, a small team of glaziers had reinstalled the eighty windows removed for safety at the outbreak of the Second World War. A list compiled by Clerk of Works W. J. Green records the many locations in the Yorkshire countryside to which the windows had been despatched. With skilled craftspeople in very short supply, Leeds resident and experienced glazier Herbert Nowland (1880–1972) came out of retirement to assist glazing foreman Oswald Lazenby (1904–83). Even before the cessation of hostilities the work of restoration and reinstallation had begun, starting with the Great East Window, a project over which the dean took increasingly direct control from 1943 onwards. In 1945 the tiny team was reinforced by the addition of apprentice Peter Gibson (1929–2016), a recent school-leaver who was to devote all but his two years of national service to the care of the Minster's glass. This was the team entrusted with the restoration and reinstallation of the St William Window in 1954, as discussed in the previous chapter.

Although Dean Milner-White remained determinedly in charge of stained-glass restoration at York Minster until the very end of his life, in his later years, as his health failed, he realised that the unparalleled skills and experience amassed in the orbit of the Minster needed to be safeguarded for the future. He did not live to see his vision of a charitable trust devoted to stained-glass conservation and preservation realised, but on 20 July 1967, thanks to the continued efforts of the Pilgrim Trust and the support of Dean Alan Richardson (1917–74), a new conservation charity, the York Glaziers Trust (YGT), came into being. The charity was expressly devoted to the care of stained glass in the Minster and at other locations with important glass throughout the UK, underlining the importance of York as a centre of expertise and excellence in conservation as well as scholarship. Peter Gibson was promoted as

Fig. 6.1
Detail of panel 7d after conservation.

secretary and superintendent of the Trust after Lazenby's retirement. It was Gibson who fought for the restoration and reinstallation of the Rose Window after the catastrophic fire of 1984, retiring in 1995 after fifty years in post. Dr Peter Newton of the University of York was appointed as art-historical adviser to the Trust, the first time that art-historical scholarship and conservation had been formally combined in a British stained-glass studio.

Restoration, Conservation, Protection: The Work of the York Glaziers Trust 1997–2007

Despite the restoration of 1954, the condition of the St William Window, located on the more unforgiving north side of the building and provided with no external protection, was already emerging as a growing cause for concern in the reports of successive Surveyors of the Fabric (Minster architects) in the 1970s and 1980s, although work on the twelfth-century glass in the nave clerestory and successive programmes of repair of the Rose Window were to be an unavoidable distraction. In 1971 three St William panels (including 15a, 15b and one other, unidentified) had been re-leaded at the direction of Surveyor Sir Bernard Feilden. In 1993 panels 24a and tracery B2 had required repair following damage by a scaffolding pole. In 1996 Penny Winton, recently appointed as head of conservation at the YGT in succession to Peter Gibson, produced a condition report on all the Minster windows, to complement the new Quinquennial Inspection of the Minster Fabric by Surveyor Ian Curry. She singled out those windows in greatest need of conservation, including the St William Window, now judged to be in a perilous state, despite the interventions of the post-war period.

In 1997 a scaffold was erected to allow closer examination of the window and Winton's more detailed report identified two panels in need of immediate attention. She also highlighted the generally weakened state of the lead matrix, attributed to poor materials and poor craftsmanship (Fig. 6.3). Numerous solder joints had failed, and in places glass was cracked and extruding from the lead. In summary, the overall lead matrix was weakened to the degree that buckling of panels was widespread and even collapse was a possibility. In places, the medieval glass was extensively cracked, heavily corroded and dangerously thin (Fig. 6.2), especially the potmetal colours, with corrosion crusts now impeding light transmission and narrative legibility (Fig. 6.4). Many of the glass plates introduced in the 1950s were failing and in some cases were admitting both dirt and moisture. In common with many Minster windows re-leaded in the postwar period, the leads used were wide, covering far more glass than the original lead matrix would have done. This obscuring of glass was exacerbated by the numerous extra mending leads (Fig. 6.5), introduced to mend breaks in original glass in the era before the availability of effective adhesives, while surface-strap leads applied over cracks added to the problem. The window was also suffering from varying degrees of progressive paint loss (Fig. 6.6).

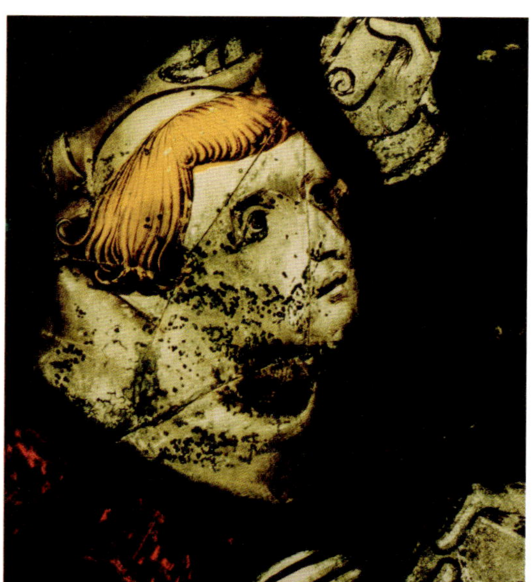

Fig. 6.2
The head of St William in panel 8b before conservation. The cracked and corroded glass is held within double plates of modern glass into which dirt and moisture has seeped.

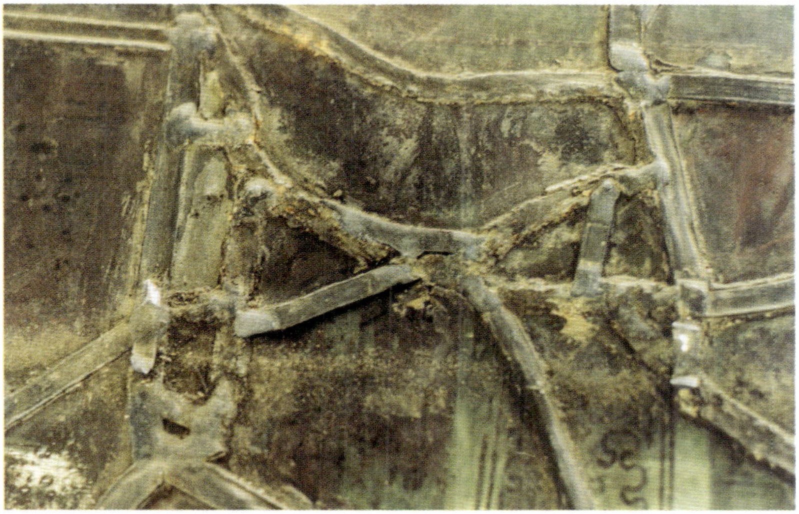

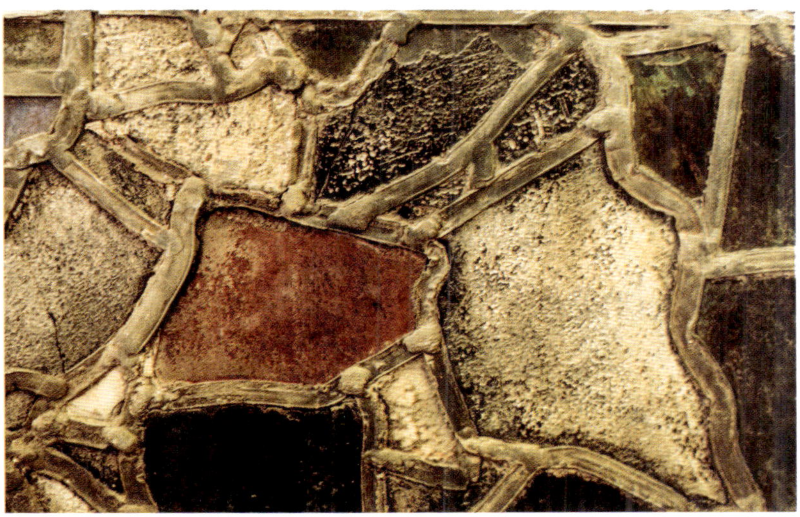

Fig. 6.3
Detail of the lead cames of panel 2b before conservation, showing broken solder joints and torn lead cames.

Fig. 6.4
The exterior surface of panel 5b before conservation, showing corrosion pits and an opaque crust of corrosion products.

Winton was invited to cost a programme of work to be funded by the Minster, the York Minster Fund (founded in the same year as the YGT itself), and the Freemasons of the Northern Province. It was originally characterised as a Millennium project, although in the event the work took far longer to complete, a measure of the unprecedented nature of the project as it evolved, which set a new benchmark for modern conservation practice at York Minster and beyond. At an early stage, the importance of complementary art-historical enquiry and advice was recognised, and a letter of advocacy was sent to the dean by Richard Marks, professor of stained-glass studies at the Centre for Medieval Studies of the University of York. This resulted in the creation of the St William Window Advisory Group (SWWAG), convened to give advice to the Dean and Chapter of York and support and guidance to the conservators of the YGT. The group first met on 1 July 1998, comprising Professor Marks and Dr Christopher Norton (also from the University of York), Tom French (now retired from the Royal Commission on Historical Monuments), YGT conservators Penny Winton and Lucy Rutherford, and Janice Smith, a trainee conservator and part-time research student working on the St William Window under the supervision of Professor Marks. The group was later joined by Sarah Brown (English Heritage), Surveyor of the Fabric Richard Carr-Archer and the Revd John Toy, Canon Chancellor of York Minster. All members contributed their time and expertise free of charge.

From the outset the group established firm objectives and underpinning principles for a project of unprecedented size and complexity in the history of the YGT, which would necessitate the re-leading of the entire window. Above all, the conservation work should halt further deterioration of the window and secure it for the future. If possible, it should render the panels more legible and redress the imbalance between glass and lead.

The conservators should fully document the window, and research into the manufacture and historiography of the window should be conducted in parallel to the conservation. In terms of the conduct of conservation practice on a day-to-day basis, it was agreed that there should be no rearrangement of original glass within the dismantled panels without consultation with the advisory group, and that the cultural significance of previous restorations should be fully investigated before intervention could be considered. Previous restoration insertions could not be removed without consultation, and all interventions should be fully documented and must be fully reversible. While these tenets are closely mirrored in the Guidelines for the Conservation and Restoration of Stained Glass, adopted in 2004 by the International Corpus Vitrearum, this careful formulation of a modern conservation policy was a new departure for the Minster's glass, ensuring widespread support for what might otherwise have been considered a controversial level of intervention. It received the approval of the Minster's Fabric Advisory Committee (FAC) and the national cathedral regulator, the Cathedrals Fabric Commission for England (CFCE).

A dossier was prepared for each panel, uniting all visual records with relevant antiquarian and historical notes and drawings. The watercolour drawings and photographs from the 1895 Knowles restoration were particularly valuable. New colour photographs were taken prior to commencement of work. The earlier lead net, so seriously failing, was carefully removed and glass pieces were laid out on rubbings (Fig. 6.7). All plates introduced in the 1950s were removed and all glass was dry-cleaned on both surfaces, with particular care taken of painted surfaces. Broken medieval glass pieces original to the window were edge-bonded where possible (Fig. 6.8), in the interest of reducing the obtrusive impact of mending leads. Three bonding techniques were used, selected on a case-by-case basis: epoxy resin, silicone and copper foil. The dismantling of the panels allowed for examination of the grozed edges of the medieval glass and in some cases provided compelling evidence that not all glass had been correctly assembled in 1895 and 1955.

Removing the mending leads and reconstituting the original pieces of glass made it possible to re-establish the original disposition of medieval glass within each panel (the original 'cutline'). However, it also

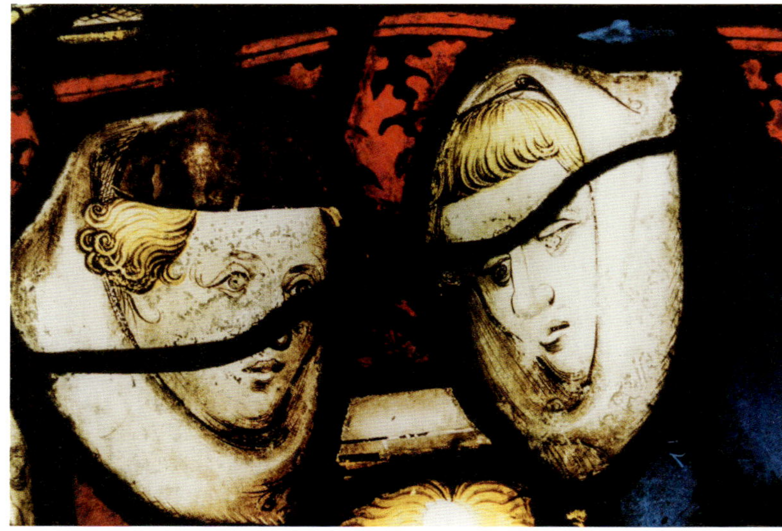

Fig. 6.5
Heavy and disfiguring mending leads in panel 3a.

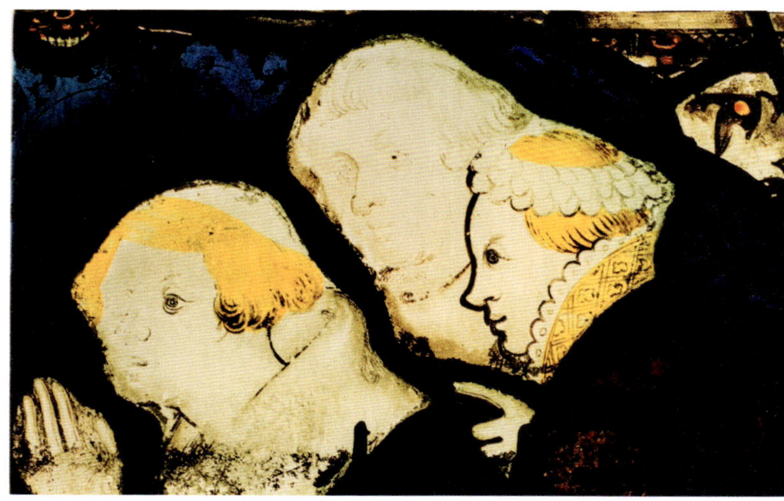

Fig. 6.6
Varying degrees of irreversible paint loss in panel 7e.

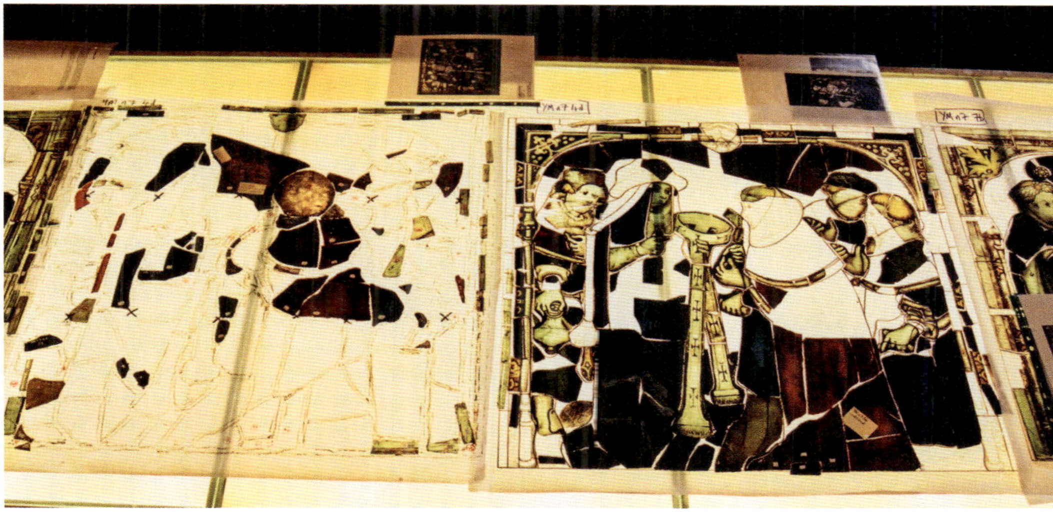

Fig. 6.7
Panel 4e after dismantling. All glass original to the panel is laid out on the rubbing on the right-hand side of the bench. Stop gaps and insertions remain on the left.

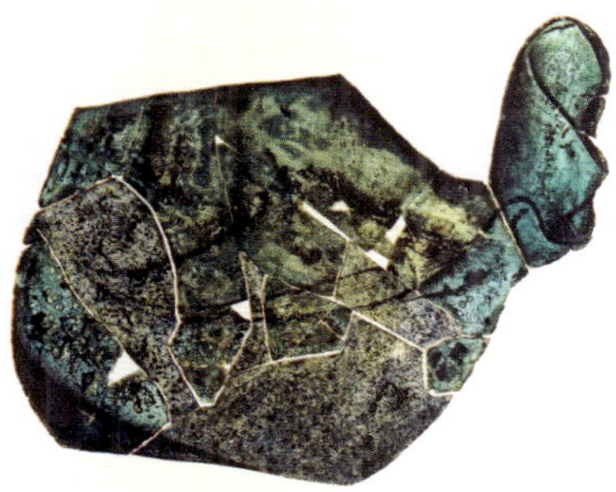

Fig. 6.8
Heavily fragmented blue drapery from the figure of the seated cardinal on the right-hand side of panel 5a prior to edge-bonding and reinstatement in the panel.

meant, not infrequently, that other pieces of glass that had been intruded during the various restorations no longer fitted. This therefore raised the question as to the degree to which glass could or should be rearranged, and on what evidence. There were also issues of legibility and aesthetics to consider. This became one of the most important ethical challenges facing the project, and was the area in which the collaboration of conservators and art historians was most critical. In the past, where original glass was missing or deemed too fragile to be retained (nowadays a very rare occurrence, thanks to modern environmental protection), it had been replaced in a number of ways, including with J. W. Knowles's newly painted pieces in1895. In the 1950s pieces lightly stippled with fired paint or unpainted glass of an appropriate colour had also been introduced, paying lip service to Winston's principles and those of the SPAB. In some cases, 'stop-gaps' of medieval glass brought from other locations had also been used. The unpainted or only lightly stippled pieces of modern glass were undoubtedly the most visually disruptive when viewed in transmitted light (Fig. 6.9).

After considerable discussion, SWWAG determined that the replacement of stippled or unpainted 1950s glass was justifiable in favour of newly painted and appropriately signed and dated pieces that restored narrative clarity. In a small number of cases, intruded stop-gaps of medieval glass from elsewhere were also removed in order to allow original glass to occupy its proper place in the panel. These pieces were logged, documented and archived. Most challenging of all, it emerged that in a very small number of cases Knowles's pieces were also no longer a good fit. Options included unaltered retention of the Knowles pieces, which meant unavoidably displacing a medieval original; total removal of the Knowles piece in order to allow the correct positioning of an original, or trimming of the Knowles piece to allow both to co-exist. Members of SWWAG decided that in order to respect the original medieval glass and to retain Knowles's thoughtful restorations, careful trimming of the latter was justified. In the event, this thankfully only affected a limited number of pieces of Knowles's drapery and 'seaweed' backgrounds.

Once the principle of replacing intrusive earlier repairs had been agreed, it needed to be applied on a panel-by-panel basis. It was decided that new insertions should normally perpetuate the colours of the earlier repairs that they replaced, since the latter often preserved evidence of the colours of the original medieval glass. Colours would only be changed on good evidence. It was also decided that earlier repairs that did not appear to make sense would not be replaced on those grounds alone, as they too might preserve evidence of original features which were no longer understood. The value of this approach is exemplified by panel 4b, where the large red repair in the middle of the panel defied interpretation. It was only many years later that it was realised that this repair, along with the piece of white fabric immediately beneath it, represented William's archiepiscopal vestments, which he was offering at the altar prior to his consecration. He is shown wearing the vestments in the next panel.

Making new painted replacement pieces for repetitive elements, such as the architectural frames and the backgrounds, was relatively straightforward. Creating replacements for missing sections of the figures and other details within the scenes was a more delicate matter. Thornton's designs rely on postures and gestures, on hair styles and clothing, and on colour contrasts to convey their message. Inadvertently altering any of them could change the interpretation of a scene. Here, the team was faced with a problem. Torre's descriptions of the panels, which contain so much information about colours, could only be used with caution, since initially there was much uncertainty as to which panels in his list were which. And in spite of all the research that had been carried out up to that point, there was still no agreement on the correct interpretation of many of the scenes.

In response to this problem, in addition to the research being undertaken by Janice Smith, SWWAG member Christopher Norton embarked on new historical research into the life and miracles of St William. In due course, his re-examination of the medieval Latin sources shed invaluable light on the window's narrative, and contributed to a proposal for the reordering of the window, which resolved at long last the vexed issue of the original order of the panels. This is discussed in more detail later in this chapter. His initial work on the Latin sources for the windows also led to a project funded by the British Academy between 2004 and 2006, which culminated in a monograph on the life and the early cult of St William, published in 2006, as the restoration of the window neared completion.

However, in the early stages of the project the solution to the problem of the original narrative order and the identification of the individual scenes had not yet emerged. With so many similar scenes, it would not have

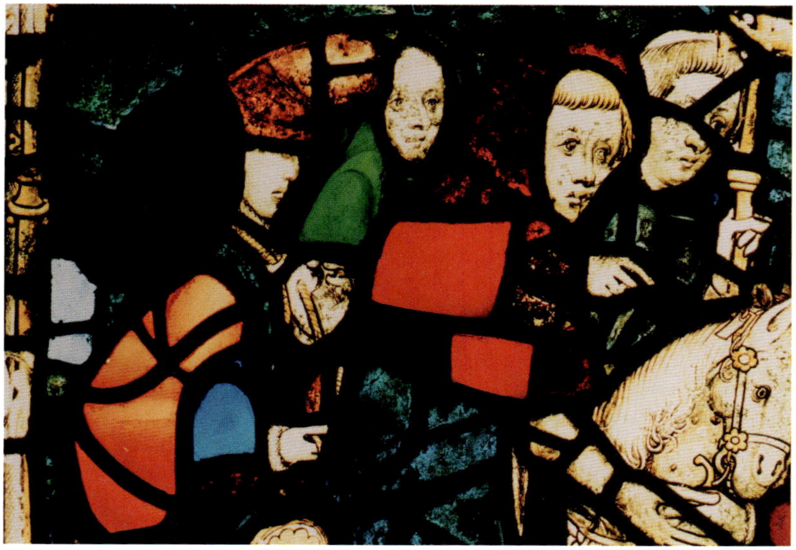

Fig. 6.9
Panel 9a before conservation, displaying the visually obtrusive unpainted modern glass used to patch the window in 1954.

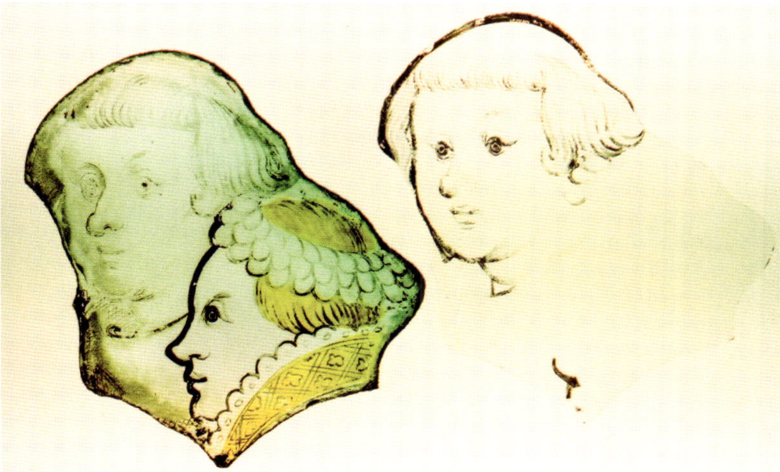

Fig. 6.10
An example of a painted backing plate (right), reinforcing lost detail in panel 7e (see Fig. 6.6).

been wise to restore the panels on the basis of speculative identifications. It was therefore decided early on that restoration of missing elements should be carried out primarily on the basis of internal evidence within each panel, drawing on the medieval sources only where the subject matter was not in dispute. Every panel was discussed individually, sometimes at considerable length. However, as the project progressed and the team became more familiar with Thornton's work, decisions were reached more rapidly. Like J. W. Knowles before them, the specialist glass-painters created carefully researched infills that took their cue from pre-existing details in the window and were a sympathetic response to the distinctive 'Thornton style'. In other places, it was possible to restore the impression of lost medieval paint by the application of small amounts of fired paint to reversible backing plates, bringing life back to faded faces (Fig. 6.10)

Two panels from early in the project illustrate the kinds of decisions that SWWAG faced. Panel 2c had been removed from the window at an early date and had missed out on the 1895 Knowles restoration. It had previously been in the St Cuthbert Window, had been restored to the St William Window in 1954 (Fig. 6.13) and was in very poor condition. Little of the medieval glass remained, apart from some of the tinted white glass, including some of the faces. Almost all of the original coloured glass had been lost, and the central figure was disfigured by an inserted, over-large and damaged medieval head. The subject matter was unknown. If re-leaded as found, the panel would have stood out from the rest of the window like a sore thumb. However, the lead lines preserved the ghost of much of the original medieval cut-line of the lost clothing, including the curving belts of three of the figures. It was therefore decided to replace the mostly lost clothing, following the original cut-lines, and the visually intrusive head of the central figure. In this way, the panel would harmonise with the rest of the window and, importantly, would not draw the eye away from the better-preserved Thornton panels. Only later was it established that the scene represents St William's education. It then instantly made sense. The central figure is the master, seated on a throne like a professor on his 'chair', with a lectern in front of him and his pupils, some of them with books, arranged around him.

Panel 4d was in much better condition and was identified as Cardinal Hincmar being entrusted with the pallium for William (Fig. 6.12). During the work, the conservators located a spare hand in the centre of the composition, which hinted at a missing figure. Draperies at the bottom of the panel also suggested an additional figure. There was no hint of a head at the top, but the background glass there had been inserted by Knowles. The Knowles photograph taken before his restoration of the panel actually shows an inserted medieval head from another window occupying this position (Fig. 6.11). The medieval Latin source for this scene states explicitly that the pallium was entrusted to Hincmar by Pope Lucius. It was therefore realised that the missing figure must have been the pope. A new head was created (signed and dated) based on original papal heads elsewhere in the window, thus reinstating

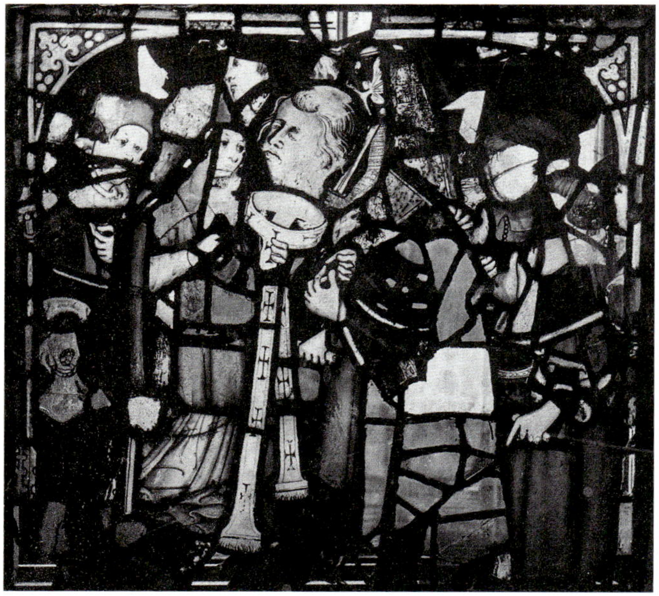

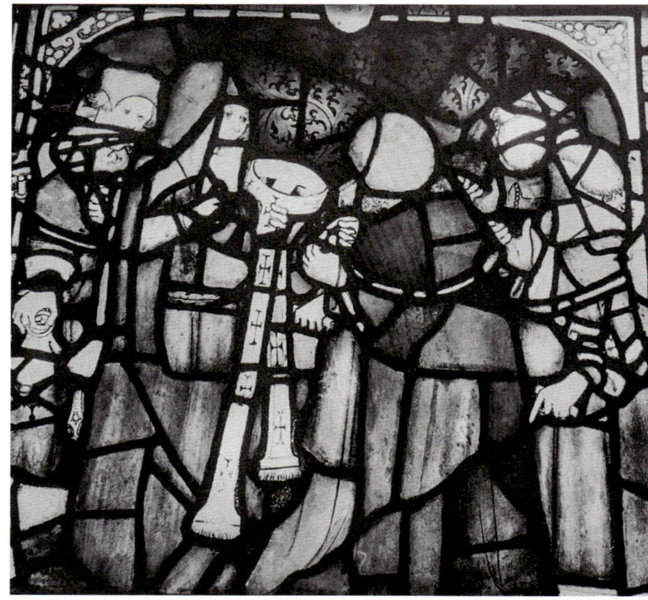

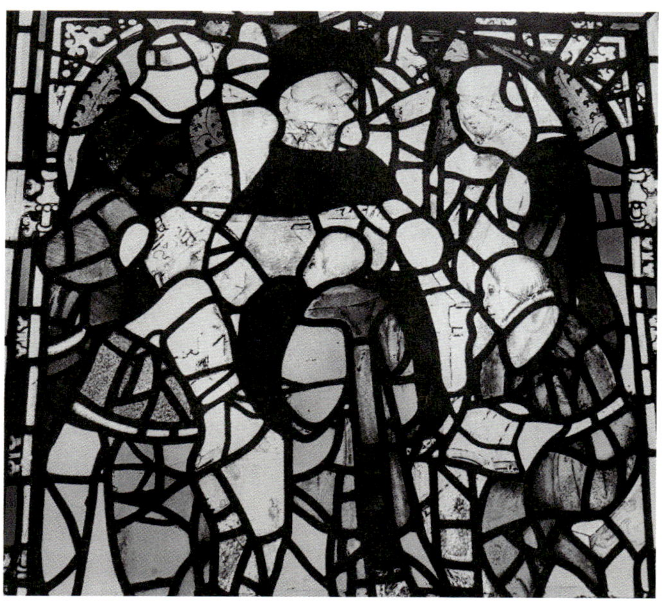

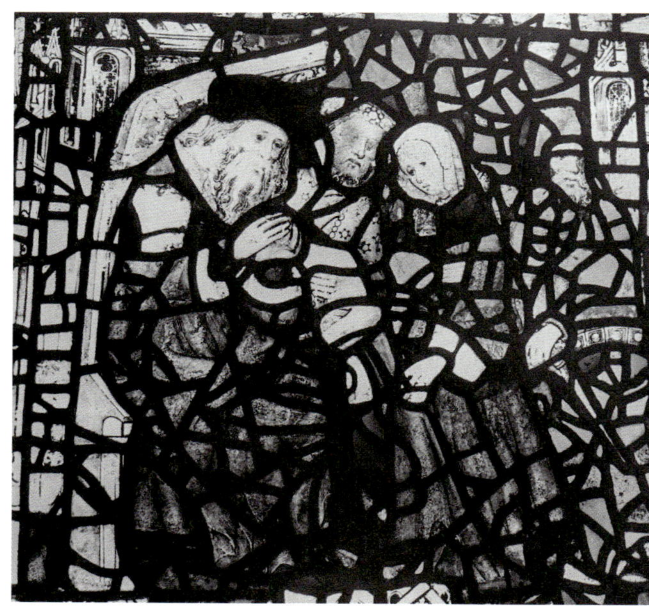

Fig. 6.11
J. W. Knowles's pre-restoration photograph of panel 4d, showing an over-large fourteenth-century head occupying the lost head of Pope Lucius.

Fig. 6.12
Panel 4d before conservation. During the 1895 restoration, seaweed diaper had been inserted in the top centre of the panel, immediately above the pallium.

Fig. 6.13
Panel 2c before conservation.

Fig. 6.14
Panel 2d (formerly 2e), alien to the St William Window but in Thornton's style. The panel was provided with a new 'St William Window frame' during conservation.

a crucial element to the scene and making sense of the transmission of the pallium, which features so prominently in the centre of the panel. Here, as elsewhere, the paint lines of the new head were toned down, so as not to draw the eye away from the Thornton glass.

In the light of new research, members of SWWAG also considered the fate of two panels known to be alien to the window, located since 1955 in positions 2e (Fig. 6.14) and 18a. Neither panel belonged here, although both were painted in a 'Thorntonesque' style. While the subjects of the missing panels could be surmised from their position in the narrative (once that had been established) and Torre had described the original panels before their destruction, there was no evidential basis on which they could be ethically recreated. The decision was made, therefore, to retain the panels for reasons of visual and stylistic harmony, and their coherence in their adopted window was enhanced by the creation of new frames for both panels copied from original St William Window designs. With the St William narrative sequence restored, these panels were placed in locations 2d and 10d, taking the places of lost St William Window scenes.

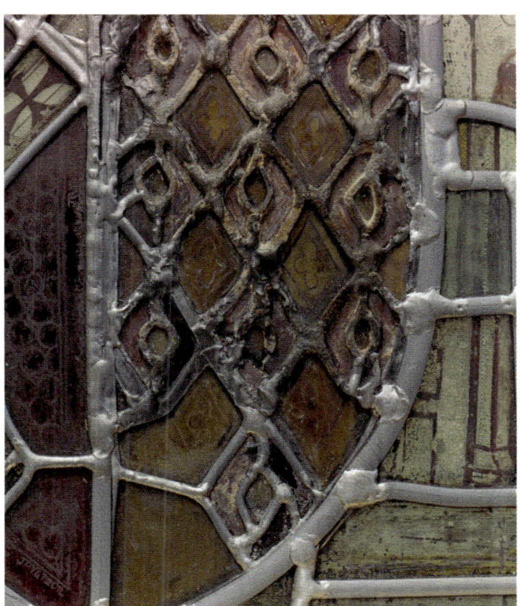

Fig. 6.15
Panel 1j of the Great East Window. Original Thornton workshop lead surviving in the shield of St William.

For many visitors viewing the conserved and reinstated St William Window, the most startling aspect of the window's transformation was the result of a new approach to leading. As inherited from the post-war restorers, the window had been weighed down with a broad, flat lead measuring 8–10mm across its flange. While this broad lead may well have been used because of limited choices of materials available to glaziers in the aftermath of the war, a long tradition of heavy leading had developed in the glazing workshop at the Minster, prompted by a belief in its strength and security, but perhaps also as a hang-over from the traditions of the Arts and Crafts movement. Medieval leads, in contrast, are known to have been much narrower across the leaf or flange, allowing for sinuous lead lines and their unobtrusive integration into the main outlines of the design. While the Minster preserves very little medieval lead as a result of generations of re-leading, a small number of surviving medieval leads, cast rather than milled, as well as painted 'fictive' lead lines, confirm their delicacy (Fig. 6.15). The window was consequently re-leaded in lead cames of 4–6mm in breadth, true to the medieval aesthetic of the window. The elimination of many mending leads through the introduction of edge-bonding techniques also contributed to a rebalancing of the relationship between glass and lead.

Environmental Protection

Probably the single-most important conservation measure adopted in connection with the St William Window, and one with far-reaching implications for the future preservation of the Minster's stained glass, was the adoption of internally ventilated Environmental Protective Glazing (EPG). Formerly known as 'isothermal glazing', this form of protective glazing relieves historic stained glass of the need to act as the interface between the external and internal building environments (Fig. 6.16). A new outer layer of clear modern glass is placed in the original glazing groove and is mortared into the stone, ensuring a weather-proof shield. The historic glass is brought slightly forwards into the building interior, supported no longer in the glazing groove but in a strong manganese bronze frame. A gap at the top and bottom of each light allows air from inside the building to pass into and out of the interspace, inhibiting, if not preventing, the deposit of any condensing moisture on either surface of the protected glass. Wetting and drying episodes are significantly reduced and are often eliminated altogether in all but the most extreme weather conditions. Importantly, if condensation does occur, it will always be on the new outer glass, and a small gap at the base of the outer glazing, supplied with a gravel-filled condensation tray and a lead-covered sill, allows any condensing moisture to exit the building without damaging the stonework. Importantly, an EPG system improves the thermal insulation of the building as a whole, and also benefits it by acting as a dehumidifier, allowing any build-up of moisture to leave the building in a self-regulating system that, unlike its electrical counterparts, requires no intervention and only minimal maintenance.

The importance of this environmental protection cannot be overstated, as moisture is the greatest enemy of stained glass. While moisture on the glass surface initially causes the migration of silica molecules to the surface of the base glass, forming a hard upper stratum, this 'gel layer' is riven with micro-cracks visible only with a scanning electron microscope. They are nonetheless large enough to admit more moisture into the body of the glass. Opaque corrosion products in solution (e.g. syngenite and gypsum) thereby enter the cracks and as they dry become crystalline in form, expanding to exert force on the surrounding glass body. This manifests as pits and craters in the glass surface, and if these pits coalesce and deepen, holes can form. This process will also eventually adversely affect the painted details on the glass surface. Moisture also encourages the growth of moulds and algae, which flourish in the presence of organic materials contained in layers of dirt and dust on the surface of a window. Mould is not only disfiguring, but also potentially damaging, as many forms of moulds and algae excrete acids that can etch the glass surface. Once medieval glass is thinned and holed by the corrosion process, it not only loses some of its artistic quality; it is also far more susceptible to wind pressure and mechanical damage.

Once a stained-glass window is protected within an EPG system, damaging rain and wind pressure will only affect the modern protective glazing, not the historic glass. Additionally, by keeping both surfaces of the historic glass dry, EPG not only creates a stable environment in which corrosion processes are halted, but also opens up a wider

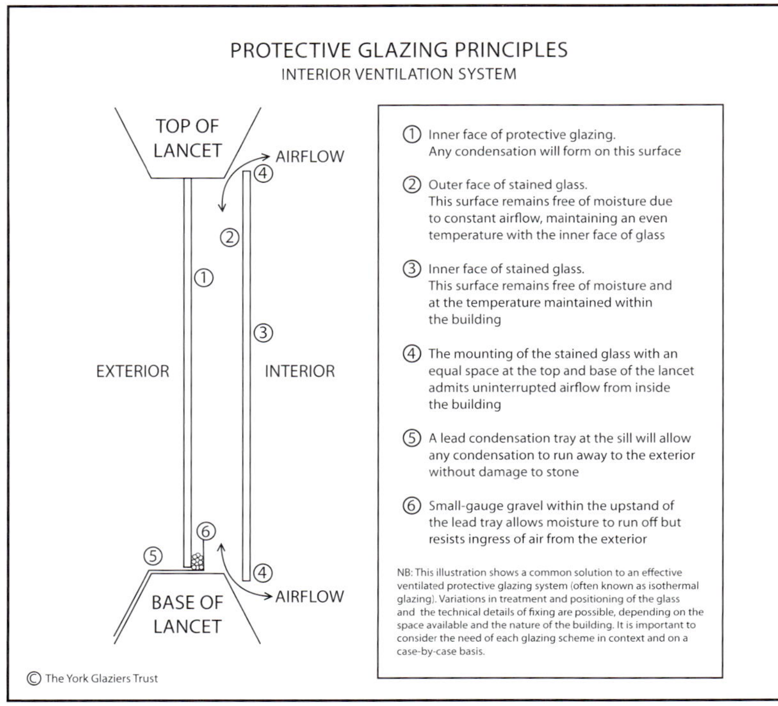

Fig. 6.16
Diagram showing the basic principles of an internally ventilated EPG system.

toolbox of conservation options, including the use of moisture-sensitive adhesives and consolidants that could not otherwise be used, and which have proved so beneficial in freeing the St William Window of mending leads.

External protection of stained glass has a long history at York Minster, having first been installed in the 1860s. The earliest versions, in plate glass and without any ventilation, were designed to keep the elements off the exterior of the windows, as the impact of internally condensing moisture was not then understood to be a threat. The greenish plate glass was unsightly and heavy, and its ferrous metal frames damaged the stone. From the early 1900s this was gradually replaced with more traditional diamond quarries set into a second glazing groove cut into the stone, although still installed without any intentional ventilation.

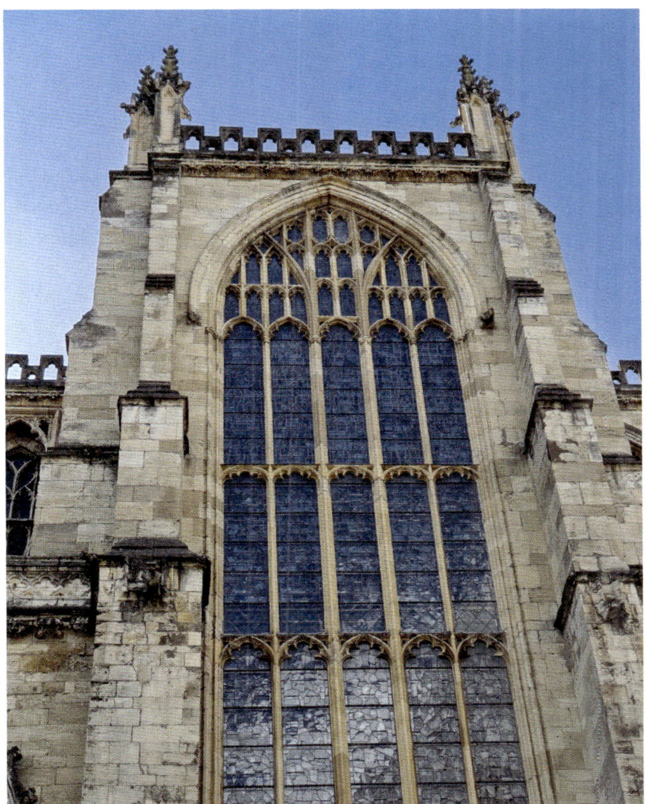

Fig. 6.17
Exterior of the St William Window showing the treatment of the exterior glazing.

From the interior these expanses of repetitive diamond quarries can cast disfiguring shadows on the medieval glass, while appearing rather lifeless from the exterior. In the design of internally ventilated EPG, great care is taken not just to create efficient ventilation, but also to maximise light transmission while minimising the negative visual impact of any large and highly reflective surfaces. The protective glazing for the St William window is leaded in a pattern that is a simplified version of the window's own lead matrix (Fig. 6.17). The glass is clear and unpatinated to ensure optimal light transmission, but is also slightly kiln-distorted to give it some movement, as would be found in a mouth-blown material.

The St William Window was the first Minster window, as well as one of the largest, to benefit from the latest Europe-wide research into the design of this approach to environmental protection. This was something strongly advocated in the subsequent 2004 Corpus Vitrearum Guidelines for Restoration and Conservation of Stained Glass, and it formed an integral part of the later and even more ambitious project to conserve and protect the Great East Window (implemented 2011–7). It is now also an integral part of the Minster's strategic plan for stained glass conservation and protection, launched in 2017.

In another crucial respect, the St William Window laid the groundwork for the Great East Window project. The St William Window Advisory Group had demonstrated the vital importance of bringing together art historians and conservators on a project of such complexity and importance. The precedent that it set was followed in the Great East Window restoration. An East Window Advisory Group (EWAG) of leading specialists was established at the very beginning of the project and helped to steer it though to its triumphant conclusion. In more ways than one, the restoration of the St William Window was a milestone in the ongoing history of the Minster's stained glass.

Restoring John Thornton's Narrative Cycle

The restoration of the original panels made them more legible. It did not, in itself, render them much more intelligible, since it was impossible to make proper sense of the scenes without knowing their original positions within the narrative cycle.

From the outset, it was recognised that one of the most far-reaching and difficult decisions facing SWWAG was the order in which to replace the panels. For the previous hundred years, since the Knowles restoration, the panels had been in the order suggested by Dr James Fowler in his 1874 article, with minor adjustments made by Dean Milner-White after the Second World War. Fowler's order was demonstrably incorrect, but restoring the panels to their pre-Knowles positions would scarcely be an improvement, since the panels were already in a considerable state of disorder by that date. Ideally, the panels would be restored to their original positions. However, the chances of doing this were slim. The recent work done by Tom French, Ben Nilson and Janice Smith, discussed earlier, had yielded valuable insights, yet no convincing reconstruction of the original lay-out had emerged. As French had concluded, with reference to his own analysis, 'Even this suggested layout has many difficulties, and must be regarded only as a starting point for establishing the original order.'

The problem seemed as if it might be insoluble. However, the restoration offered the last chance for generations to restore the window to its proper narrative sequence. So it seemed worth making one further attempt. Against expectations, this succeeded. SWWAG therefore recommended to the Dean and Chapter that the panels be returned to their original positions; permissions were granted by the Fabric Advisory Committee and the Cathedrals Fabric Commission for England, and, for the first time in centuries, the panels could be seen in the positions intended for them by John Thornton. How was this achieved?

It should be said at the outset that examining the panels in the studio gave us a huge advantage over previous scholars who had studied the window by means of black-and-white photographs or at a distance in the Minster. Knowing exactly which pieces of glass were original, establishing the medieval cut-lines, and uncovering previously obscured details such as the missing figure of Pope Lucius in panel 4d, all greatly helped in making sense of the scenes. However, the bottom half of the window was due to be reinstalled first, so a decision had to be made about re-ordering when half of the panels were still unrestored. And the window presented major challenges which could not be overcome simply by studying the panels in the workshop.

In the first place there is the sheer size of the window. The ninety-five narrative scenes (not counting the five donor panels in the bottom row) form one of the largest cycles of the life and miracles of a saint in any medium – perhaps the largest. Even the St Cuthbert Window opposite had only seventy scenes. Ninety-three of the panels, fortunately, are original. The other two (panels 2d and 10d), as we have seen, were inserted by Dean Milner-White to replace lost originals. An additional level of uncertainty, however, related to the five panels in row 14, which consisted entirely of plain diamond-shaped quarries. This row, at the bottom of the third section of the window, cannot be seen from the ground, as it is obscured by the large projecting transom that separates the second and third sections of the window. It could therefore have been left blank from the beginning. Alternatively, it had been suggested that it could originally have contained narrative panels, which would have been moved at some point to fill gaps left by other panels that had been damaged or destroyed. This would indicate a major reorganisation of the window, in whole or in part. If so, the change had been made before the end of the seventeenth century, since row 14 was recorded as blank by Torre. On this hypothesis, there would have been 100 narrative panels, of which seven were lost – a much more daunting prospect. In the event, it turned out that row 14 had almost certainly been blank from the beginning, but until this had been established, the possibility of a further five missing panels had to be borne in mind.

Many of the surviving ninety-three panels are very similar in design. For instance, there are several scenes showing the pope in Rome seated on a throne and accompanied by ecclesiastics (panels 3d, 3e, 5c, 5d, 8b and18a). The differences in the figures and the variations in their postures and gestures are difficult to interpret when the scenes are considered on their own, out of context. Their significance only really becomes apparent when the panels have been placed in their proper positions in the cycle and can be read, as intended, as part of an unfolding narrative. Many of the posthumous miracle scenes at the shrine are very similar. Some even copy elements from other panels in the window, which adds to the difficulty of identifying particular episodes and positioning them correctly. Reconstructing the narrative involved a constant two-way process of trying to identify the scenes in order to place them in their correct position, and trying to place them in their correct position in order to identify the scenes.

One well-established method for working out the imagery in the Minster windows is to compare them with other examples. The St Cuthbert Window, for instance, belongs to a long tradition of narrative cycles of the life and miracles of the saint, which can be traced back to illuminated manuscripts of the twelfth century. Comparison with the other known cycles is extremely helpful in deciphering the damaged panels in the window. For the St William Window, by contrast, there is little to be gained from comparative iconography. Images of St William's life and miracles are almost unknown outside the Minster, and within the Minster, as we have seen in Chapter 3, they consist mostly of the miracle of Ouse Bridge and the story of Ralph and Besing. The late-thirteenth-century window dedicated to St William in the Chapter House (CHn3) originally contained twenty scenes, but it is so damaged as to be of little use. Indeed, if anything, it is Thornton's window that helps to make sense of the Chapter House window.

The Torre manuscript might seem an obvious way in to reconstructing the narrative. However, the panels were not always easy to identify from Torre's somewhat wayward descriptions, particularly the scenes with similar compositions and the most damaged panels. Once they had all been identified (including the two now-lost panels), it was still not clear how many of them had been displaced by the time Torre recorded them, without corroborating evidence of the original order from other sources. It was only once the correct panel order had been worked out that it became clear that a fifth of the narrative panels were already out of position by 1690 (Fig. 6.18). Torre was not a shortcut to a solution.

The medieval texts relating to St William are crucial to understanding the window, but they present difficulties of their own. The broad outlines of the story had long been known, and most of the scenes could be assigned either to William's lifetime or to the posthumous miracles. The ones that include the shrine or portable reliquary must be posthumous, whereas scenes including groups of ecclesiastics should belong to his life. Even here, however, caution was necessary. Panel 4b, for instance, could be interpreted as a scene at the shrine like 15d, but is in fact an incident from William's life. Panels 18a and 20c are very similar to some of the lifetime scenes, but belong much later.

From John Browne and Dr James Fowler onwards, the texts have been scrutinised with the aim of identifying individual scenes. Some panels could be identified with confidence; some interpretations had not stood the test of time; some panels defied interpretation. There was no easy way of reconstructing the window from the texts. A number of different texts relating to St William were available at the time the window was made. They are all in Latin, and most of them have still not been translated into English. Some recount episodes from William's life; some recount posthumous miracles; some cover elements of both. Some of them exist in more than one version. Equally, some parts of the story appear in more than one source, and the details differ from one text to another. A further complication is that some scenes have no relationship to any known text, and were probably based on oral traditions handed down in York. It would be no easy matter to tease out which of the texts (and which versions of them) were consulted for the window, and how they were combined with each other and with oral traditions to construct a coherent narrative. In fact, it was only after the original order of the panels had been reconstructed using other evidence that the intricacies of the relationships between the texts and the images became apparent. The next chapter explores the light this sheds on the creation of the window.

In view of these various difficulties it was decided to focus attention on evidence internal to the window, all the while continuing to work on Torre and the medieval texts, as time allowed. Identifications of individual scenes would be taken into account only when they were beyond reasonable doubt.

The main lights of the window are divided into four sections, each surmounted by a stone transom. The number of panels in the different sections is not uniform. The bottom section has four rows of narrative scenes, in addition to the donor panels in the bottom row. The second section has six. The third section starts above the major transom with the blank row 14, followed by four rows

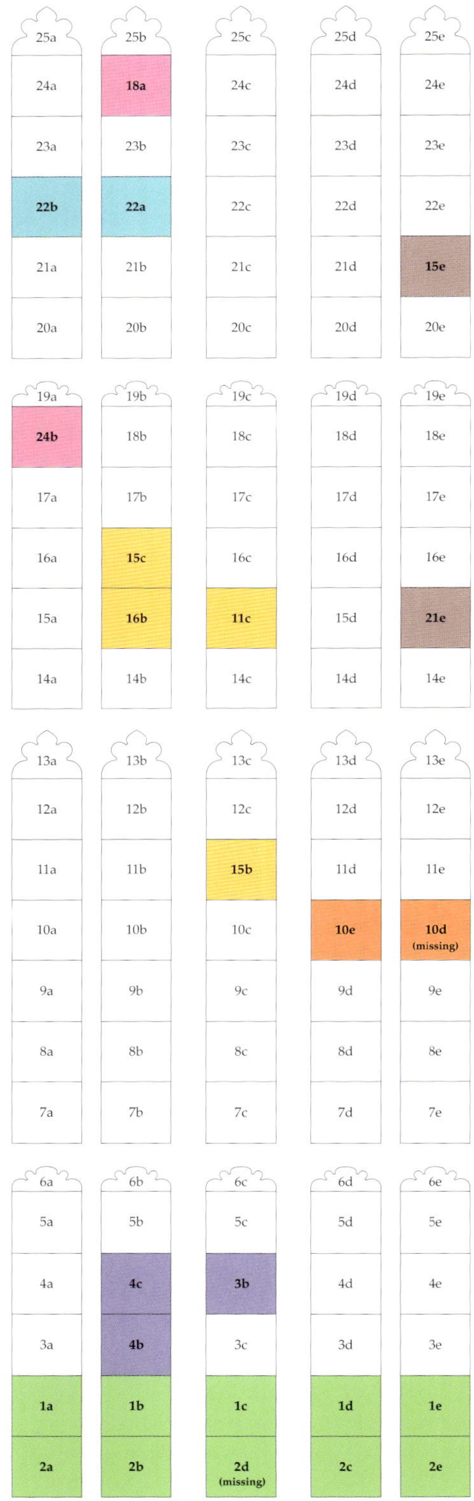

Fig. 6.18
Diagram showing which panels were out of place by the time James Torre recorded the St William Window, *c.*1690.

of scenes; the top section has five rows.

The first step was to identify the panels belonging to the four rows at the tops of the four sections (rows 5, 12, 18 and 24). All of the narrative panels are framed by fictive architectural surrounds. Vertical shafting on either side supports a canopy over the top. In most cases this consists of a horizontal flat-topped canopy, which frames the panel at the top and provides a base for the scene in the row above. The top row of each main section, however, is capped by a row of cinquefoil-cusped panels corresponding to the stonework cusping at the head of each light (rows 6, 13, 19 and 25). The shape of the cusping is different in each case, so the cinquefoil panels from each row are of a different shape. They therefore cannot be moved from one row to another. The narrative panels in the rows immediately beneath are designed as a single unit with the cinquefoil panels. They lack the usual horizontal flat-topped canopies. Instead, the coloured backgrounds run up to the top of the panel and continue onto the cinquefoil panels above, while the flanking shafts support elaborate architectural canopies, which fill the cusping of the cinquefoil panels with gables and finials. The design of the window requires twenty panels to fill the top rows of the four sections, and there are indeed precisely twenty panels that lack the flat-topped horizontal canopies.

These twenty panels form four sets of five corresponding to the four rows that they occupied. The most striking is the set of five that occupy row 12 and depict the early miracle story of Ralph and Besing, vividly depicted in their bright red duelling costumes. These form a distinct episode, and the order of these five panels can be confidently established. Another set of five, which belong in row 18, can be identified without difficulty from the Latin text of the *Translation of St William*. The Translation ceremony of January 1284 itself is preceded by a story of Edward I escaping unharmed from an accident on a mountain in Wales through the intervention of St William. This is depicted in panels 18b–18e, where the order again is not in doubt. Panel 18a seems at first sight anomalous. It depicts a seated pope accompanied by ecclesiastics, and looks like several scenes from St William's life. However, the Translation narrative starts with a brief mention of the official canonisation of St William by the pope in 1226, and this is what is shown here. So this must be the first scene in the row. Row 5 contains five scenes dominated by popes, which must belong to William's life, though their order within the row could not immediately be determined. With rows 5, 12 and 18 forming a clear chronological progression, it is evident that the story read from bottom to top, as suggested by previous scholars. The five miracle scenes in row 24 must therefore have come at the end of the posthumous miracles, though their subject matter and order within the row was yet to be established. Thus, it was possible at the outset to assign twenty of the ninety-three extant narrative panels to their correct rows, and ten of them (12a–12e and 18a–18e) could be placed in their proper positions within the rows.

These four rows are key to unravelling the sequence in the rest of the window. Medieval windows usually have backgrounds of more than one colour, arranged in some sort of regular pattern. The most common colours in the fifteenth century were dark blue and dark red, and these are the colours used in the St William Window. In row 12 the colours alternate:

red, blue, red, blue, red

This may be called a red row, and row 5, with three reds and two blues, must have been the same. Row 18 is a blue row:

blue, red, blue, red, blue

and row 24 must have been the same. Of the remaining seventy-three original panels, thirty-six are blue and thirty-seven red, with two other panels lost. If all the rows in the bottom half of the window were red rows, and all the rows in the top half were blue rows, this would have required thirty-seven blue panels and thirty-eight red. Alternatively, there could have been a chequer pattern throughout. Both schemes were tried but only a chequer-pattern produced a workable result. The narrative panels in John Thornton's Great East Window also have an alternating blue-and-red chequerboard pattern.

As well as alternating background colours, medieval windows often have variations in the designs of their fictive architectural frames. These too are usually arranged in a regular pattern. A common arrangement for a five-light window would be an alternation of designs:

a b a b a

Rows 5, 12, 18 and 24 (and the cusped panels that go with them in the rows above) all contain two different frame designs, but they are not arranged in the normal manner. In row 12, where the narrative order is not in doubt, the pattern is:

a a a b b

Row 18, on the other hand, has:

a a b b b

Rows 5 and 24 can be deduced to have had three of one design followed by two of another, like row 12. Similar patterns existed elsewhere in the window. Even before they could be allocated to specific rows, some panels could be identified that must have belonged to pairs or triplets of adjacent panels with the same frames. Examples are the two panels showing the pallium being sent to William (panels 4d and 4e), the woman who swallowed a frog (panels 17a and 17b), the man with a bad leg (panels 21a and 21b), and the three scenes of the man knocked off a ladder by a falling stone (panels 22c–22e). This rules out a chequer pattern of frames.

These patterns are most unusual and rather surprising. On closer inspection, however, they provide a crucial clue to the arrangement of the rows. Combining a chequer-board pattern of coloured backgrounds and the usual arrangement of frames gives a standard layout on a blue row of the following:

a	**b**	**a**	**b**	**a**
blue	**red**	**blue**	**red**	**blue**

In this case the first, third and fifth panels could be swapped without disrupting the pattern; likewise, the second and fourth panels. The same would apply with a red row. The patterns in the St William Window give a different result. For blue rows, they would be:

a	**a**	**a**	**b**	**b**
blue	**red**	**blue**	**red**	**blue**

or

a	**a**	**b**	**b**	**b**
blue	**red**	**blue**	**red**	**blue**

The only panels that can be swapped without disrupting the pattern are the first and third panels in the first example, and the third and fifth panels in the second example. Again, the same applies if the row starts with a red panel. Consequently, there is very little possibility of movement of panels within each row – though they could still of course be moved to another row with the same pattern. What this means is that the number of possible permutations is very significantly reduced.

The analysis of the frames can be taken further. There are eleven different frame designs in the window (Fig. 6.19). In addition to those with the cusped heads at the top of each section, there is a very ornate frame design in the bottom row (Type A), which

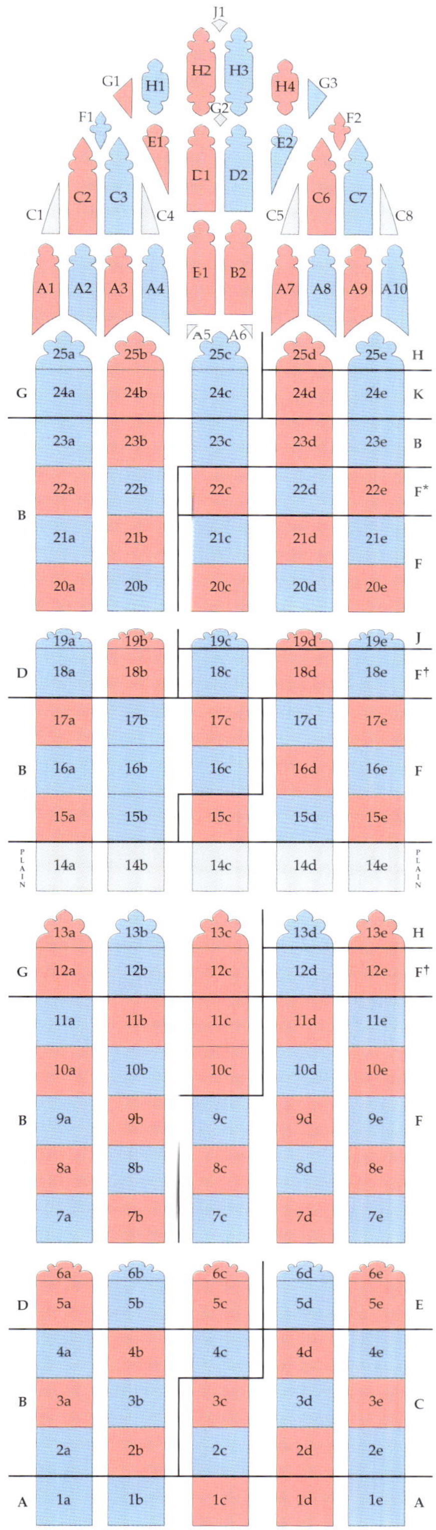

Fig. 6.19
Diagram showing the original disposition of background colours and canopy designs in the main light panels.

emphasises the importance of the Roos donors. The architectural frames on the seventy-three surviving narrative panels with horizontal canopies are of three types (B,C and F plus variant F*). There are thirty-eight examples of Type B. They include identifiable subjects ranging from the marriage of William's parents to miracles that post-date the Translation of the relics in 1284. They therefore cover the whole chronological span of the cycle, and must have been spread across all four sections of the window. There are only seven extant examples of Type C, all with scenes from William's life, including the two scenes of the sending of the pallium (panels 4d and 4e), which belong early in his archiepiscopate. There are twenty-eight examples of Type F and F* combined. They include a number of lifetime scenes, some of them definitely from the end of William's life such as the Ouse Bridge miracle (panel 9c), together with many miracle scenes, some of them post-dating the Translation of the relics. Thus, Types C and F/F* combined cover a chronological span equivalent to that of the Type B panels, and must likewise have been spread across the full height of the window.

How then might the frames have been arranged? They could not have been arranged with one frame per row, since that would require multiples of five of each type of frame, which was not the case, even if the two missing panels were added in. In any case, rows 5, 12, 18 and 24 suggested two frames per row. If the two missing frames were of Types C or F/F* (as in fact turned out to be the case), there would have been thirty-eight panels with Type B and thirty-seven with Types C and F/F* combined, i.e. as near as possible half each. If a chequer-board pattern was ruled out, how else might that have been achieved? The breakthrough came when it was realised that each section might contain rows with the patterns

a a a b b
and
a a b b b

Having thus postulated a structural pattern for the cycle based on an analysis of the objectively quantifiable coloured backgrounds and frame designs, the next step was to start arranging the scenes to see if a plausible sequence could be constructed. The initial focus was on the scenes from William's life and early miracles from the bottom two sections of the window, since these were due to be reinstated first. Initially, scenes that could be identified with reasonable confidence were provisionally positioned at appropriate points. Other panels were then placed around them. After much trial and error and much shuffling of paper – this being done before digital photographs were available – a sequence finally emerged in which the coloured backgrounds formed a regular chequer pattern of alternating red and blue and the frames fall into a discernible pattern, as shown in Fig. 6.19. The bottom section contained seven Type B panels and eight Type C panels (including the missing panel in 2d), arranged in the order BBCCC in rows 2 and 3, and BBBCC in row 4. A similar pattern emerged in the second section, with twelve Type B panels to the left, and thirteen Type F panels to the right (including a lost panel in 10d), arranged in order BBFFF in rows 7, 8 and 9 and BBBFF in rows 10 and 11.

The result is an unusual but nonetheless regular sequence. Frame Type B is on the left in both sections and is paired with another frame on the right – Type C in the lowest section, Type F in the second section. In both sections, the layout changes from two Type B panels at the bottom to three Type B panels at the top, where the layout matches that of the rows beneath the transoms, namely three panels of one type followed by two of another. In terms of the story, the narrative moves from the marriage of William's parents in panel 2a to his death in 10e, followed by the earliest miracles in row 11 and the Ralph and Besing story in row 12.

There are two anomalies. Firstly, the coloured backgrounds of row 1 do not match the chequer pattern of the rows above. This is very obvious in the diagram, but is barely discernible in the window, since the coloured backgrounds are all but obscured by the fictive hangings (Fig. 4.6). Secondly, panel 11c is red instead of blue, forming a cross of red panels at the top of the second section. This was probably deliberate, to emphasise the first of the posthumous miracles. It is one of the very few in which St William himself appears, and the orange rays stand out vividly against the red background.

To test the validity of the reconstruction, the re-ordered lower sections were first compared with the sequence recorded by Torre *c.*1690 (Fig. 6.18). The bottom two rows were already known to have been swapped over and disordered. In the rest of the lowest section, three panels were not in the positions noted by Torre, and in the next section only a further three differed from Torre's order.

It was only at this stage that the reconstructed cycle was compared with the Latin texts. The result was surprising. The window followed the narrative in the written sources remarkably closely. Almost every single panel was directly based on the texts (as set out in Appendix Two), and the scenes that share very similar compositions all fall into place, the subtle differences between them making sense when read in the light of the textual sources. The fit between the texts and the window is so close as to be compelling.

Once the code had been cracked for the lower half of the window, it was relatively easy to apply the results to the upper two sections. The Type B frames go on the left, the Type F and F* panels on the right, with the central light changing from F at the bottom to B at the top. The top section was fairly straightforward, with the post-Translation episodes in rows 20

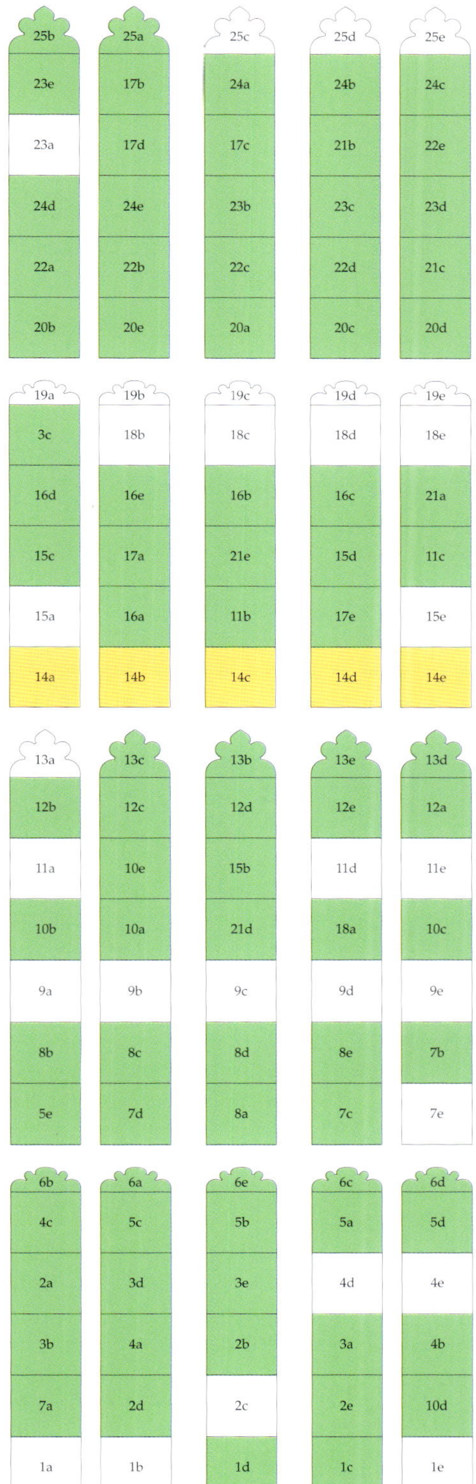

Fig. 6.20
Diagram showing panels out of sequence by 1954.

–22 falling into place without much difficulty. The miracle scenes in row 23 and in most of the third section of the window are complete in one panel and could potentially be moved around, but they could be placed by reference to Torre. Only nine panels in the upper half of the window are not in the locations recorded by Torre (Fig. 6.18). In the top section there are some anomalies in the patterns of the coloured background and the frames, but these can be ascribed to haste in completing the window, as will be discussed in the next chapter. The blue background of panel 16b is probably a simple mistake. Minor anomalies can be found even in John Thornton's Great East Window.

Comparing the reconstructed original sequence with the state of the window over the centuries shows how badly disordered it had become. In Torre's time, out of 100 figurative panels (including the donor panels at the base), twenty-five were no longer in their original positions. When the window was taken out for restoration in 1997, seventy-six out of the ninety-eight surviving panels were out of position (Fig. 6.20). The proportion of out-of-position panels had increased from one-quarter to three-quarters in 300 years. Reconstructing the original order makes it possible not only to identify the individual panels, but to also appreciate the challenge presented to John Thornton by this commission, and the thoroughgoing and imaginative design process he went through, a subject that we pursue in the next chapter.

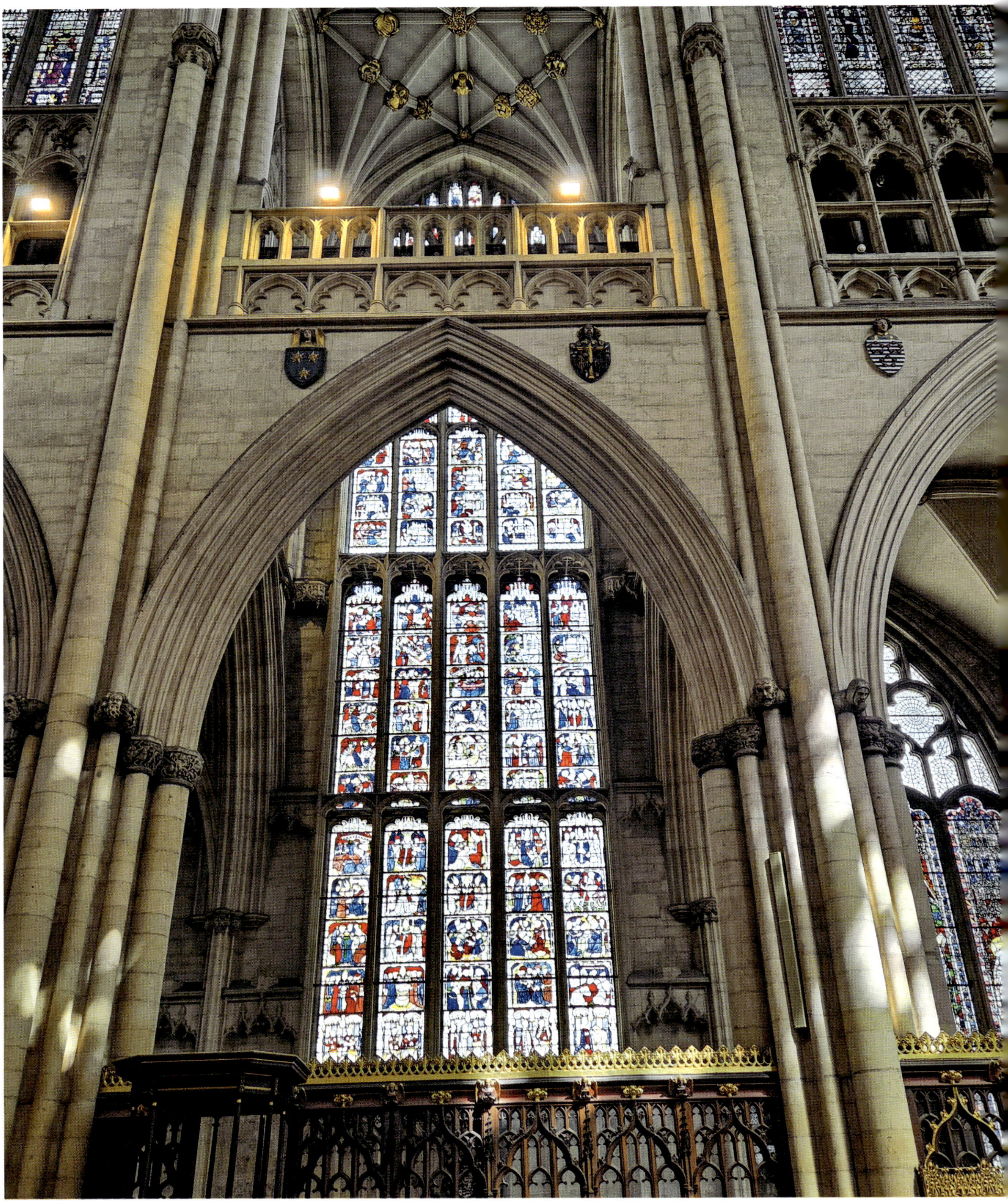

Chapter 7

The Creative Genius of John Thornton

The restoration of the St William Window has transformed the way we look at it. Studying the glass on the bench in the studio and subsequently in high-resolution digital photographs has revealed countless details that were previously invisible, while the reinstatement of the panels in their original order enables us at last to follow the narrative right through from beginning to end as John Thornton intended it. We have gained precious insights into the process of creating the window, and can begin to appreciate the scale of Thornton's achievement.

Collecting Stories of St William

The sheer size of the window presented practical challenges that would have daunted a lesser man: supply of materials, finding skilled craftsmen, running a large workshop, delivering the finished product on time, and so on – to say nothing of the artistic challenges involved. Thornton, however, had already demonstrated his abilities with the Great East Window and the choir clerestory windows. He had presumably developed good working relationships with the Minster clergy and the masons working on the building. The Great East Window, of course, surpassed all others in its size, its artistic ambition, its theological sophistication, the variety of its panel designs, the richness of its colours and the quality of its execution. Yet in one respect the St William Window presented more of a challenge than the Great East Window. There was already a long-established tradition of biblical illustration in a variety of different media, which Thornton was able to draw on when designing the scenes in the window. For instance, there was a rich tradition of illuminated manuscripts of the Book of Revelation, with up to eighty separate miniatures, which Thornton referred to when designing the eighty-one scenes of the Apocalypse in the window. Thornton's brilliance in the Great East Window was his ability to adapt the existing artistic tradition for a new, monumental context with astonishing assurance and vitality.

Fig. 7.1
View into the north-east transept, with the St William Window beyond.

For the St William Window, on the other hand, the case was rather different. In the first place, there was no precedent for a window containing ninety-five scenes from the life and miracles of a single saint. Secondly, the existing iconographical tradition relating to St William was slight, consisting for the most part, as we have seen, of just a few scenes, such as the miracle of Ouse Bridge. Only the Chapter House window had a more extended cycle, but even this contained only twenty scenes. As far as we know, there were no illuminated manuscripts of the life and miracles of St William. Thirdly, there was no single written source with enough material on St William's life and miracles to fill the whole window. A great deal of preliminary research on the sources would be needed.

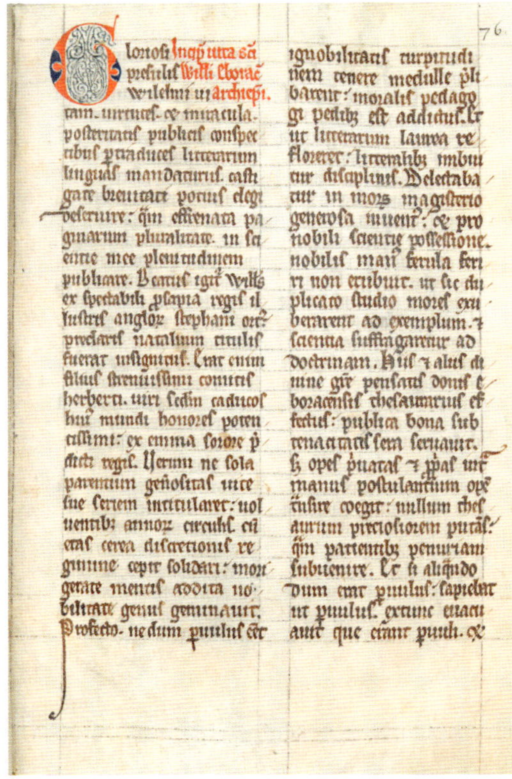

Fig. 7.2
The opening page of the thirteenth-century *Life of St William* from Thornton Abbey. British Library, MS Harley 2, f. 76r.

Information about St William's life and miracles could be found in various texts, all of which had been written at the Minster, and all of which were in Latin. These are discussed in greater detail in Appendix Two, which includes a table listing the textual sources for the individual panels. In order to have access to this material, Thornton must have collaborated with someone who had a good grasp of Latin and was familiar with the York sources. Here again he could build on previous experience, since he must have engaged in similar collaborations over the choice of seated figures from the history of the Minster in the bottom row of the Great East Window (Fig. 1.5) and the standing figures in the choir clerestory (Fig. 4.2), all of whom are taken from Latin sources. For these earlier projects, however, Thornton would have needed only lists of names. For the St William Window he needed stories, episodes and vignettes, which he could transpose into a visual medium and combine into an overarching narrative. This presupposes a much closer collaboration.

The Minster produced few scholars of any significance in the Middle Ages. One such figure who was active at exactly this time was Canon John de Neuton. Like William three centuries earlier, he was treasurer of the Minster during a major campaign of rebuilding and thus must have been closely involved in the work on the fabric. He also had a considerable personal library, including historical works, and he was the driving force behind the construction of a new, dedicated library building, which now houses the Minster shop and the choir-practice rooms. He died in 1414, as the window was taking shape in Thornton's workshop. The preliminary research on the texts must have been completed by the time he died, and he must be considered a strong candidate for Thornton's collaborator, both on the St William Window and on the earlier glazing projects. The collaboration between Thornton and a scholar at the Minster found an echo in the collaboration between conservators and art historians on the St William Window Advisory Group during the recent restoration.

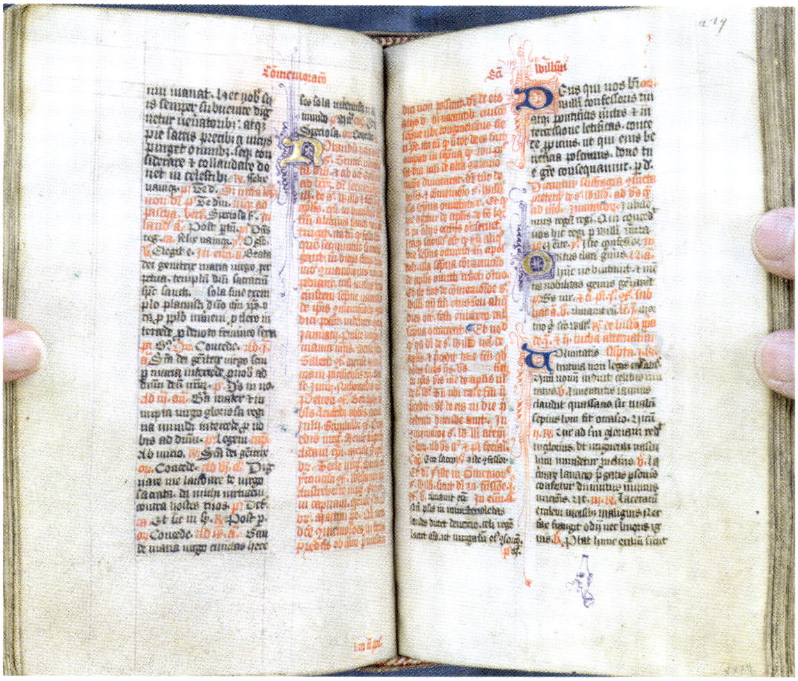

Fig. 7.3
Early-fifteenth-century York *Breviary* open at the readings for the Feast of St William. York Minster Library, MS Add. 383, ff. 228v–229r.

The principal text used for the first three sections of the window was the *Life of St William*, written probably in the 1220s around the time of the papal canonisation (Fig. 7.2). This is not a biography in the modern sense. Rather, it belongs to the traditional genre of saints' lives. Saints' lives were designed to honour the saint and inspire devotion among the faithful, and they are normally composed of two sections: the life of the saint, and the posthumous miracles. Substantial extracts from William's *Life* were incorporated into the York *Breviary* (Figs. 3.23 and 7.3) and would have been read out every year at the appropriate points in the liturgical calendar. It was an obvious source to use for the window, whose two-part structure of life and miracles follows the established convention.

However, the *Life* did not provide sufficient material for such a vast window. It had to be supplemented from other sources. For William's childhood and early career (row 2), no information was available beyond the brief account in the *Life*, and it was the principal source for the final year of William's life in rows 7–10. For the intervening years, however, Thornton was fortunate to be able to draw on the *Chronicle* of John of Hexham. This covers the period of the civil war between King Stephen and the Empress Matilda, and is particularly well informed about events in the North of England. The Minster possessed (and still possesses) a unique abbreviated version of the *Chronicle* consisting of verbatim extracts from John of Hexham relating to William and Archbishop Murdac (Fig. 7.4). This *York Abbreviated Chronicle* was no doubt the version of John of Hexham that was consulted for the window. The format of the *Chronicle*, in which events are recorded in chronological order, year by year, made it particularly suitable for the narrative in the window, and it is the principal source for rows 3–5. In addition to these two main sources, some episodes from William's later life are derived from the Minster's own *Chronicle of the Archbishops*. This is a composite chronicle, which traces the history of the Minster from Paulinus onwards, archbishop by archbishop.The entries on William and Archbishop Murdac belong to the section of the *Chronicle* attributed to Thomas Stubbs in the later fourteenth century.

It is evident from reading these Latin sources that they have been carefully collated to form a single narrative for the window. The correspondence between the texts and the window is striking. Of the forty scenes of the life of St William in rows 2–10, only five (panels 2b, 3b, 4b, 8e and 9e) have no direct parallel in the texts, and all of them are necessary or plausible additions to the story. Equally, there are very few incidents in the texts that are not depicted in the window. For instance, the *York Abbreviated Chronicle* reports that a cross was seen in the sky above the Minster when William was elected archbishop. Since this redounds to the glory of the saint and could have made a memorable scene, it is perhaps surprising that it was omitted. Another omission is the return of Cardinal Hincmar to Rome with William's pallium following the death of Pope Lucius (panel 5a). The *York Abbreviated Chronicle* blames William for having delayed collecting his pallium from Hincmar – a somewhat unfair criticism, since no one could have foreseen that Pope Lucius would be killed, but perhaps sufficient reason to leave it out of the window. For whatever reason, the consequent gap in the narrative means that the renewal of opposition to William, leading to his deposition (panels 5b–5e), is left unexplained.

In places, it seems that Thornton was not merely aware of the sequence of events, but was familiar with the actual wording of the texts. The extraordinary triple deathbed scene in panel 7c is one example. William's three Cistercian opponents, Bernard of Clairvaux, Pope Eugenius and Archbishop Henry Murdac, all died within a short space of time in 1153. Their deaths were a turning point in the story and they might have been expected to be shown individually. However, the *York Abbreviated Chronicle* recounts their deaths in consecutive sentences, while both the *Life* and the Stubbs *Chronicle* actually say that Eugenius and Murdac died on the same day (they don't mention Bernard). The texts seem to have prompted Thornton to create a scene which is unique in medieval European art, showing three deathbeds in three different countries at the same time. Another suggestive example is panel 8c. Between 1142 and 1154 William made no fewer than four return journeys to Rome. All of them are mentioned in the texts, but in no case is the actual journey mentioned, except for the return journey in the early spring of 1154, which is mentioned in passing in the Stubbs *Chronicle* ('returning to England'). The journey itself was of no significance, but Thornton seems to have seized the opportunity to display his artistry in the memorable image of William sailing back to England wearing full archiepiscopal vestments (panel 8c).

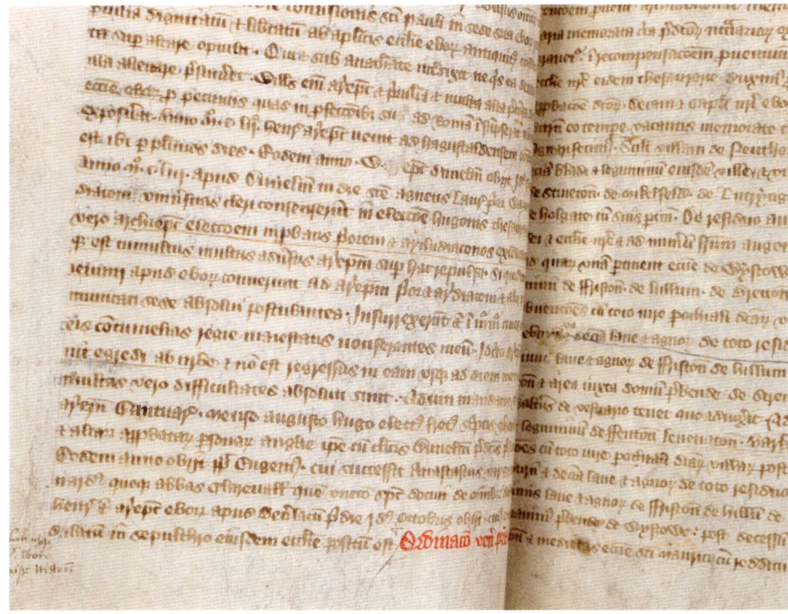

Fig. 7.4
The *York Abbreviated Chronicle* of John of Hexham in the Minster's *Registrum Magnum Album*, York Minster Library, Ms. L2(1) f. 61v. The text concludes at the bottom of the left-hand page with an account of the deaths of Pope Eugenius, Bernard of Clairvaux and Henry Murdac.

In the second half of the window, there is a less clear-cut correspondence between Thornton's scenes and the written sources. The Latin *Life* is again the principal source for the early posthumous miracles in rows 11–17. Some of them are also mentioned in the Latin source known as the *Miracula,* preserved in the Dodsworth manuscript. This is a composite text, which starts with a long list of the miracles at the tomb in 1177 that led to William being revered as a saint. Other early miracles follow; and there are later additions down to the fourteenth century. The early parts of the *Miracula* were probably known to the author of the Latin *Life*, and the whole text would have been available to John Thornton as it had been written out on a wooden panel, which was displayed in the Minster, probably at the tomb-shrine in the nave, as documentary evidence of William's miracles. The *Miracula* text gives dates and names, including the names of the protagonists of the story in row 12, Ralph and Besing, but the miracles are mostly recorded very briefly. The *Life*, by contrast, contains a smaller number of early miracles, but they are treated at greater length as a series of vignettes, which lent themselves better to being transposed into a visual medium. In fact, though often cited as a source, none of the miracles in the window are definitely based on the *Miracula* text rather than the *Life*, with the possible exception of panel 17c.

The window depicts only a selection of the miracles in the *Life*. After the first two (panels 11c–11e), the window departs from the sequence of miracles in the *Life*, which makes identification of the rather similar miracles at the tomb in rows 16–17 more difficult. Some of the miracles have no equivalent in the *Life* or the *Miracula*, namely the man attacked by a devil (panel 15a), the ship with the broken mast (panel 16e) and the man thrown from his horse into a river (panel 17d). A Latin hymn to St William praises him in passing for his help to sailors, which perhaps alludes to the incident in 16e. Otherwise, no textual sources are known for these scenes. It is probably no coincidence that these three miracles all took place away from the Minster. They therefore perhaps did not merit a mention in the records of miracles kept at the tomb. They may well derive from stories passed down by word of mouth rather than written down.

Rows 18–21 are based on a Latin account of the Translation of St William's relics in 1284, written not long after the event. It survives in the form of extracts, which were incorporated into the York *Breviary* as readings for the Feast of the Translation in January. Different versions of the *Breviary* contain different extracts, which, when combined, enable the original text to be reconstructed with reasonable confidence.

Row 18 starts with the papal canonisation of St William in 1226 (panel 18a). Given the repeated emphasis on papal involvement in the scenes from William's life, it may seem surprising that the canonisation is covered in just a single scene. However, Thornton was merely following his source, since the readings for the Translation in the *Breviary* start with a very brief mention of the canonisation, before proceeding to the episode involving King Edward I in Wales, which occupies the rest of row 18.

The top section of the window starts with the ceremony of the Translation of the relics (row 20). Given the emphasis accorded to Edward I in row 18, it is odd that he is not shown carrying the reliquary containing the saint's bones in panel 20b, even though he is specifically stated to have done so in the Translation account. Perhaps the manuscript of the *Breviary* consulted for the window omitted this detail. Or perhaps the king was omitted deliberately in order to focus attention on the clerical participants in the Translation in panels 20a–20c and on the miracle that took place on that day (20d–20e). Row 21 includes two miracles that took place not long after the Translation, and which are mentioned in one version of the *Breviary*.

Rows 22–24 have no known written sources. It seems likely that there never were any. The miracle of the man hit on the head by a stone while up a ladder in panels 22c–22e ends with him carrying the stone to give as a thank-offering for his miraculous deliverance. Scarcely less miraculous is the survival of what appears to be the very same stone at the Minster (Fig. 7.5). It bears an inscription in Latin

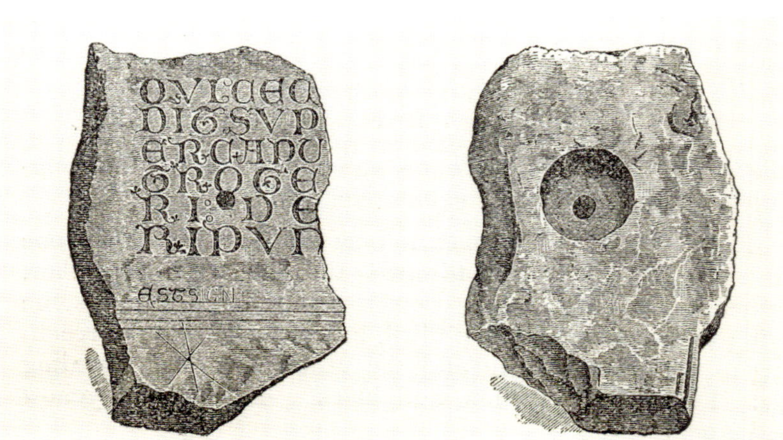

Fig. 7.5
The Roger of Ripon stone, apparently the stone related to the miracles in panels 22c–22e or 20d–20e. Engraving illustrated by Dr James Fowler, 1874.

stating that it was the stone 'which fell on the head of Roger of Ripon'. An archdeacon called Roger of Ripon is attested in the mid-fourteenth century. Could this be the man in the miracle story? The figure on the ladder is not in clerical garb, but appears to be a servant. The style of the lettering, which is rather amateurish in its execution, would fit a date at the end of the thirteenth century or the early decades of the fourteenth, whereas Archdeacon Roger of Ripon died in 1386. It is conceivable that the miracle occurred while he was a young man, prior to becoming a clergyman, but it seems unlikely that it is the same man. Alternatively, the Roger of Ripon stone could be the one that fell on the head of one of the servants during the Translation ceremony (20d–20e). The 1284 date might fit the style of the lettering better, though according to the *Breviary* the stone in question was part of a column, which is not the case with the Roger of Ripon stone. Either way, the stone would have stood out from the more usual votive offerings at the tomb, which mostly consisted of models of parts of the body that had been healed, as can be seen in panels 21b and 22b. The stone was solid evidence of the miracle, and its intriguing inscription was bound to prompt questions, so the story was very likely repeated to pilgrims at the tomb long after the event. Similarly, the chains offered by the released prisoner in panel 22b could also have been the subject of an oral tradition.

Panels 23a–24c are very different in character. They depict individual episodes at the tomb, comparable to many of the miracle scenes in rows 15–17. Indeed, although panels 23c and 24c are new designs, the others are actually composed of elements copied from some of the earlier scenes at the tomb. Depictions of the tomb and figures from the earlier panels are recombined to make new scenes, not always successfully, as explained in the Catalogue. These panels seem to have been intended as generic miracle scenes, without any reference to specific incidents,

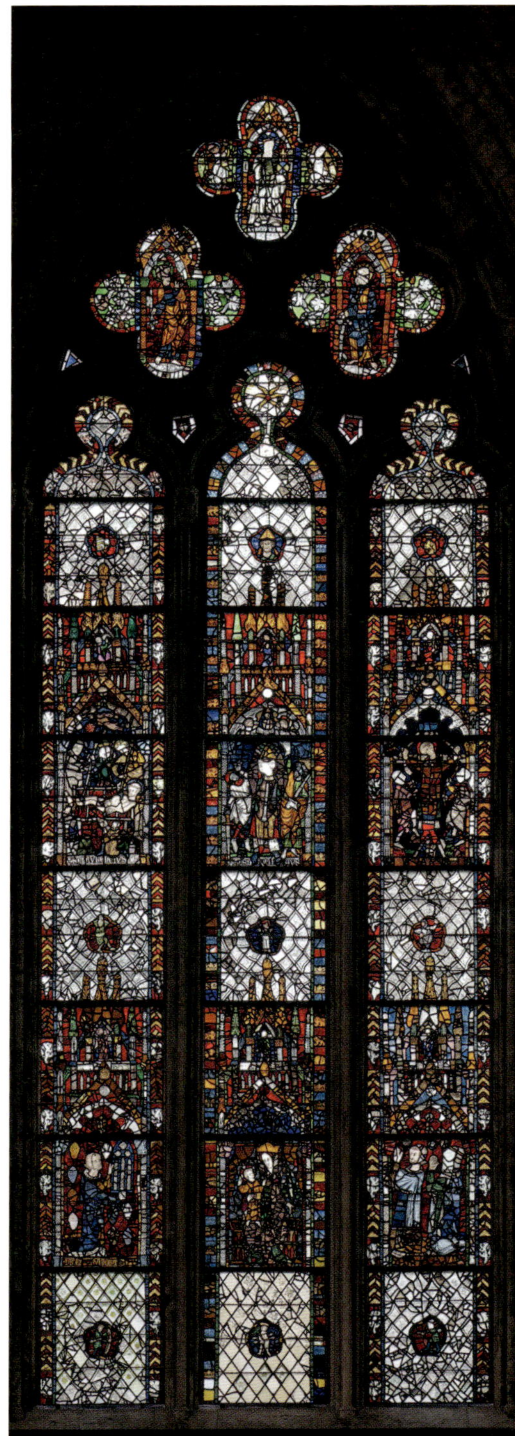

Fig. 7.6
The Martyrdom Window (n26) of *c.*1320, typical of the 'band window' design that predominates in the nave. Donor figures kneel in the lower register of the window.

the visual equivalents of remarks in the texts that many other miracles took place whose details had not been recorded in writing. In this context, it is all the more striking that the last two scenes in the window, panels 24d and 24e, depict a quite specific story involving a lady falling from a horse and giving thanks at the tomb for her deliverance. If we are correct in thinking that the lady in question is none other than Beatrice de Roos, the donor of the window, then she herself must have been the source of the story. In the last three rows, Thornton was drawing on a living oral tradition to bring the story right up to date.

Having thus traced as far as possible the sources of the scenes depicted in the St William Window, we can now appreciate the huge amount of research that went into collecting the stories of William's life and miracles. Thornton then had to arrange them into a coherent narrative.

Designing the Window

The contract for the Great East Window, which Thornton signed in 1405, stipulated that he had to design all the panels himself. The same very probably applied for the St William Window. Before he could design the individual panels, he needed to know their position in the window. Although the Latin sources provided him with subject matter and a chronology, it was up to him to devise a scheme that fitted the window.

By its unusual position within the building, the St William Window has a dual aspect, as an aisle window (Fig. 1.2) and as a large transept end-wall window (Fig. 3.8). There were earlier examples of both in the Minster. The aisle windows are so high above the floor that the eye is naturally drawn first to the bottom of each window, before being led upwards to the tracery at the top. This upwards movement is reflected in a vertical hierarchy in the imagery. In the nave aisle windows, for instance (Fig. 7.6), the lower band of figural panels normally includes the donor(s) and the upper band depicts scenes from the earthly life of Christ or the saints, while the tracery lights contain a vision of saints, angels and God in heaven. The West Window has a similar arrangement on a much larger scale, with standing figures of archbishops at the bottom, a row of apostles in the middle (Fig. 3.13), and above them four scenes of the life of Christ and the Virgin, who are shown seated in glory in heaven at the top of the main lights. For the Great East Window, however, Thornton had adopted a different layout. The bottom row contains the figure of the donor, Bishop Skirlaw of Durham (see Fig. 4.4), flanked by archbishops (including St William, Fig. 1.5) and other leading figures from the early history of the Minster. The huge tracery section of the window depicts a vast assembly of saints in heaven beneath God or Christ and his angels at the top. But the central section is filled with the cycle of scenes from the history of the world from Genesis and the Apocalypse, which read, unusually, from the top downwards. This makes sense for a window that is normally viewed from a certain distance and where the central narrative can be read like the page of a book from top to bottom. At the same time, there is a circularity in the imagery, since beginning and end are united by the theme of Alpha and Omega, which is cited at the bottom right-hand corner of the window and links the entire cycle to the figure of Christ at the apex of the window.

The general format of the St William Window follows that of the Great East Window: a single row of donor figures at the bottom, an enormous narrative cycle filling the rest of the main lights and a vision of heaven in the tracery. Yet here, unlike the Great East Window, the narrative reads row by row, left to right, from the bottom up to the top. This makes it easy for the viewer from the aisle to follow the story up the window – but only so far: the upper parts of the cycle are not visible from the aisle. Conversely, from in front of the high altar, the whole of the narrative can be seen (Frontispiece), but might perhaps more easily be read from the top down, like the Great East Window. The tension between the two viewpoints has not been resolved. But in another respect the St William Window does follow the example of the Great East Window. Again, there is a certain circularity, since the end of the narrative cycle at the top right-hand corner is linked back to the bottom right-hand corner through the figure of Beatrice de Roos, who appears (if the identification is correct) as a young woman in panels 24d and 24e and as the matriarch of the family in panel 1e.

The St Cuthbert Window opposite makes an interesting comparison. There, the whole of the bottom section is filled with the figures of the donor, Bishop Langley of Durham, and his Lancastrian associates, all kneeling before a standing figure of St Cuthbert (Fig. 7.7). This effectively forms a self-contained unit when seen from the aisle. The upper three sections containing scenes from the life and miracles of St Cuthbert can be read together from in front of the high altar, and they originally read from top to bottom, like the Great East Window. This arrangement reconciles the two different viewpoints more satisfactorily than the St William Window. Indeed, it can be seen as a critique of the St William Window. It had the further advantage that the cycle of Cuthbert scenes could be kept to more manageable proportions.

Thornton used the physical structure of the window with its three transoms as a means of structuring his narrative. The four sections of the main lights can be read as separate chapters, each of which ends at the top right-hand corner with a pair of scenes of particular significance. The bottom section traces William's life up to the decisive turning point when he was deposed and replaced as archbishop by Henry Murdac (panels 5d–5e). The larger second section takes the story from his retirement to Winchester up to his death, concluding with the first three posthumous miracles. At the top of this section Thornton placed the story of Ralph and Besing, the only one of the miracle stories to occupy a complete row by itself. It concludes with a pair of panels showing Ralph's miraculous healing at the tomb (panels 12d–12e). The Ralph and Besing story comes almost at the end of the Latin *Life*, but Thornton has placed it earlier in the sequence to provide an emphatic ending to the second section. The third section presents a further selection of early miracles, culminating with the only miracle involving a king. The four panels depicting the memorable incident of Edward I's fall on a mountain in Wales conclude with two scenes showing the king giving thanks before a statue of St William and hastening to give honour to the saint at York (panels 18d–18e). The final section begins with the Translation of St William's relics, followed by post-Translation miracles, some of which now feature the portable reliquary. The final pair of scenes depicting Beatrice de Roos's riding accident (panels 24d–24e) are emphasised by subtle differences of design. They have a type of frame that is found nowhere else in the window;

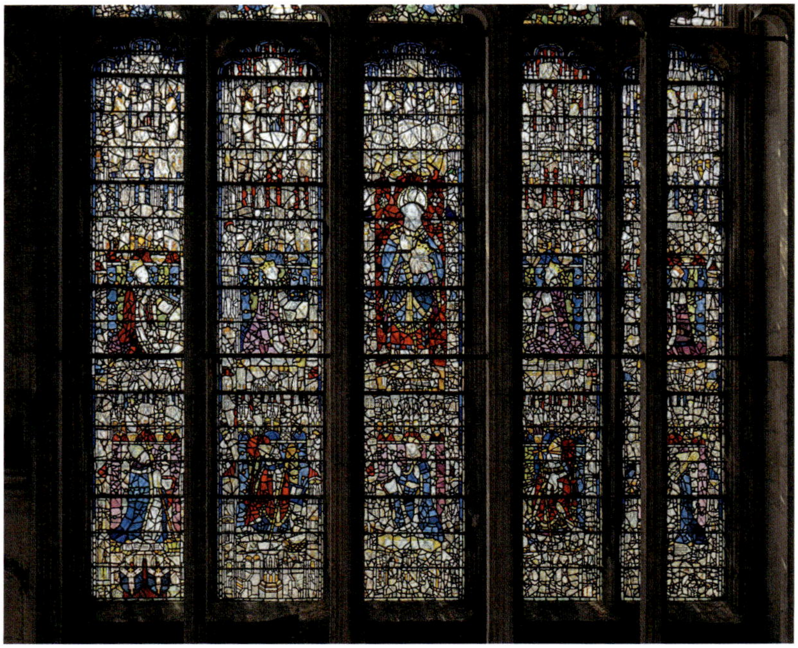

Fig. 7.7
The lower section of the St Cuthbert Window (s7). St Cuthbert surrounded by historical figures.

they are slightly larger than the other panels, and the figures of Beatrice are larger in scale and consequently more prominent. In these ways, and by their position at the very end of the narrative, these two panels are marked out from the rest as being of special significance.

The importance accorded to the scenes in the top-hand right corner of each section points to another distinctive feature of Thornton's design. In medieval windows with an odd number of lights, it was common practice to emphasise the central light, both by the overall composition of the window and by placing the most important figures in the centre. This can be seen, for instance, in the three-light windows in the nave aisles and in the five-light choir clerestory windows. Thornton had also emphasised the central light of the nine-light Great East Window. Thus, Bishop Skirlaw, the donor, is in the middle of the bottom row (Fig. 4.4). Immediately above him is the figure of Christ in the Last Judgement. Other important scenes of Christ in the Apocalypse cycle are also positioned in the central light, and the strong central axis concludes with the figure of Christ at the very apex of the window.

In the St William Window, by contrast, there is a marked emphasis on the right-hand light. In many of the rows, thematically linked scenes culminate in the fifth light. And some of the panels in the right-hand lights depict pivotal episodes that determined subsequent events, thus linking one row to the next and driving the narrative forward. These features are particularly apparent in the lower two sections of the window. Row 2, for instance, covers the whole of William's life before he was elected archbishop, and it ends with the death of Archbishop Thurstan (2e), which set in motion all the events that were to follow. In panel 3e, the pope gives his judgement on William's election, and the figure half-concealed on the right sets off for England carrying the papal letter, which is then delivered in panel 4a. Row 9 groups together five scenes of William's return to his diocese in 1154, culminating with his enthronement in the Minster in panel 9e. This is followed in row 10 by five panels from the last ten days of William's life, ending with his death at the end of the row in panel 10e. At the end of the next row, panel 11e is the first depiction of the tomb where most of the miracles were to take place.

The central light does contain some important scenes, such as William's consecration in panel 3c and the first posthumous miracle in which St William appeared to the blind girl, in panel 11c – but these in no way diminish the emphasis given to the right-hand light. The relative unimportance of the central light is also demonstrated more subtly by the frames of the panels. As we have seen in the previous chapter, the usual pattern in medieval windows is for frames to be arranged symmetrically around the central light. In the St William Window, however, the first two frames in each row are always the same, and the last two are also always the same, but the central light sometimes has the same frame as the first two panels, sometimes the same as the last two (Fig. 6.19). This arrangement, which is hard to parallel elsewhere, imparts a sense of instability to the central light, which detracts from its importance.

The most obvious consequence of the prioritising of the right-hand light can be seen in the bottom row. The normal pattern, which can be seen in many windows in the Minster, is for the principal donor, or donors, to be placed at the bottom of the central light, or in adjacent lights facing towards the centre. In the St William Window, Beatrice de Rocs is in panel 1e, kneeling and facing towards the right, and the younger members of the family are all lined up behind her, facing in the same direction (Fig. 4.6). She is placed unquestionably at the head of the family, and most unusually she looks out beyond the frame of the window. This seemingly odd arrangement makes more sense if we look to panel 24e at the top of the window, where the lady we assume to be Beatrice is again depicted kneeling and facing right, but here she is looking at the tomb of St William. In the bottom row, Beatrice should be understood as looking out of the window towards the reliquary of St William behind the high altar. She and her family are like the donor figures on the wing of a triptych, looking towards the figures in heaven in the centre of the composition. In this way, Beatrice and her family are linked to the relics of the man whom they could claim as their family saint. We may wonder whether Beatrice herself insisted on being represented in this way.

The more we look at the window, the more we can admire Thornton's skill in composing such a vast narrative cycle, all the while adhering closely to the Latin texts that underlie the story. His artistic flair is also apparent in his designs for the individual scenes.

Designing the Panels

Although Thornton's narrative cycle was entirely new, when it came to designing the individual panels he was able to draw on existing artistic traditions, and on some of his own compositions in the Great East Window. The marriage of William's parents, for instance, in panel 2a, the enthroned archbishops in 3b, 4c, 5e, 9e and 20c, and the deathbed scenes in 2e, 5a and 10e are all versions of common designs. The window contains several scenes of clergy before the pope (3d, 3e, 5c, 8b and 18a) whose composition is essentially a variant of Moses and Aaron before Pharaoh in the Great East Window (Fig. 7.8). The circular compositions of the groups in panels 3a and 3c have a precedent in the scene of St John teaching in the Great East Window (Fig. 4.16). Where appropriate, Thornton adopted and adapted earlier traditions and compositions for the St William Window.

The majority of scenes in the window are interiors. This is denoted in the simplest manner by patterned pavements, and, very often, by just a single prominent piece of furniture. This is usually a throne or an imposing seat, or a bed, or, in the miracle stories, the shrine. Apart from the floor, the interior of the building is not usually represented, nor for the most part are other interior details shown. There are a few exceptions, where there are few figures and the story demands or permits additional elements. Panel 17a, for example, shows the woman who swallowed a frog in an elaborately panelled setting, with food set out on a table in front of her. She is the only figure in the scene, which allows her to be shown twice. Panel 21a shows the man having his leg measured lying in a bed with a panelled headboard, with elaborately patterned bed-clothes and a well-stocked bedside table, all details that suggest a man of some status able to afford the life-size model of his leg depicted in panel 21b. Panel 22a likewise suggests a man of some standing, albeit a prisoner. Panels 22c and 22d depict tapestry hangings, but they are an essential part of the story. The only other panels to feature similar interior decorations are the donor panels in row 1. These combine with exceptionally elaborate architectural frames to convey the sense of a fictive architectural interior of great richness whose purpose is to show off the wealth and status of the Roos family. The donor figures themselves make an interesting contrast to the figures in the rest of the window. They are essentially static, and do not relate to one another. By contrast, what emerges from the narrative panels is Thornton's mastery of group scenes and his fascination with the interactions between individuals in the group. Superfluous detail would detract from the focus on the human interest of the scene.

Thornton uses a variety of devices to convey the meaning of the scenes and to enhance their visual interest. One is his use of colour. Many of his scenes are quite crowded, and one way of defining the individual members of a group is to give adjoining

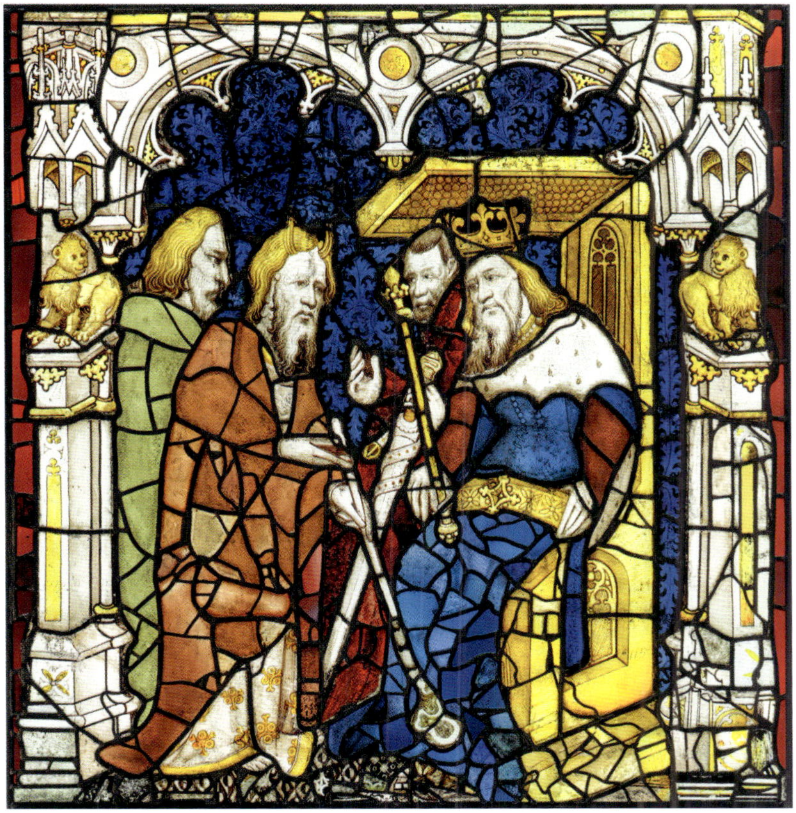

Fig. 7.8
The Great East Window, panel 13c. Moses and Aaron before Pharoah.

figures different coloured clothes or, in the case of individuals who are wearing clothes of more than one colour, to make sure that the colours of adjacent figures are counter-changed. Panel 3d is one example among many. Different styles of clothes and vestments are an important indicator of the relative status and identity of different individuals. Hairstyles and head-gear are very carefully considered as identifiers, particularly when it comes to the many ranks of clergy in the scenes. Panel 5d is an excellent example. In the middle is the pope wearing the papal triple tiara. Standing next to him are two cardinals, identified by their red cardinals' hats with long red tassels. Standing just behind them, one on either side, are two bishops or archbishops. They are not wearing vestments (the scene is not in church) but are identifiable by their mitres. On the left-hand side are five senior clergy wearing clothes of two contrasting colours. The one in the foreground clearly has a clerical tonsure, with shaven crown and hair covering the ears. The two seated figures opposite are lesser clergy or acolytes, untonsured and wearing robes of a single colour, belted at the waist. The adjacent panel 5e contains a similar grouping of clergy, but they are quite different. The figure seated on the throne is an archbishop (Henry Murdac) identified by his episcopal mitre and his archiepiscopal pallium, prominently displayed over his blue vestments. The figures gathered around him are all monks, identifiable by their monastic tonsures, consisting of a thin circle of hair above the ears and below the shaven crown. And being robed in white, they are Cistercians, monks of Murdac's order, as no doubt are the two at the back wearing blue copes with green collars.

These conventions produce some striking results. Archbishop Thurstan in panel 2e dies with his mitre on, as does William in 10e. Pope Lucius in 5a wears the papal tiara on his deathbed, as does Pope Eugenius in the triple deathbed scene in 7c. Bernard there is bare-headed to show his monastic tonsure and has his crozier beside him to denote his abbatial status, while Archbishop Murdac has his mitre on and his pallium draped over his bed-clothes. The art of John Thornton does not aspire to realism. Nor was he aiming at historical accuracy. The papal triple tiara, for instance, was only introduced in the fourteenth century, while Bernard's highly ornate, late-medieval-style crozier would have been anathema to the man himself in the twelfth century. Throughout the window, hairstyles, vestments, clothing and other accoutrements of the clerics and lay people alike are convenient props, in contemporary style, for Thornton to convey the essentials of the scenes with maximum economy and visual clarity. In one respect Thornton's desire for visual clarity conflicts with the story he is presenting. Sailing home to England in panel 8c, William shows off the pallium that he has just, at last, received from the pope in the previous scene. Yet in 3b and 4c Thornton depicted William at his election as archbishop and at his consecration wearing the pallium. This is entirely consistent with artistic convention and indicates clearly that this is William as archbishop. With most archbishops this would not be a problem. But in William's case it contradicts the historical facts described in the Latin sources and makes a nonsense of the immediately following scenes in which Pope Lucius sends the pallium to William (4d and 4e). If Thornton was aware of this, he may have felt (not unreasonably) that most viewers would not appreciate the niceties of the arguments over the pallium, and decided that the clarity of the individual scenes should take precedence over narrative coherence.

Being able to identify the figures in the scenes is essential for making sense of them; the character and meaning of the scenes depend on the postures and gestures of the figures. It is here that Thornton's skill as a designer is most apparent, as can be seen by comparing two pairs of very similar scenes in row 3. Panel 3a shows William's election as archbishop, by the York Chapter. The figures are arranged in a circle, like the canons in the Chapter House, with no individual figure elevated in status above the rest. They are differentiated by different tonsures and head coverings, with contrasting colours of clothes in the usual Thornton manner. A sense of calm deliberation is conveyed by their upright seated postures and the varied positions of their hands as the different speakers make their points. The result of their decision is seen in the next panel, where William is enthroned as archbishop and swears an oath of office on the Gospels. Panel 3c shows William's opponents conspiring to have his election nullified. The figures are again arranged in a circle, but here everything is confusion. In the centre, several figures are huddled together, standing or leaning forward in their agitation and their eagerness to affix their seals to a letter. In the background to the right two of the conspirators are whispering together. The only two calm figures are the two scribes in the foreground who are writing down the appeal and preparing the letter to send to the pope, which appears in the next panel. The next two panels are extremely similar in composition, but subtle differences convey their meaning. In 3d William and one of his opponents kneel to present their separate petitions to the pope, the standing figures in the background indicating by their gestures that this is a matter of great significance. In 3e the pope hands down to the two appellants a single document containing his decision, while a messenger behind the throne sets off for England with the judgement. In this row, as elsewhere, authority and judgement are key themes, emphasised by the prominence given to the archiepiscopal and papal thrones as seats of authority and the written word as conveying official communications and divine or papal imprimatur.

The scenes at the shrine are generally less crowded. Partly, this is because they depict the miraculous healing of a single individual, but the main reason is that the shrine itself is the principal actor in the scenes, being a surrogate for St William and the locus of divine healing power. To avoid repetition and maintain visual interest, Thornton designed no fewer than seventeen different views of the shrine. Only in the top row did he repeat some of the designs, and even then the details were painted differently. The shrine is placed in the centre of the panels or on the right-hand side, thereby maintaining the left-to-right movement of the narrative. It is presented from different angles, sometimes with the altar, which stood at one end, sometimes with a priest in attendance. The quatrefoils on the base of the shrine in panels 17b and 23e recall the quatrefoils on the base of Archbishop Melton's fourteenth-century tomb-shine in the nave (Fig. 3.7), but there the resemblance ends. The shrine in the window is depicted as a solid structure with a gabled roof, whereas the actual tomb-shrine had an openwork structure with shafts that revealed the lid of the sarcophagus and supported an upper storey with a platform where the reliquary was housed. Thornton's shrines are conventionalised, and if anything resemble more clearly the later high altar shrine with its solid base with niches where pilgrims could kneel (Fig. 3.20). As elsewhere, Thornton was not concerned with representational accuracy, but rather with the human drama of the miracles performed at the shrine.

The choice of miracles focused on people with visible illnesses and deformities – swollen limbs and bodies, paralysis and curvature of the spine, people on crutches, with skin diseases, and so on. There are a number of stories in the texts of deaf and dumb people being cured, but these are less easy to depict and are avoided, with the possible exception of panel 17c. Family, friends and bystanders provide assistance, point to the miraculous events or display their astonishment by their expressions and gestures. By such methods Thornton introduced variety and human interest into what could easily have become a monotonous sequence.

The exterior scenes provide visual variety and offered Thornton the opportunity to show off his skill in design. The exterior setting may be indicated by nothing more than the grass and foliage beneath travelling figures (panels 4e, 8a and 9a). A landscape with trees is evoked in the two riding accidents in 17d and 24d. Panels 7b and 7d depict William in a chapel in a wooded landscape. Here again Thornton has created two different designs, the details in the chapel in 7b being reminiscent of the buildings in the Great East Window. Other memorable scenes include the man attacked by a devil in panel 15a, the shipwreck in 16e, the girl rescued from drowning in the river in 17e and King Edward I falling from a mountain in Wales in 18c. Comparison of this panel with the same scene in the fifteenth-century alabaster (Fig. 7.9) highlights the brilliance and energy of Thornton's design, compared with the extremely wooden figure of the king in the alabaster.

Row 9 illustrates the way in which Thornton drives the narrative forward across the row, as William makes his final return to York before his death. In the first four scenes, as often throughout the window, the direction of movement is from left to right, drawing the eye across the row until it comes to rest on the final, more static scene where William is enthroned in the Minster. Panels 9b–9d depict three of the most important structures in the medieval city: Micklegate Bar, Ouse Bridge and the Minster itself. All are represented schematically, particularly the Minster (which also appears in 11d), which could never be identified from its appearance in the panel alone, independently of the sequence in the narrative. Ouse Bridge is shown as being constructed of stone, as indeed it was at the time the window was made (Fig. 3.4), although the Latin texts make a point of saying that the bridge that broke as William and his retinue passed across it was made of wood. Thornton is not interested in historical exactitude, but in presenting the story vividly. In this row his focus is on the welcome William received from dignitaries and clergy who greeted him on his return. In the first two panels the interactions between the figures on horseback are enhanced by the carefully observed (and different) interactions between the horses. Thus row 9 brilliantly encapsulates the narrative drive of Thornton's window, the energy and vitality with which he imbued the scenes and the human interest that he imparted to the story.

Creating the Window

It is apparent from the study of both windows attributable to John Thornton that the members of the workshop operated as a

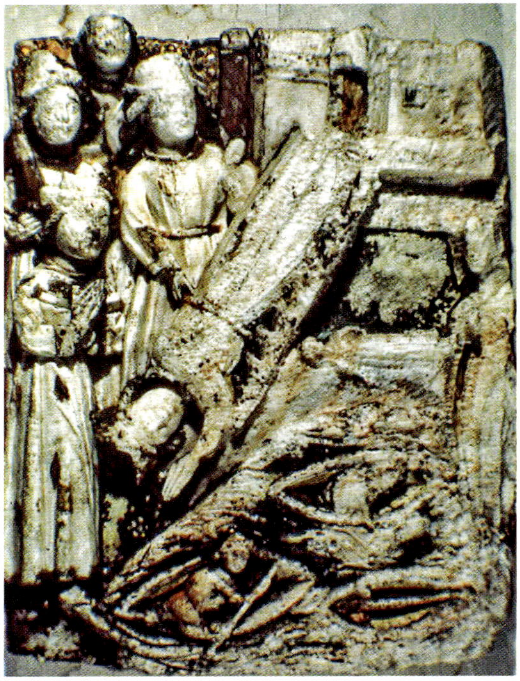

Fig. 7.9
A fifteenth-century alabaster panel found in Peaseholme Green in 1957, depicting King Edward I falling from a mountain in Wales.

close-knit team, under the oversight of a single controlling master. This relatively small number of artists and craftspeople needed to work together closely and in harmony in order to create these huge windows within a remarkably tight time frame – in the region of three years in the case of the Great East Window, and perhaps over an even shorter period for the smaller St William Window. The St William Window provides a number of clues as to how the work was organised.

As we have seen, the Dean and Chapter valued Thornton's skills as a designer extremely highly, and certainly in the making of the Great East Window, and probably in the St William Window too, expected him to devote himself to the crucial process of designing the individual narrative panels and preparing the full-size 'cartoons' from which they would be made. The setting out of the 1:1 scale designs was both artistically and technically the most demanding part of making a window, ensuring not only that the patron's intentions, recorded in the small-scale vidimus, were translated into the full-scale panels, but also ensuring that the panels would actually fit the window openings with the necessary precision. For much of the medieval period, this drafting process was executed on a whitened 'glaziers' table', as described in a twelfth-century text by the pseudonymous author Theophilus and illustrated in the two sections of a table preserved in Girona in Catalonia (Fig. 4.10). While cumbersome to a degree, these whitened boards, supported on trestles (called 'portraying tables' in some of the medieval accounts), served as both cartoon and glazing bench, guiding the cutting, painting and leading-up of the glass. The Girona tables bear the physical evidence of all three processes taking place at the table (Fig. 7.10). Theophilus also describes how they could be washed to allow new designs to be laid out in successive phases of work, and on the Girona tables it can be seen how new subjects were marked out on the table, while repeated elements of the design, notably the architectural frames, were retained for use over several panels.

This process would have required careful organisation to achieve the matching up of frame and figure in the correct sequences. In the Great East Window, where each row had its own distinctive canopy design, the YGT noticed evidence that this process did not always run smoothly, as a number of scenes were found to have been framed by the wrong architectural canopy, an error best explained by the incorrect 'slotting' in of new scenes under the retained canopy frames, as the glaziers' tables were adapted and reused. The rationalisation of the architectural framing of the St William Window, with most of the scenes placed within three rectangular frames of a simpler design (Fig. 5.15), not only gave the window a strong visual coherence, but also probably sped up the design process and minimised the risk of error, allowing a larger number of narratives to be inserted within the framing templates marked out on the whitened glaziers' tables.

However, even in the St William Window, this did not always proceed without a hitch.

Close analysis of the Girona tables and the numerous panels made on them that survive in the cathedral has shown that within a single workshop, the director of the team allowed its members a considerable degree of autonomy, e.g. in the cutting and leading patterns within a panel. This was also the case with the St William Window. Comparison of the better-preserved examples of frame Types B and F demonstrate that the cut-lines are not always in the same positions. This can be seen, for instance, with the cut-lines in the top corners of the frames. Similarly, the boss in the centre of the canopy in Type F is usually positioned on a separate piece of glass, but in some cases, parts of the adjacent mouldings are included on the same pieces (e.g. panels 9c, 9d and 15e). Similar variation was also observed in relation to the Great East Window. In reality, even panels with repeated/reused elements in common are always bespoke objects, a version but never a replica. This means that every panel is vulnerable to disruption at the point that its pieces are removed for firing in the kiln. The need to match up the individual glass pieces belonging to so many complex and novel narratives as they came out of the kiln and returned to the glaziers' benches for re-assembly and leading-up required meticulous attention to detail if chaos was not to ensue.

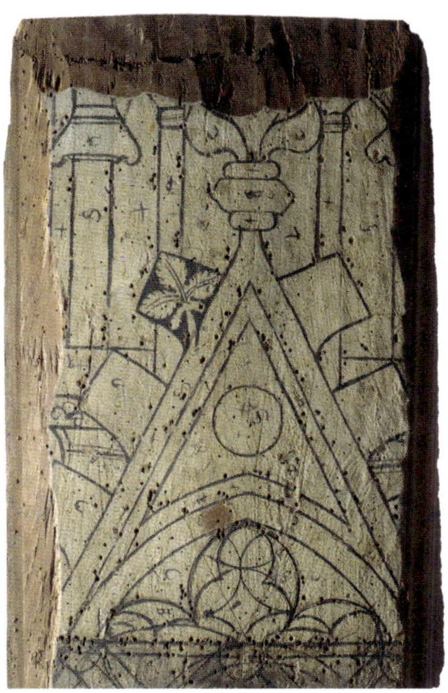

Fig. 7.10
The Girona glaziers' table c.1340 (canopy detail). Letters and symbols, presumed to be instructions relating to glass colour, can be clearly seen.

Janice Smith's analysis of the very numerous glaziers' marks found in the paint across the St William Window has suggested that these marks were not particular to an individual painter, nor were they a means of locating a panel within the overall window scheme, unlike the sequential assembly numbers cut by the masons into adjoining stone and commonly used in the assembly of timber structures (Fig. 7.11). Rather, they were used as the means of identifying glass pieces that belonged to the same panel, ensuring that pieces taken away from their unique template during the firing process were safely reunited with it in time for the glazier to lead-up the panel ready for installation. The large number of marks, far more numerous than on the glass of the Great East Window, suggests that panels were being painted, fired and glazed at a considerable pace. This is further evidence, therefore, of an exceptionally well-organised and professional team at the top of its game, for which Thornton as presiding master must take considerable credit.

It was J. A. Knowles who first suggested that, in contrast to the cartooning practice of the Great East Window, more than one master may have been involved in the drafting of the cartoons on the tables. This was certainly the practice observable in the fourteenth-century accounts for St Stephen's Chapel, Westminster. And after the completion of the Great East Window, Thornton would have had every confidence in his tried and trusted assistants. Knowles forwarded this hypothesis based on what he perceived to be some discernible differences in cartooning style, such as in the density of figure grouping and the use of miniaturised architectural structures. The bottom row, containing the donors, certainly seems to have been drawn up by a single draughtsman. The panels are larger and have more complex frames than any other row, although this is hardly surprising given their proximity to the viewer and their importance to the patrons of the project. They also lack any glaziers' sorting marks, which may be indicative of a slower and more careful manufacturing process, perhaps hardly surprising as these would have been the first panels to be made, and the ones subjected to the greatest scrutiny by clients and patron. However, this interpretation can be countered by the fact that some of these distinctions reflect the requirements of the narrative. Furthermore, the number of cartoons assigned to the three draughtsmen proposed by Knowles are not equal in number and are found scattered throughout the window, making any interpretation of their significance for our understanding of workshop practice difficult. They are certainly not proof that Thornton was delegating the cartooning process to any appreciable degree. Evidence for the dominant role of a single designer in the preparation of the 'cartoons' can be found in the extreme precision with which colour changes and costume details were organised. Theophilus explains that it was the master who should mark up critical colour choices on the glaziers' tables for the benefit of those cutting and painting the glass, and the Girona tables are annotated with letters and symbols (Fig. 7.10).

Now that the correct narrative order of the panels has been restored, it is possible to confirm that the window was created from the bottom to the top, as French had suggested – in other words progressing in the order of the narrative. This was also the case with the Great East Window, although here it was read from the top to the bottom. Several pieces of evidence point to this conclusion. The Type C frames, which were used only in the right-hand half of the bottom section (Fig. 6.19) incorporate thin strips of coloured glass flanked by tinted white glass pieces. The colours contrast with the backgrounds to the scenes: red strips for panels with blue backgrounds, blue strips for panels with red backgrounds. These frames would have been fiddly to make. In the other sections of the window they are replaced by Type F frames. The designs of the frames are similar, but they omit the coloured strips, which are replaced by painted cross-hatched lines. Composed entirely of tinted white glass, the Type F frames would have been much easier to make, and evidently replaced Type C frames in order to save time and money.

Further up the window, there are signs of haste and lack of quality control. At the top of the second section, panels 12d and 12e were originally made with Type F frames, closed at the top with a canopy. As discussed in the Catalogue, the panels were then altered to give them open tops supporting Type H canopies in row 13. The same thing has happened with panels 18c–18e at the top of the third section, though here the cusped panels 19c–19e have canopy Type J. At the start of the row, panels 19a and 19b reused the Type D canopies from row 6, though the cusping is of a slightly different shape and does not fit the design so well. Similarly, the cusped panels in row 25 at the top of the main lights reuse Type G and H from row 13, though they do not fit the cusping in row 25 so well. The reuse of canopies from lower down in the window clearly points to a bottom-up manufacturing process.

Within the top section (Fig. 7.12) the normal pattern of the frames breaks down in rows 22 and 23. Panels 22c–22e, which depict the miracle of the man hit on the head while hanging tapestries, have a variant of Type F frames (Type F*). These have the usual canopies over the top, but they are supported on each side by a single circular column instead of the usual side-shafts. Another

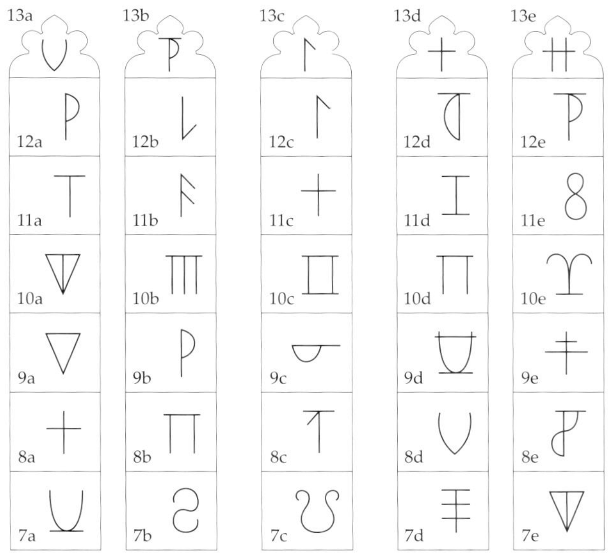

Fig. 7.11
Glaziers' marks, recorded during conservation, in section 2 of the window.

anomaly is that the lower sections of these columns are painted on the same pieces of glass as the adjacent portions of the chequered pavement. This is the only time in the entire window where parts of the frame are combined with parts of the scenes they contain. In every other case, the frames are entirely separate. Why the difference? One possibility is that the three Type F canopies that had been removed from panels 18c–18e were reused here, but were given different shafts. This has intriguing implications. It suggests that the workshop had run out of Type F frames and it was decided in this case to make the requisite shafts as part of the scenes. The fact that in every other case the frames and the scenes are painted on separate pieces of glass suggests that Thornton had divided his workforce into different teams, one working on the frames and one working on the scenes. This would be a sensible division of labour. Glass-painters who were adept at painting frames would not necessarily have been skilled at painting figures or backgrounds, and vice versa. The repetitive work of creating the frames would have advanced more quickly than the larger, more complex figurative scenes. So, by the time they reached the top of the window, the frame painters would probably have been well ahead of the scene painters. Having frames painted and fired but not yet leaded-up would make it all the more important for the different examples of the frames to have distinguishing glaziers' marks on them.

As noted in the previous chapter, there are thirty-eight Type B frames and thirty-seven of Types C and F/F*/F† combined. This suggests that the numbers of frames of each type had been decided in advance. This would explain why row 23, uniquely, contains five frames of Type B. They had no more Type F frames left, but enough of Type B to fill the row.

These anomalies therefore provide fascinating insights into the working practices of Thornton's studio. They also indicate a loss of quality control in the upper parts of the window. This is equally apparent with the coloured backgrounds. Panel 16b is blue instead of red. The chequer pattern of colours breaks down at the top of the window, since rows 23 and 24 are both blue rows. These are simple mistakes. More intriguing still are some unique features of the scenes in rows 23 and 24. Panels 23e and 24c are new designs, as are the pair of scenes depicting the riding accident of the lady presumed to be Beatrice de Roos (24d–24e). The other six scenes are composed entirely of shrines and figures copied from panels lower down the window and recombined in different ways, as described in the Catalogue. All of them are taken from rows 15–17, except for the shrine in panel 24a, which is copied from the one in 21b. The shrines in these two panels, which are reasonably well preserved, are identical in design, but they show some differences in their cut-lines, indicating that the glaziers had some discretion as to the cutting of glass and thus the positioning of leads (Fig. 7.13). There are also some differences of detail, notably on the roofs of the two shrines and the decorative circles on the base of the altar, showing that the painters were allowed some freedom to paint decorative details, as seems to have been the case with

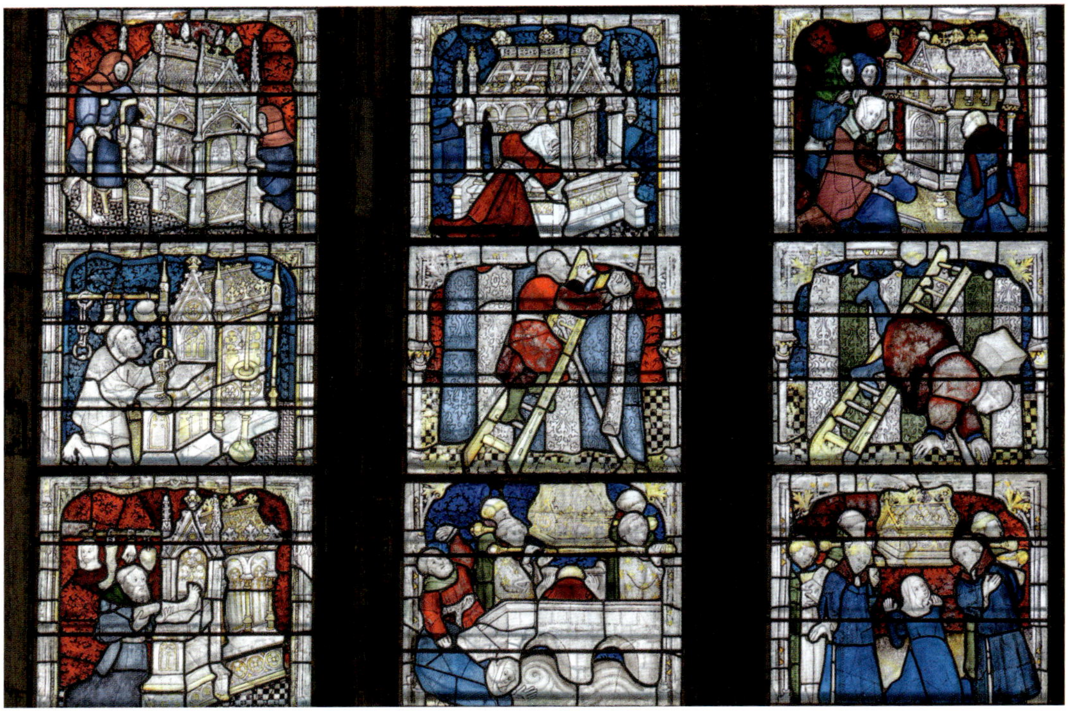

Fig. 7.12
The St William Window, rows 21, 22, 23, lights b–d.

the panels made on the Girona tables. The shrines in 16c and 23e are practically identical, but close inspection reveals differences of detailing on the roofs. The shrines in panels 15b and 23b are identical in conception, but have differences in cut-lining and decorative detailing, including the absence in 23b of the spouts from which the holy oil is issuing in 15b.

Most intriguing of all are the figures in panels 23a–23b, 23d–23e and 24a–24b. They are less well preserved than the shrines because much of the coloured glass of the clothing has been replaced, but their outlines and most of their faces and hands survive. Although some minor details have been changed, there is no doubt that they were copied from earlier scenes. Thus, the woman at the shrine in 16c appears again in 23e (with the addition of spots on her skin), and reappears, reversed, in 24b. The woman who swallowed a frog is shown in 17a holding her belt, which she has taken off to relieve her discomfort. She reappears in 24a with the same gesture (and a slightly more swollen stomach), but without the belt, rendering the gesture of her left hand meaningless. The disabled man crouching in front of the shrine in 15b holds up his hand to collect the holy oil issuing from the tomb. He reappears in 24b with the identical gesture, but this is now redundant, as there is no holy oil for him to collect. In 16c one of the men points at the boy on the floor. The same man reappears in 23e with the identical pointing gesture, which is now pointless, as the boy is missing. The fact that the figures with pointless gestures are all in rows 23 and 24 proves (should there be any doubt) that it is these panels that were copied from scenes lower down the window, not *vice versa*. Although this kind of copying could often be attributed to the re-use of cartoons, it seems unlikely that many of the cartoons from rows 15–17 would have been kept for long. So many full-size cartoon tables would have caused serious problems of storage. It seems more likely that the figures and shrines in rows 23 and 24 were copied from the finished panels, presumably still awaiting installation in the building.

These six panels are evidence of more than just haste. They evince a different mind at work. Throughout the window up to this point, Thornton had gone to great lengths to avoid repetition, even in scenes with very similar compositions. He had also consistently used gestures in a thoughtful manner to highlight the action and convey interactions between different characters in the scenes. These characteristics are still evident in the four new scenes in rows 23 and 24. Even if faced with a deadline to get the job finished, it is hard to believe that Thornton would have come up with scenes that mechanically copy elements from earlier panels and show a complete misunderstanding of the significance of gestures. If we are to look for panels in the St William Window that were not cartooned by Thornton himself, it is surely these.

By their very inadequacy, these six panels demonstrate Thornton's quality as a designer and explain why the Dean and Chapter were so insistent that he alone should cartoon the panels in the Great East Window. There seems little doubt that Thornton was under pressure to complete the St William Window as soon as possible. The anomalies in the frames and the coloured backgrounds and the scenes copied from earlier panels in the window all point in the same direction. All the same, it may seem surprising that Thornton allowed the six second-rate scenes in rows 23 and 24, even if they were to be placed at the top of the window where their inadequacies would escape notice. No amount of analysis can account for the vagaries of life. Perhaps Thornton was detained in Coventry, where he is known to have maintained a workshop, or perhaps he fell ill and was forced to delegate the cartooning. Whatever the reason, he did make sure that the last two panels in the story (24d–24e), showing (as we suppose) Beatrice de Roos's riding accident, were of the highest quality. By this time, Beatrice was well on in years, probably over seventy, and Thornton perhaps made these two scenes earlier on so that she could examine all the panels depicting her and her family in the workshop. The death of her son, William Lord Roos in 1414, which resulted in the changes in heraldry in the bottom row discussed in Chapter 4, must have increased the urgency to get the window finished. Hopefully Beatrice saw it installed in all its glowing splendour before she died in April 1415.

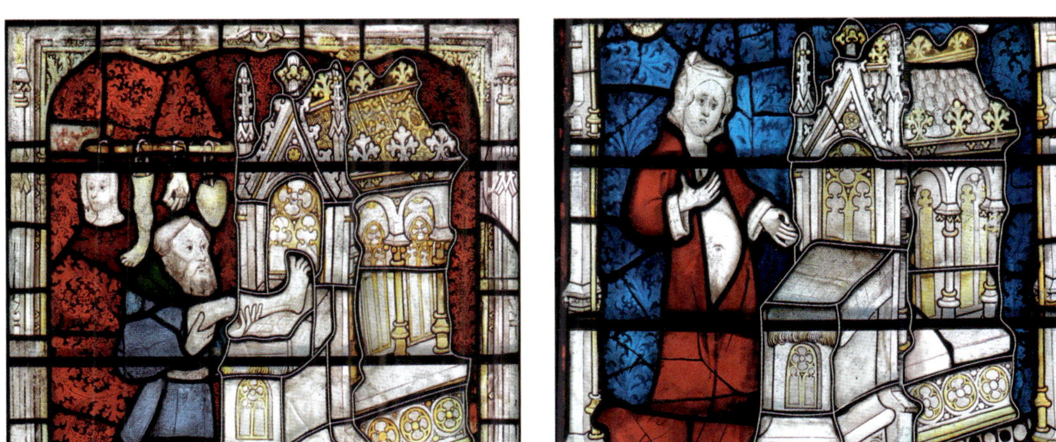

Fig. 7.13
The cut-lines of panels 21b and 24a, displaying only minor discrepancies in the cutting and leading of the two shrines.

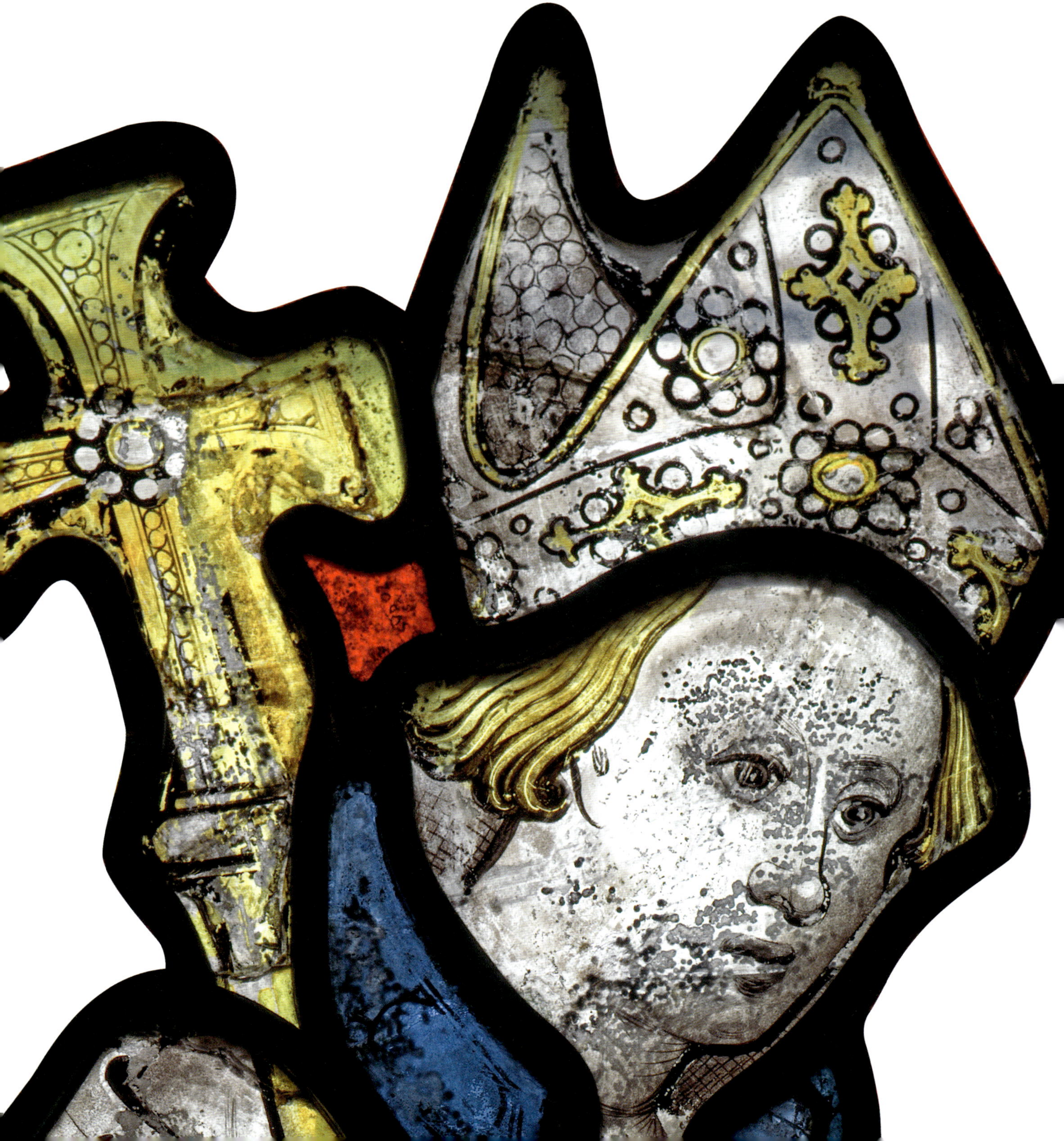

Catalogue

The catalogue describes and illustrates every panel in the window. It is divided into five sections, corresponding to the four sections of the main lights and the tracery lights. Each section has a brief introduction. Appendix Three gives a concordance of the present panel numbers with their pre-restoration positions, which correspond to the panel numbers published by French in 1999. During the recent restoration all of the panels were photographed and documented in the workshop of the York Glaziers Trust before and after restoration and all records have been deposited in the York Minster Archive. At the start of the project photographs were taken with traditional colour film. About halfway through, a digital camera was introduced. Consequently, the workshop photographs were of variable quality. Subsequently, the whole window has been photographed *in situ* using a high-resolution digital Hasselblad camera. These are the photographs reproduced in this book. Having been taken *in situ*, in a few cases, the edges of the panels are obscured by stonework or glazing bars, and in some cases there are shadows from the external environmental protective glazing. The digital photographs can also be accessed online at: https://stainedglass-navigator.yorkglazierstrust.org/window/st-william-window.

The main light panels are all about 830mm wide. The donor panels in row 1 measure approximately 860mm in height. The remaining panels measure between 750mm and 790mm in height.

For the diagram showing the panel numbers, the coloured backgrounds and the frame types, see Fig. 6.19.

Rows 1–6

The bottom section of the window starts in row 1 with five donor panels depicting members of the baronial family of Roos of Hamlake (Helmsley), arranged from left to right in ascending order of seniority. Each panel shows the figures in a fictive chapel (denoted by the elaborate architectural frame of Type A) decorated with hangings in the background. Laymen in heavy gowns trimmed with fur and armed with short daggers stand in niches in the side shafts of the canopies, and gesture towards the hangings with one arm and the kneeling figures with the other. All the members of the family kneel in attitudes of prayer and look towards the east – the location of the principal altars. The eye is naturally led to the right-hand panel (1e), which Lady Beatrice de Roos, the principal donor of the window, occupies on her own. Originally, an inscription probably ran across the base of the panels, but nothing survives. The bottom row of panels, the most accessible from the ground, has been one of the most heavily damaged.

The narrative starts in row 2 with the marriage of William's parents (panel 2a). The rest of row 2 covers the first five decades of his life, from his baptism and education at Winchester (2b and 2c) to his time as treasurer of York Minster (panel 2d, a replacement for a lost original) up to the death of Archbishop Thurstan in 1140 (2e). Rows 3–5 depicts the events of William's first archiepiscopate between 1141 and 1147. Row 3 starts with William's election as archbishop in January 1141 (panels 3a–3b). His opponents then appeal against his election to the pope (3c–3e). Row 4 depicts William's vindication, his consecration as archbishop at Winchester in September 1143 (panel 4c), and the pope sending him the pallium from Rome (4d–4e). Row 5 focuses on the papacy in Rome: the death of the pope (5a) is followed by a renewed appeal to his successor (5b–5c), who formally deposes William (5d). The bottom section concludes with William's successor, Henry Murdac, enthroned as archbishop of York (5e).

Rows 2–4 have much simpler frames than row 1, of two different designs: Type B on the left and Type C on the right. In row 5, which is underneath the transom, the coloured backgrounds run up to the top of each panel and continue into the cusped panels of row 6 immediately above them, and the scenes are framed at the top by the elaborate architectural canopies within the cusping. The panels within rows 5 and 6 are thus designed as single units, and there are two different frame designs, Type D in lights a–c and Type E in lights d–e.

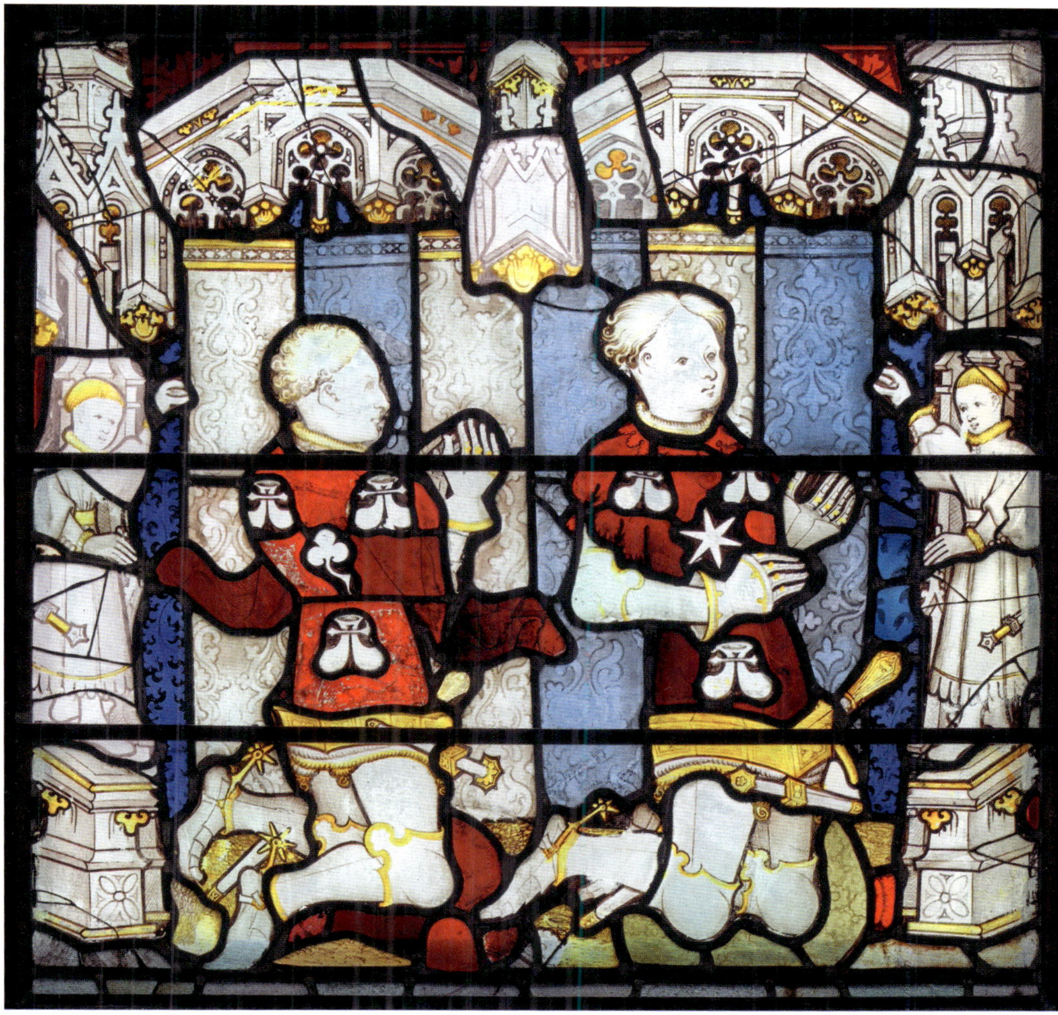

1a The first donor panel: Robert and Richard de Roos

Two beardless young men in plate armour kneel in attitudes of prayer. Both are bareheaded. Their surcoats bear the family arms, *gules three water bougets argent*, differenced by the addition respectively of a mullet (or star) and a trefoil, for Robert and Richard, fourth and fifth sons of William, 6th Lord Roos. Both boys are depicted as grown men, despite being boys at the time of the window's creation.

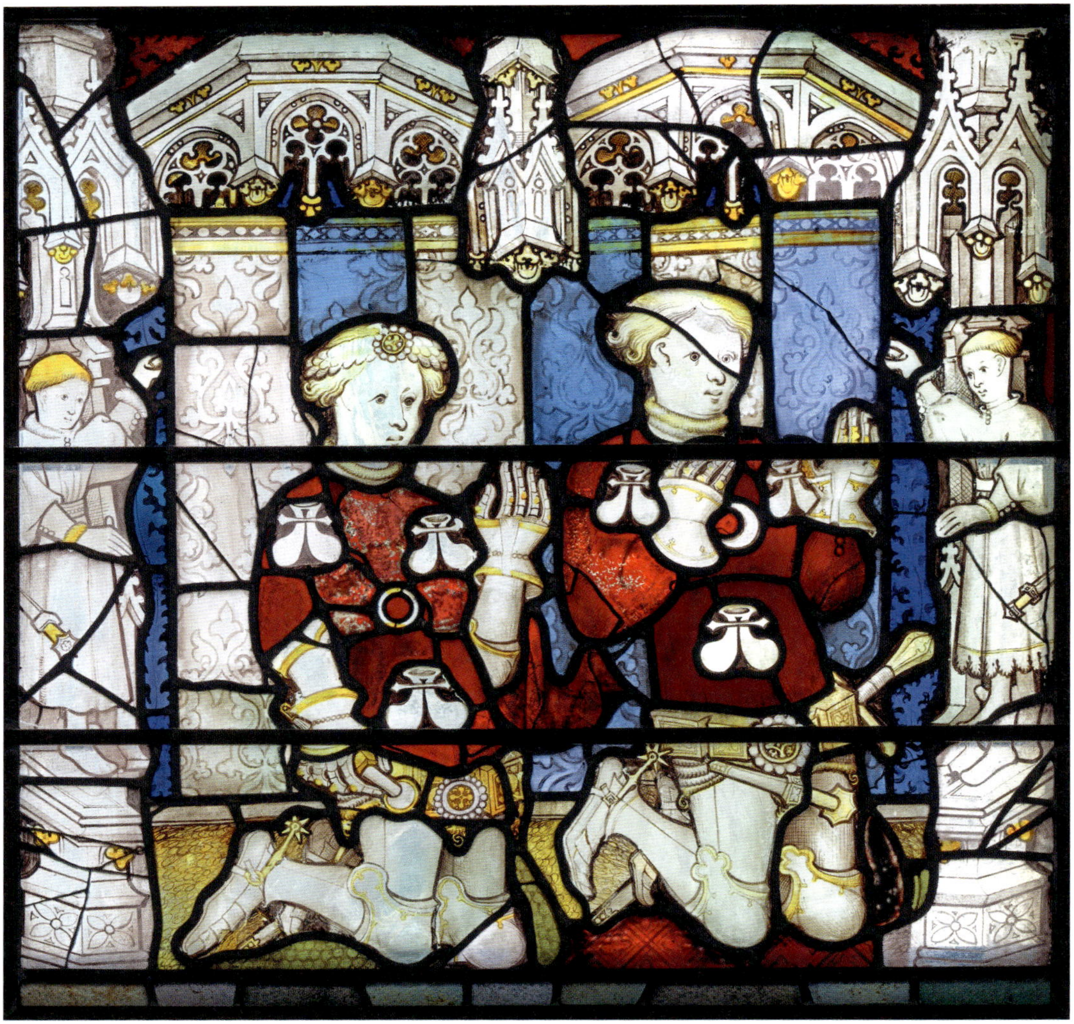

1b The second donor panel: William and Thomas de Roos
The design is very similar to panel 1a. The arms on the surcoats are differenced by a crescent and an annulet, for William and Thomas, second and third sons of William, 6th Lord Roos. Thomas wears a circlet on his head, while William is bareheaded.

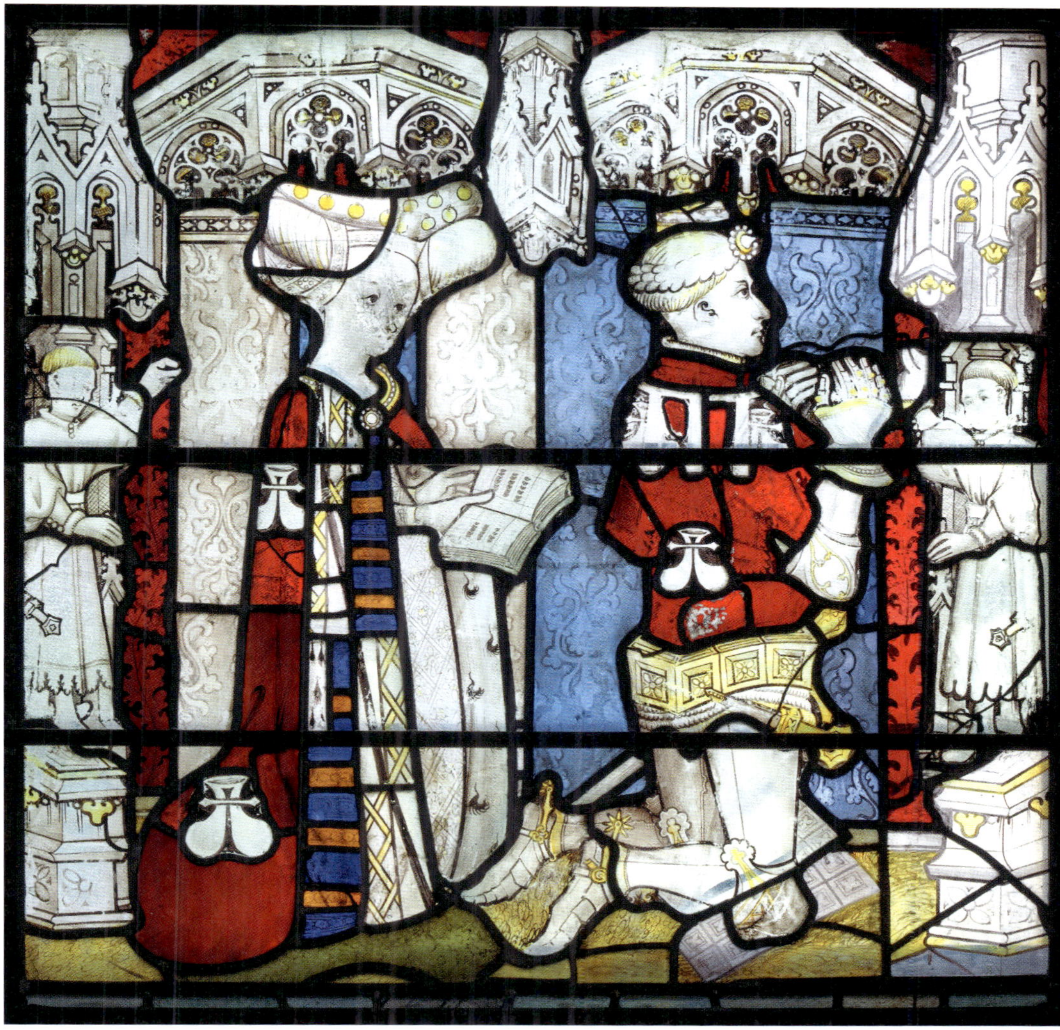

1c The third donor panel: John de Roos and Margery, his wife

The surcoat with a label of three points denotes John, the eldest son and heir of William, 6th Lord Roos. The lady is his wife, Margery, *née* Despenser, identifiable by her cloak, which bears the arms of Roos impaling the arms of Despenser of Goushill, whom he had married in 1404. John is clean-shaven and dressed in plate armour, with a circlet on his head. Margery wears a fashionable horned headdress covered by a veil to which coins are sewn, meaning that none of her hair is visible. She holds an open book.

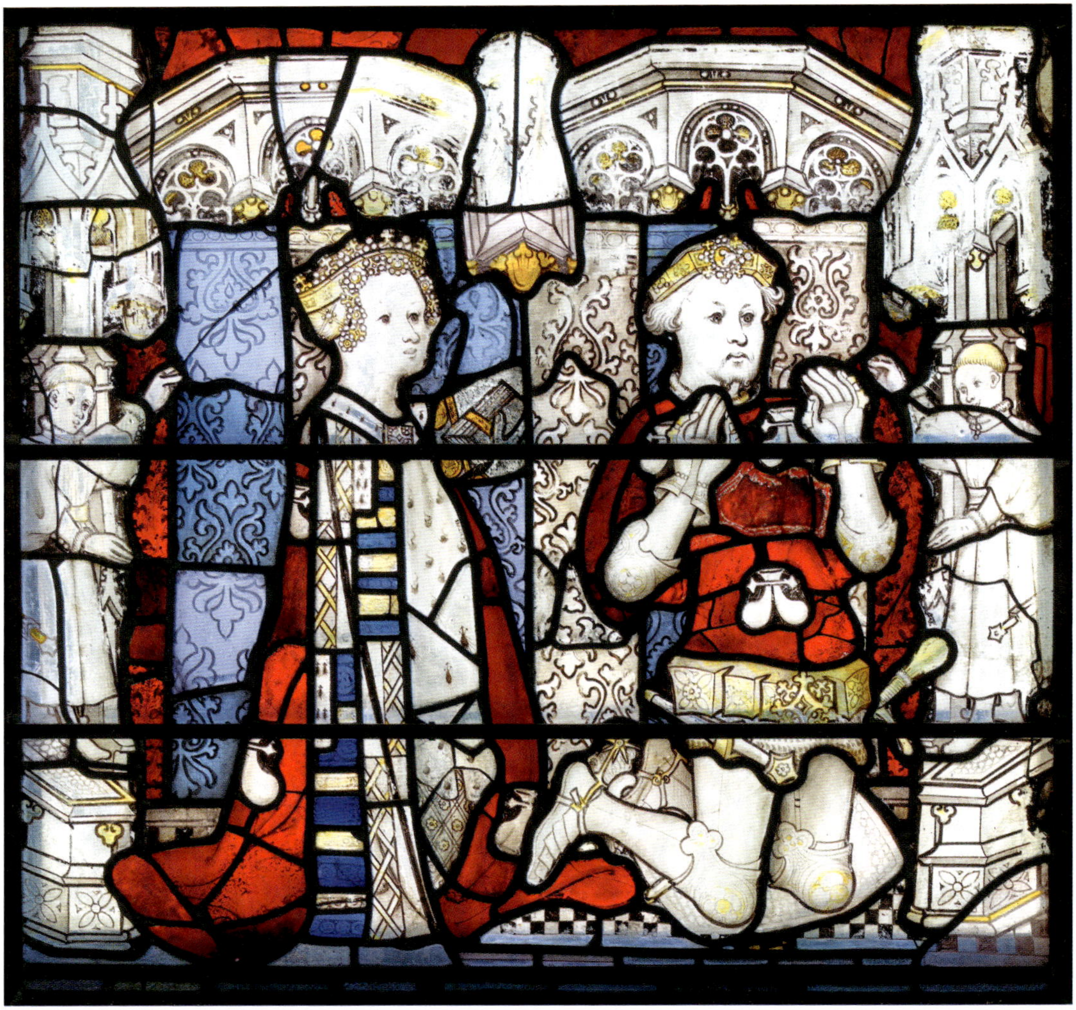

1d The fourth donor panel: Lord Roos and his wife

The surcoat with the arms of Roos with no mark of difference denotes the head of the family. This should be William, 6th Lord Roos (d.1414) whose five sons are depicted in 1a–1c. Lord Roos, bearded and wearing plate armour, wears a more substantial circlet than those worn by other male members of his family, and his wife wears a similarly richly jewelled coronet. She holds a book, although it is not original to the panel. Both kneel on cushions. Strangely, however, the lady is dressed not as William's wife, Margaret, *née* Arundel, but as his daughter-in-law, Margery, as she bears the same arms as the lady in panel 1c. The explanation may be that William, 6th Lord Roos, died in the early stages of the window's creation, and that arrangements were quickly made to show his son, John, now 7th Lord Roos, as the new head of the family, meaning that John and his wife are shown a second time. An alternative explanation is that the glaziers made a mistake in the cartooning of the heraldic dress of Margaret Arundel, mistakenly decorating her gown with the arms of her daughter-in-law.

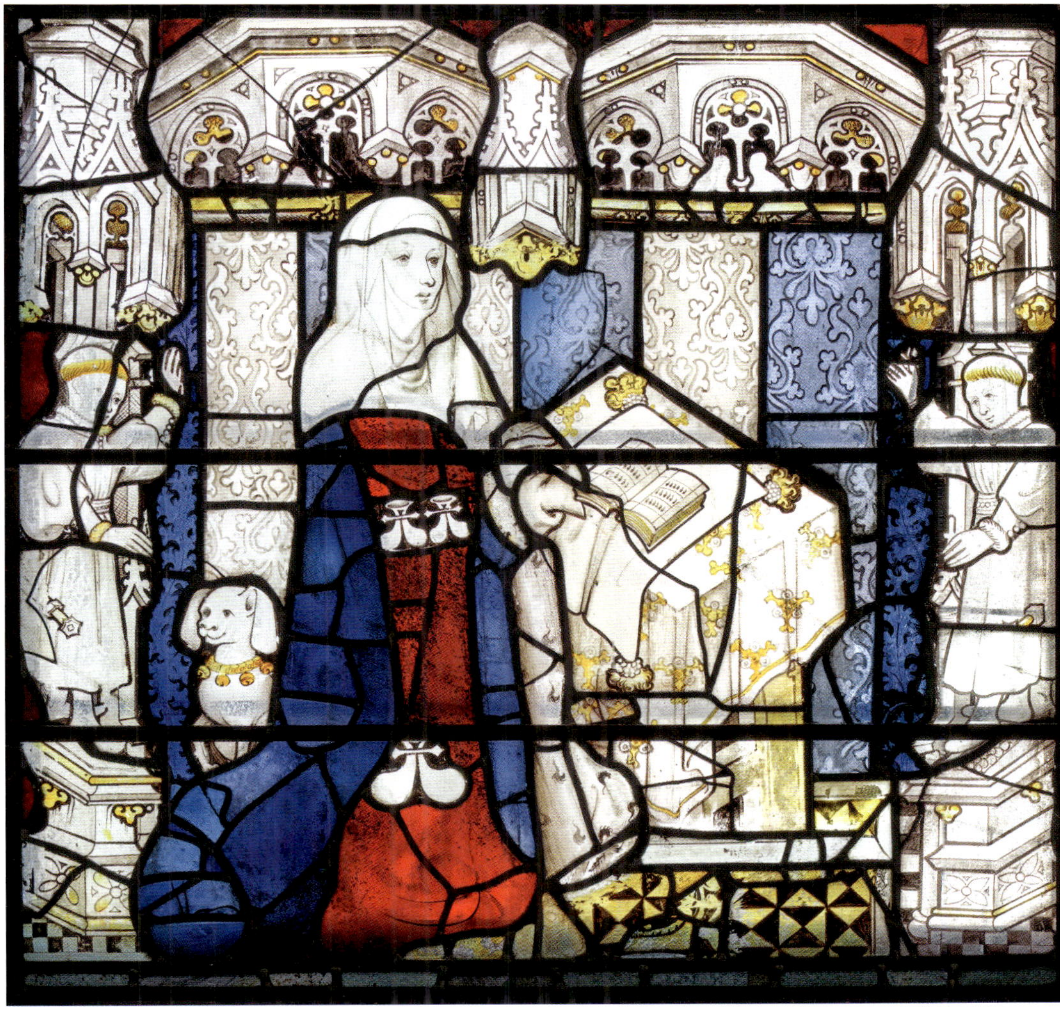

1e The fifth donor panel: Beatrice, Dowager Lady Roos

The lady kneeling before a richly draped wooden prayer desk, on which lies an open book, is Beatrice, *née* Stafford, widow of Thomas, 4th Lord Roos (d.1384). Her cloak formerly bore the arms of Stafford impaling Roos. In contrast to the other panels in row 1, Beatrice is alone, accompanied only by a small dog wearing a collar decorated with golden bells, who looks back at the other members of the family. Unlike the other women in the row, she is rather soberly dressed, with a veil and chin cloth, as befitted her widowed state. Her position, at the head of her family, placed closest to the altar, means that she was almost certainly the initiator of the commission, and she may be the lady who appears in the last miracle story at the top of the window in panels 24d and 24e. She died in 1415. It is the most restored of all the donor panels.

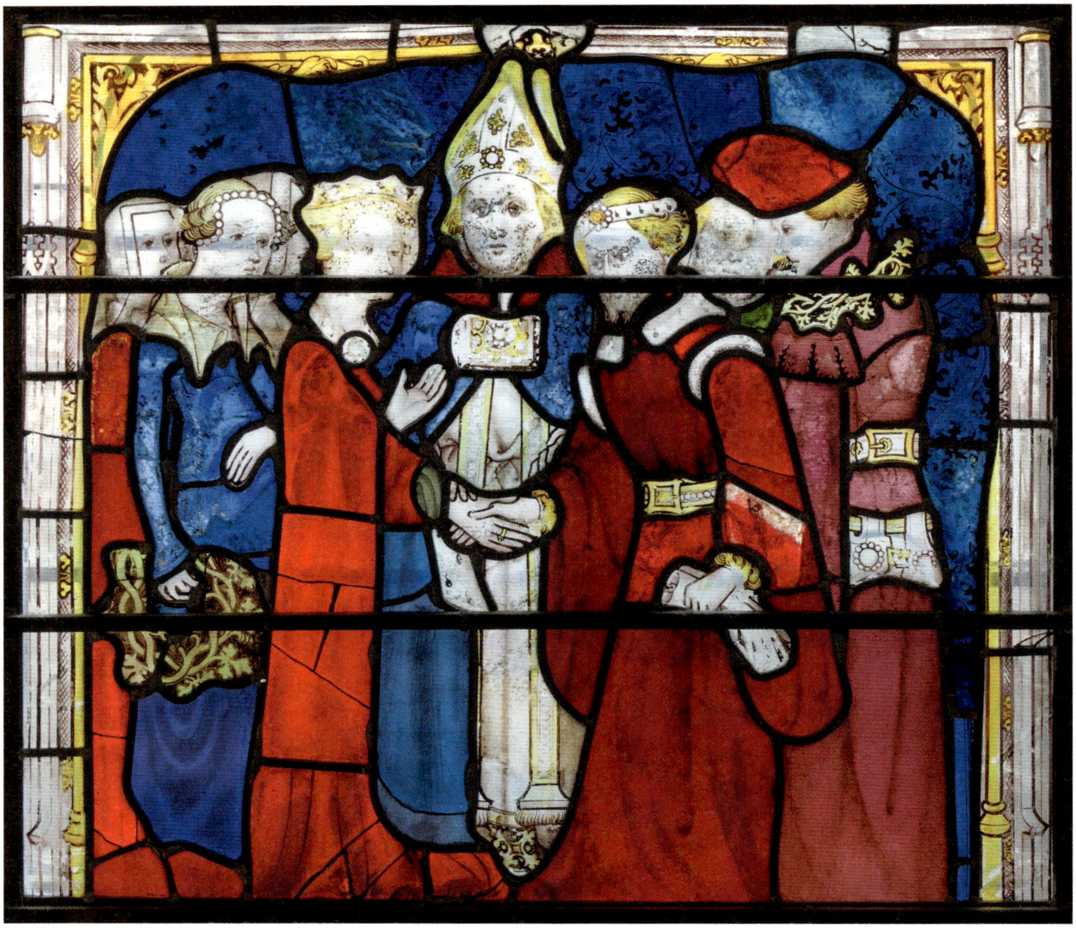

2a The marriage of William's parents

The narrative section of the window starts with the marriage of William's parents, Herbert and Emma, a relative of King Stephen. Both are richly dressed in the fashion of the fifteenth century. Emma wears a coronet and Herbert's heavy garment is fur-trimmed. They stand in front of a bishop, who has brought their hands together as they make their vows. A ring is clearly shown on Emma's middle finger. One of the stylishly dressed bridesmaids holds a leafy garland, and one of the men behind Herbert wears a similar garland round his neck. This standard depiction of a medieval marriage is not explicitly described in the *Life of St William* but is essential to introducing the narrative.

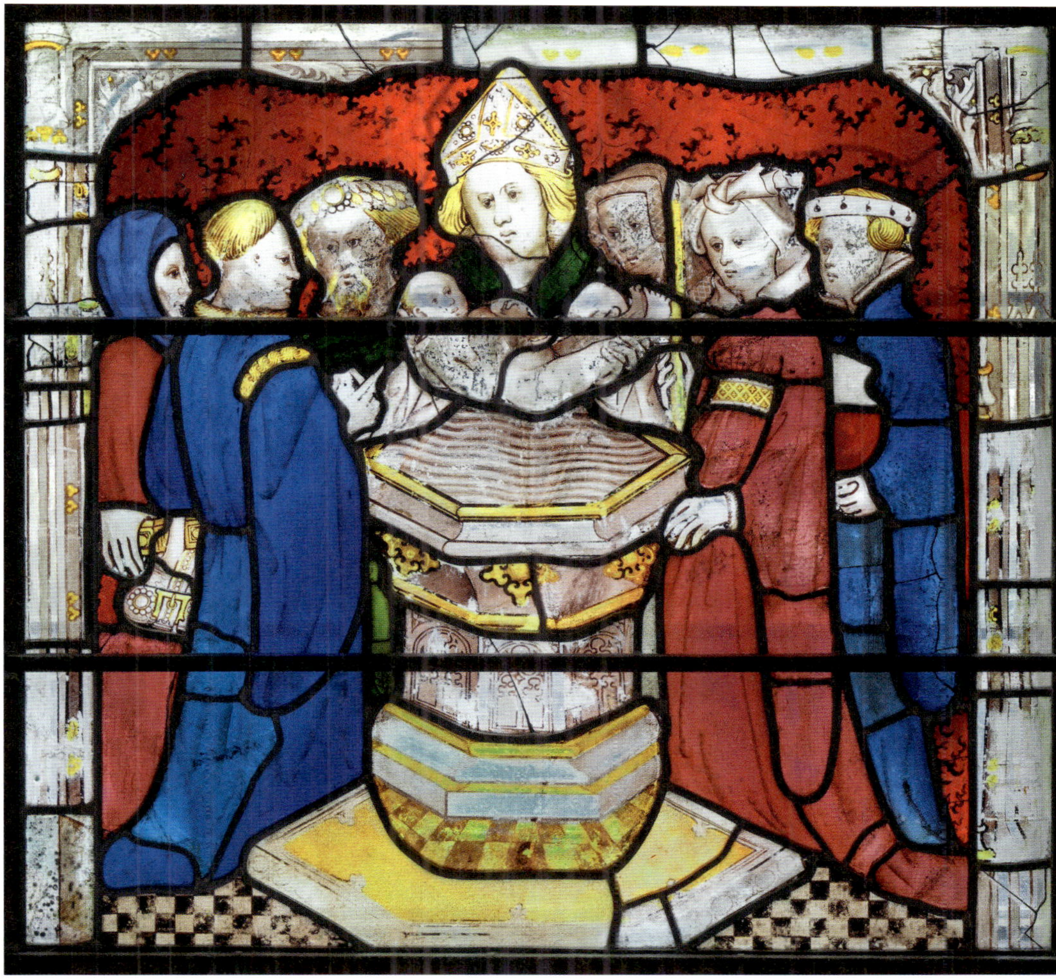

2b William's baptism

As with the previous scene, William's baptism is not specifically mentioned in the written sources but is an appropriate way to introduce the future archbishop and saint. A bishop holds the infant William over a brimming font. Herbert and Emma (who holds a candle) are accompanied by (presumably) William's godparents. William was born in the 1080s, but the characters in the scene are all modishly dressed in a variety of fashions of the fifteenth century. While much of the upper half of the panel is well preserved (except for the central section of the bishop's face), the lower part has suffered extensive damage.

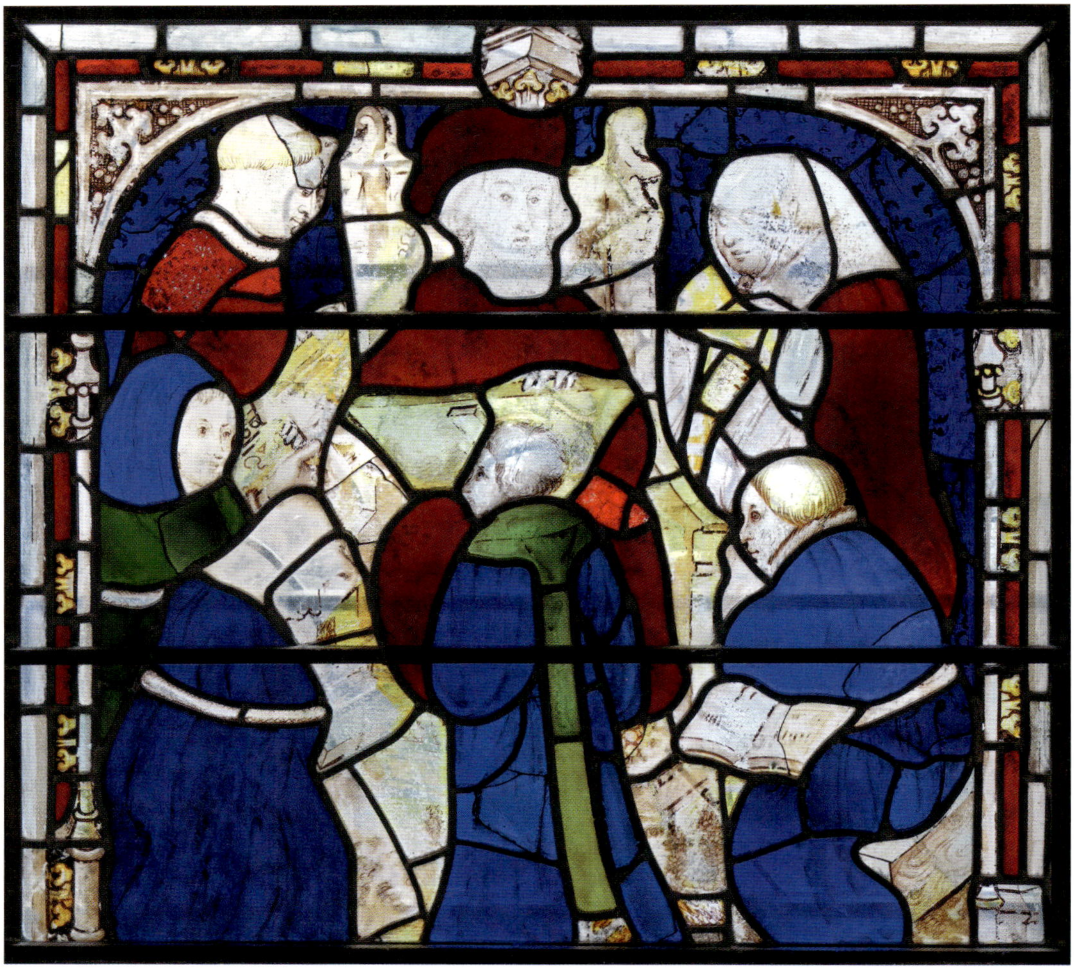

2c William's education

William stands with his back to the viewer, in front of a master who is seated on an imposing chair and places his hand on a lectern. Other members of the class, some with their heads studiously bowed over their books, stand or perch on stools to either side. If the head is original, the female figure standing at the back on the right is probably William's mother, who has brought him to the teacher. William grew up in Winchester. This panel was reinstated in the window in 1954, having previously been in window n3. It has been considerably restored, and suffers from paint loss, but the original frame design proves that it belongs to the St William Window.

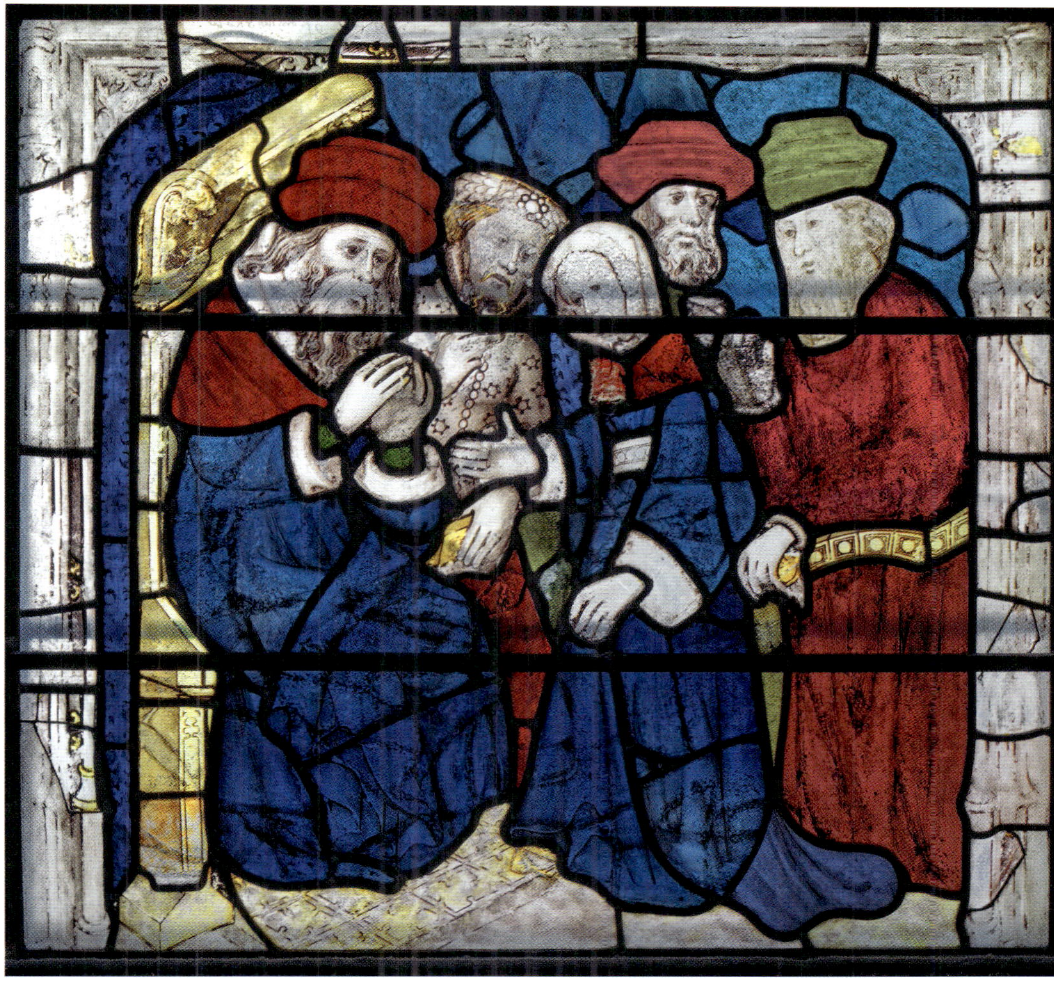

2d (Replacement panel for William as treasurer of York Minster)

William's long career as treasurer (*c.*1108–41) is covered in the *Life* in just a few conventional sentences extolling his character and conduct, husbanding the Minster's resources and using his private wealth for the relief of the poor. The original glass is lost but Torre *c.*1690 recorded five figures in the panel, one dressed in red, the others in white, probably representing William and four needy people receiving alms. The present panel incorporates some fragmentary figures of similar style and date which were brought from the south transept (window s23) in 1954, but do not belong to the St William Window. At an earlier date they had been intruded into the St Cuthbert Window, although they are not part of the Cuthbert narrative either. They have been much restored and set within a modern background and frame so as to harmonise with the rest of the window. The original panel would have had frame Type C, and a red background.

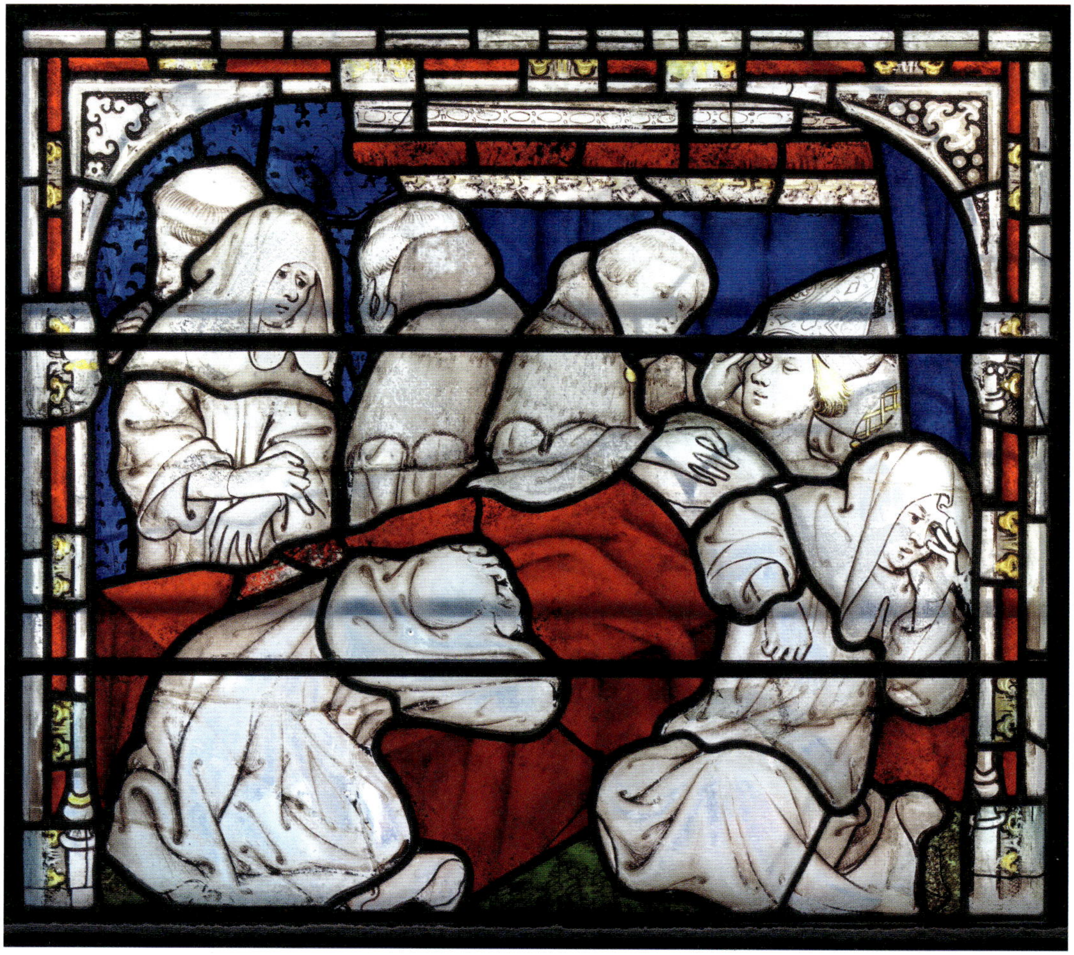

2e The death of Archbishop Thurstan

Archbishop Thurstan (1114–40) lies on his deathbed, conforming even in death to the artistic convention that archbishops wear mitres. Around him are canons of the Minster in varied and expressive postures of grief. One prostrates himself on the bed. Two have turned away. Two canons behind the bed wear white robes with ermine tippets; others have sleeved robes with hoods of white fabric. The canon closing Thurstan's eyes, who wears a silver-stained brooch at his neck, may be intended to be William.

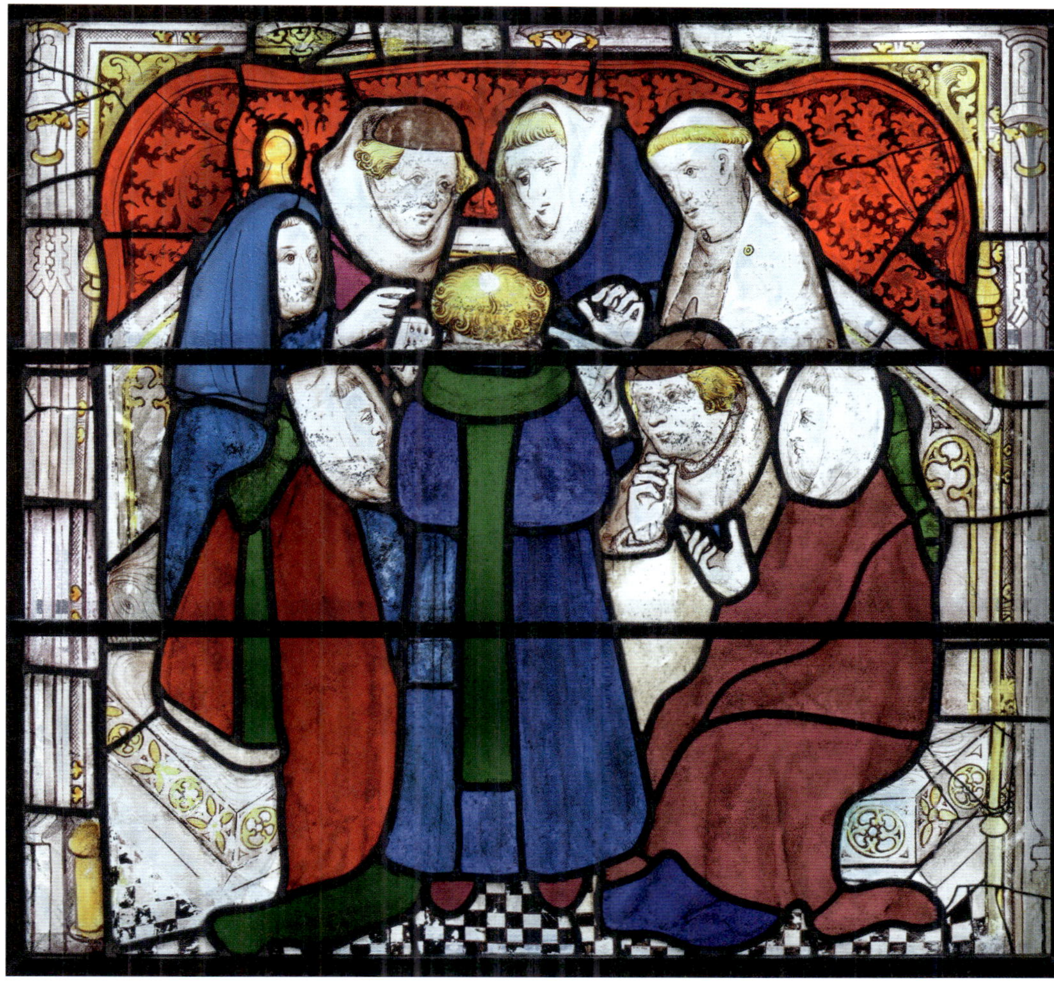

3a The canons elect William as the next archbishop

Seated in a polygonal space, which recalls the Gothic Chapter House, the canons meet to elect William as the next archbishop. In typical Thornton style, the scene is animated by the gestures of the figures, and by the contrasting colours of their robes and the variety of their headgear. With characteristic attention to detail, the figure in white with a monastic tonsure (a thin circle of hair with shaved crown and neck) represents one of the monastic members of the Chapter. A junior cleric standing in the middle apparently reads from a book or letter.

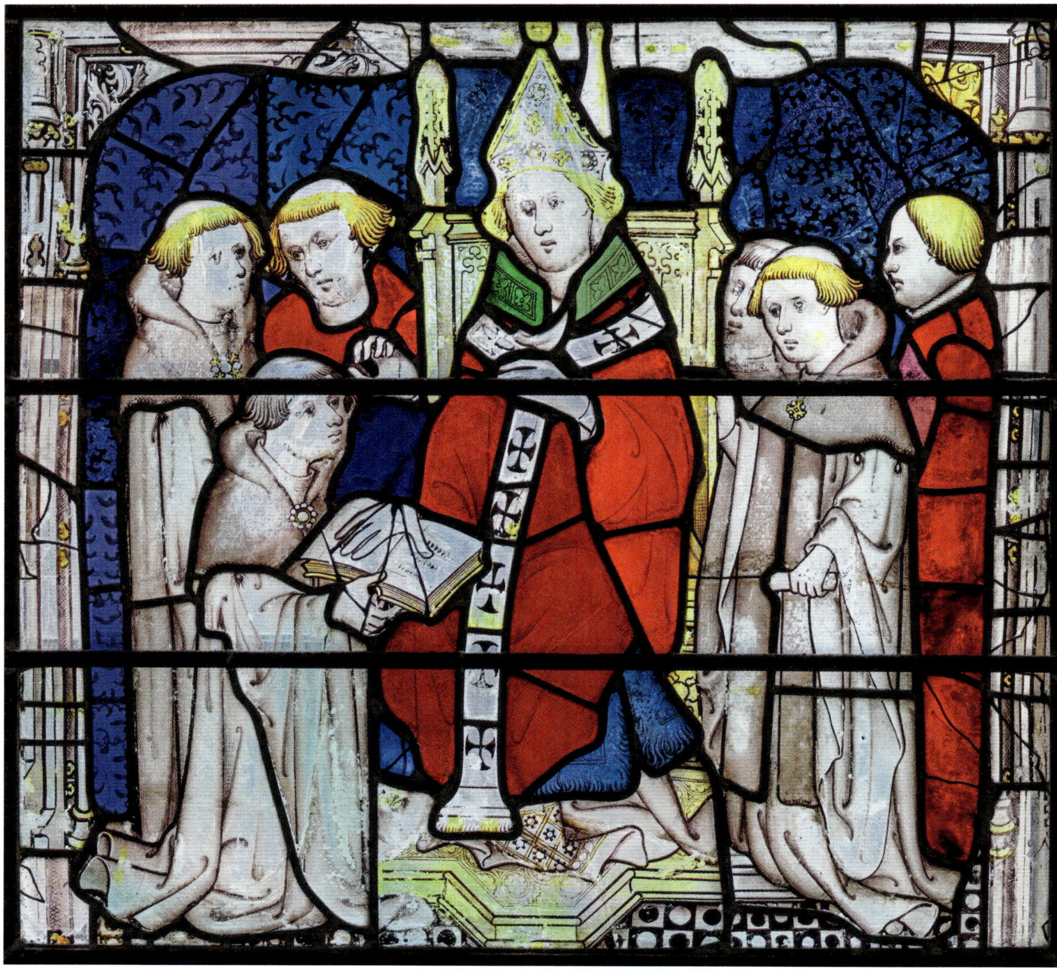

3b William takes the oath of office

Seated on the archiepiscopal throne, William takes the oath of office, with his right hand on the Gospels. He is watched by a group of canons with characteristic tonsures, consisting of a shaved crown above long hair covering their ears and necks. They mostly wear white choir robes. To the right is a lesser cleric in red without the tonsure. William is depicted wearing the standard archiepiscopal vestments, including the pallium (a strip of white cloth with black crosses, which encircles the shoulders and hangs down in front and behind), even though in reality he had not yet received the pallium from the pope (see panels 4c–4e and 8b). This scene is not mentioned in the written sources, but serves to introduce William as archbishop for the first time.

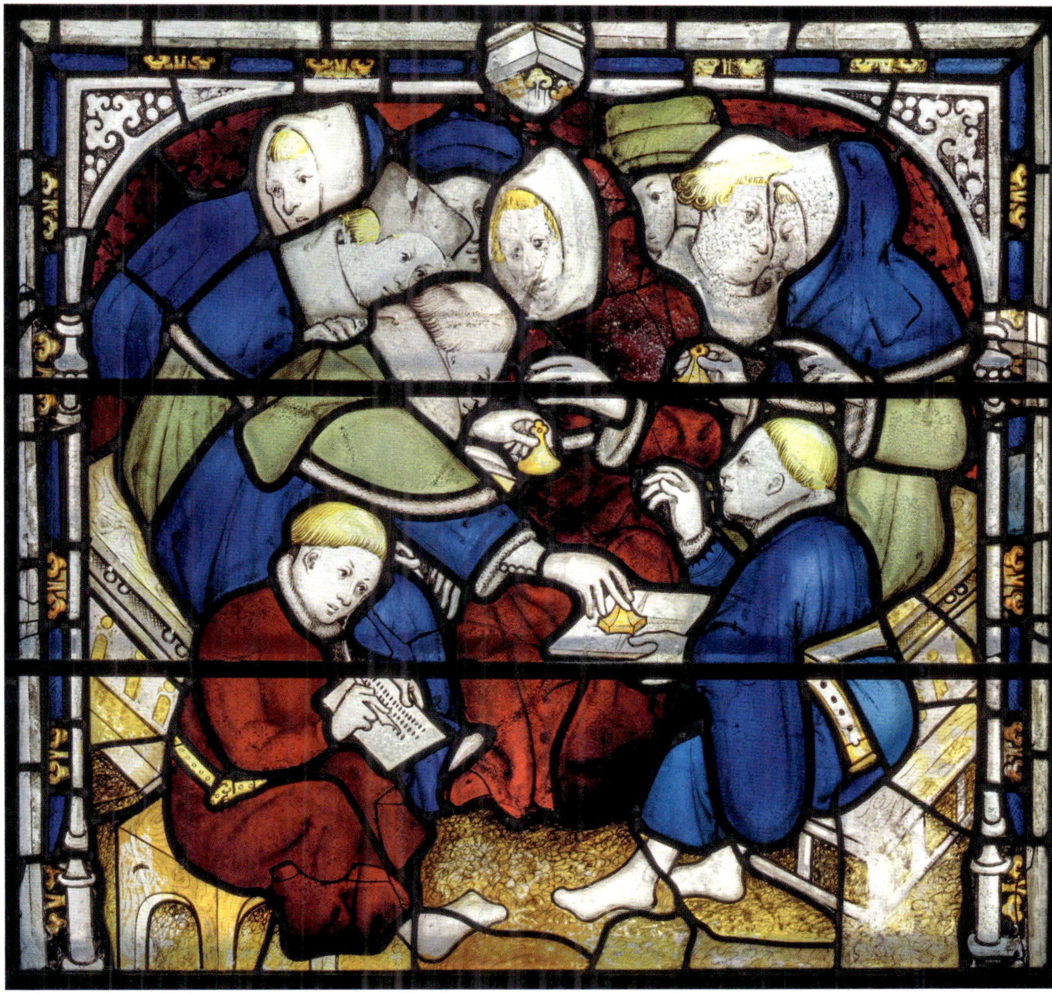

3c William's enemies conspire against him

A minority of the canons contest William's election, alleging improper secular interference. They are encouraged by two figures lurking at the back, identifiable by their green and blue hats as laymen. Two lesser clergy acting as secretaries sit on stools to left and right. The canons affix their seals to a letter of appeal to the pope. The animated gestures and private conversations of the conspirators contrast with the calm deliberations of the canons in panel 3a.

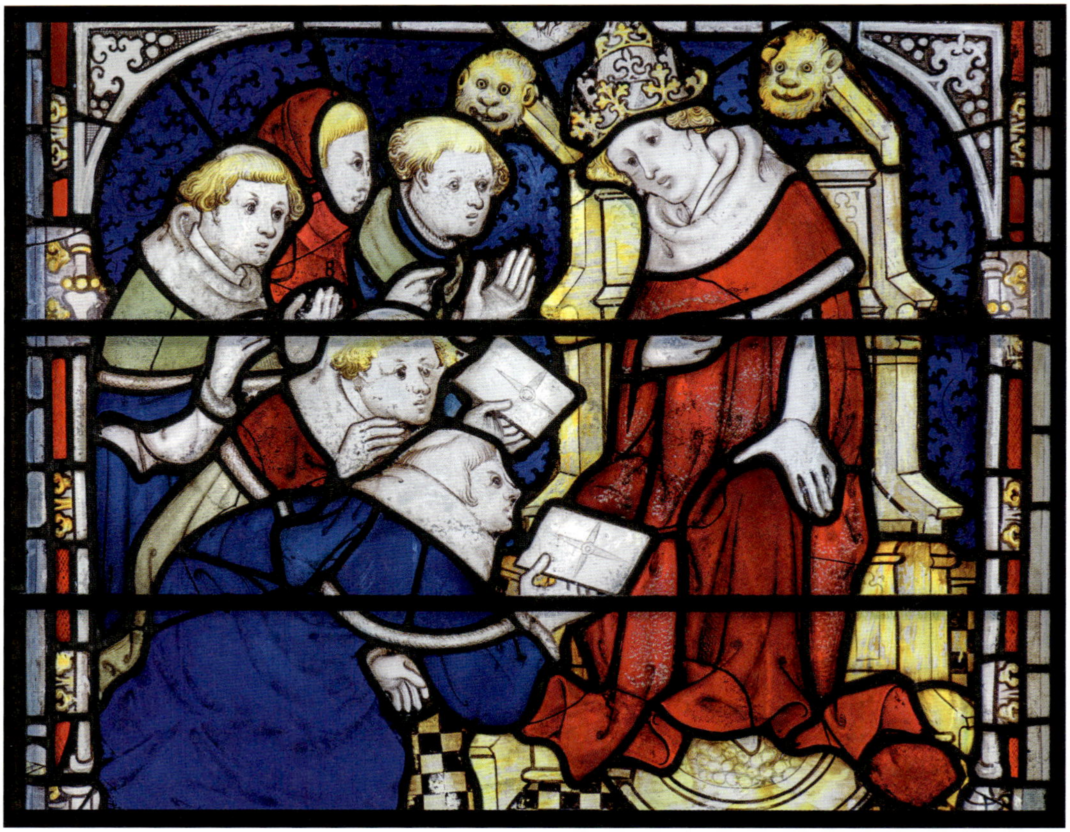

3d William and his enemies petition the pope
William (dressed here in blue) kneels to present his petition to Pope Innocent in Rome (identified by his triple tiara). Behind him, Archdeacon Walter of London presents a counter-petition, accompanied by three representatives of William's other enemies.

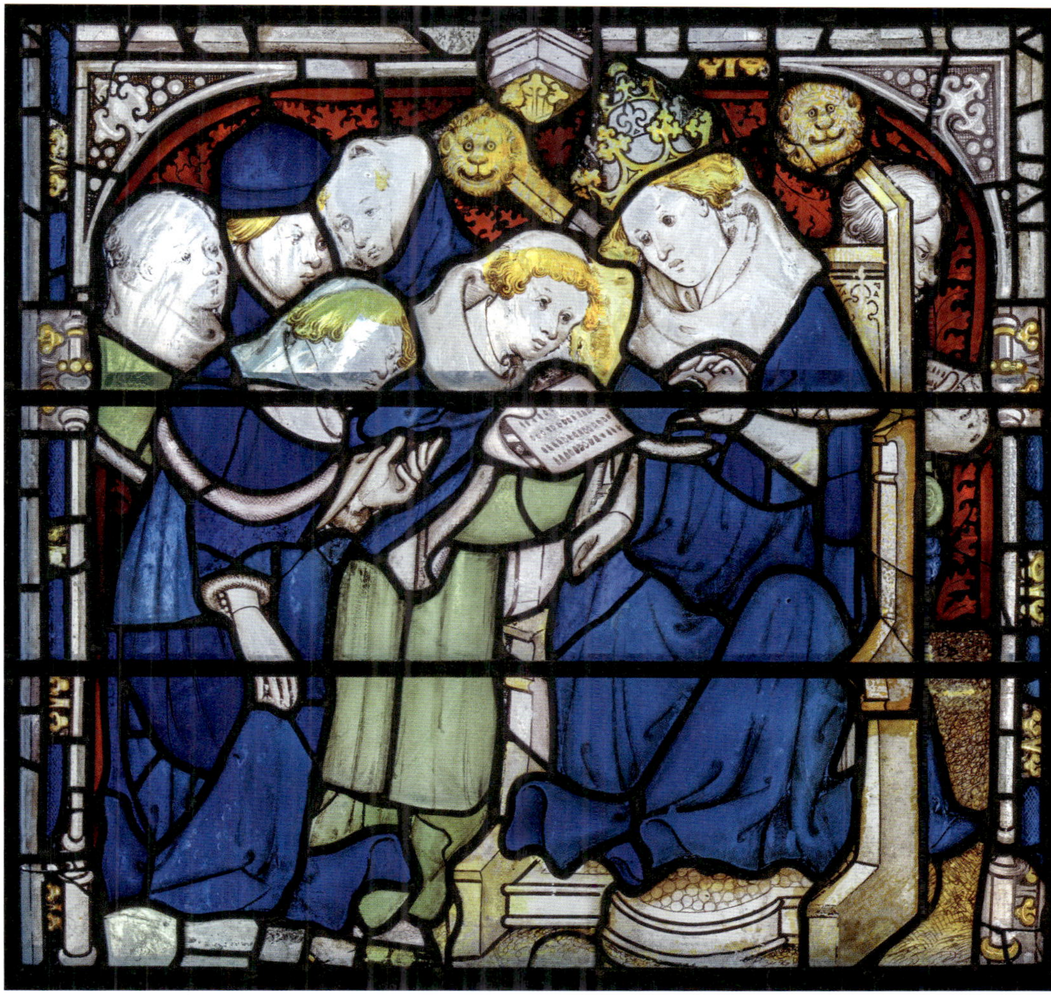

3e The pope gives his judgement

William and Walter of London again appear before Pope Innocent, with three figures again behind them. This scene is very similar to panel 3d, but the single document and the postures and gestures of the figures show that in this case the pope is handing down his judgement to the petitioners. An additional figure on the right (largely concealed by the papal throne) sets off to England, with the pope's letter, its green circular seal just visible.

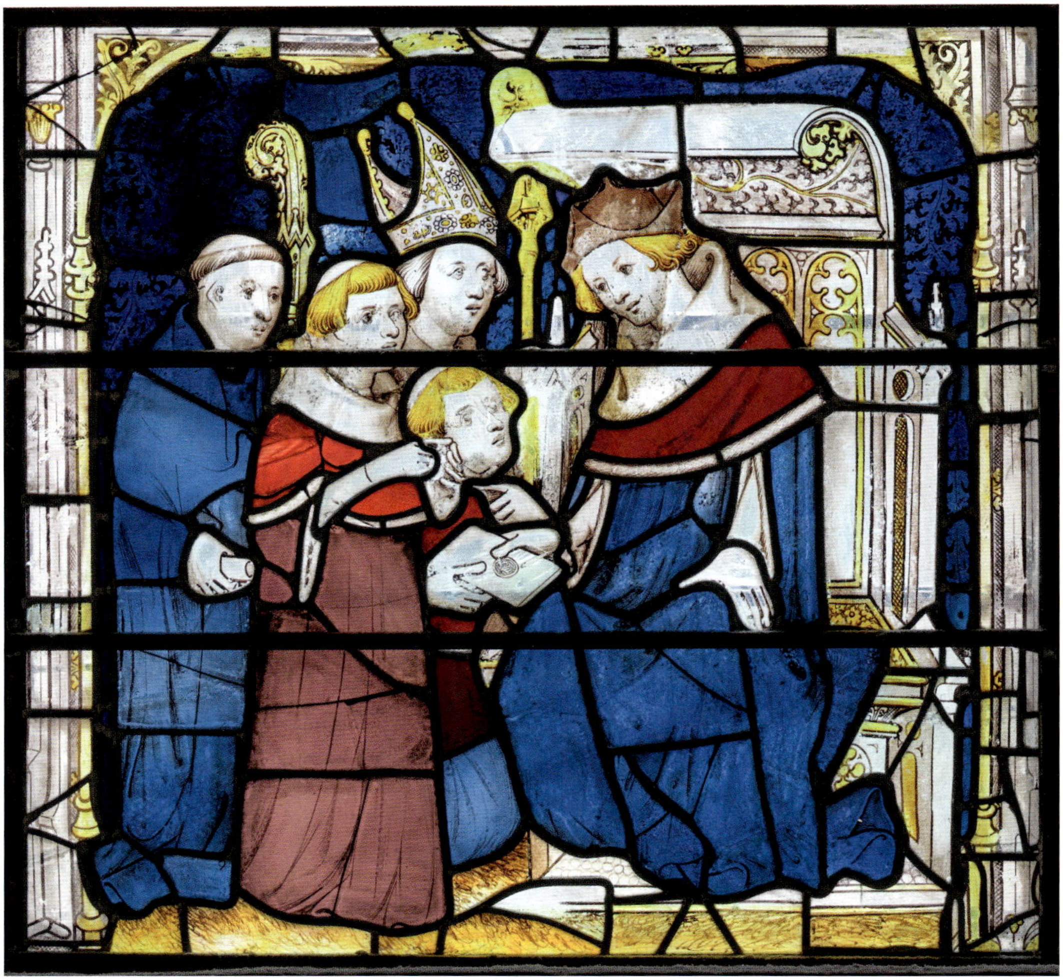

4a The pope's letter is delivered to the dean of York

The seated dean, robed like a canon but distinguished by his hat, is handed the pope's letter by a kneeling cleric who points to William (standing in front of him). The letter states that William's election should stand so long as an oath is sworn by the dean, or another appropriate person, that the election was valid. The bishop in the background and the abbot (with blue habit, monastic tonsure and crozier) represent Ralph Nowell, the bishop of the Orkneys, and a Benedictine abbot, both of whom subsequently swore the oath in lieu of the dean.

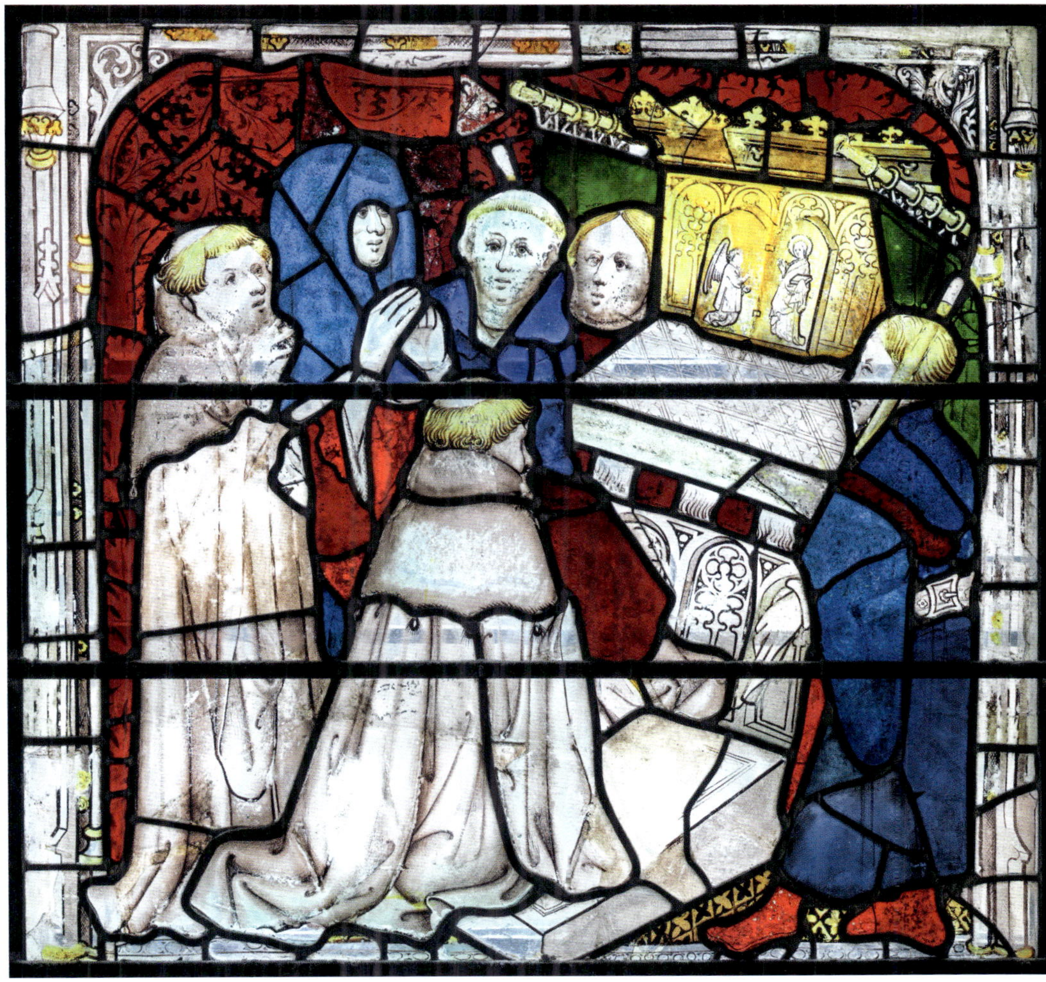

4b William prays before his consecration at Winchester

William kneels in prayer before an altar, on which is a diptych of the Annunciation. Green curtains hang on either side. He offers in front of the altar the red-and-white vestments with which he will be vested as archbishop. He is accompanied (from left to right) by a canon in white robes, a hooded figure, a Benedictine monk (with blue habit and monastic tonsure), a lesser cleric and (on the right) a verger holding a staff. The monk represents one of the monks of Winchester Cathedral, and the hooded figure with hands raised may represent Henry of Blois, the bishop of Winchester and papal legate, who was himself a Benedictine monk. The large blue hood is a repair.

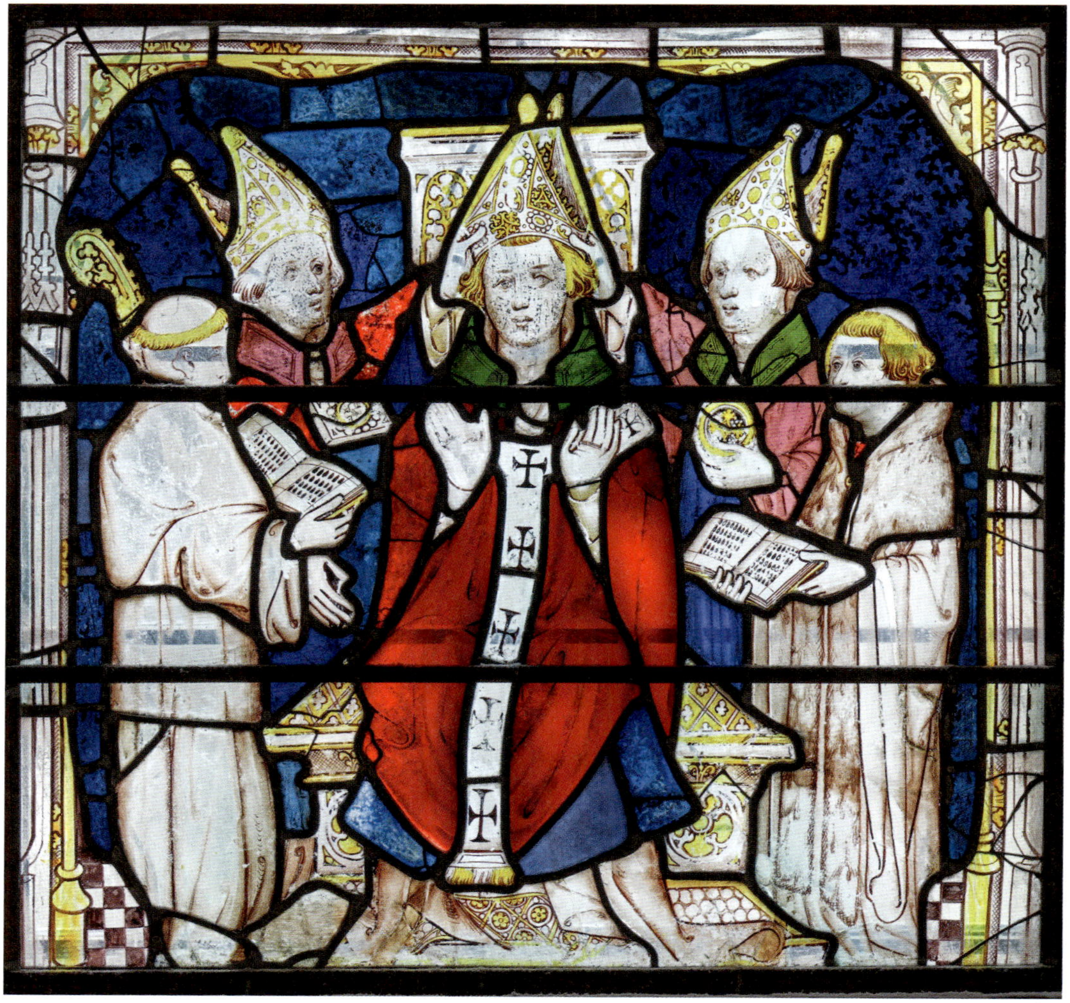

4c William is consecrated archbishop

William, seated on a throne, is consecrated in Winchester Cathedral by Henry of Blois and another bishop, who place his mitre on his head. On the left stands an abbot, identified by his monastic tonsure and crozier. On the right is a canon dressed in white robes. As in panel 3b, William's archiepiscopal status is signified by the pallium, even though he had yet to receive it (see panels 4d and 4e). Artistic convention conflicts with historical fact. William was consecrated in September 1143.

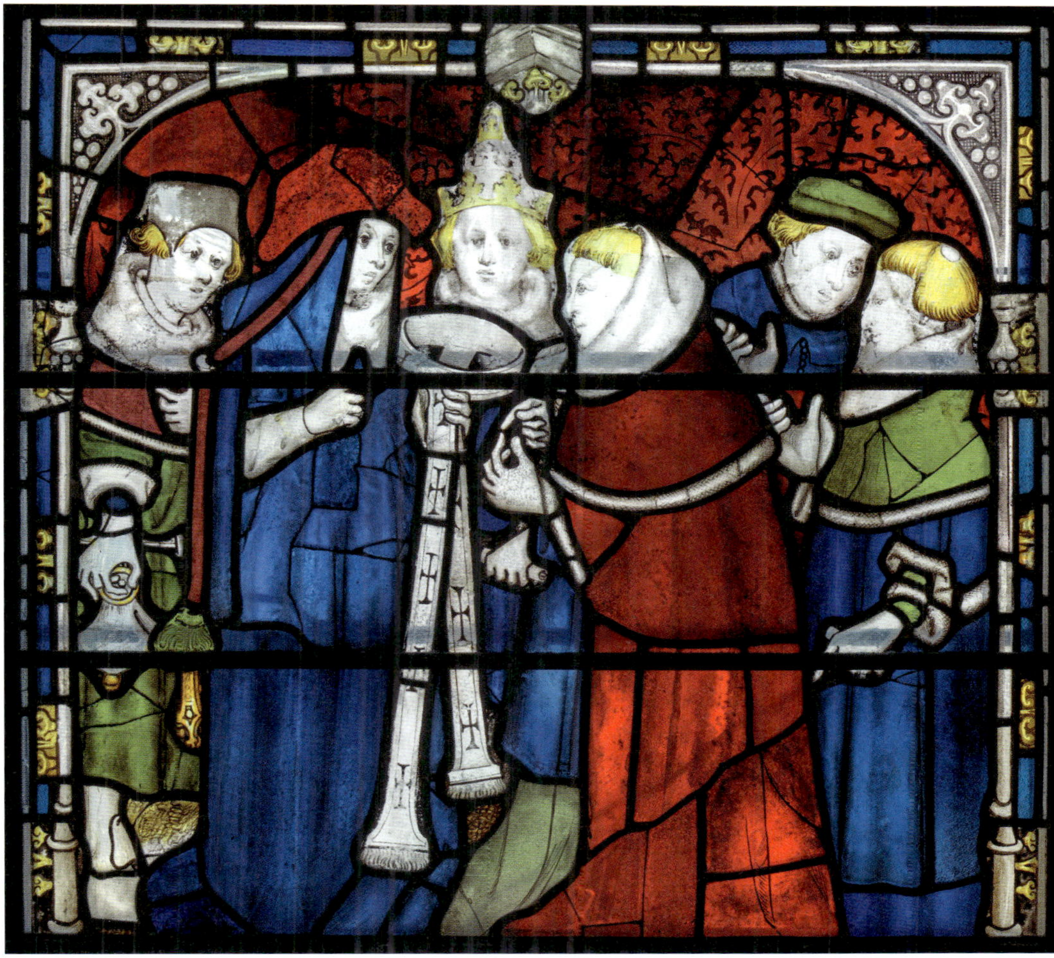

4d The pope sends the pallium to William

In Rome the new pope, Lucius, orders his legate, Cardinal Hincmar, to take the pallium to William, as a definitive sign of papal approval. Lucius (whose head is a restoration) stands behind in the centre, Hincmar (robed in blue) is identified by his red cardinal's hat, and the prominent figure in red standing opposite him probably represents an envoy from William. Other figures look on and gesticulate. The focus of the scene is the pallium itself, which is rarely depicted, as here, showing the circular band that went around the shoulders and the vertical bands that hung down in front and behind. It is usually only represented when worn over a chasuble, in which case only the vertical band at the front is visible, as in 4c.

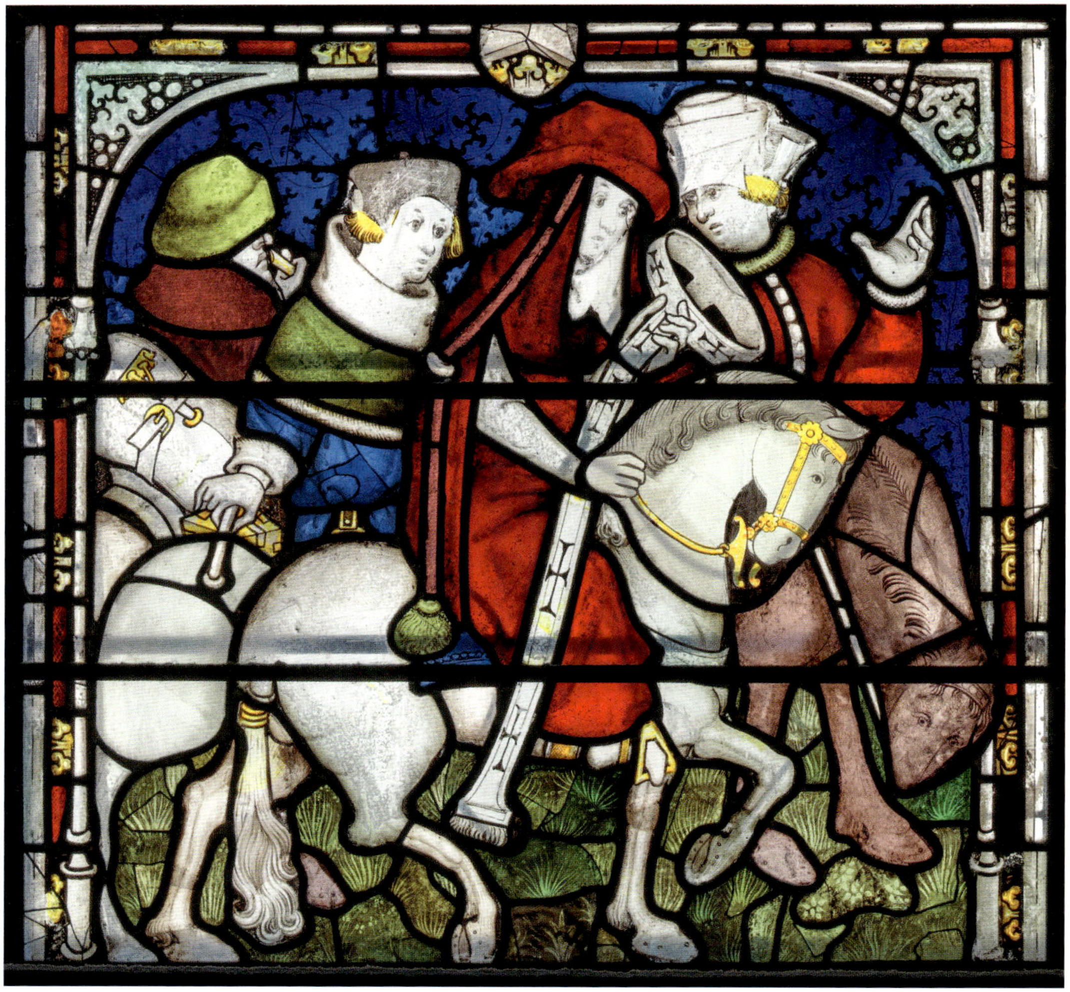

4e Cardinal Hincmar carries the pallium to England
Wearing his red cardinal's hat and robes, Hincmar displays the pallium as he rides along. His well-laden mounted retinue comprises a canon (on the left) and two laymen, who appeared in the previous scene. The direction of travel and the gesture of the man on the right lead the eye onwards past the end of the row.

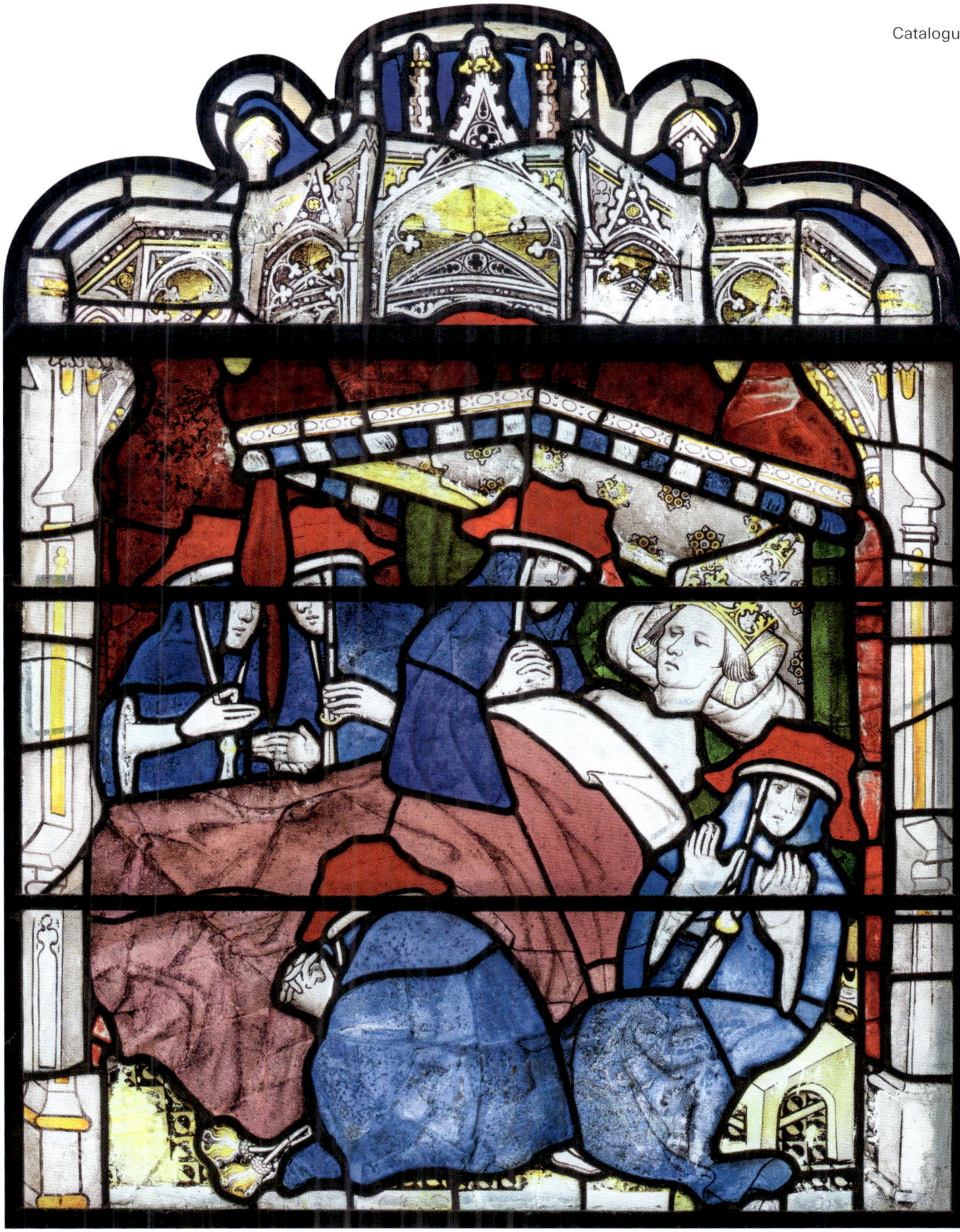

5a–6a The death of Pope Lucius

Even on his deathbed, the pope is shown wearing the papal triple tiara. His sumptuous canopied bed, with purple bedspread and green curtains, is also indicative of his status. He is surrounded by grieving cardinals robed in blue and wearing red cardinals' hats. With the pope's death, Cardinal Hincmar's legatine commission lapsed, and he returned to Rome without having delivered the pallium to William. However, his return journey is not depicted.

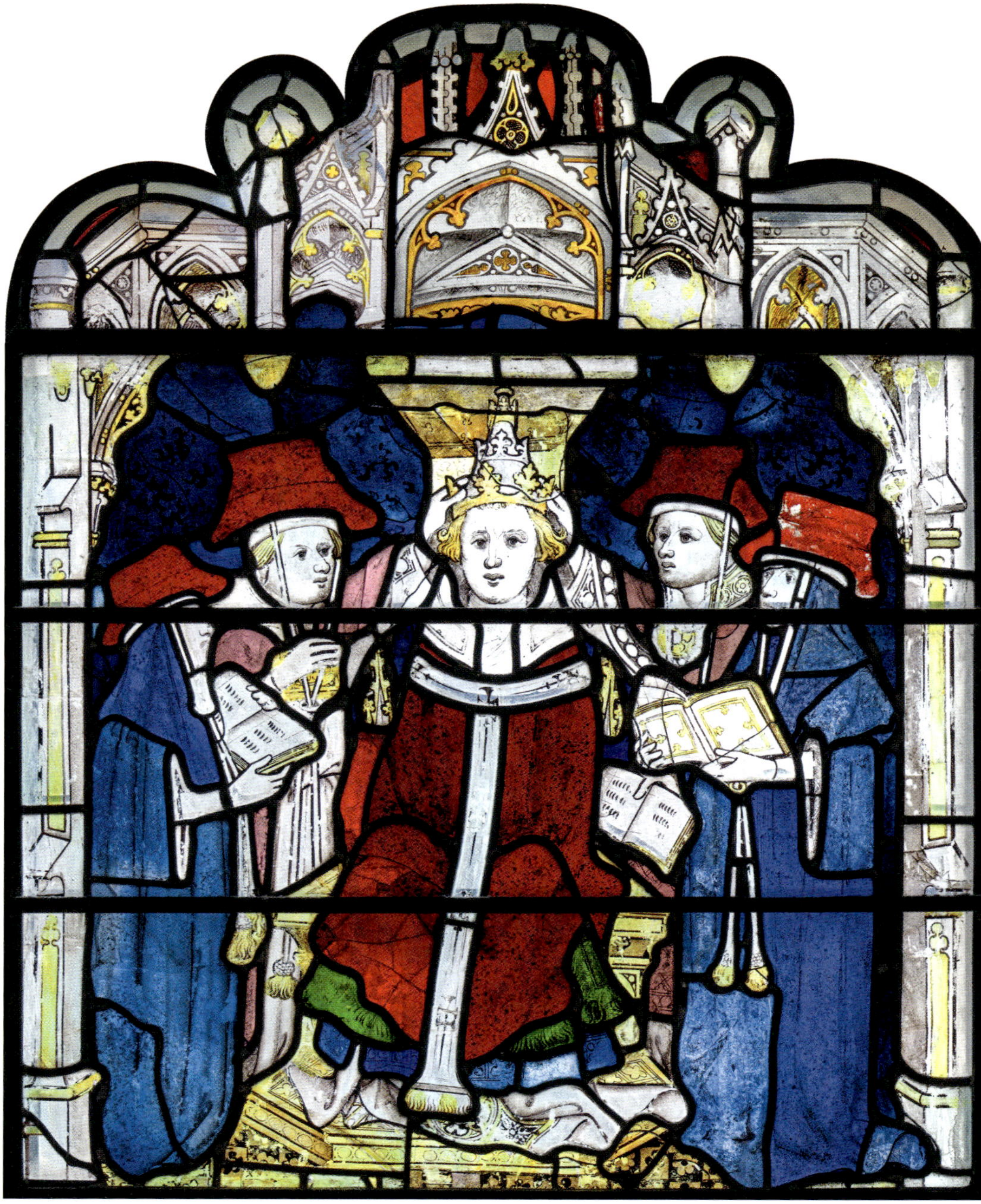

5b–6b The consecration of Pope Eugenius

The new pope is seated on the papal throne as two cardinals wearing liturgical vestments place the triple tiara on his head. The pope, like an archbishop, wears a pallium. Two other cardinals to left and right robed in blue participate in the ceremony. Three of the figures hold open books. Pope Eugenius, a Cistercian and a former monk of Clairvaux under St Bernard, became pope in February 1145.

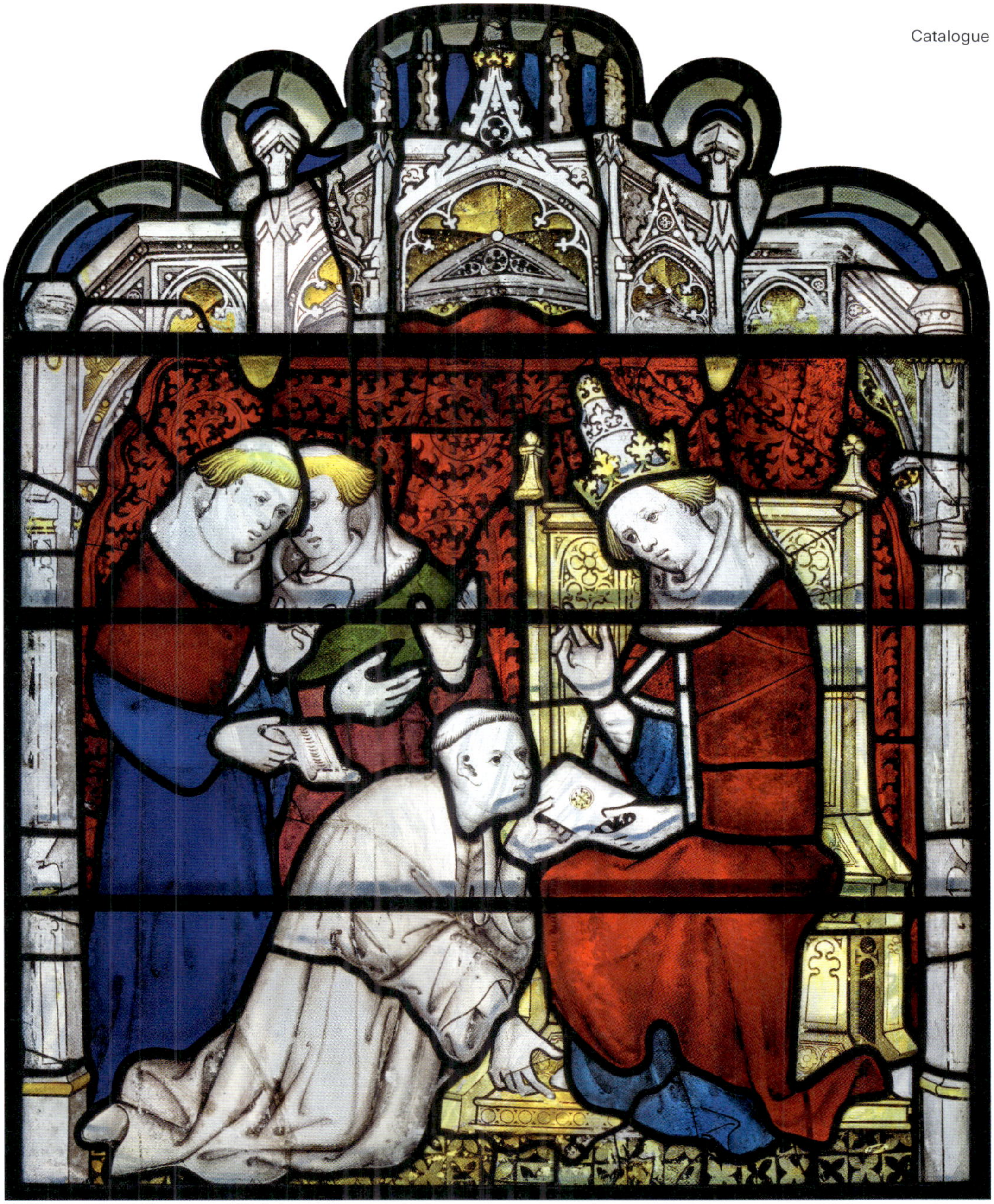

5b–6c The Cistercians appeal to Pope Eugenius against William

The revived opposition to William was spearheaded by St Bernard and by Henry Murdac, the new abbot of Fountains Abbey, who was another former monk of Clairvaux. Here, the Cistercian pope receives a letter from a kneeling monk wearing a white Cistercian habit. Two senior clerics in coloured robes discuss this new turn of events.

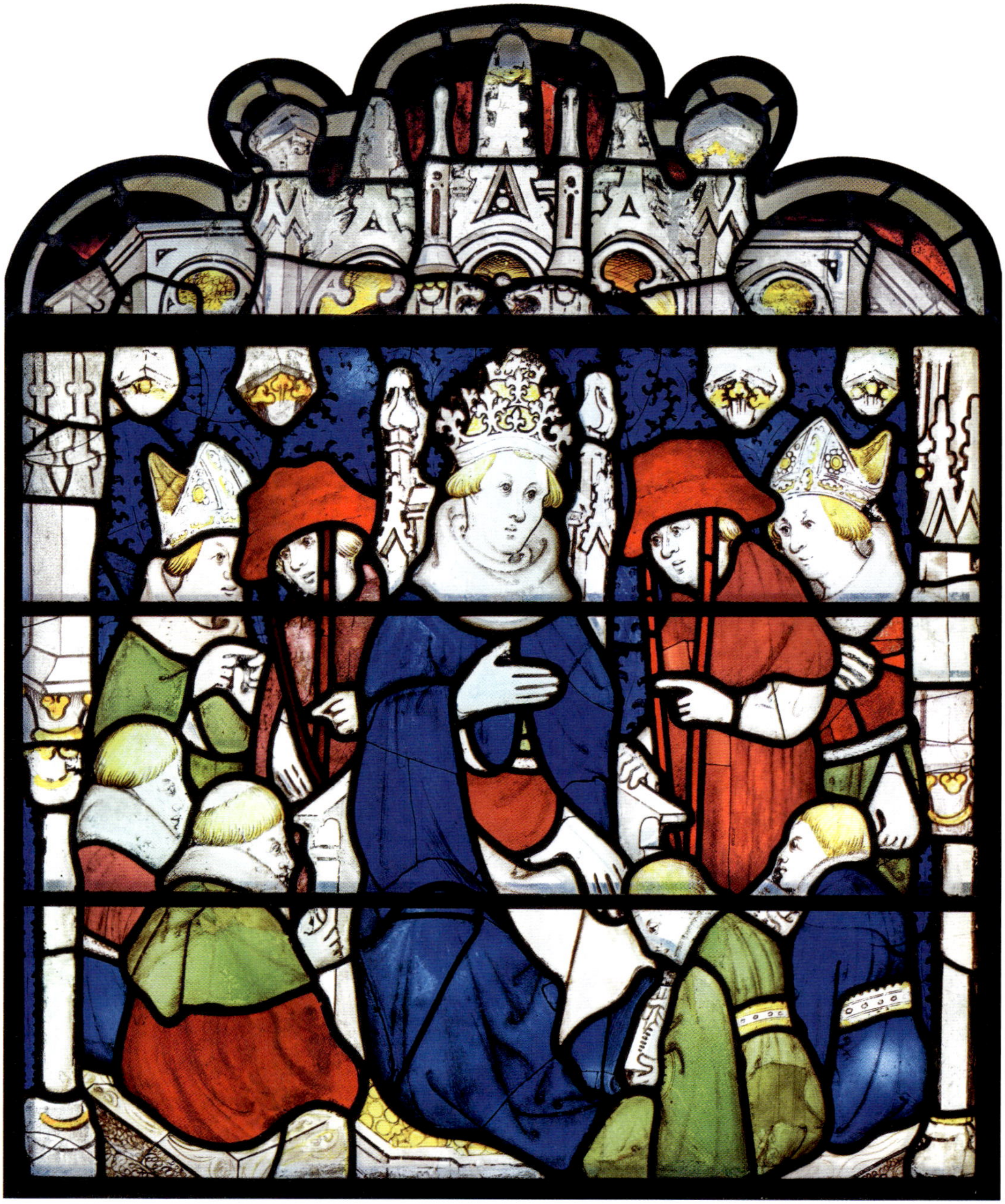

5d–6d Pope Eugenius deposes William

The pope formally deposes William. His judgement is witnessed by two cardinals standing next to the throne, two bishops and two canons or senior clergy seated in the left foreground. Two junior clerics in the right foreground, wearing monochrome robes with belts, record the judgement.

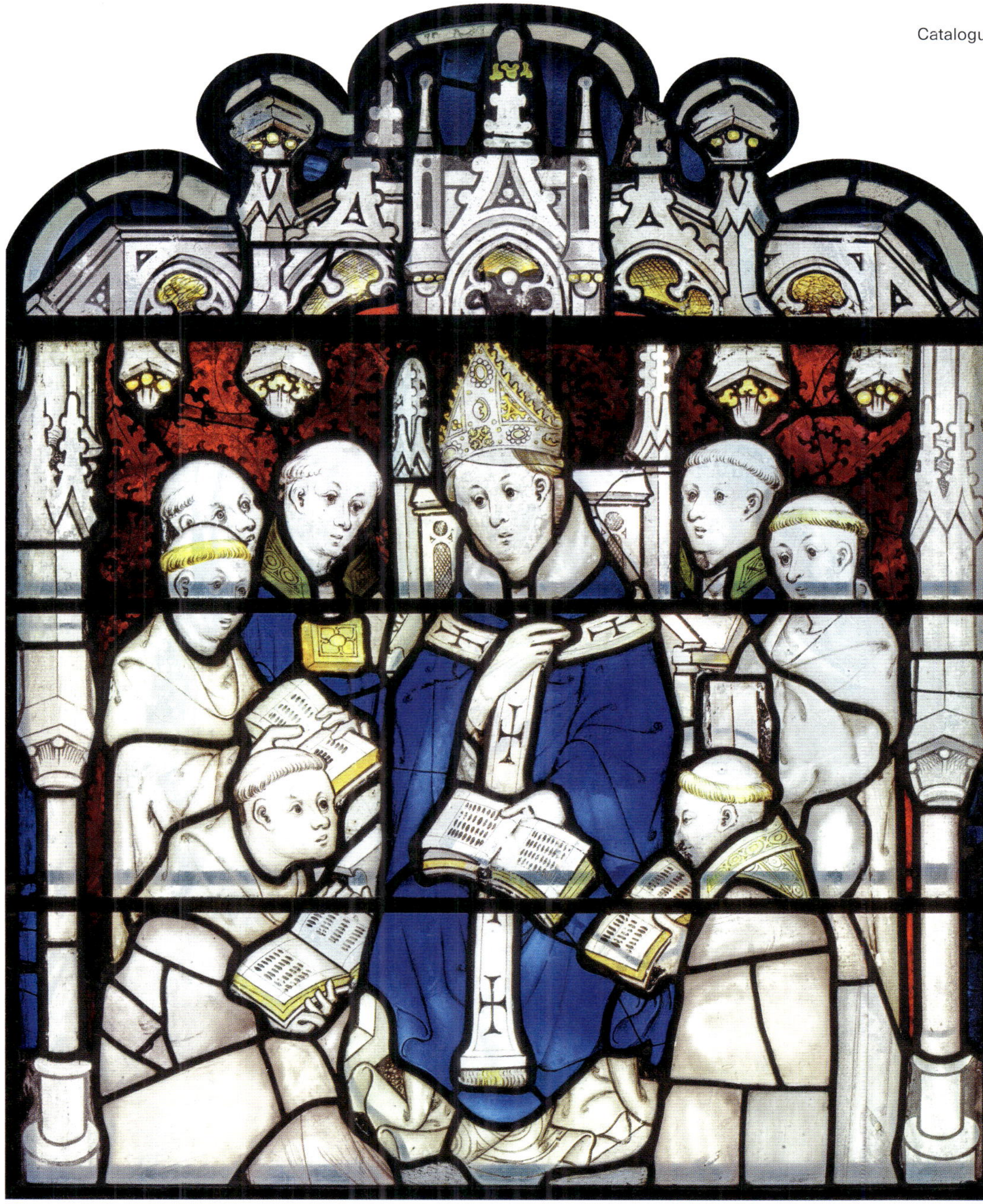

5e–6e The new archbishop, Henry Murdac, teaches his flock
William's successor, Henry Murdac, teaches his Cistercian monks, who all have monastic tonsures. He wears the archiepiscopal pallium and holds an open book. The Cistercian monks in their white habits gather round him, several of them also holding books. The two at the back next to the throne wear coloured copes. By choosing this scene, Thornton avoids yet another consecration scene, and emphasises Murdac's Cistercian connection. The bottom section of the window thus ends with the triumph of William's enemies in 1147.

Rows 7–13

The next section of the window contains six rows with narrative scenes. Rows 7–10 cover the final years of William's life: indeed, they focus almost entirely on the year before he died. Rows 11 and 12 introduce the first of his posthumous miracles.

Row 7 begins with William returning to Winchester in 1147 after being deposed as archbishop of York and withdrawing from public life (panels 7a–7b). Then, in the autumn of 1153, his three principal opponents all died within a few weeks of each other, as depicted in a unique triple deathbed scene (7c). William then came out of retirement to take up the office of archbishop again (7d–7e). He travelled to Rome once more, where he received the pallium from the new pope (panels 8a–8b), and then returned to England (panels 8c–8e). Row 9 depicts William travelling around his diocese (9a) before returning to York, where he was greeted at Micklegate Bar by civic dignitaries (9b). The miracle at Ouse Bridge is depicted next (9c), before his reception by the clergy at the entrance to the Minster (9d). The row ends with William enthroned within the Minster (9e).

The final days of William's life are shown in row 10. He celebrates Mass in the Minster on Trinity Sunday (10a) and welcomes his guests to a celebratory feast (10b), but he is taken ill and retires to his bed (10c), where he remains for some days (panel 10d is a replacement for the lost original). He dies in the archbishop's palace on 8 June 1154 (panel 10e).

Row 11 starts with William's burial in the Minster (11a). Soon after, a terrible fire causes burning timbers to fall on his tomb and the lid is broken, but his body is unharmed (11b). In the next scene William appears to a blind girl in a vision and heals her (11c) – the first of the posthumous healing miracles, which took place in 1177. This is followed by the story of a hydropsical woman who is brought to the Minster and healed at the tomb, which appears here for the first time as a shrine-like structure. The whole of row 12 is taken up with the story of Ralph and Besing, which likewise ends with a miracle at the tomb.

In this section, rows 7 to 11 employ two different frame designs: Type B on the left side, as in the bottom section, and a new design, Type F, on the right. As with rows 5 and 6 at the top of the bottom section, the panels in row 12 are topped by architectural canopies set within the cusped panels of row 13, beneath the transom. Panels 12a and 13a to 12c and 13c have Type G frames by mistake. The side shafts are of this type, and the outlines of the original canopies across the top can still be seen in the leadlines in the coloured backgrounds. Once the mistake had been realised, the canopies were removed, and the side shafts and the backgrounds were carried on up to the top of the panels. These are designated as Type F† on the diagram, and they support Type H canopies in the cusped panel 13d and 13e.

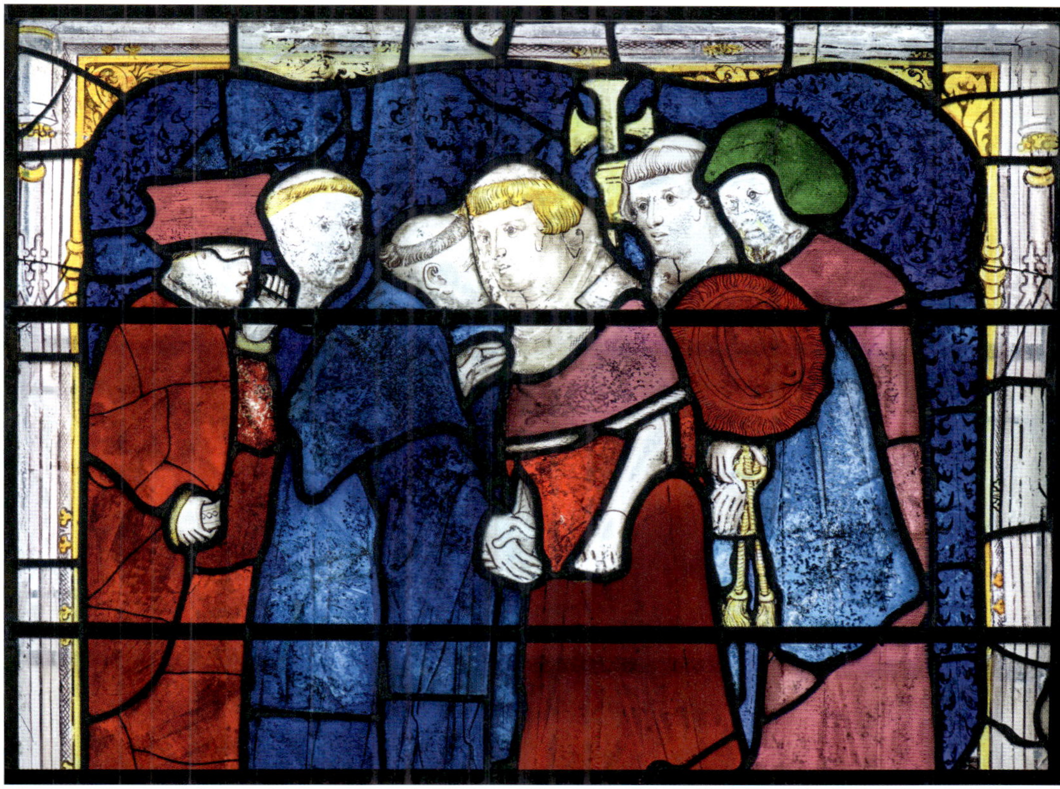

7a William retires to Winchester

William, robed in red, retires to Winchester, where he is greeted by Henry of Blois, dressed here as a Benedictine monk in a blue habit. Behind Henry stand another monk and a layman in a red robe. William is accompanied by another layman and by a cleric holding an archiepiscopal cross-staff. The robes of the figures are heavily restored.

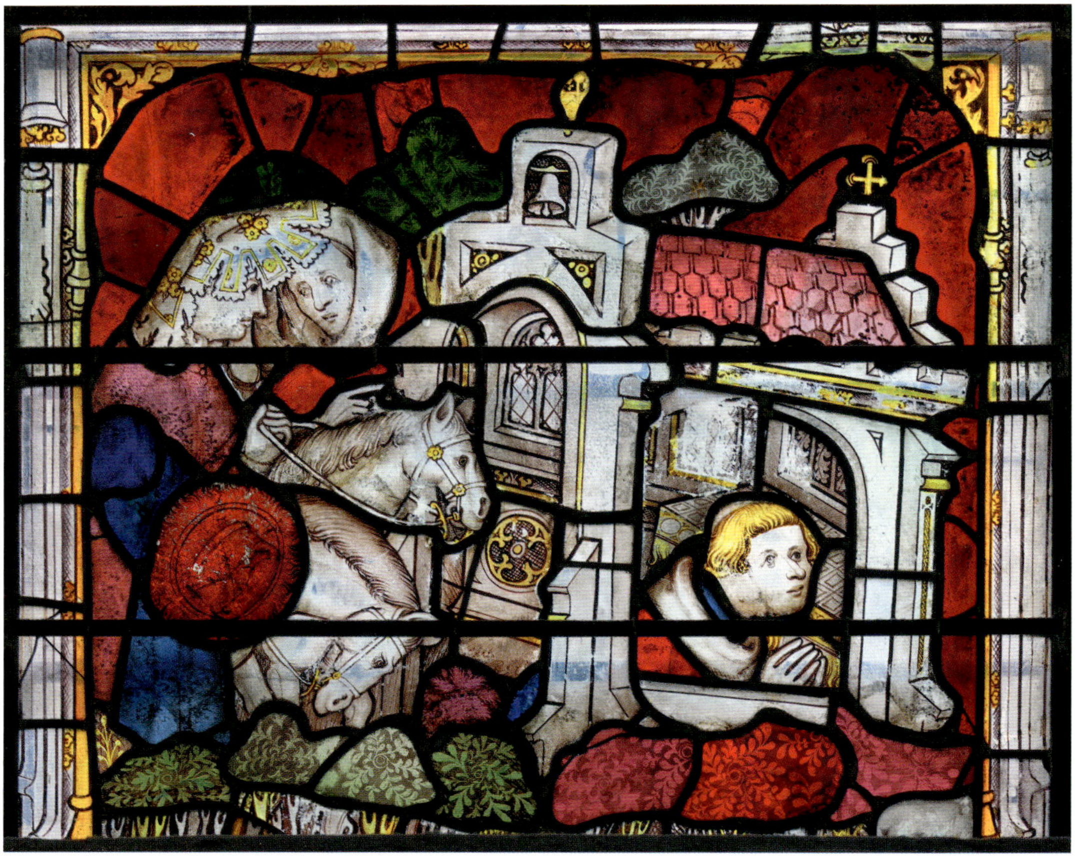

7b William withdraws from the world
William devotes himself to a life of penitence and prayer at Winchester, retreating from worldly cares. He kneels inside a small chapel set amidst trees, turning his back on the fashionably dressed couple on horseback outside who gossip about him.

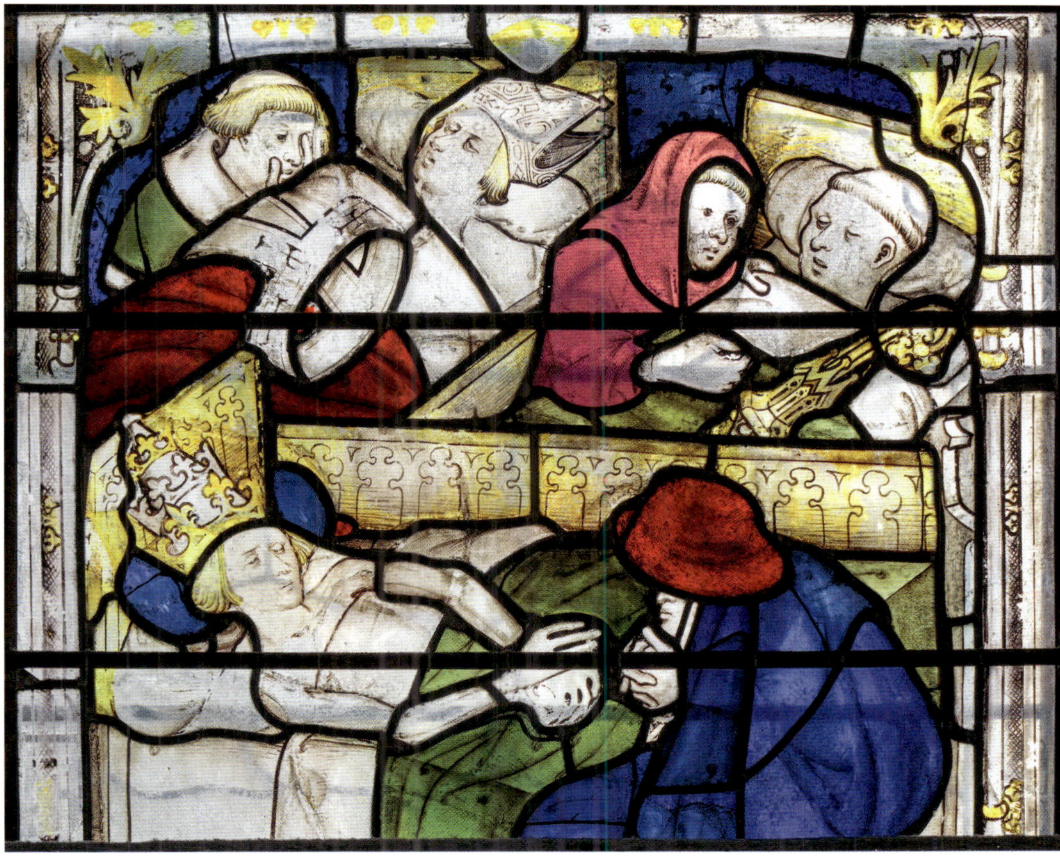

7c The death of William's opponents

This unique triple death bed scene shows the death of William's three principal Cistercian opponents, who all died within a few weeks of each other in 1153. Across the bottom is Pope Eugenius in Rome, wearing his papal tiara and with a grieving cardinal by his bed. Behind and to the right is St Bernard at Clairvaux, identified by his tonsure and his abbatial crozier, accompanied by a monk. To the left is Archbishop Henry Murdac in Yorkshire, with his mitre on his head and his pallium draped over the bed, with a canon at his bedside.

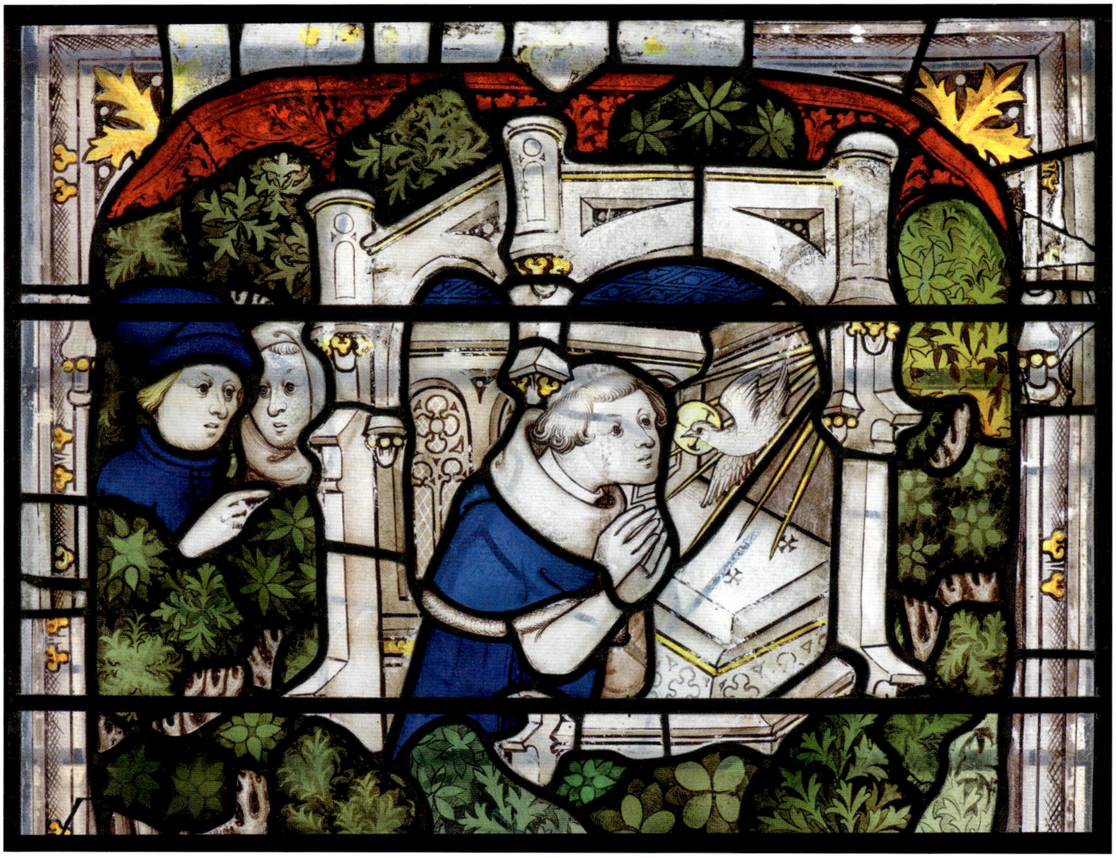

7d The Holy Spirit reveals the news to William

The Holy Spirit in the form of a dove reveals the news of his opponents' deaths to William as he kneels in front of the altar of a small chapel. As in panel 7b, the chapel is set in the middle of a wood, which here surrounds it on all sides. Two men peering through the foliage witness the event.

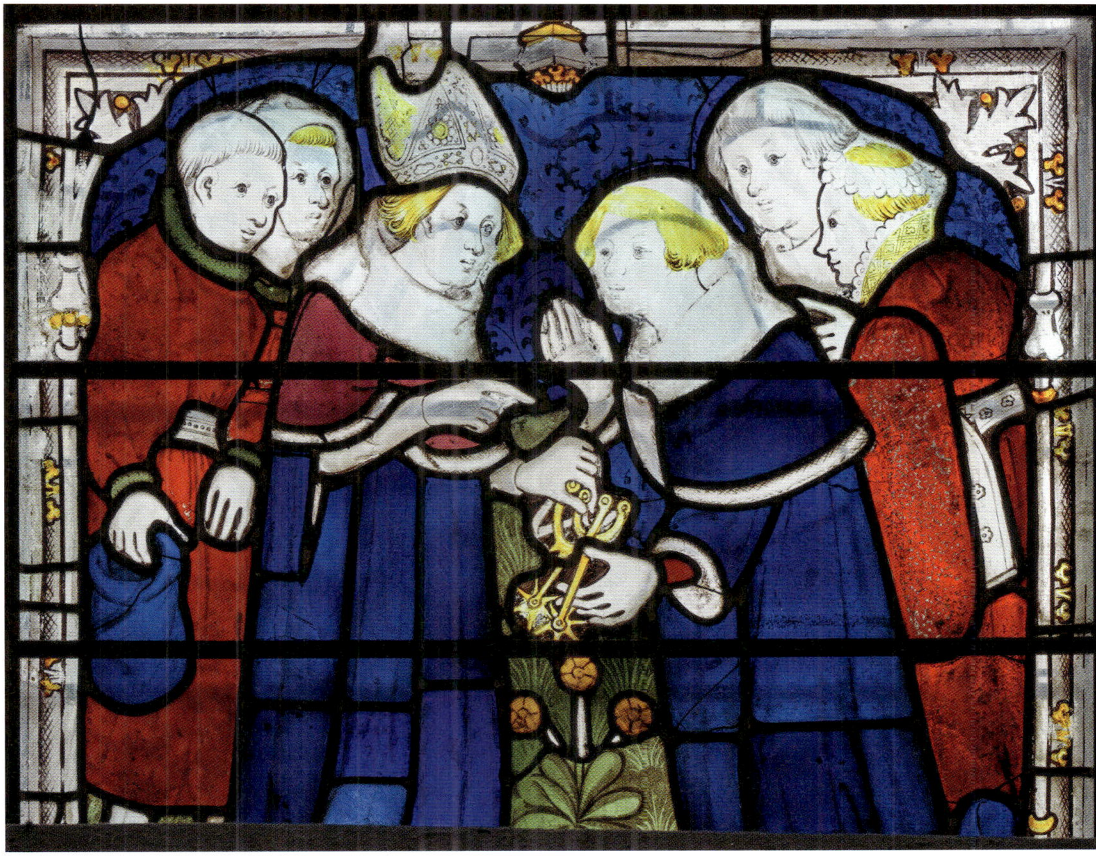

7e William is given spurs by Henry of Blois

Henry of Blois (this time in episcopal garb) gives William a pair of exquisitely ornate spurs. William asks Henry if God has revealed to him that William is about to go on a long journey. He tells Henry not only that his opponents are dead, but that one of the cardinals who had previously supported him during the election dispute is the new pope. The four bystanders listen intently.

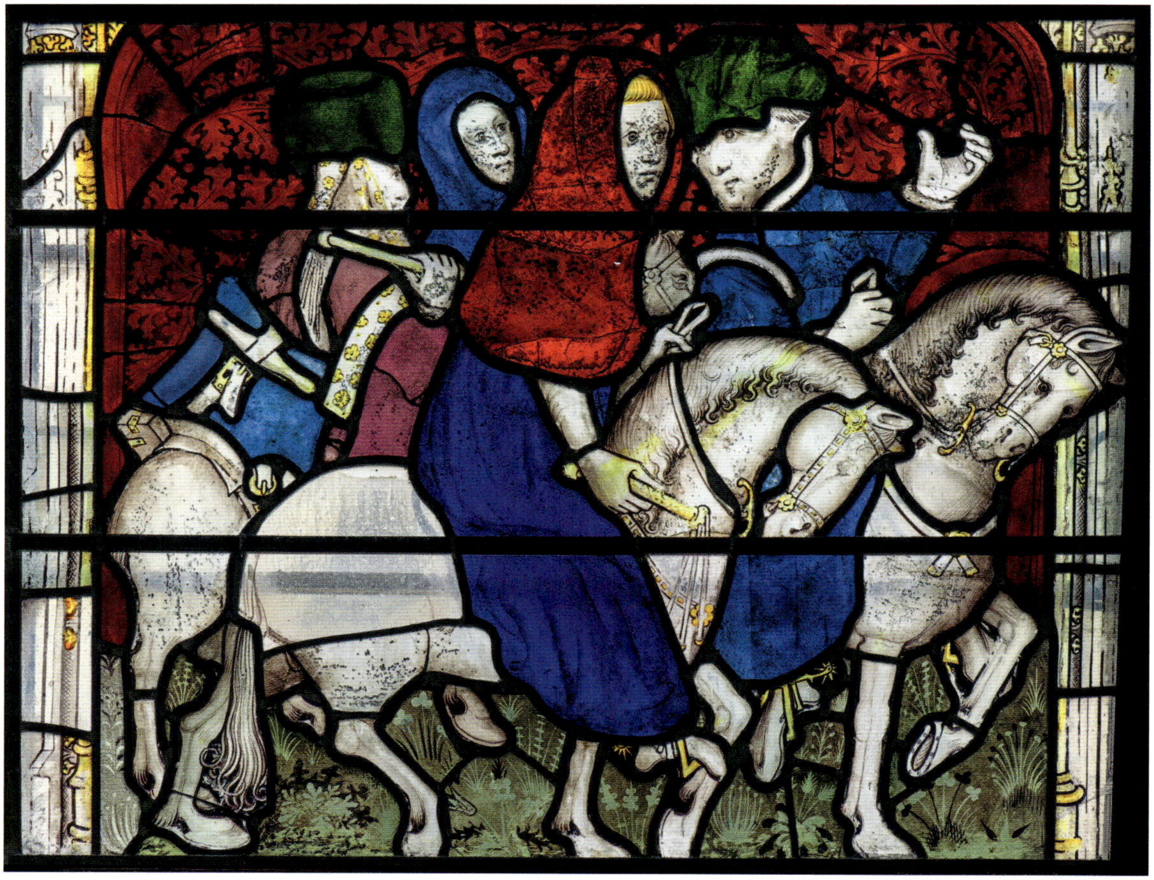

8a William travels to Rome again

Once again William undertakes the arduous journey to Rome in order to gain papal approval for his reinstatement as archbishop of York. He and his entourage are mounted on white horses, whose harnesses are shown in some detail. The man in front engages William in animated conversation.

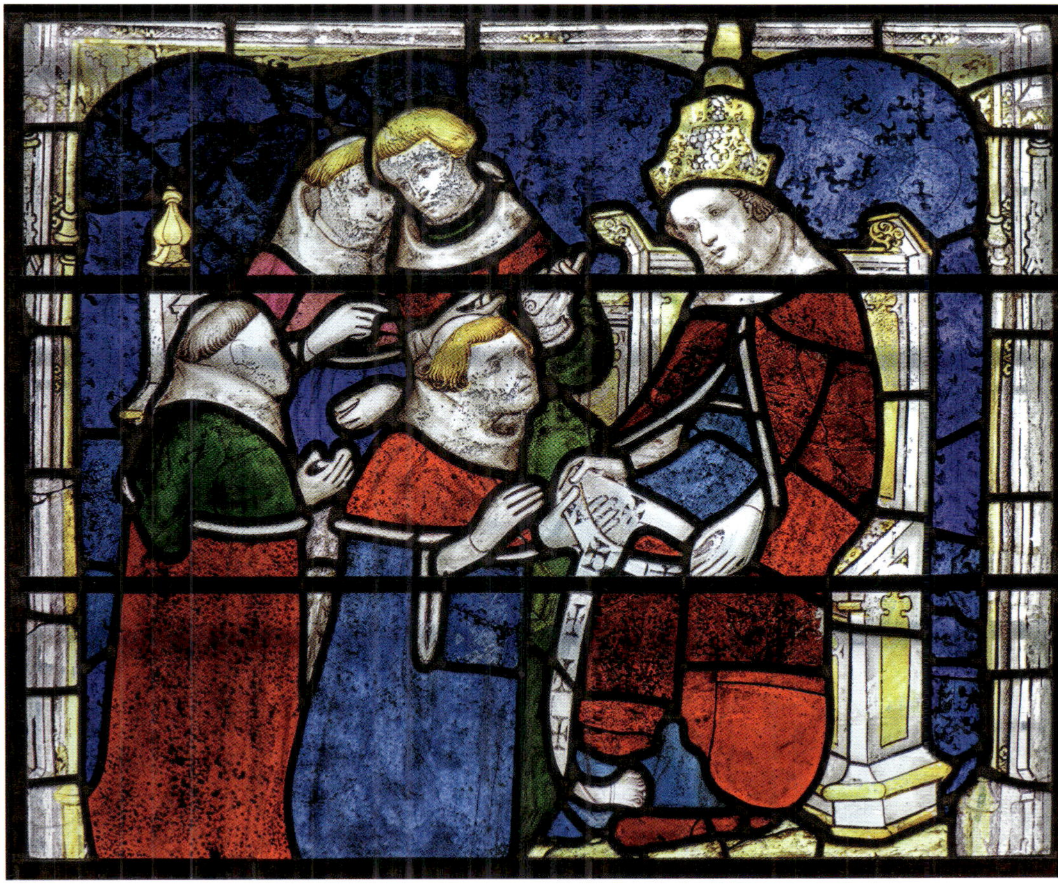

8b William receives the pallium from the pope

In Rome the new pope, Pope Anastasius IV, gives William the pallium, which is shown prominently in the centre of the panel. William kneels to receive it, while three clerics look on.

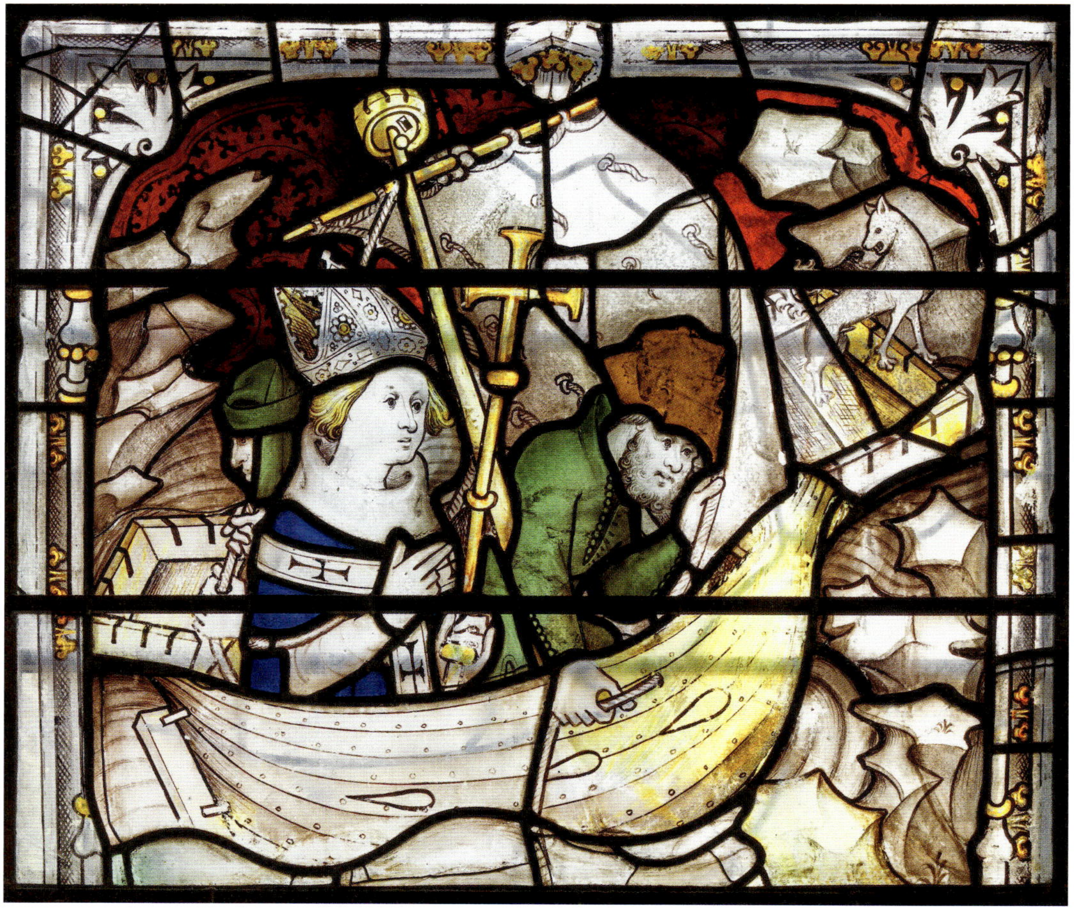

8c William sails back to England

William crosses the Channel in a single-masted boat, its sail fully unfurled. The sea is represented by a brown wash on white tinted glass, with dramatic craggy shores on either side. Flanked by the ship's captain and a sailor, both dressed in green, William shows off his archiepiscopal insignia: mitre, cross-staff and pallium. A dog stands in the prow.

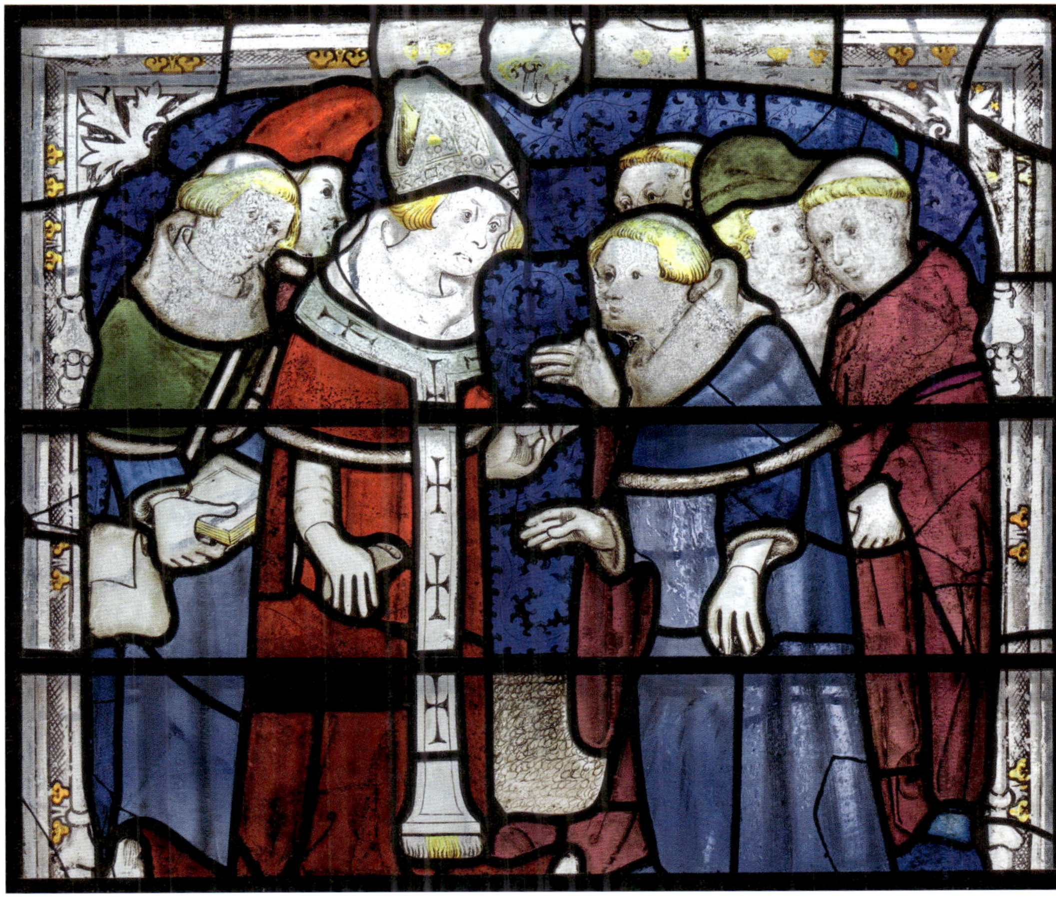

8d William meets Roger of Pont-l'Evêque at Canterbury

Passing through Canterbury, William (distinguished by his mitre and pallium) meets the archdeacon of Canterbury, Roger of Pont-l'Evêque (robed in blue). William is accompanied by a cleric with a satchel and a book. A layman with a red hat stands behind. Behind Roger are a layman and two monks of Canterbury, in purple robes, identifiable by their monastic tonsures. William announces that Roger will succeed him as archbishop of York.

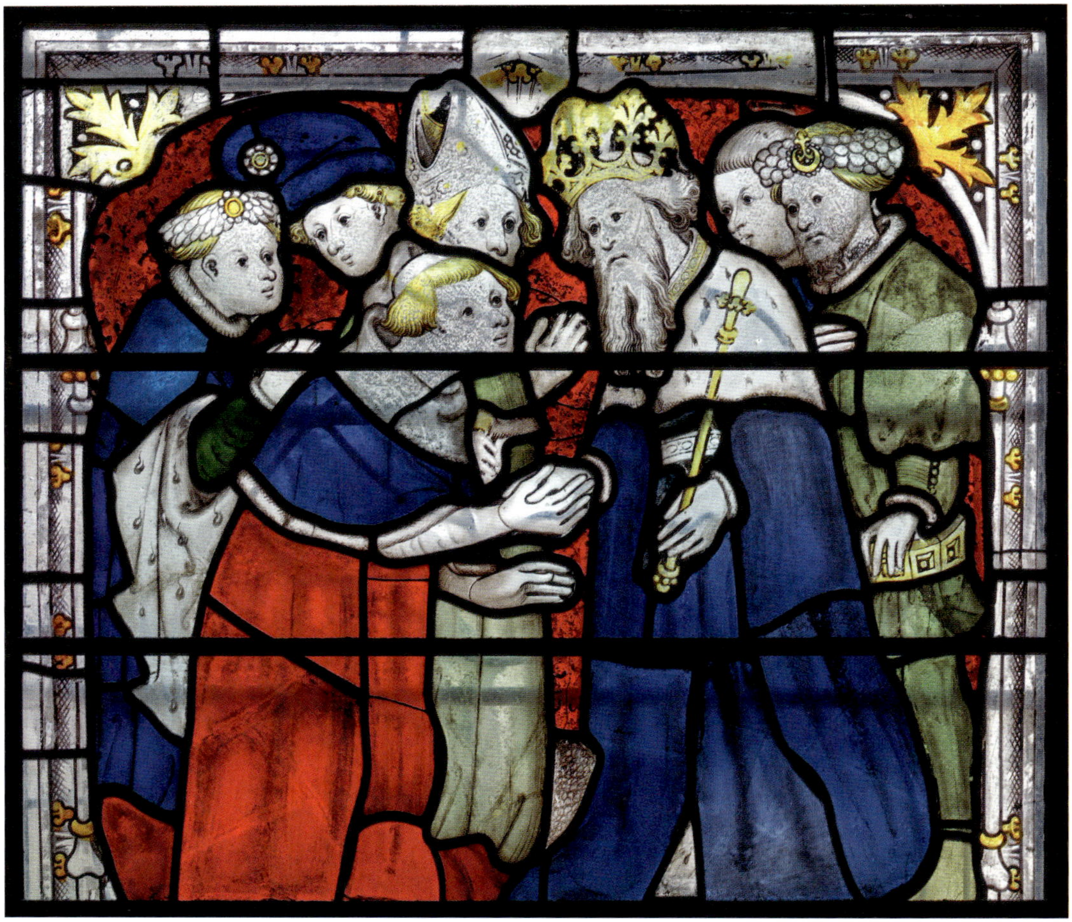

8e William is greeted by King Stephen

William, here in everyday clothes, is greeted by the king. Henry of Blois, wearing a mitre, stands behind, while richly dressed courtiers look on. William spent Easter 1154 at Winchester, and this scene effectively demonstrates royal as well as ecclesiastical approval for William's return to York.

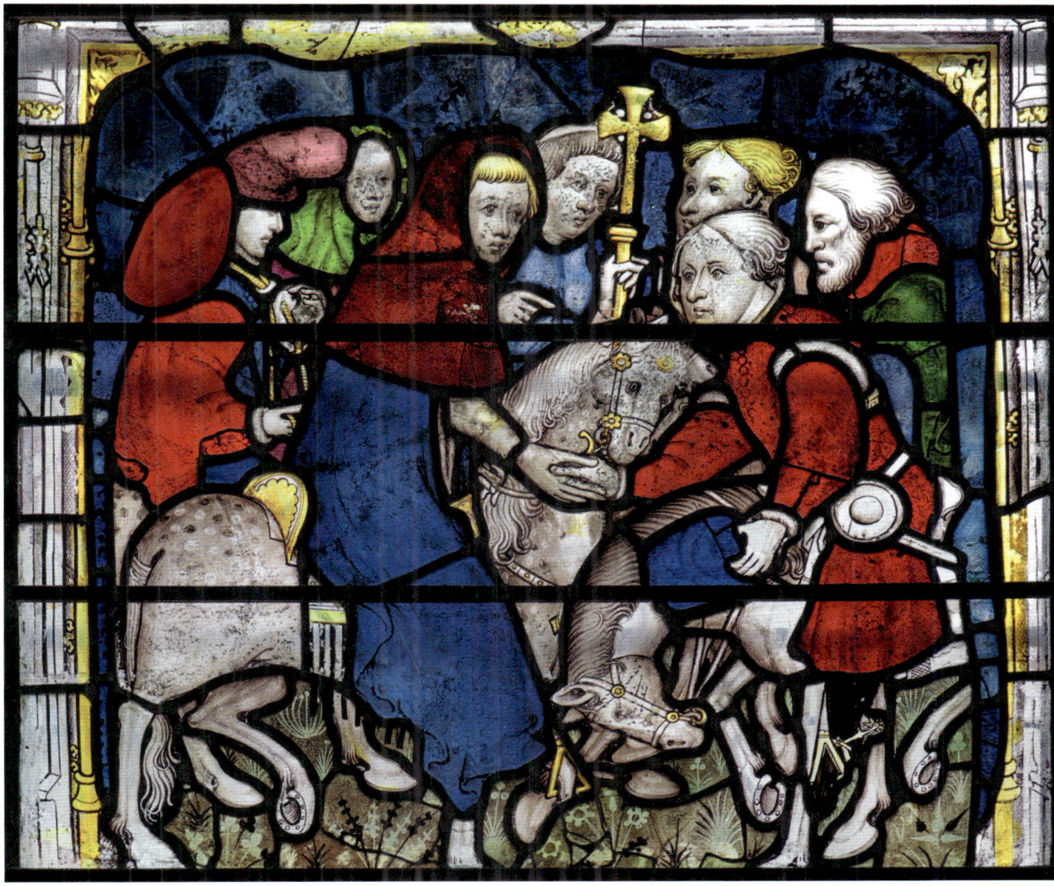

9a William travels round his diocese
Before returning to York, William made a tour of the diocese. Accompanied by his cross-bearer and two laymen, he is greeted by three laymen on horseback, one of whom doffs his hat and shakes William by the hand.

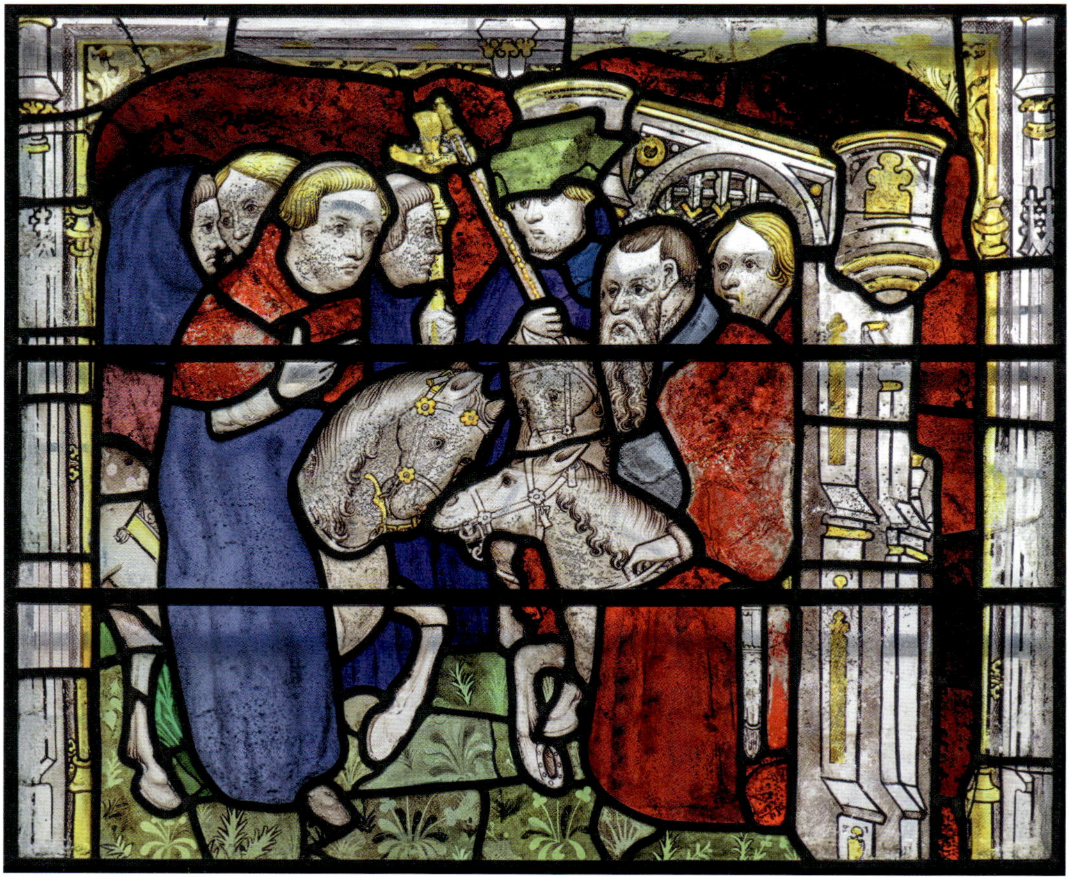

9b William is greeted at the gates of York by the leading citizens

It was customary for distinguished visitors to be greeted by the civic authorities outside Micklegate Bar. William approaches on horseback, accompanied by his cross-bearer and two laymen. The mayor, with a long forked beard, emerges from the gateway with two other officials, one of whom holds the sword of state, an anachronistic symbol of civic authority, which was only granted to the mayor in the late fourteenth century.

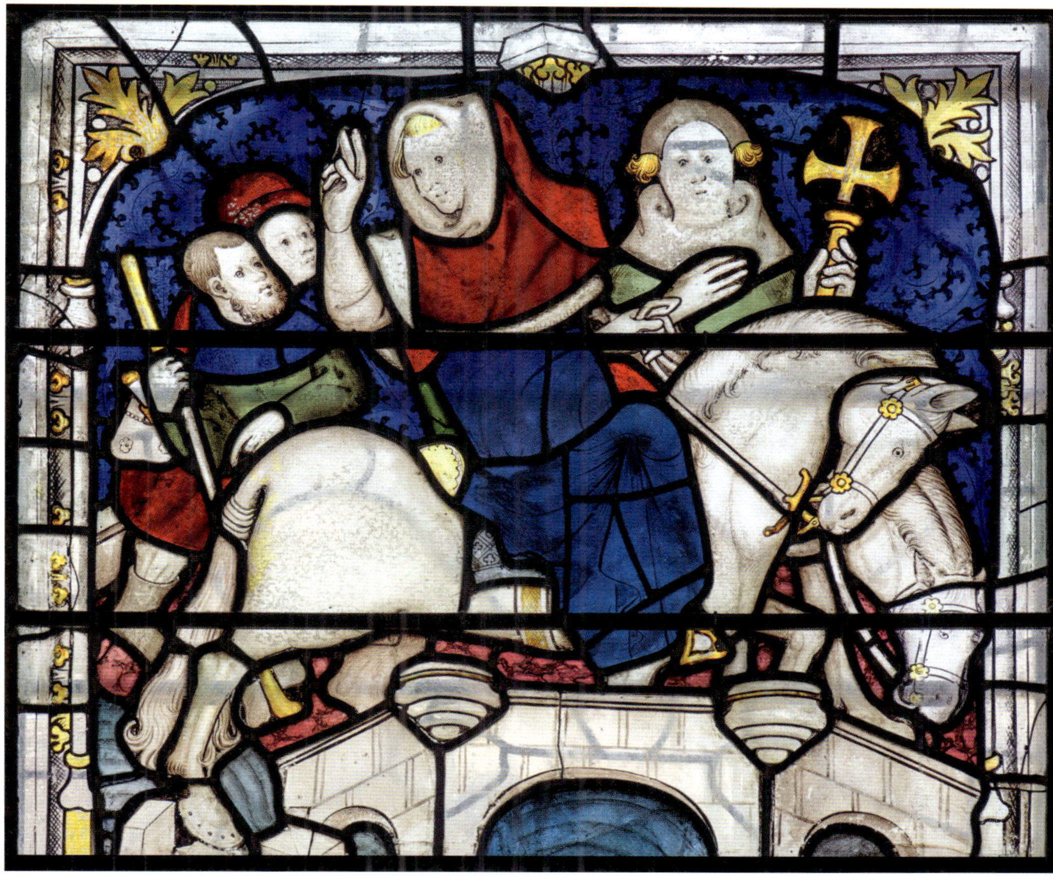

9c The miracle of Ouse Bridge

As William crossed Ouse Bridge ahead of a large crowd, the bridge (which was made of wood in the twelfth century) gave way, catapulting people and horses into the river. William turned round, made the sign of the cross, and prayed that no one should be drowned. William and his cross-bearer dominate the scene, leaving little room for the crowd, none of whom have been thrown into the river by the modest damage to the bridge. The bridge is shown anachronistically as made of stone.

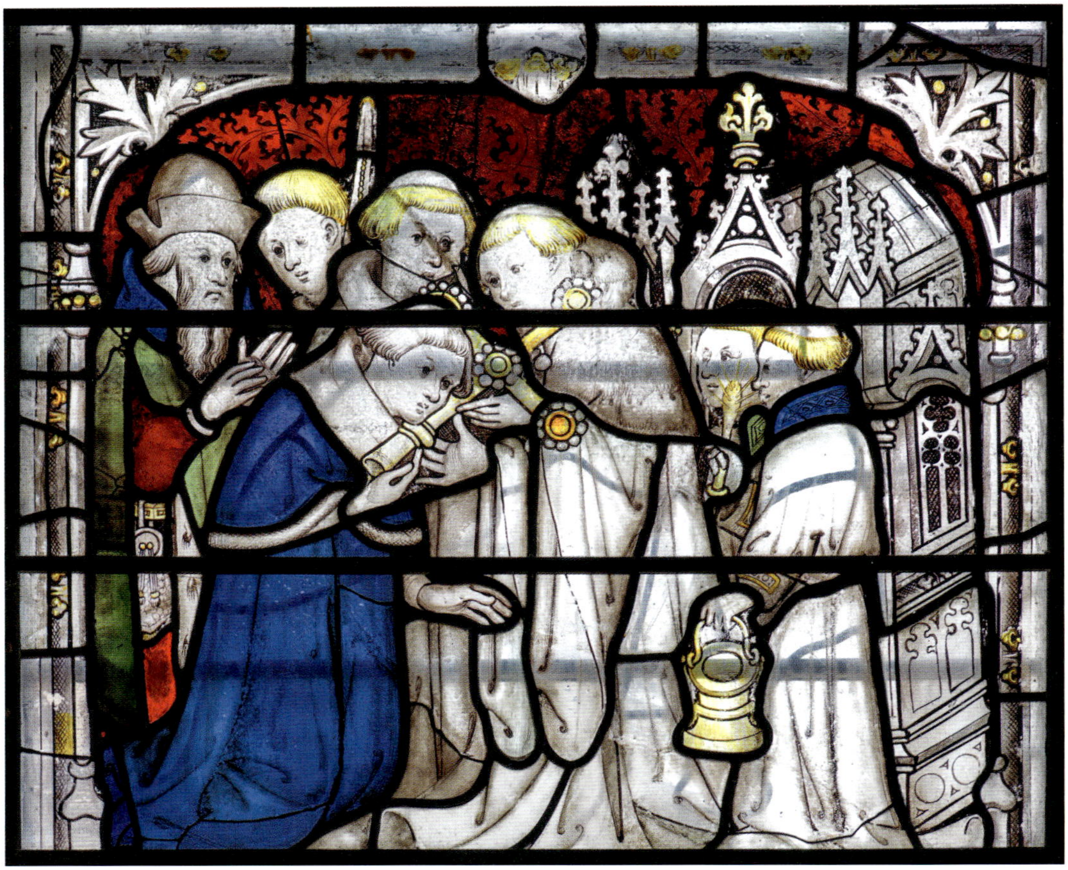

9d William is greeted at the entrance to the Minster by the clergy

William arrives at the Minster followed by the mayor with his long beard and his attendant sword-bearer. Two canons in choir robes welcome William, and one of them offers him a jewelled cross to kiss. Behind them stand two young acolytes, one of whom holds a holy water vessel and an aspergillum. It was customary in the fifteenth century for a new archbishop to be met by the Minster clergy at the west door, where he would be sprinkled with holy water and offered a cross to kiss, before entering the Minster for his enthronement.

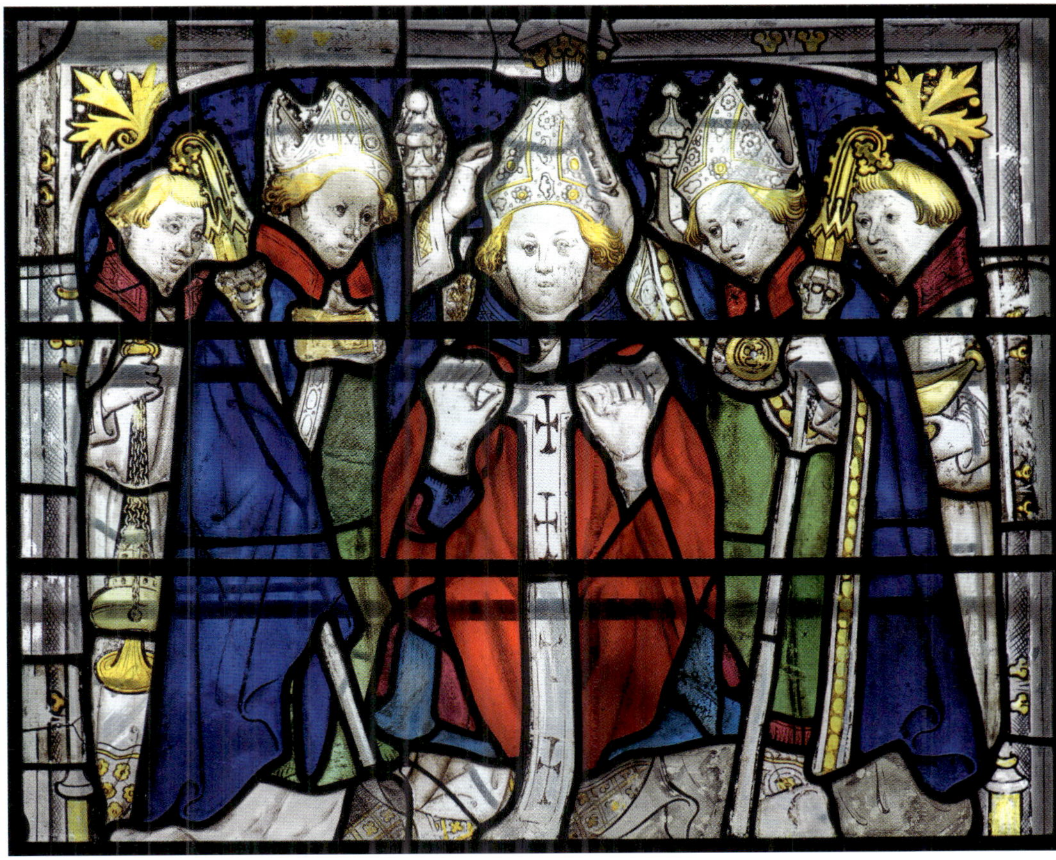

9e William is enthroned in the Minster

Wearing his pallium over his vestments for the first time in the Minster, William is enthroned by two bishops, who place his mitre on his head. The clergy on either side carry an ncense boat and a thurible.

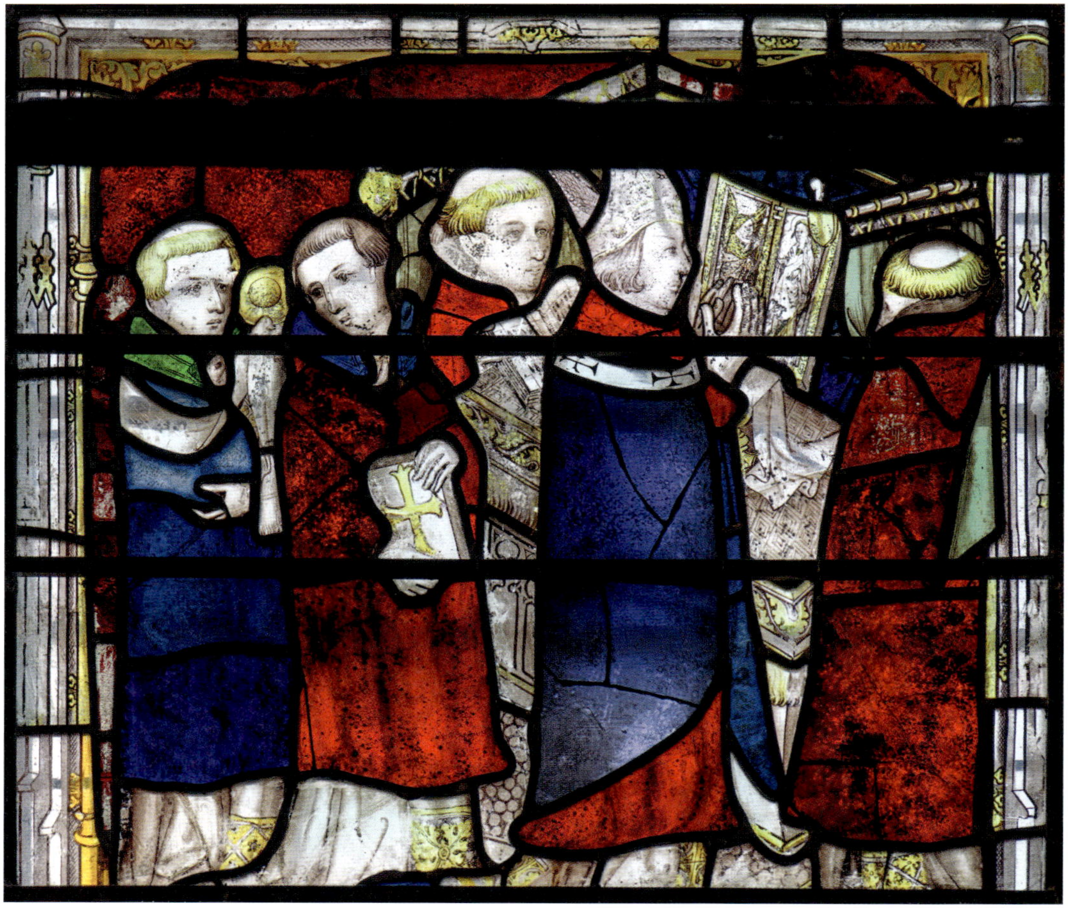

10a William celebrates Mass in the Minster on Trinity Sunday
Wearing his mitre and pallium, William celebrates high Mass in the Minster on Trinity Sunday. On the altar is a portable altarpiece with the Annunciation. Just visible below William's hands are a chalice and paten covered with a cloth. Two clerics stand at either end of the altar, the one to the left holding the missal open for William. Behind William are a deacon holding the Gospels and a subdeacon.

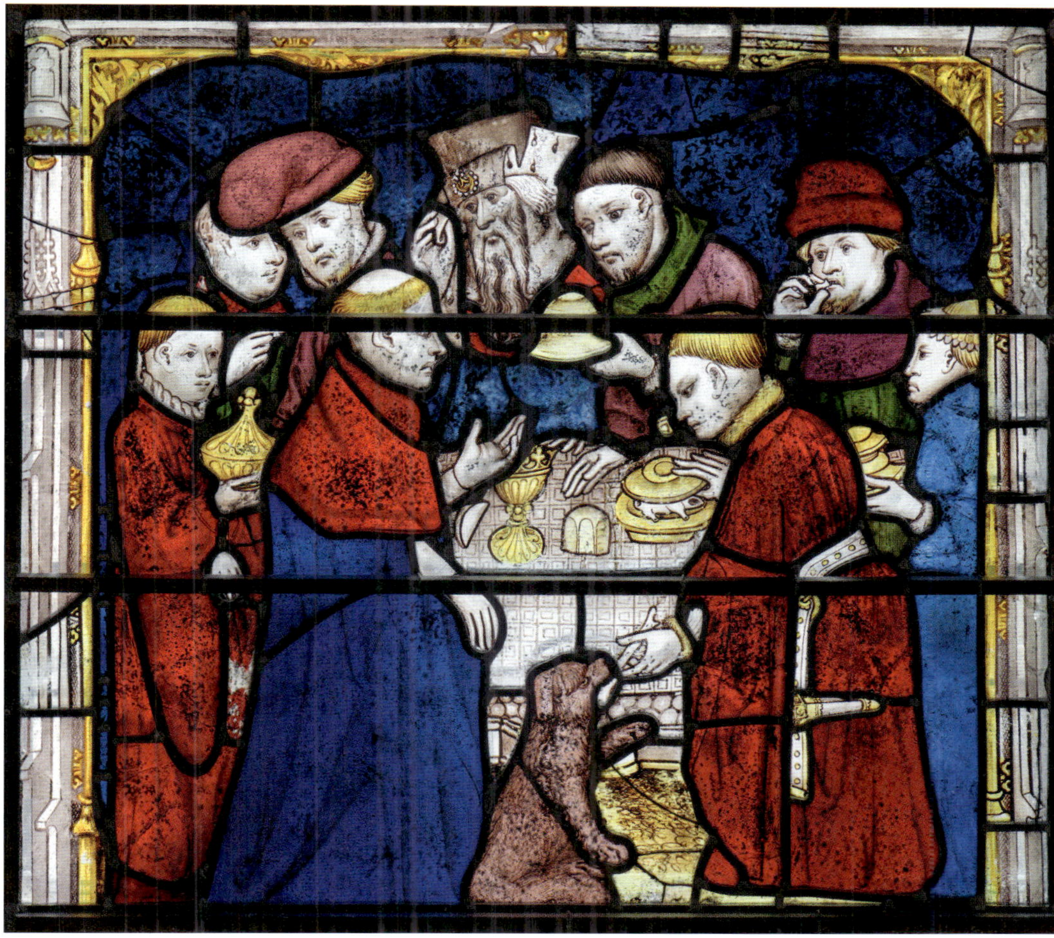

10b William welcomes his guests to a feast

After the service, William, standing centre-left having taken off his vestments, welcomes his guests to a feast in the archbishop's palace. The mayor, with the long beard, is seated in the middle, with other lay guests on either side. William orders the servants, who stand at either end, to serve the meal. In the foreground, a dog is being given a bone.

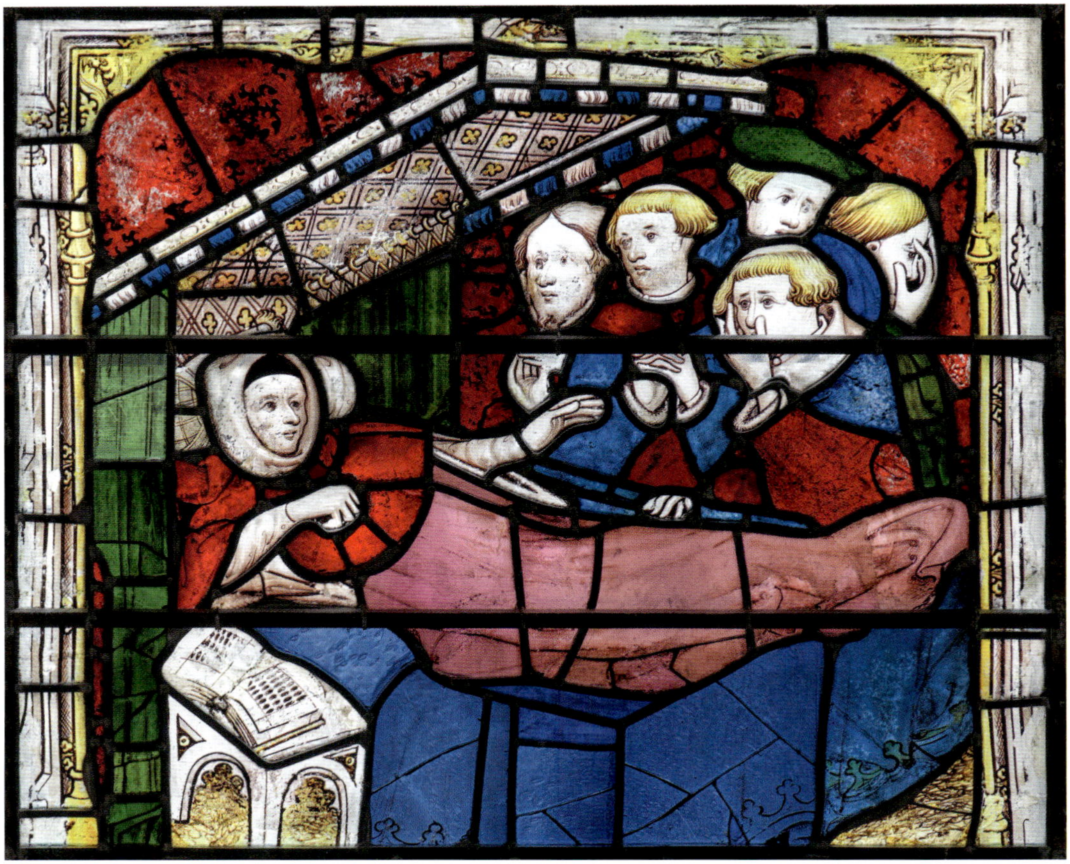

10c William takes to his bed and prophesies his death
Too ill to join the feast, William returns to his chamber, takes to his bed and prophesies his approaching death to members of his household. These include laymen as well as two clerics. They express their consternation and distress by their gestures.

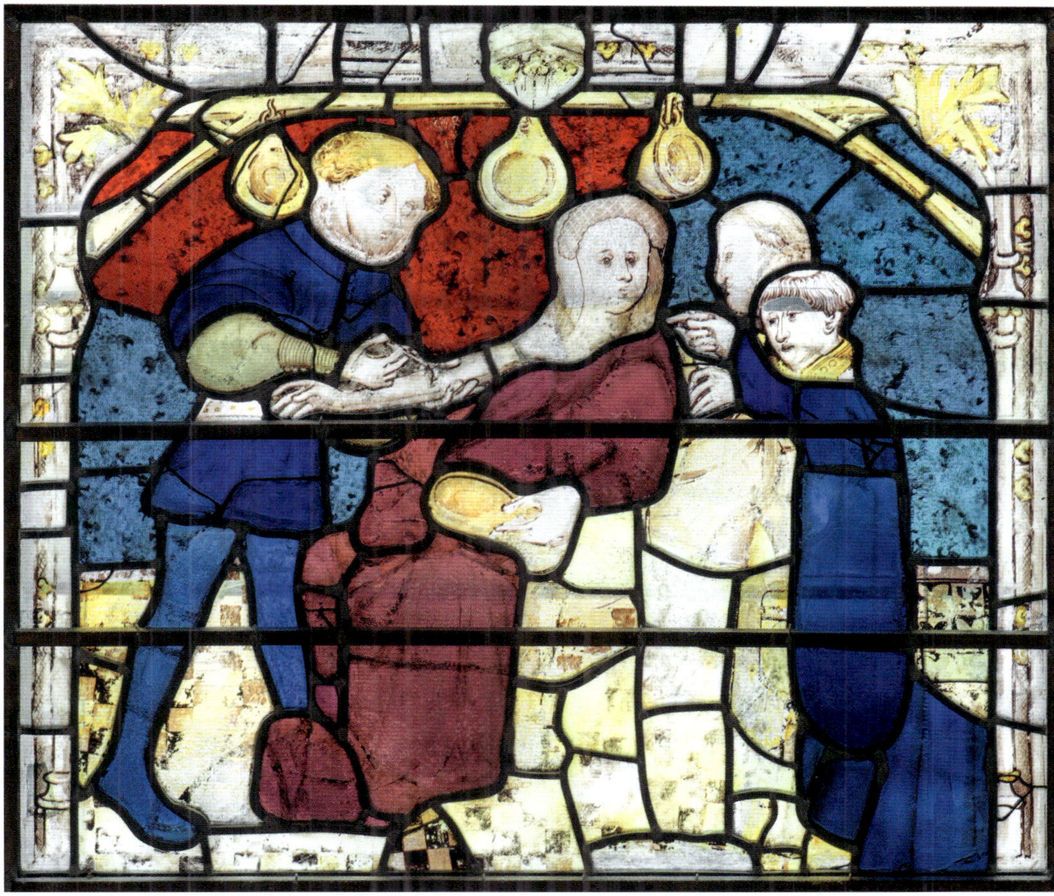

10d [Replacement panel for William during his final illness]

William lay on his sickbed for over a week. The original panel depicting this is lost but in about 1690 Torre recorded a scene similar to 10c showing an archbishop sick in bed, with a weeping figure clothed in white on either side. The present early-fifteenth-century panel, showing a woman being bled, was inserted into the St William Window in 1954, having been previously in the St Cuthbert Window. Although it does not belong, it is a not inappropriate stop-gap for the missing panel. Its original location has not yet been identified. The original panel would have had a Type F frame and a blue background.

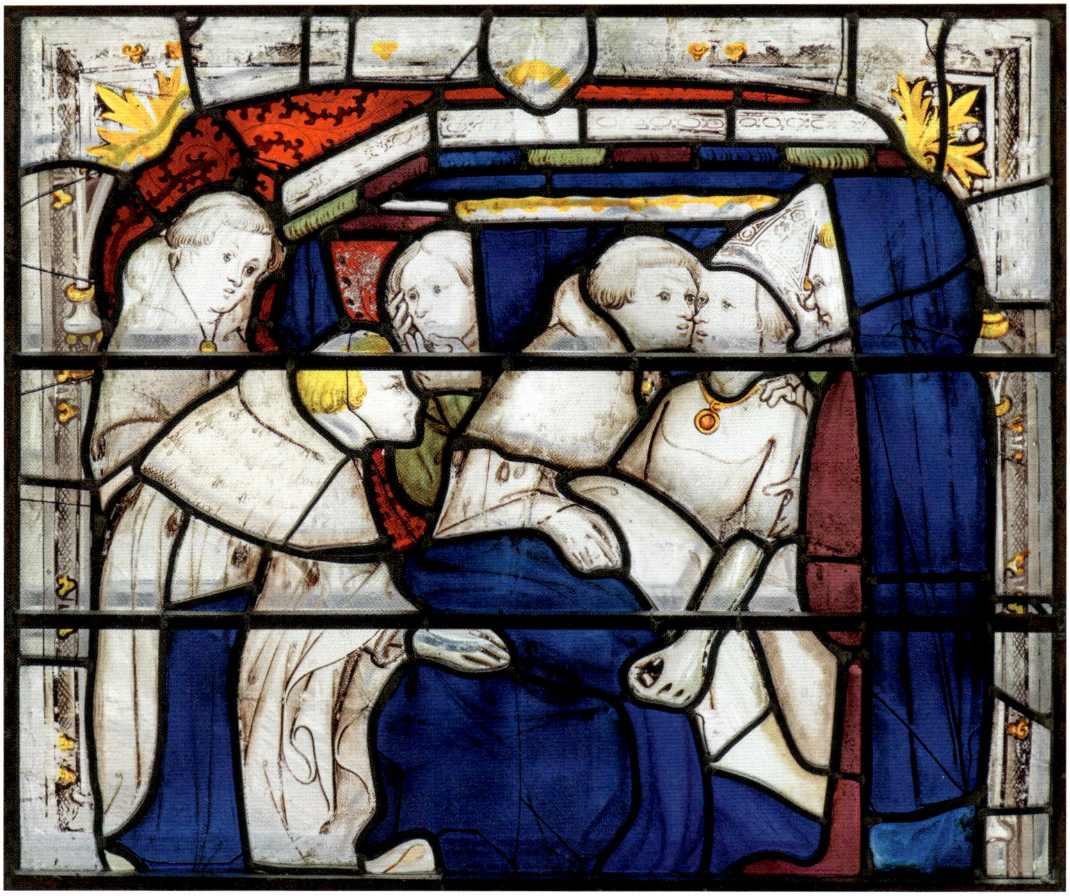

10e William's death

On the ninth day of his illness (8 June 1154), William, seeing that his end was near, said farewell to his brethren, and passed away. Propped up in a canopied bed by a half-concealed servant dressed in red, William, wearing his mitre, kisses one of the canons. Two other canons and another member of his household look on.

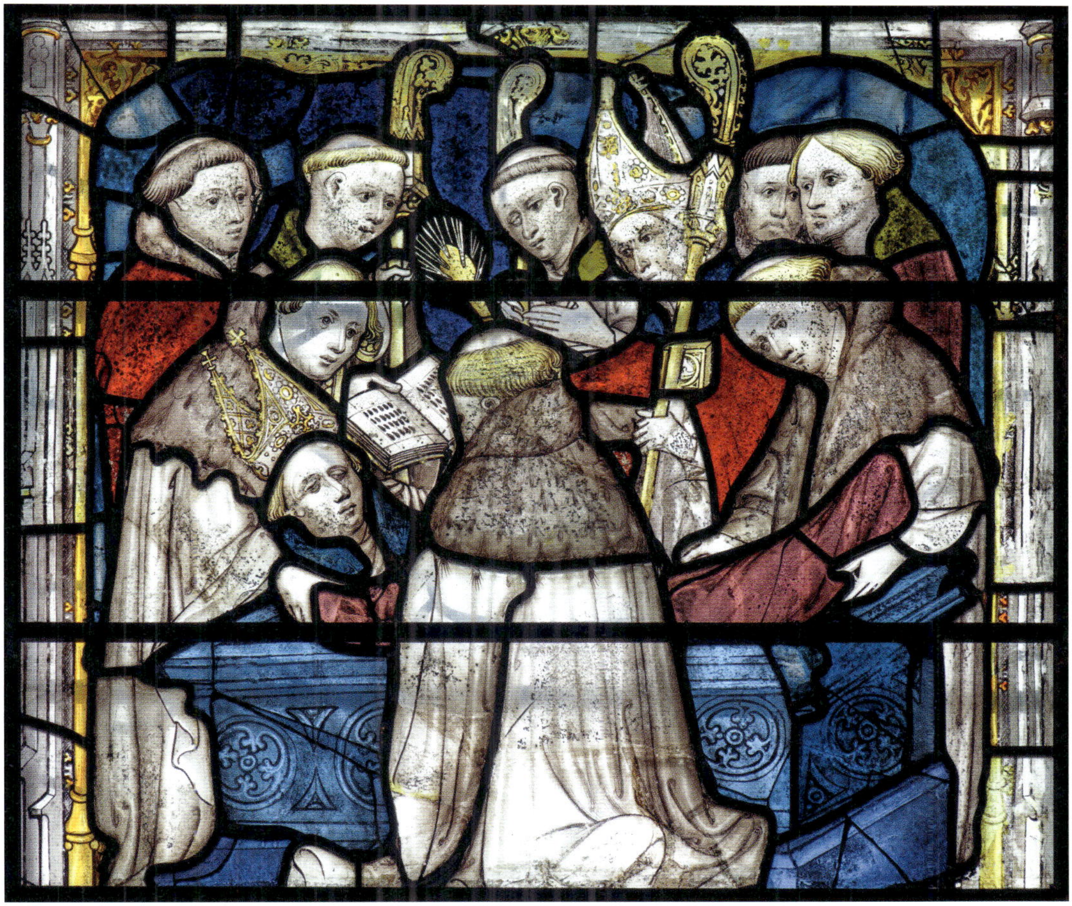

11a William's burial

William was buried in a reused Roman sarcophagus at the east end of the nave. Wrapped in a purple shroud and with his mitre on his head, William is laid to rest in an ornate blue sarcophagus by three kneeling canons, wearing white robes with ermine tippets. Behind stand (from left to right) another canon (in red), two abbots (with monastic tonsures and croziers), a bishop and two laymen. One of the abbots holds an open book, while the bishop stretches out his right arm to sprinkle holy water on the corpse. The aspergillum is visible between the two abbots.

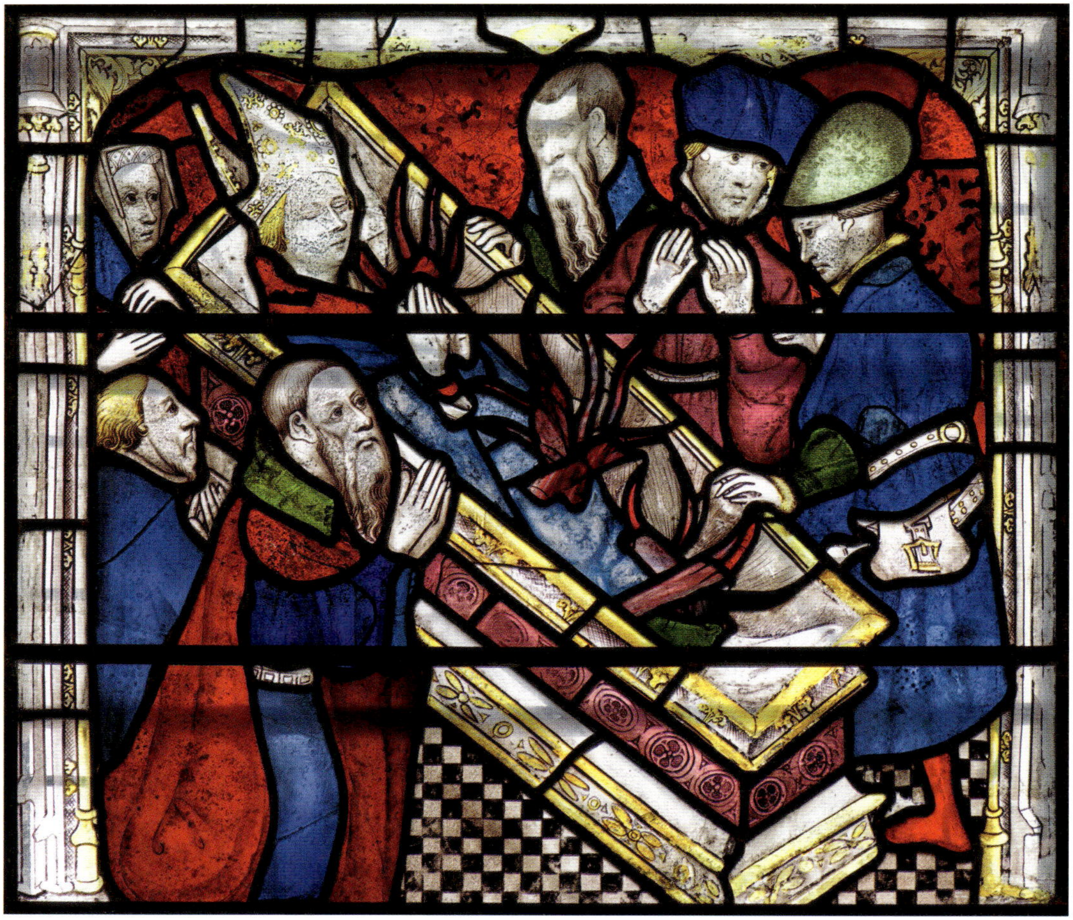

11b William's body unharmed during a fire in the Minster

Not long after William's death, a catastrophic fire broke out in the Minster and a huge timber fell on the sarcophagus (which stood proud of the floor) and broke the lid. Burning wood fell on William's body, but neither his vestments nor his body were harmed, to the astonishment of all. The panel shows William's body intact, with red flames rising from it in three places. The crowd of witnesses are all lay people, five men and one woman. This was the first of William's posthumous miracles, according to the *Life*.

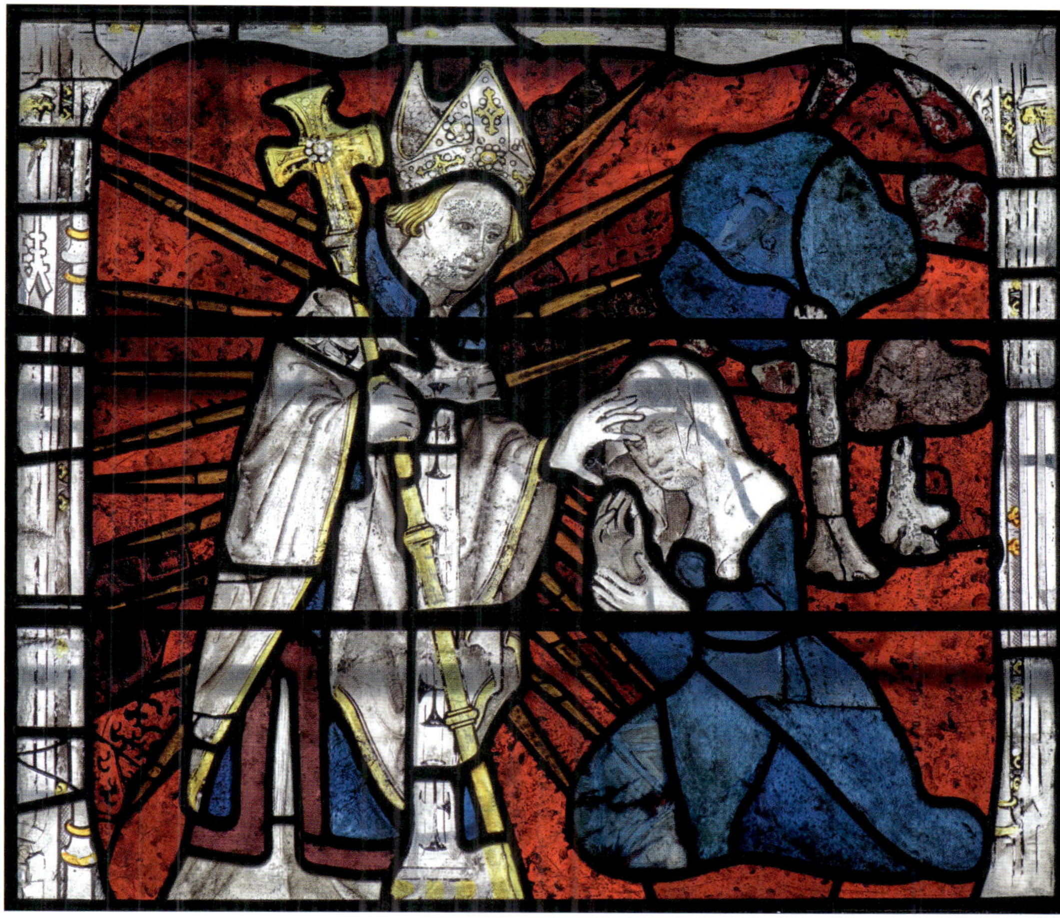

11c The healing of a blind girl

William's first healing miracle, which is dated to 1177, concerned a young girl who had been blind for seven years. During a vigil at William's tomb, she had a vision of a man, venerably attired and of dazzling brightness, who touched her eyes, and she regained her sight. The panel shows William in full archiepiscopal garb and holding his cross-staff, with rays of light emanating from him. In order to emphasise the visionary nature of the miracle, the figure of William dominates the scene and the tomb is not shown.

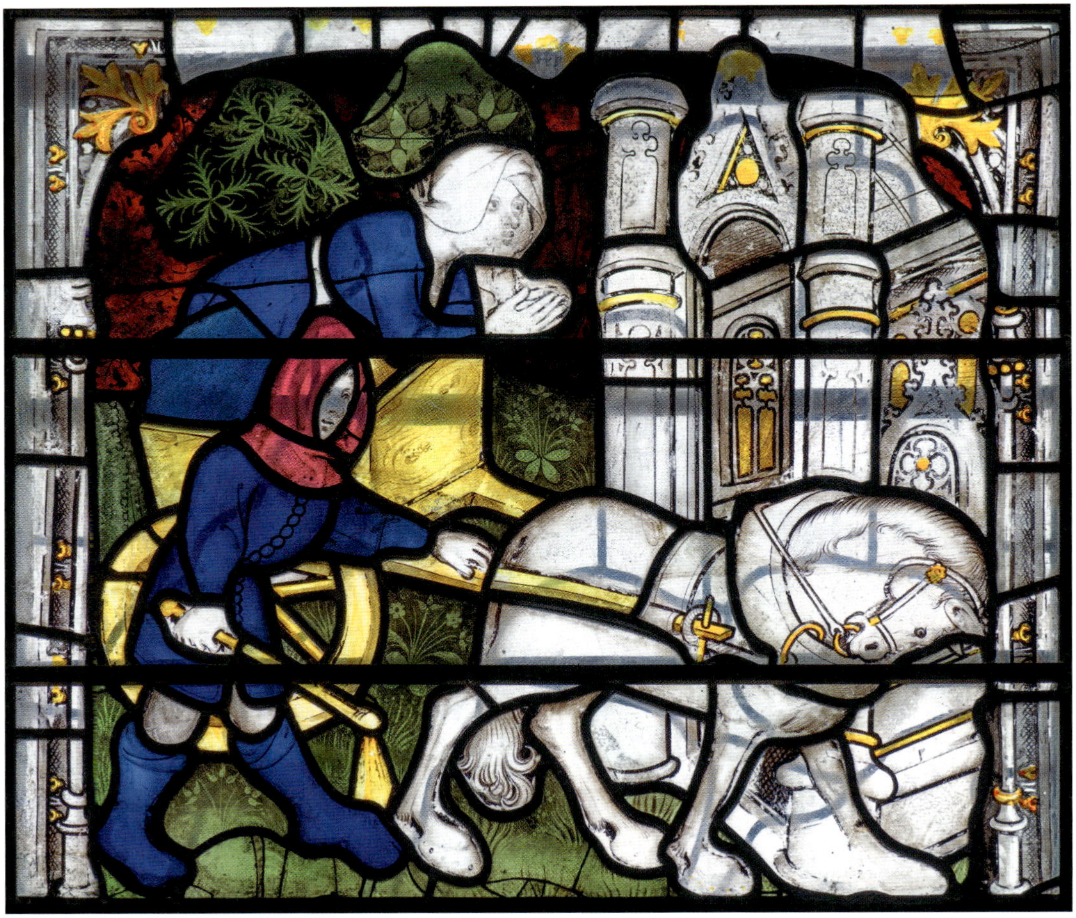

11d A hydropsical woman is brought to the Minster

The second healing miracle recorded in the *Life* is spread over two adjacent panels, 11d and 11e. A hydropsical woman with grossly swollen body and limbs is brought to the Minster in a cart, where she was deposited with great difficulty before being taken to the tomb. The Minster is depicted rather as it is in panel 9d.

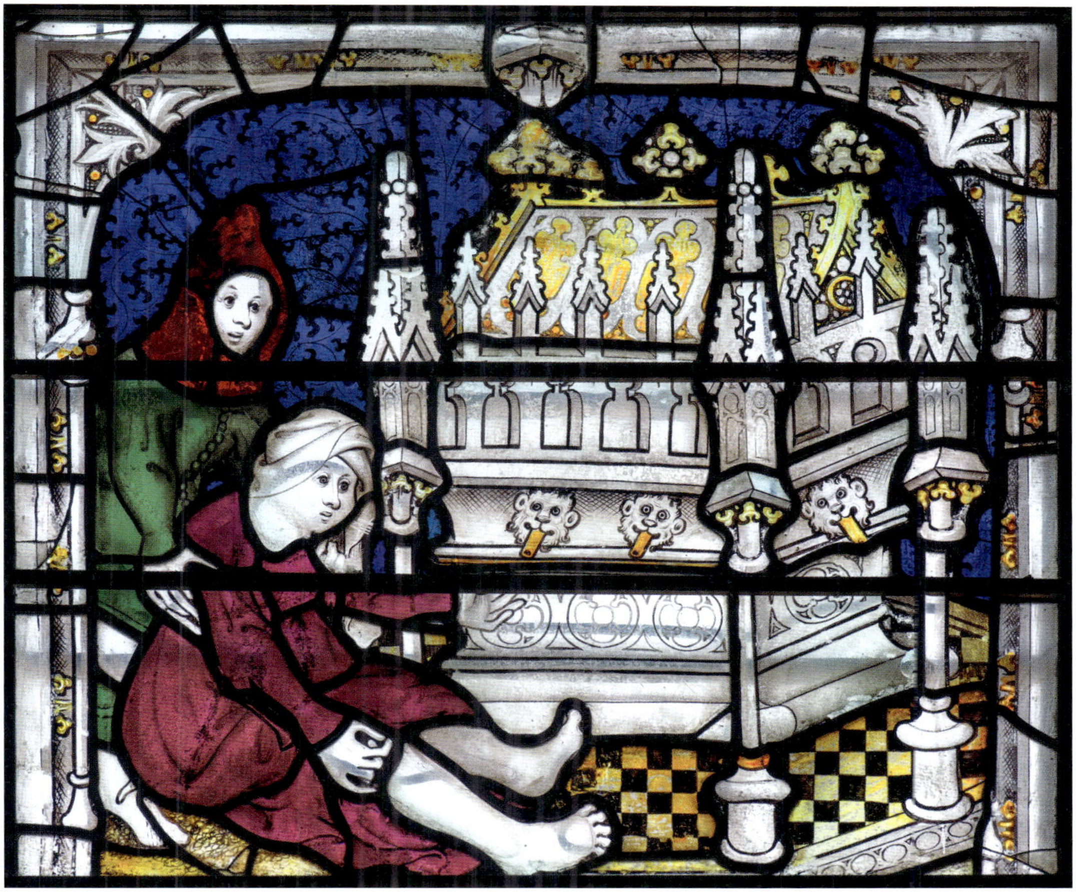

11e The hydropsical woman is cured at the tomb

This concludes the story begun in panel 11d. At the tomb, helped by the man who brought her in the cart, the woman anoints herself with oil emanating from the tomb. She stretches out her hand towards one of the pipes emerging from the mouths of lions from which the oil seeped, as can be seen in panel 15b. Once recovered, she was lighter and stronger than she had been before the illness. From now on, the tomb is always represented as an elaborate gabled and pinnacled shrine.

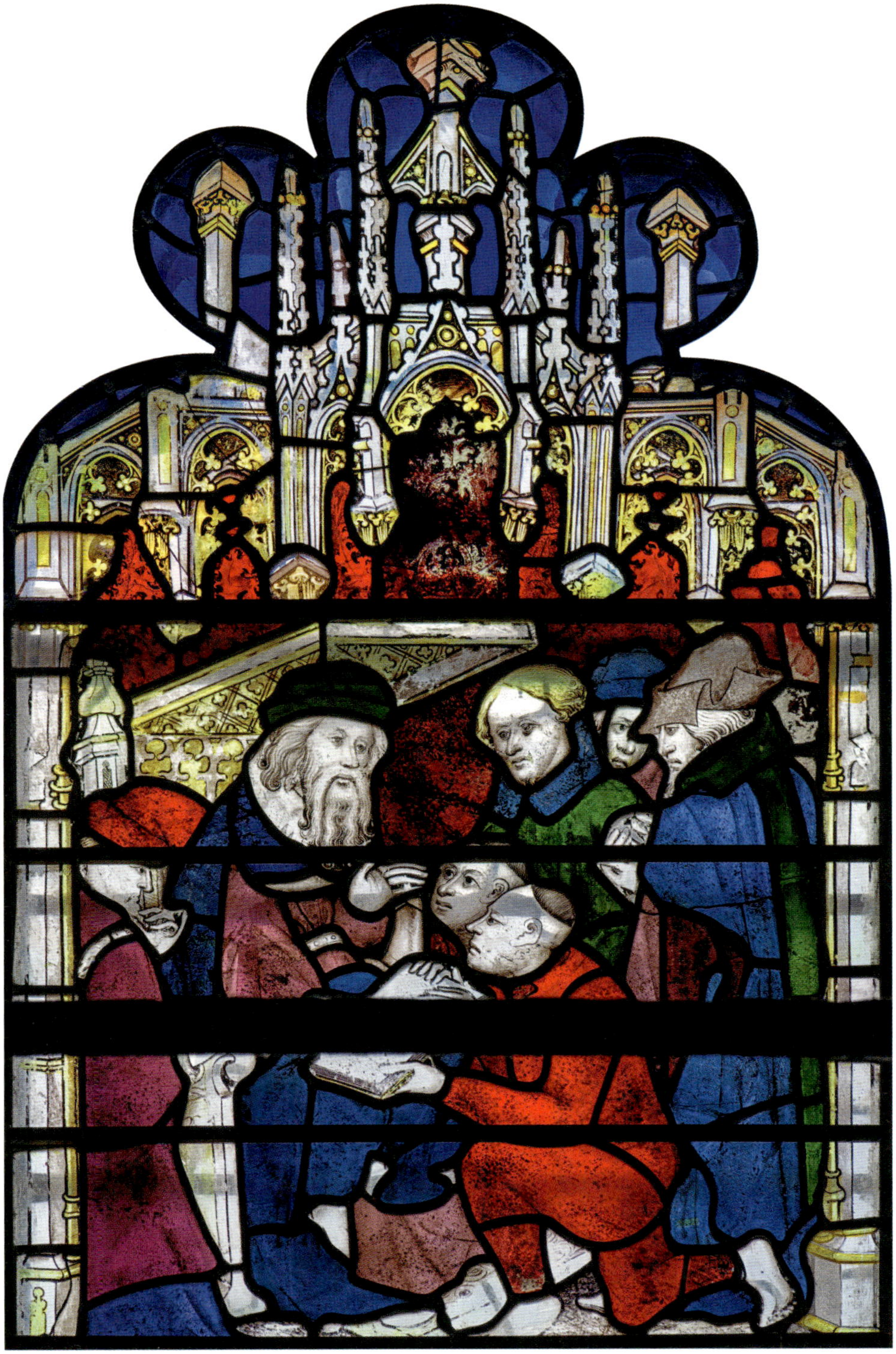

12a–13a Ralph and Besing appear before a judge

The story of Ralph and Besing is spread over the whole of row 12. An innocent man called Ralph was unjustly accused of arson by a jealous neighbour named Besing. The case was to be decided through trial by combat. The two men kneel before the judge, placing their hands on an open book to swear an oath, while officials and bystanders look on.

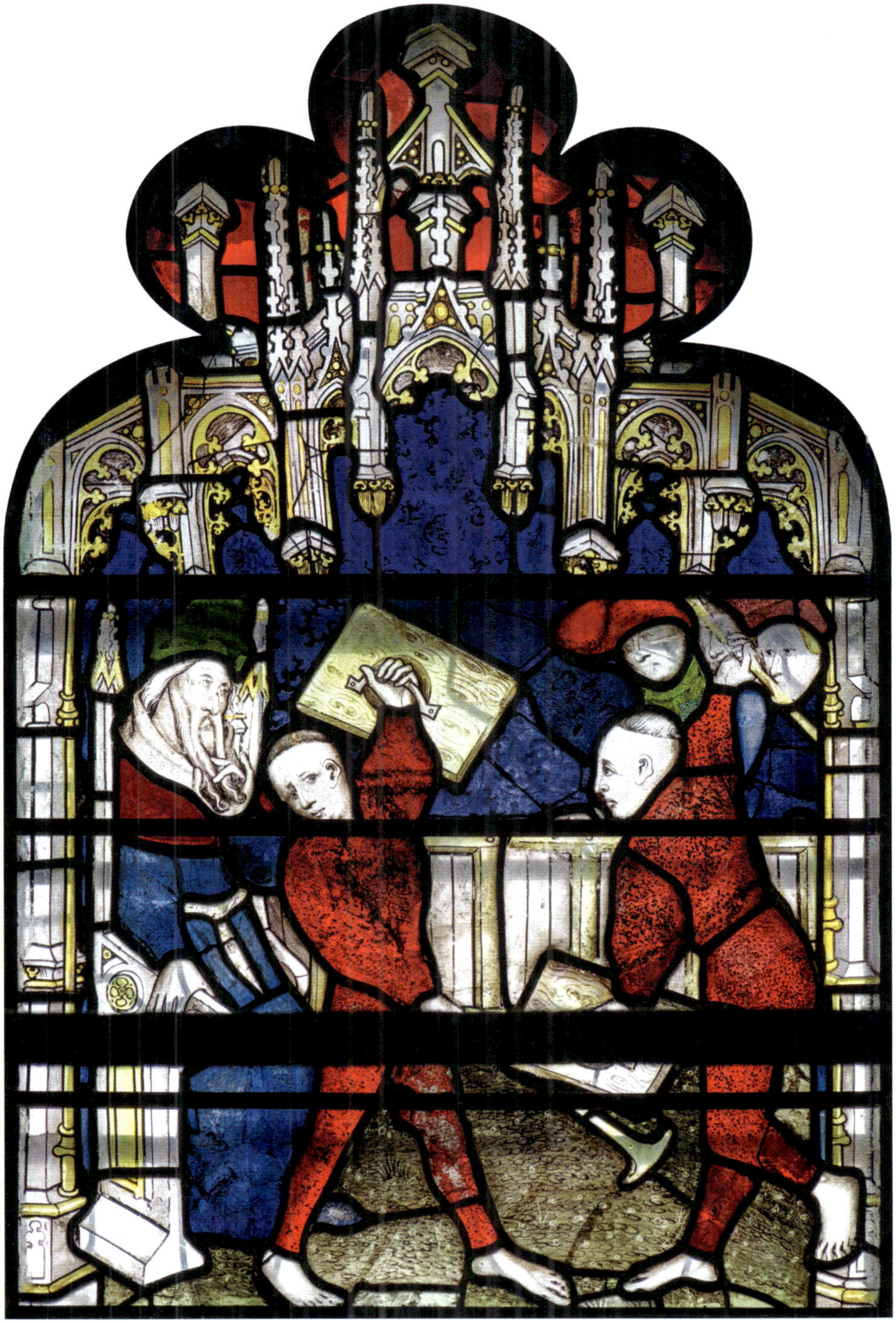

12b–13b Ralph and Besing fight

Watched by the judge, Ralph and Besing fight. They wear red combat suits and are equipped with identical rectangular wooden shields and duelling weapons like pick-axes with short, sharply pointed heads. The duel takes place outside, and spectators look on from behind a barrier.

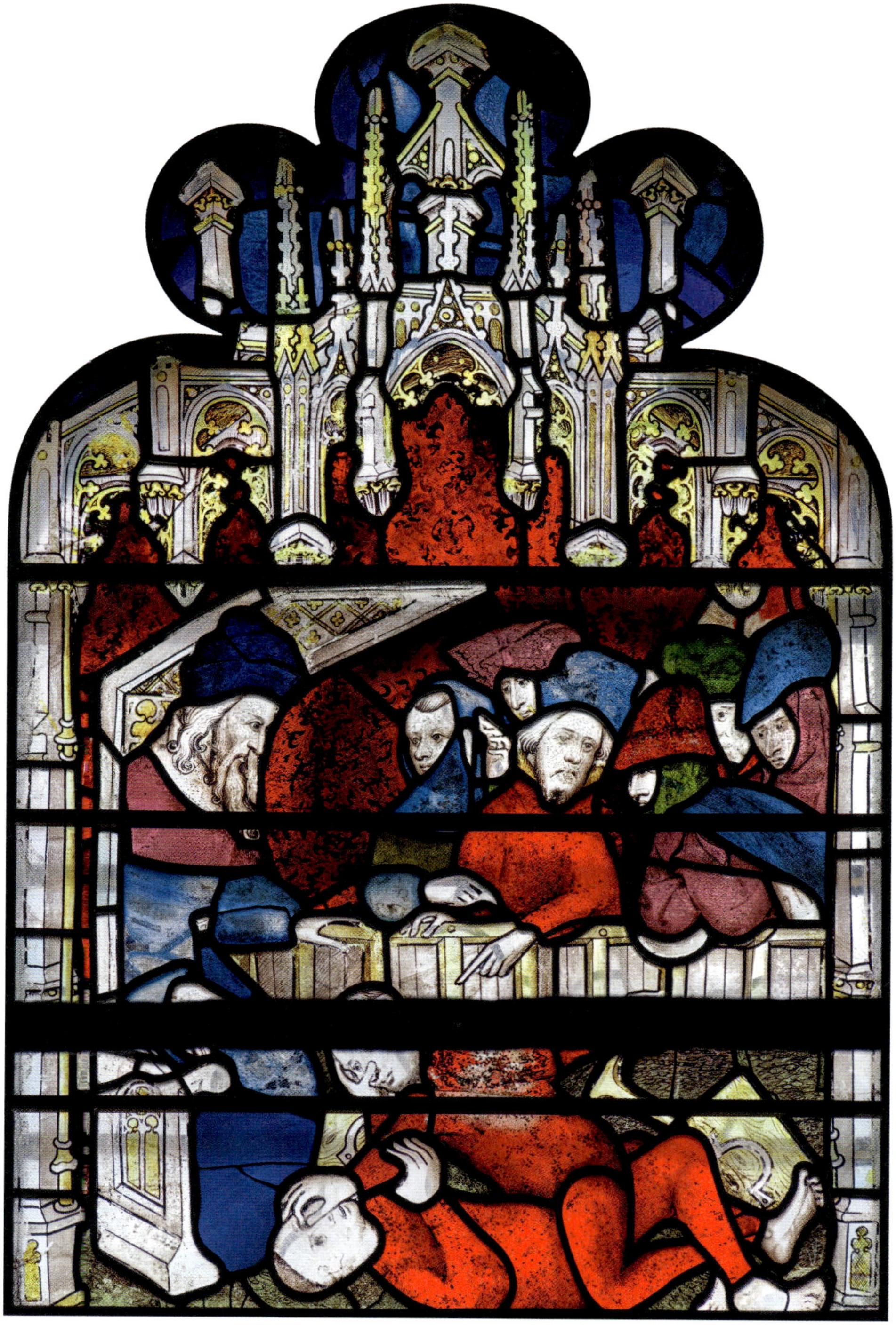

12c–13c Ralph is blinded by Besing

Still under the eye of the judge and watched by the crowd, the two men wrestle on the ground, their weapons discarded. Ralph tries to fend Besing off, but Besing plucks out Ralph's left eye with his right hand. In his left hand (obscured by the glazing bar) he already holds Ralph's right eye. The spectator in the middle points at the horrific conclusion to the duel.

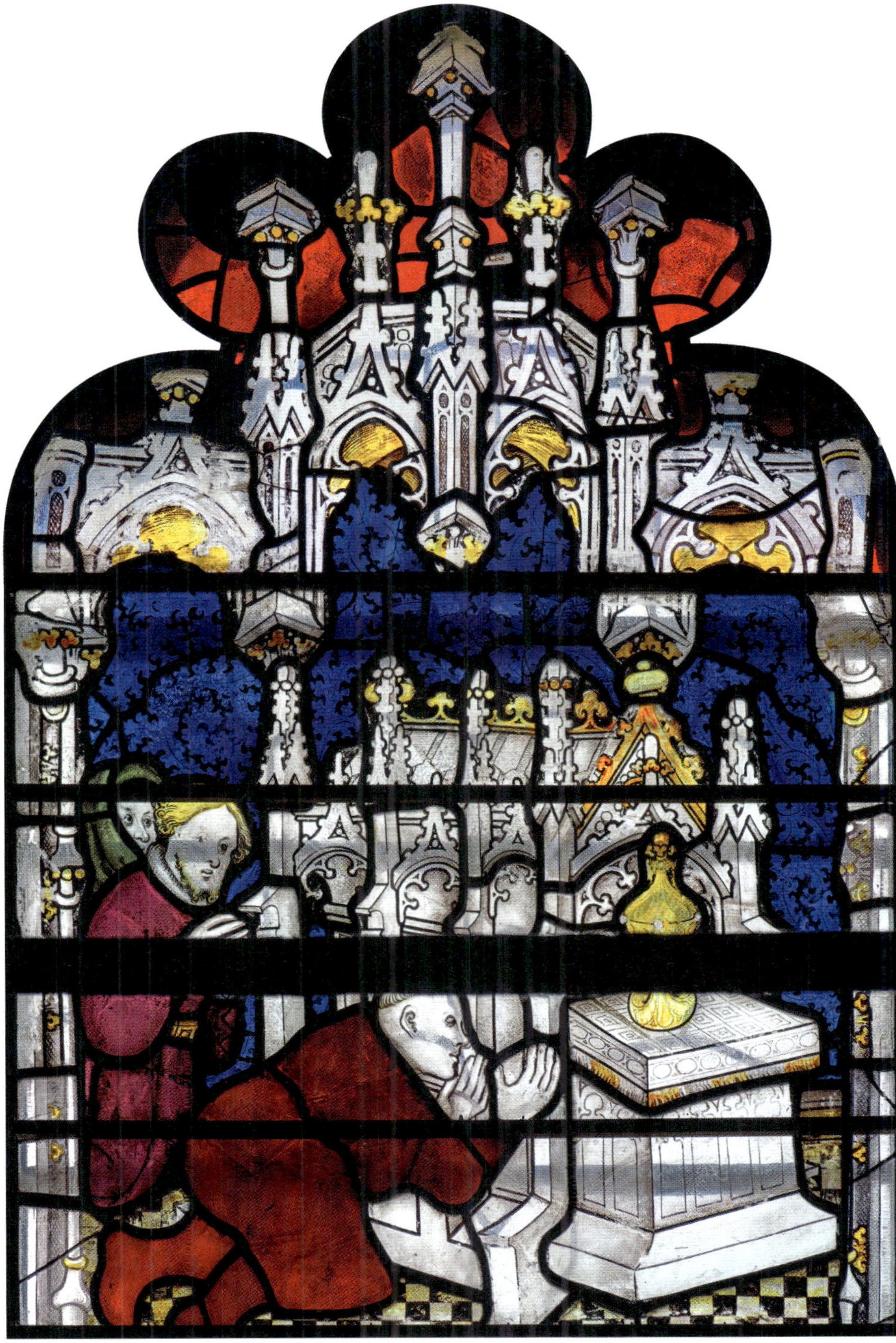

12d–13d Ralph prays at St William's tomb
Still in his red suit, the blinded Ralph prays at the tomb of St William, accompanied by two laymen. The small altar that stood at one end of the tomb is clearly depicted.

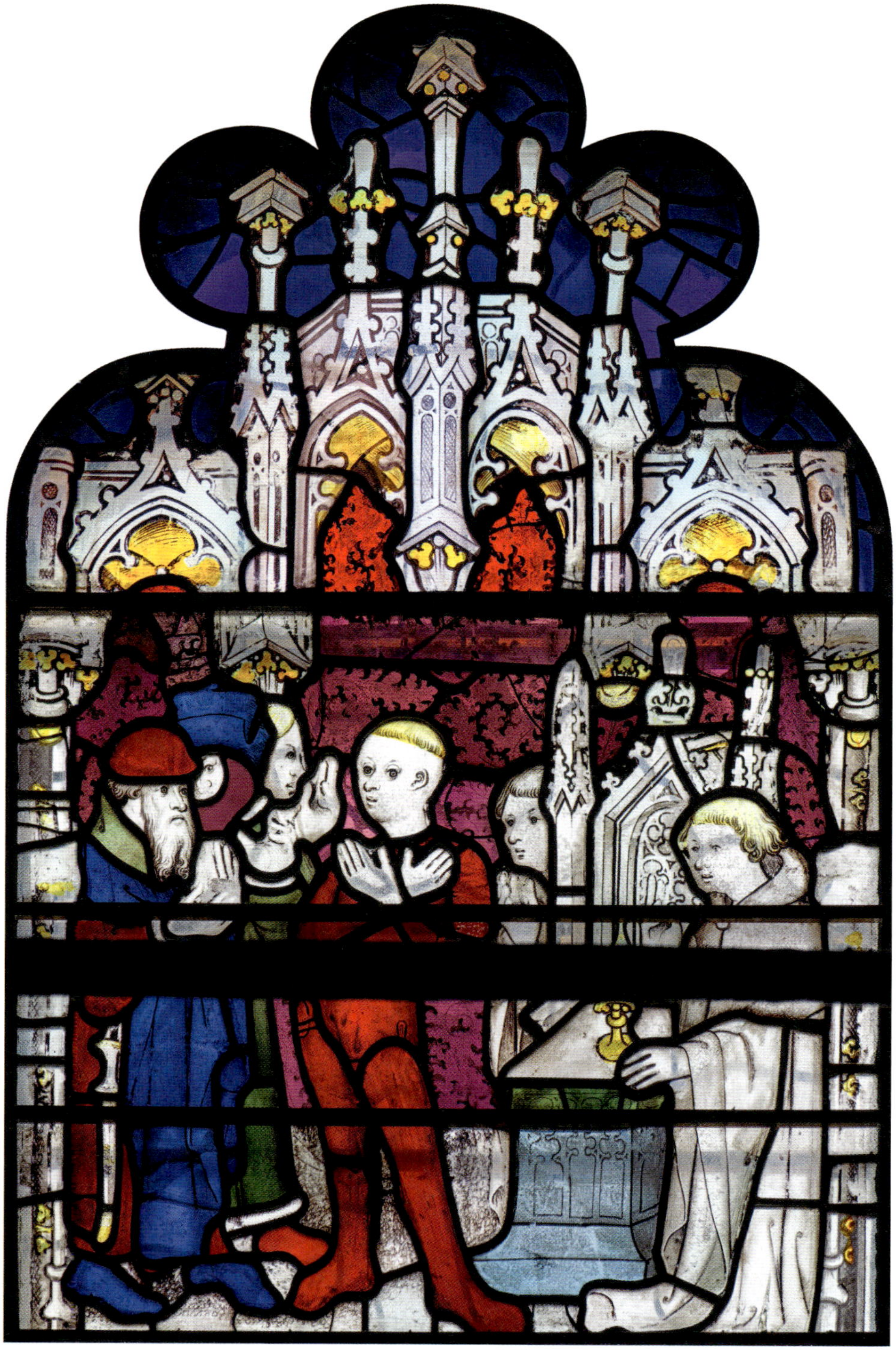

12e–13e Ralph is given new eyes

Ralph's prayers are answered and he is given new eyes, which, according to the *Life*, were smaller than his old ones and of a different colour, but gave him clear, sharp sight. Ralph stands in the centre with his hands crossed on his chest. His eyes are given special emphasis. Two Minster clergy standing by the tomb witness the miracle, and the onlookers register their amazement. This concludes the second section of the window.

Rows 14–19

The third section has just four rows of narrative scenes (rows 15-18). Row 14 is almost totally obscured from floor level by the stonework of the projecting transom beneath it. It never contained any narrative scenes, and it is currently glazed with plain glass incorporating quarries recording the names of the donors to the most recent restoration. It is not illustrated here.

Rows 15–17 contain miracle scenes. Panels 17a and 17b are a pair illustrating the story of a woman who swallowed a frog. All the other miracles are complete in a single panel. The majority of them take place at William's tomb, but they also include a boy drowned in a well (15c), a man thrown from a horse (17d), a ship saved in a storm (16e) and a girl saved from drowning (17e). The majority of these miracles are recounted in the early-thirteenth-century Latin *Life* and can be dated to between 1177 and *c*.1220, prior to William's formal canonisation by the pope.

In row 18 the subject matter changes. Panel 18a depicts William's papal canonisation in 1226. The narrative then jumps forward to 1283–4 and the events surrounding the Translation of William's relics. The rest of row 18 depicts an episode involving King Edward I. While on campaign in Wales in 1283, he and Queen Eleanor of Castile are invited to the Translation ceremony (18b). He then falls from a mountain (18c), gives thanks to William for his deliverance (18d), and the section ends with him and Queen Eleanor hastening to York to attend the Translation ceremony (18e).

Rows 15–17 have the same frames as rows 7–11: Type B on the left and Type F on the right. In rows 18–19 lights a and b have the same frames as panels 5–6a to 5–6c (Type D), though the cusping in row 19 is of a slightly different shape from row 6. Panels 18c–18e, like panels 12d and 12e, were originally made with Type F frames, but were altered to make them open-topped panels supporting Type J canopies in the cusped panels 19c–19e.

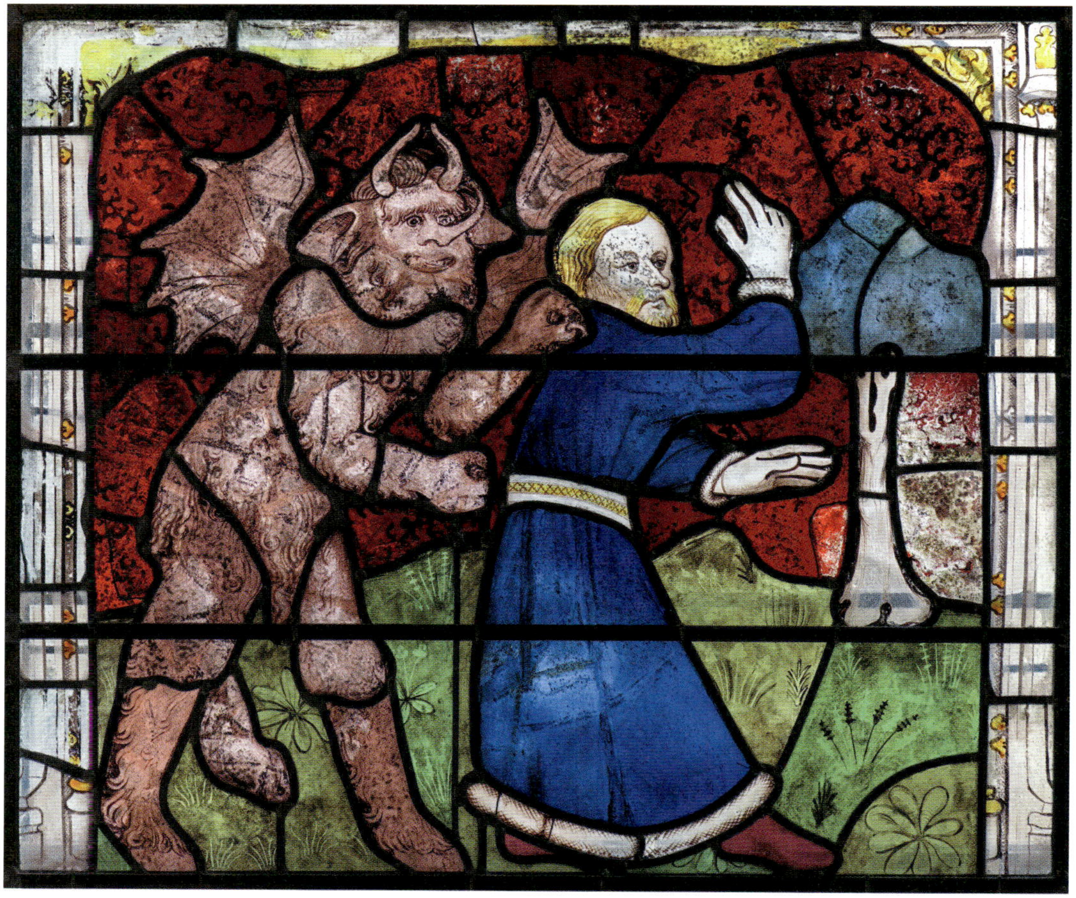

15a A man attacked by a devil
A man out for a walk is attacked from behind by a devil. The devil has wings and a tail and is covered in hair. He has two horns, large ears and a long, upturned nose. He is the only devil in the window. This episode does not feature in the extant Latin texts and its interpretation is uncertain.

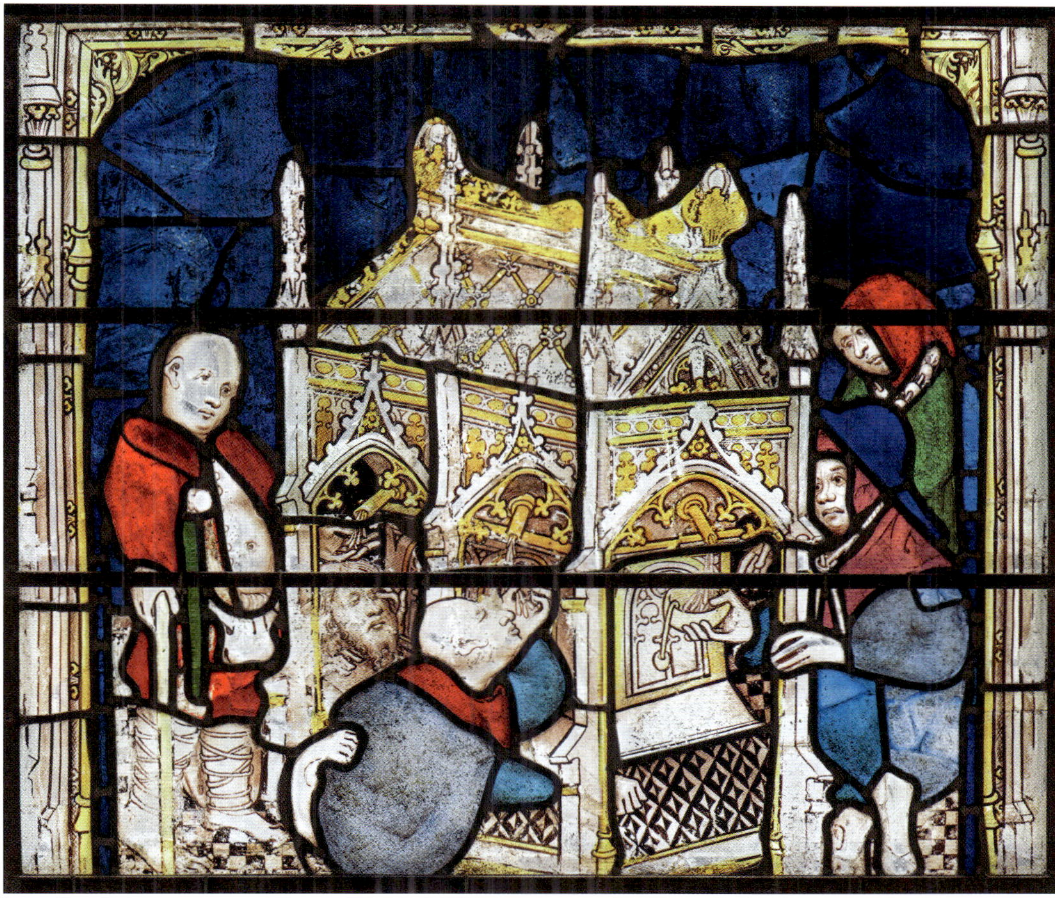

15b Disabled men collect holy oil seeping from the tomb
Five men with disabilities of various kinds stand or kneel around the tomb and collect oil, which issues from it. This panel seems to be a conflation of various different reports of holy oil issuing from the tomb and disabled people being cured there. To the left, a man with a swollen belly and swollen, bandaged legs stands with a crutch. The figure in the middle is unable to stand because of his contorted limbs and body. The shorter figure standing on the right with stumpy legs enclosed in some sort of strapping is probably a double amputee.

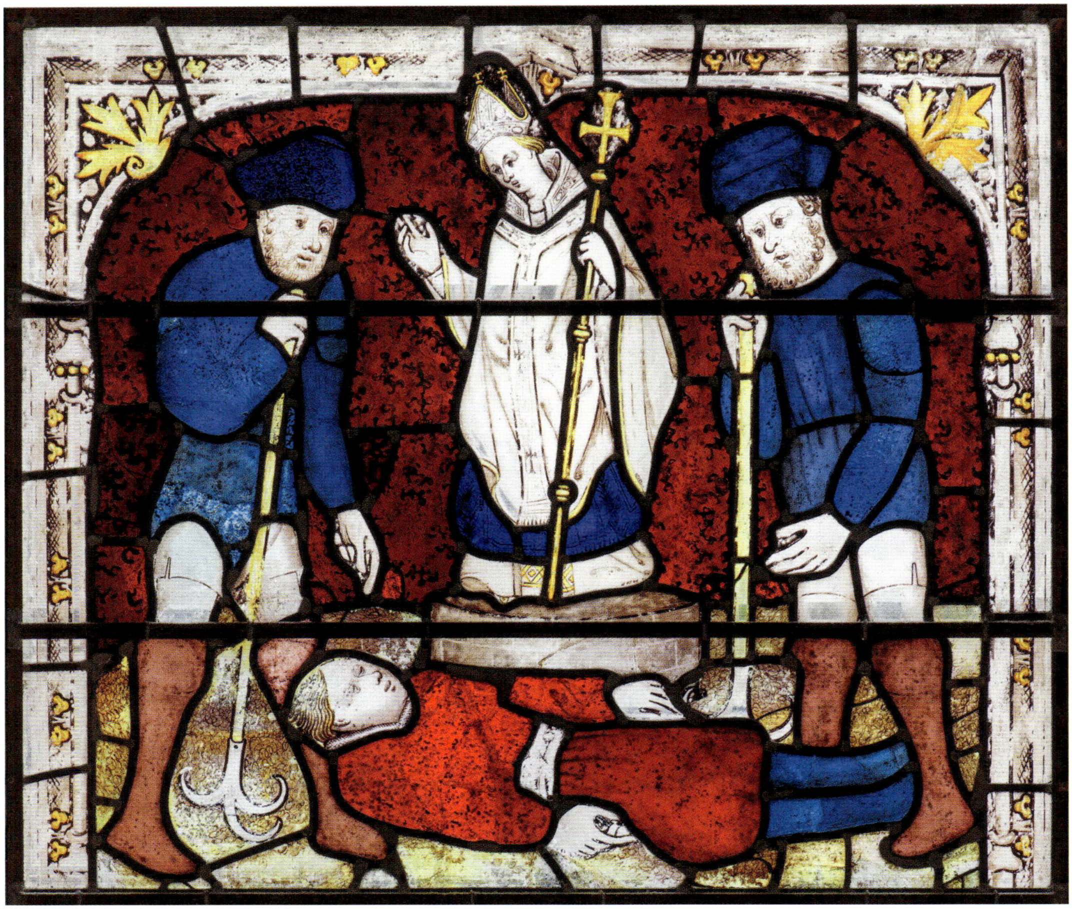

15c A boy drowned in a well is revived by St William

This panel was badly damaged and the upper part is largely a restoration. It depicts the story of a boy who fell into a well and was drowned. He was fished out dead and was restored to life by St William in response to his mother's prayers. The men who rescued the boy hold large grappling hooks, but the mother is not represented. In the centre St William appears in a vision above the circular well-head.

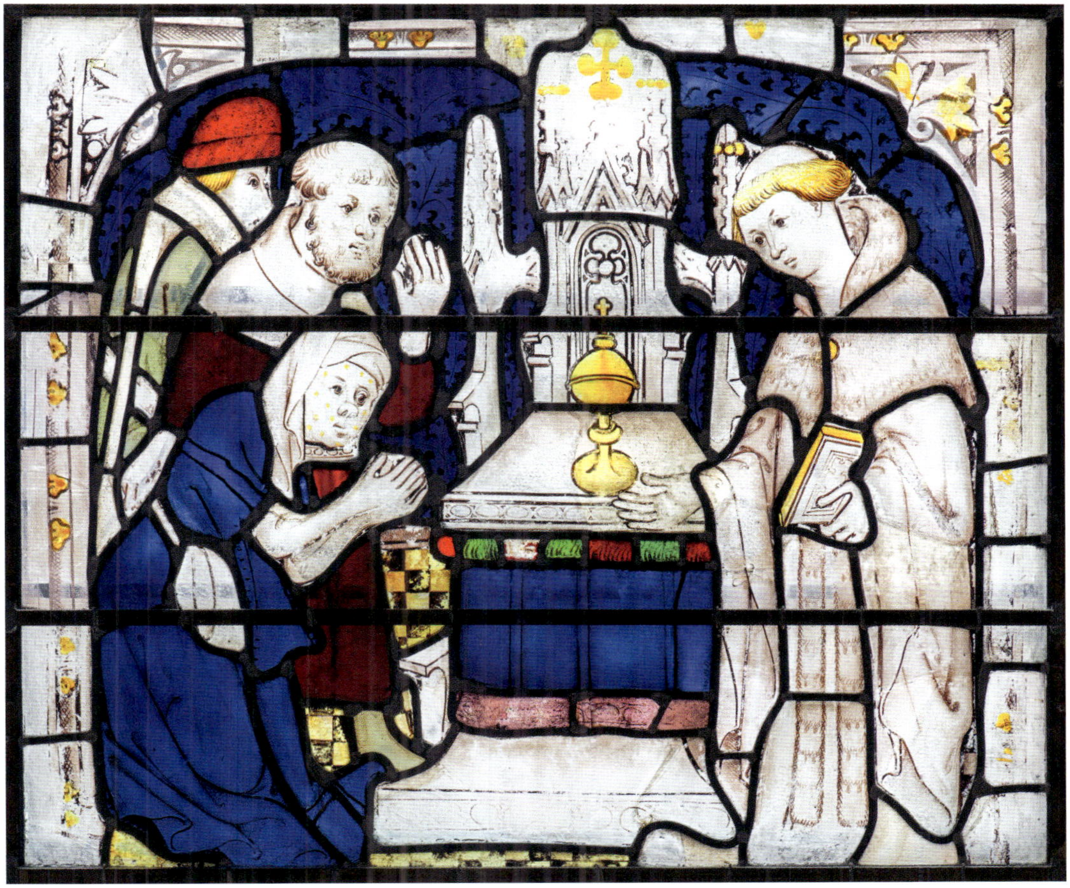

15d A woman with leprosy comes to the tomb to be healed

This panel depicts the story of a woman who was so badly afflicted by leprosy that she was unable to appear in public and was estranged from her husband. Kneeling in prayer at the tomb, she reveals her scarred nose, blotchy face and withered arms. Her husband, robed in red, stands behind her and places his hand on her back, presenting her to the priest at the tomb. The tomb is shown in an unusual end-on view, with the altar in front of it.

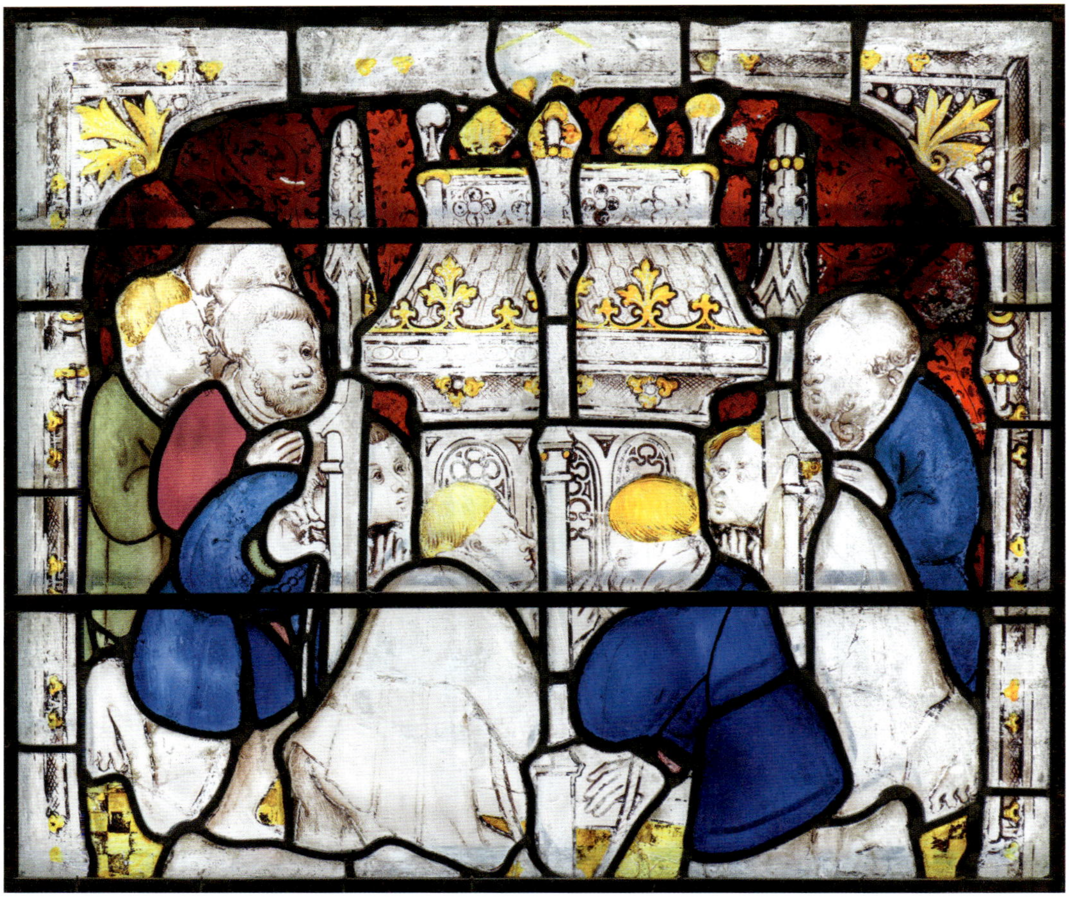

15e Eight one-eyed men at the tomb

The *Life* tells of eight one-eyed men who were healed at the tomb. In this panel a group of eight men gather round the tomb. All of them have a rope round their necks. The figure in blue on the left has a white rope hanging down in front of him, and the two in the centre are joined together by a rope that hangs down in a loop between them, showing that they are linked together. Although there is some paint loss on their faces, some of the men are definitely shown with one eye, whereas the kneeling figure on the left has already had his sight restored, as both eyes are visible.

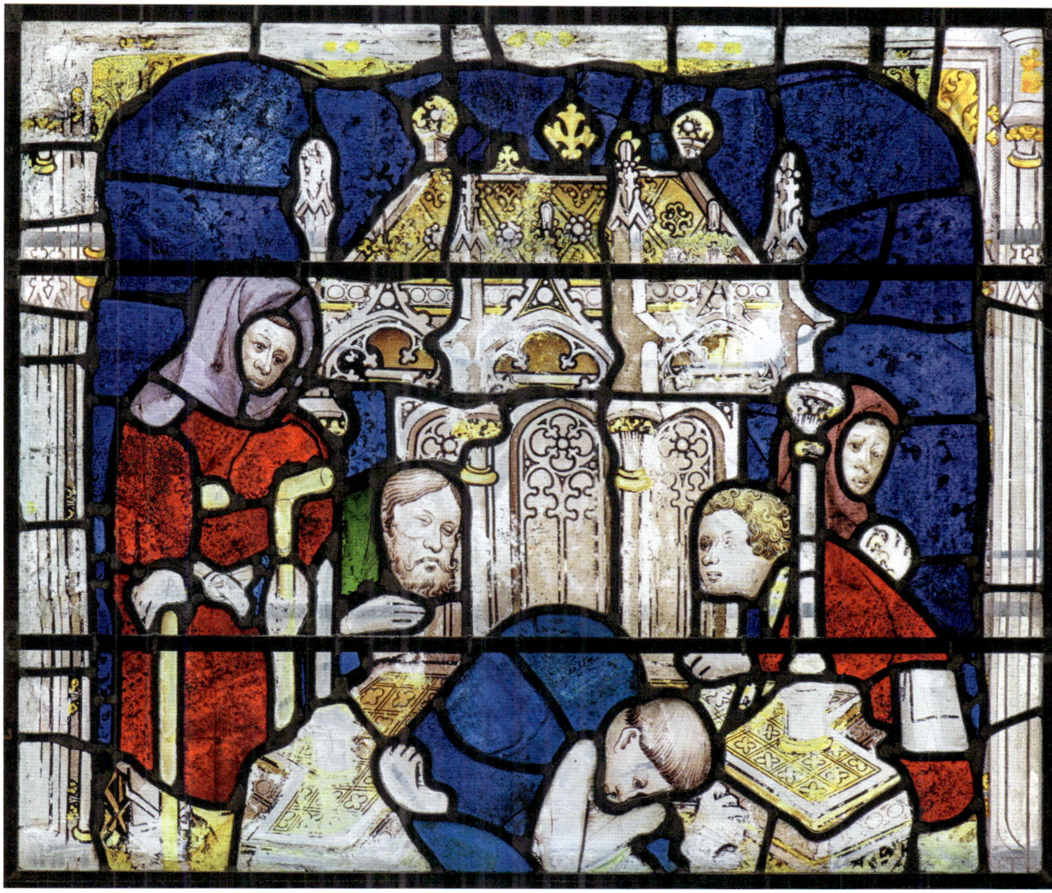

16a Five disabled men come to the tomb to be healed

As in panel 15b, five men with various afflictions gather round the tomb, but this time no holy oil is emerging from it. The man on the left supports himself with crutches and has a bandaged leg. The central figure s probably the man mentioned in the *Life* whose body was contracted into a ball and who was unable to lift his eyes from the floor. Another miracle story mentions a man with two crutches being healed at the tomb.

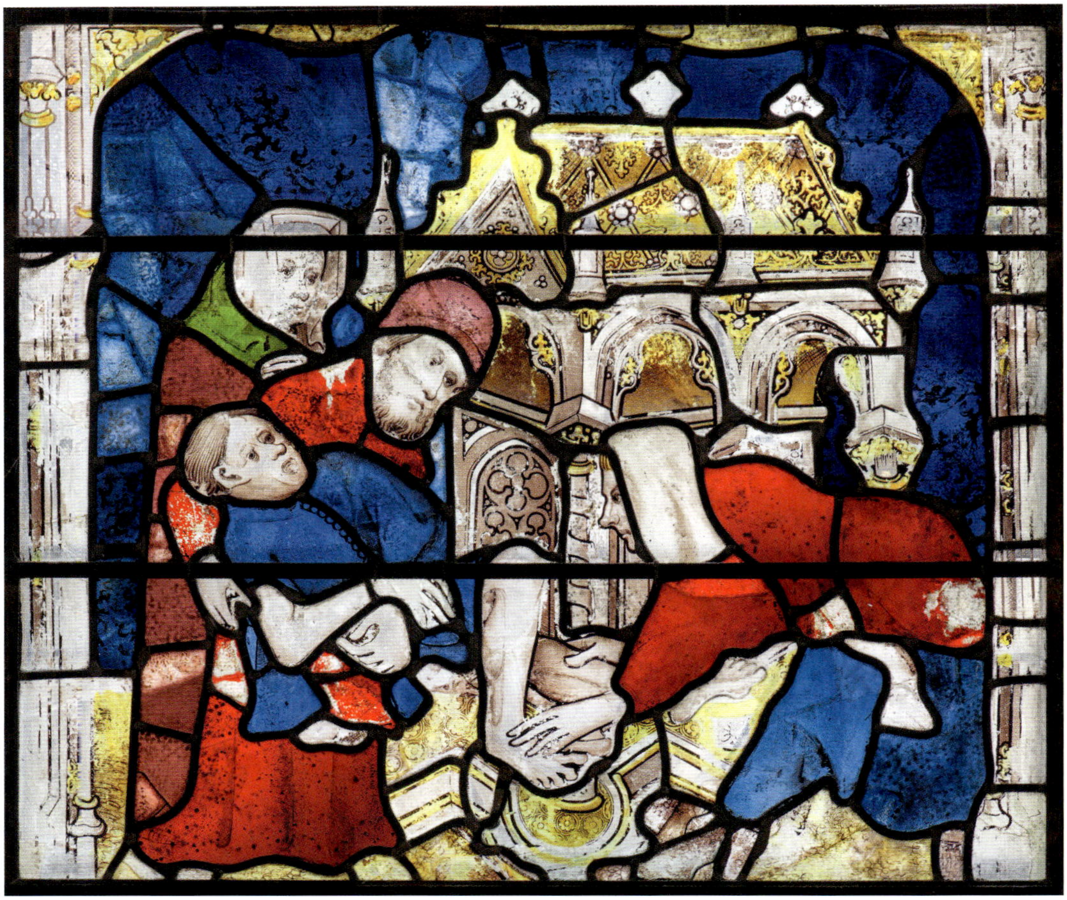

16b A paralysed man is brought to the tomb

The *Life* recounts how a man who was totally paralysed was carried to the tomb by his family, and was cured. The man on the left supports the sick man, while the figure on the right starts to relax his stiffened legs.

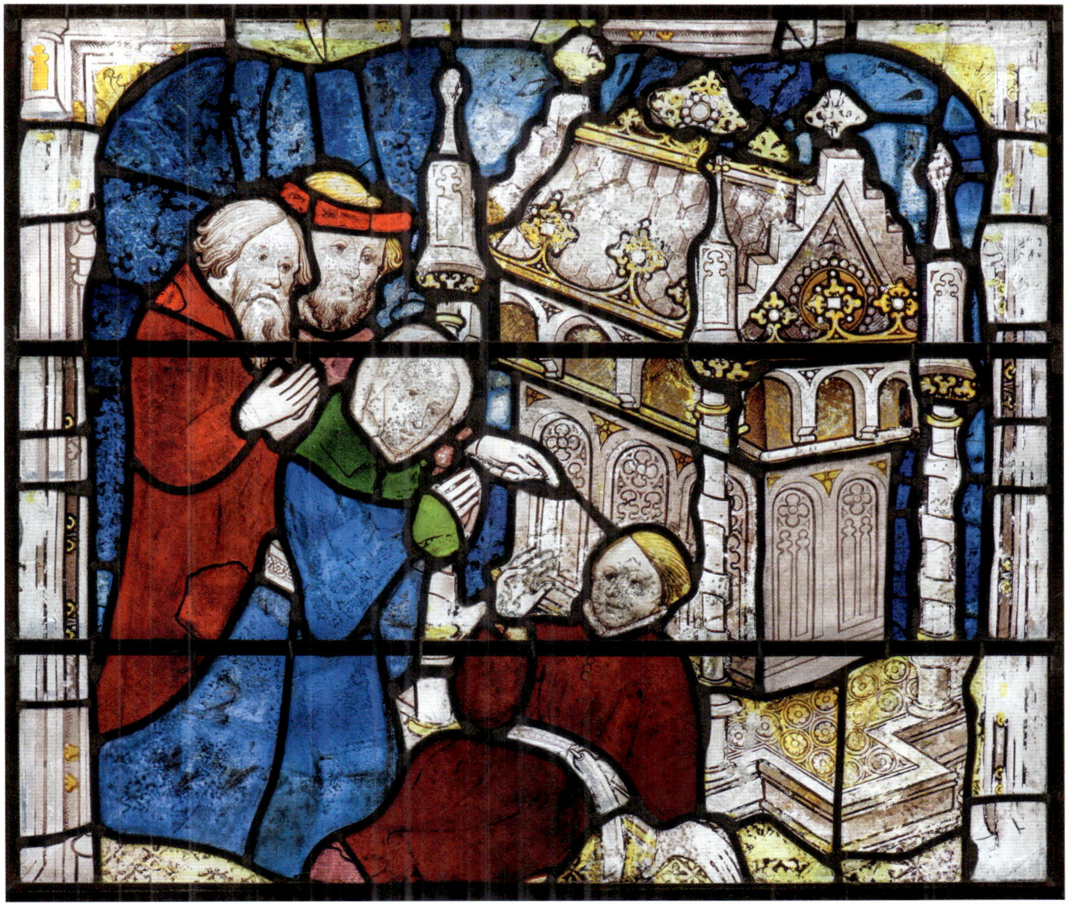

16c A boy with a deformed hand is cured at the tomb

A boy whose right hand was permanently tightly contracted into a fist was brought to the tomb and healed. The boy lies in front of the tomb and raises his right hand to show that it has been cured. His parents look on devoutly and the man in the background points at the miracle.

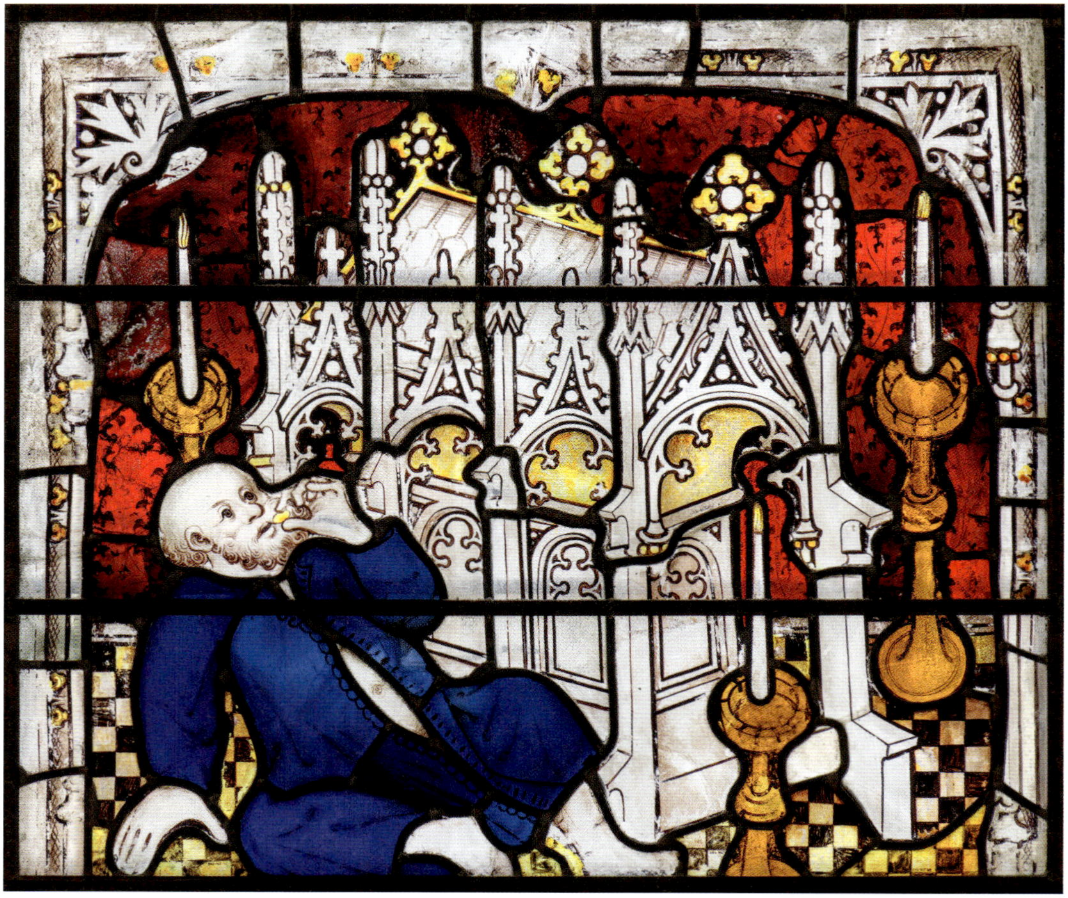

16d A man with a stomach complaint at the tomb

The miracle stories tell of many people with hydropsy or other stomach complaints cured at the tomb. This man is semi-recumbent in front of the tomb, his unbuttoned robe showing his painful stomach. He is about to eat something that he holds in his left hand. This is probably the story of a man suffering from stones, which is alluded to in some Latin verses in honour of St William. He ate some mortar from the tomb, which turned into bread, and he was cured.

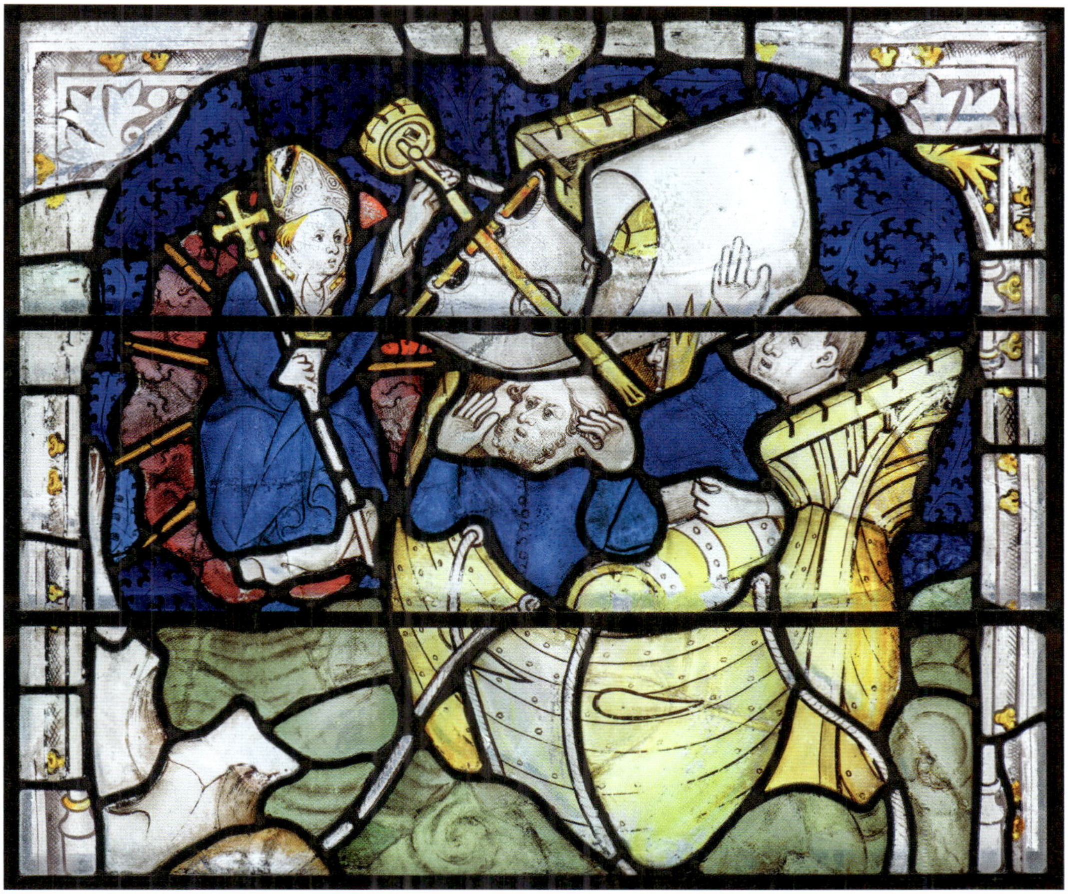

16e St William saves a ship with a broken mast

St William appears dramatically in a vision. He grasps the top of the broken mast and prevents the ship from being driven onto a rocky shore. Two merchants seated beside a barrel containing their goods throw up their hands in amazement. A third man can just be seen in profile next to the broken stump of the mast. No such incident is mentioned in the surviving miracle stories, but some verses in honour of St William praise him for his help to sailors.

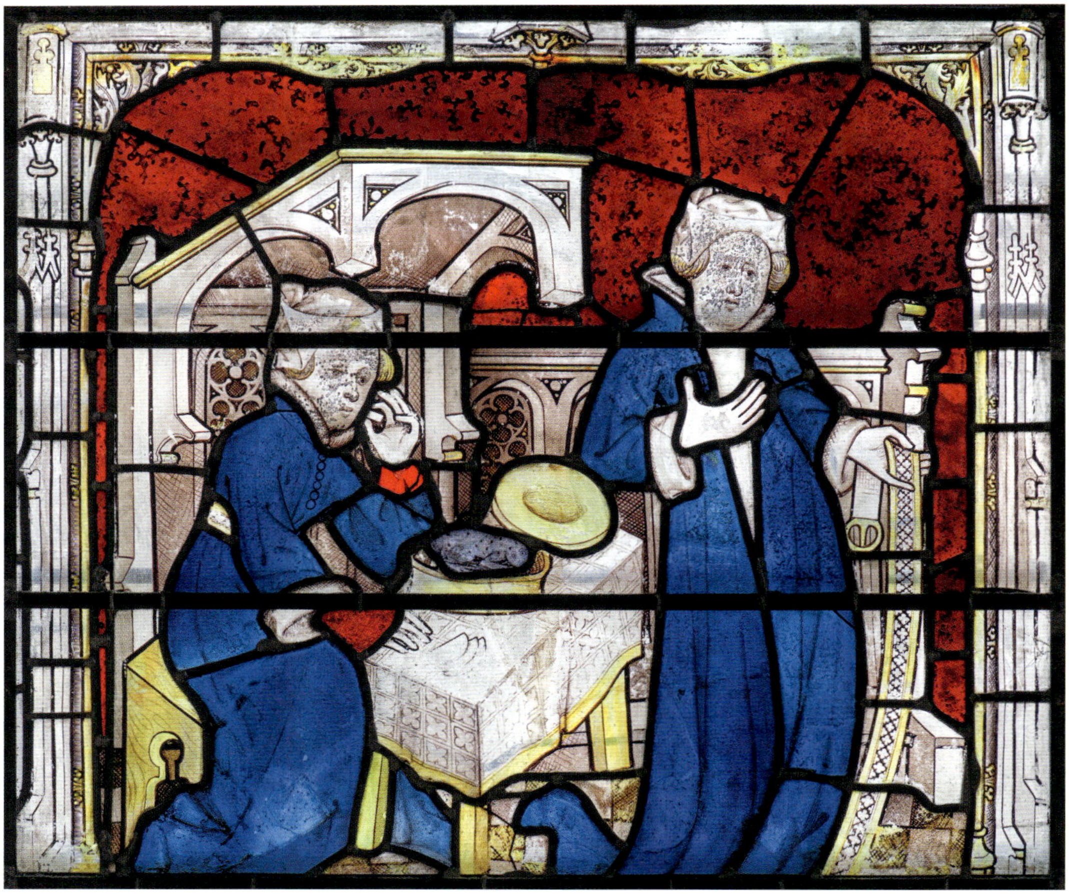

17a A woman who swallowed a frog

This miracle is spread over two panels (17a and 17b). According to the *Life*, during her evening meal, a woman swallowed a frog, which had inadvertently been mixed in with her food during cooking. Soon afterwards she fell ill. This and panel 21e are the only scenes where the same figure appears twice in the same panel. On the left, seated at table and wearing a narrow-waisted blue dress, she is eating her meal, and a large, purple, spotted frog can be seen in the dish on the table. On the right, she has stood up and taken off her belt to relieve her pain, and presses her hand to her chest.

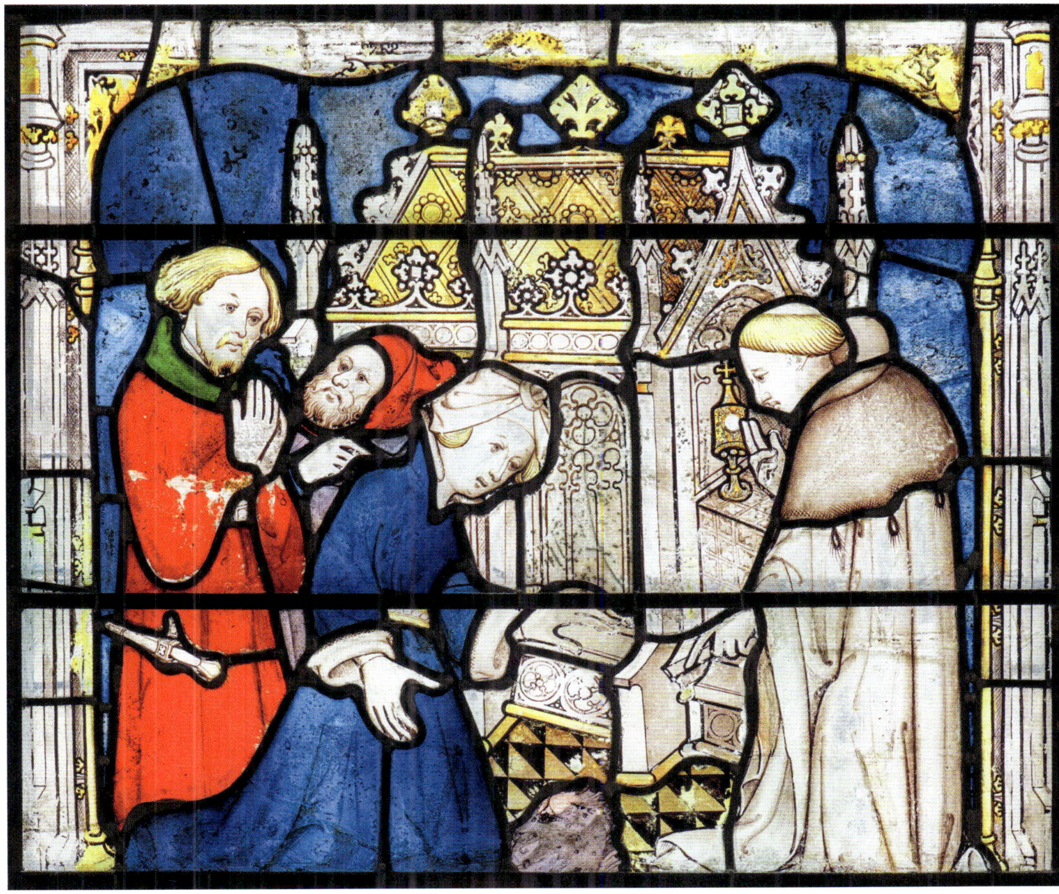

17b The woman is cured at the tomb

This is the sequel to panel 17a. Wearing the same blue dress, the woman is taken to the tomb by her husband, where she throws up and is restored to health. The priest points to the purple frog, which has been vomited up in the middle of the floor, and a bystander witnesses the miracle.

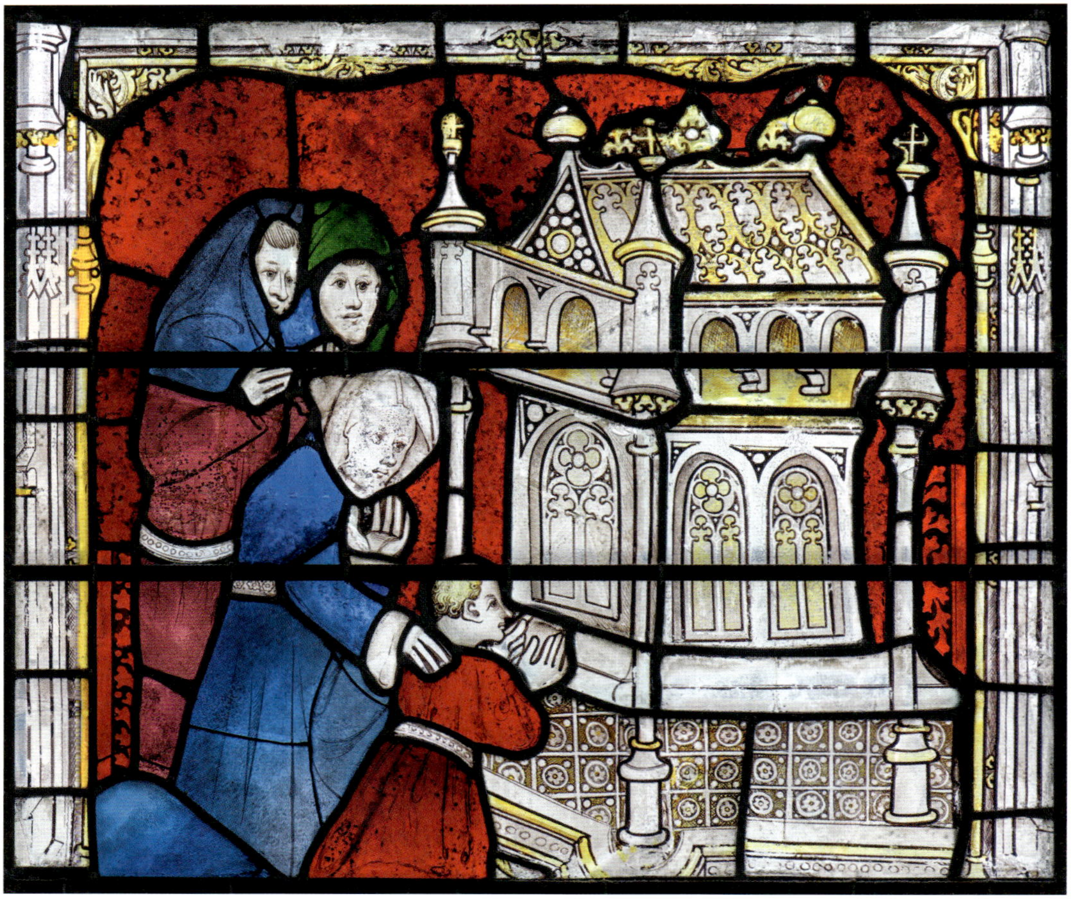

17c A boy is cured at the tomb

A boy is taken to the tomb by his mother, while two men look on. The prominence given to the boy's profile head and his right ear suggests that it could be the miracle of a deaf boy cured at the tomb mentioned in one of the sources.

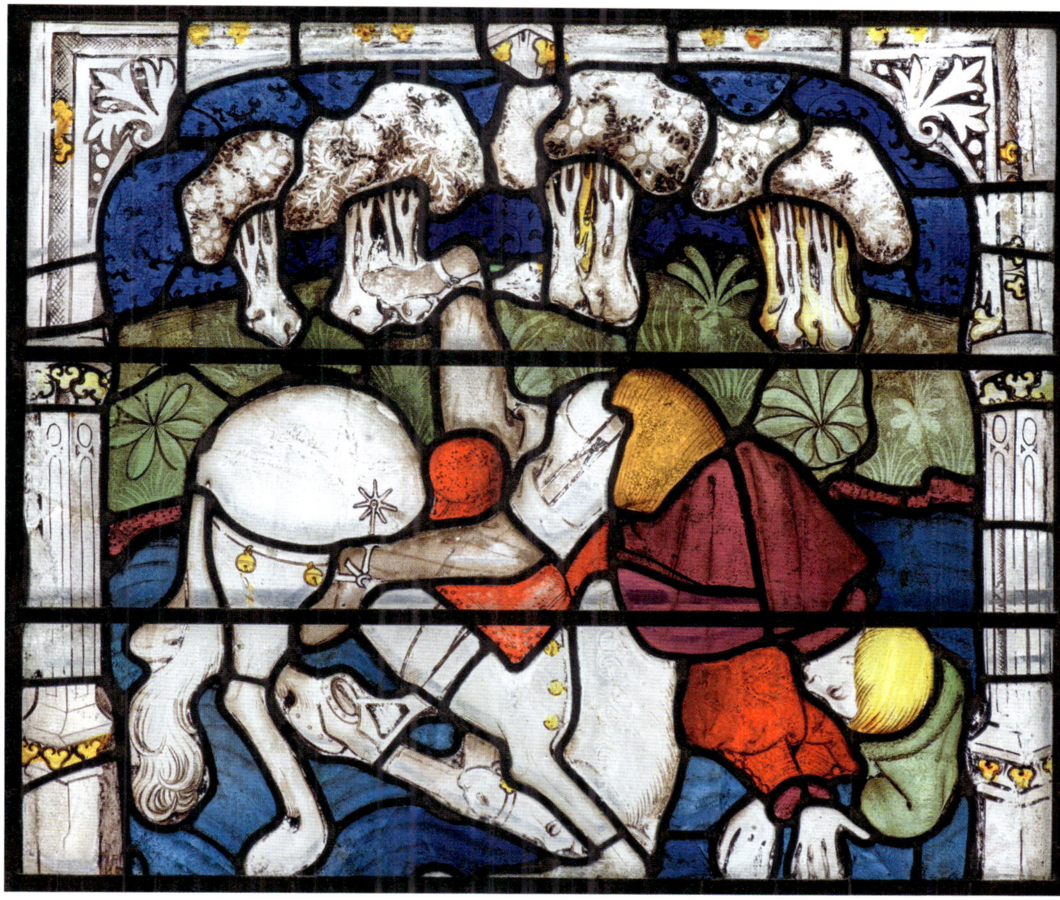

17d A man is thrown from his horse into a river

There is no known textual source for this scene. A rider is thrown head-first into a river when his horse stumbles. The man is richly dressed and is depicted wearing a very prominent rowel spur. The horse has a harness with gold bells on it and its front legs have given way, revealing the nails on the horseshoe and the empty stirrup. The wavy blue glass of the river is separated from the landscape beyond by a brown strip representing the riverbank. There is no sequel to the incident.

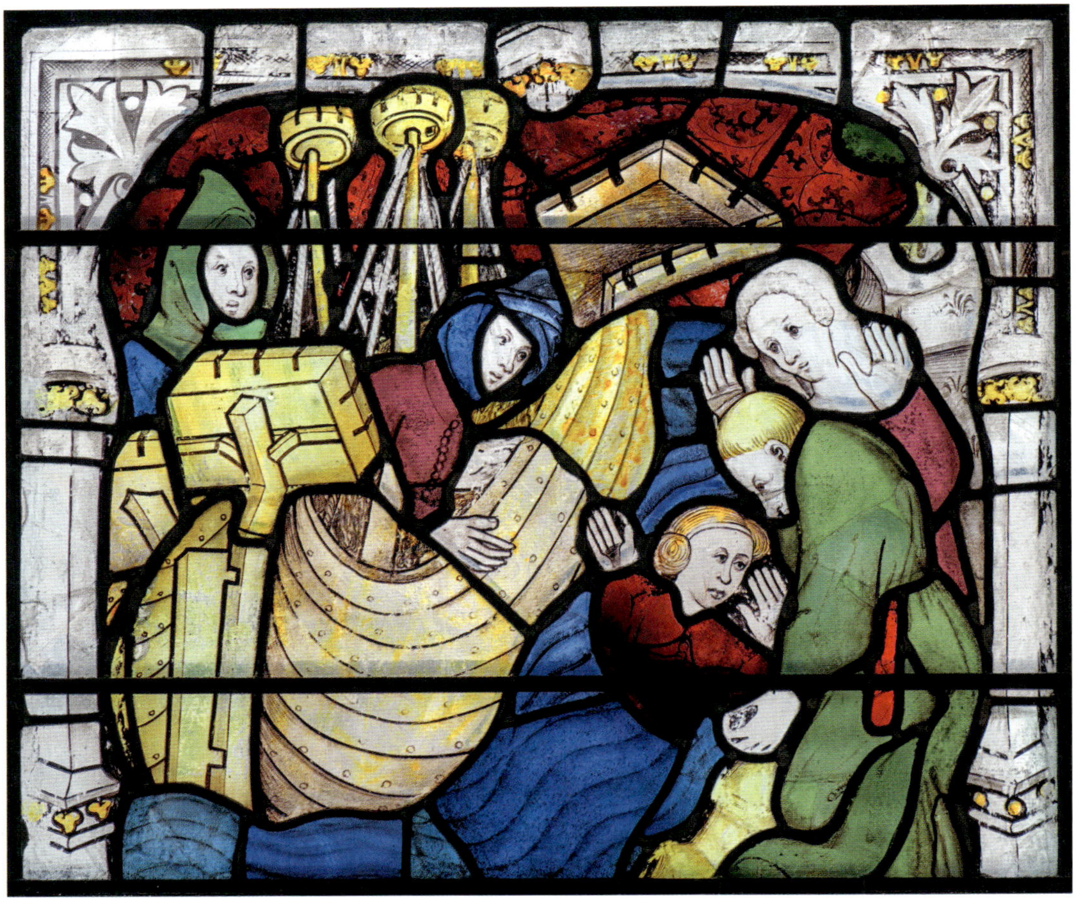

17e A child is saved from drowning in a river

The child is hauled out of a river by a man in green, while a distraught woman looks on – perhaps the parents. Across the water three boats are moored together, and two men watch the rescue. The final miracle in the early-thirteenth-century *Life* concerns a fisherman's son who was trapped between two boats on the River Ouse and was drowned, and an antiphon in honour of St William tells of a drowned boy being returned to his mother. The child appears to be a girl, but the head is an early repair and was probably originally a boy.

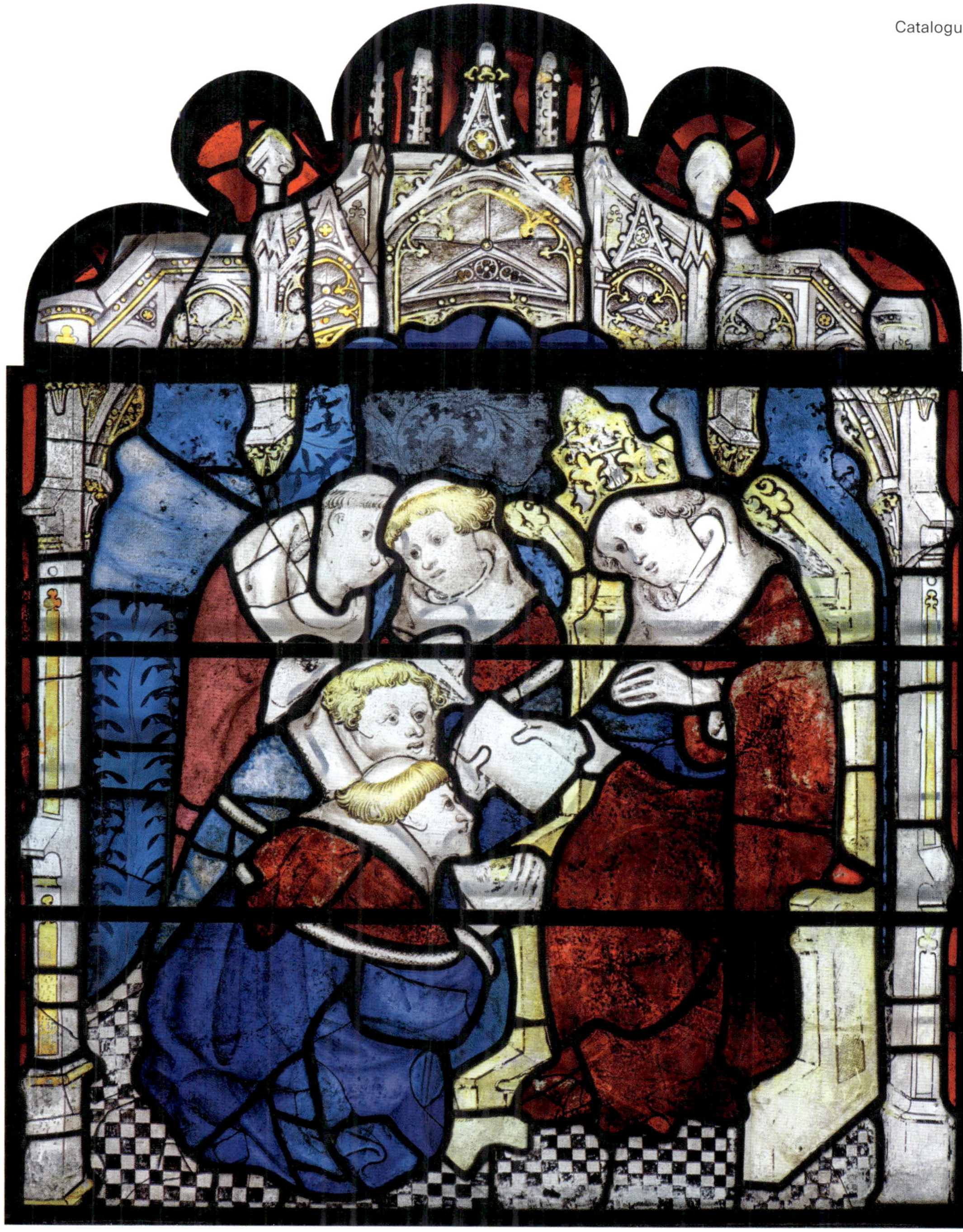

18a–19a William is canonised by the pope

Rows 18 and 20 follow the readings for the Feast of the Translation of St William in the York *Breviary*. The sequence starts with William's canonisation, which was proclaimed by Pope Honorius in 1226. Seated on his throne, the pope gives the bull of canonisation to two kneeling canons. Behind them stand another senior cleric and a monk, distinguished by their tonsures.

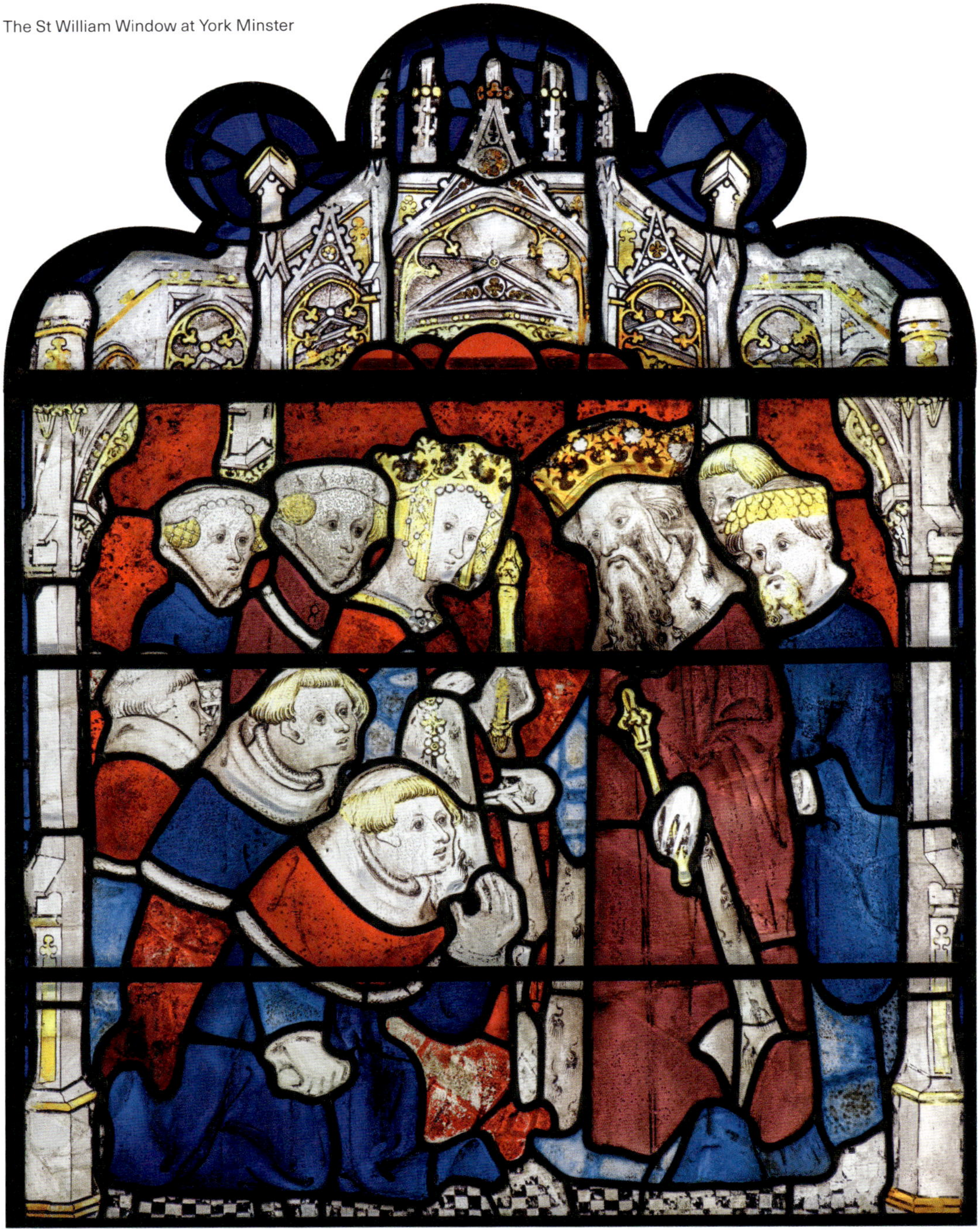

18b–19b King Edward I and Queen Eleanor of Castile are invited to the Translation of William's relics
The narrative jumps to 1283, when an invitation was issued to King Edward and Queen Eleanor to attend the Translation of the relics of St William. Three kneeling canons address the king, who is accompanied by two courtiers. The queen stands behind, accompanied by two ladies-in-waiting. The king wears a crown and an ermine-lined purple robe and holds a sceptre in his left hand. The queen also carries a sceptre and wears an elaborate headdress surmounted by a crown.

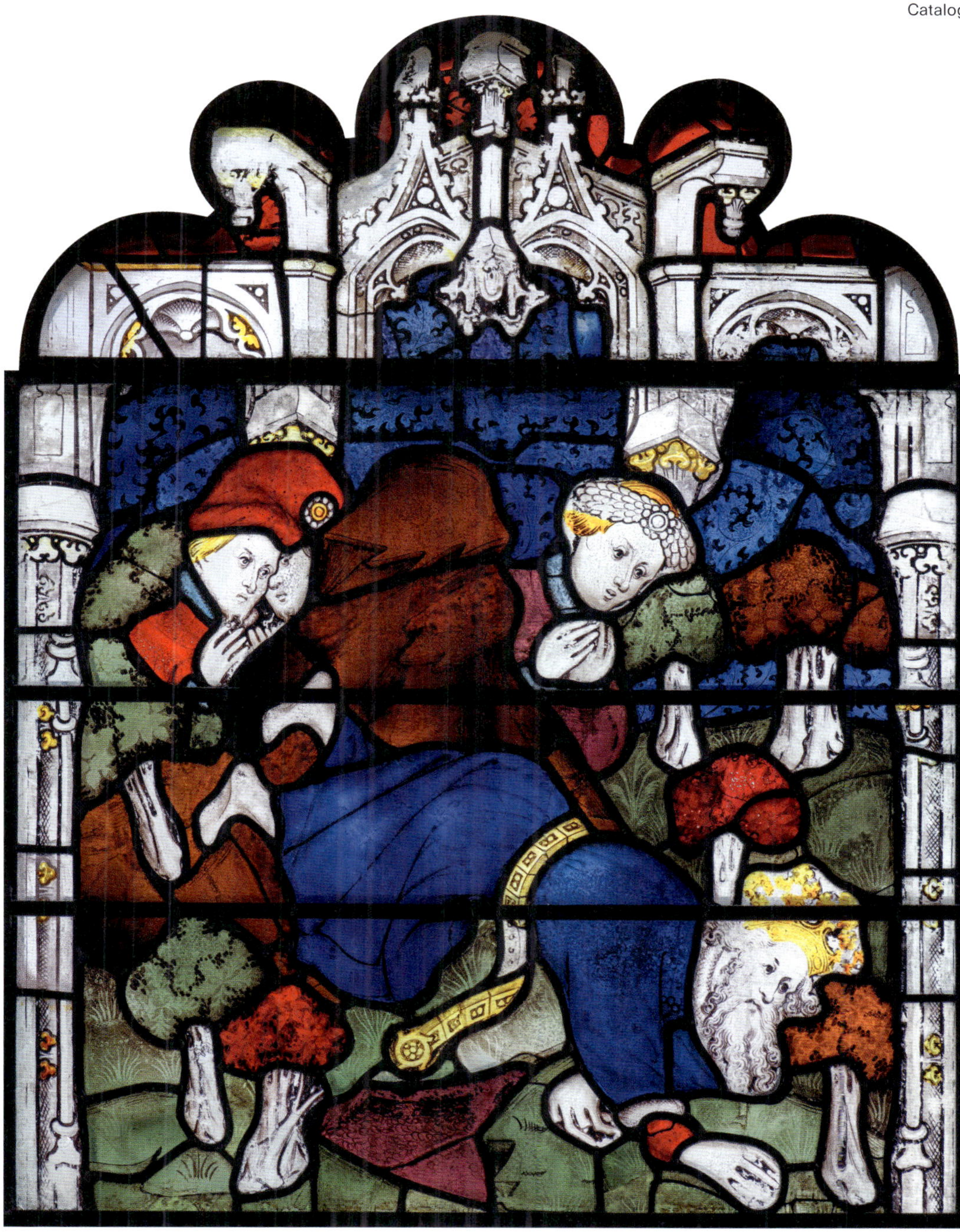

18c–19c King Edward falls from a mountain in Wales
Having accepted the invitation, the king has a bad fall from a mountain, which looms up in orange glass in the middle of the scene. Three members of his retinue, fearing him to be seriously injured, peer anxiously round the mountain. Edward I was in Wales at the time, engaged in his campaign against the Welsh.

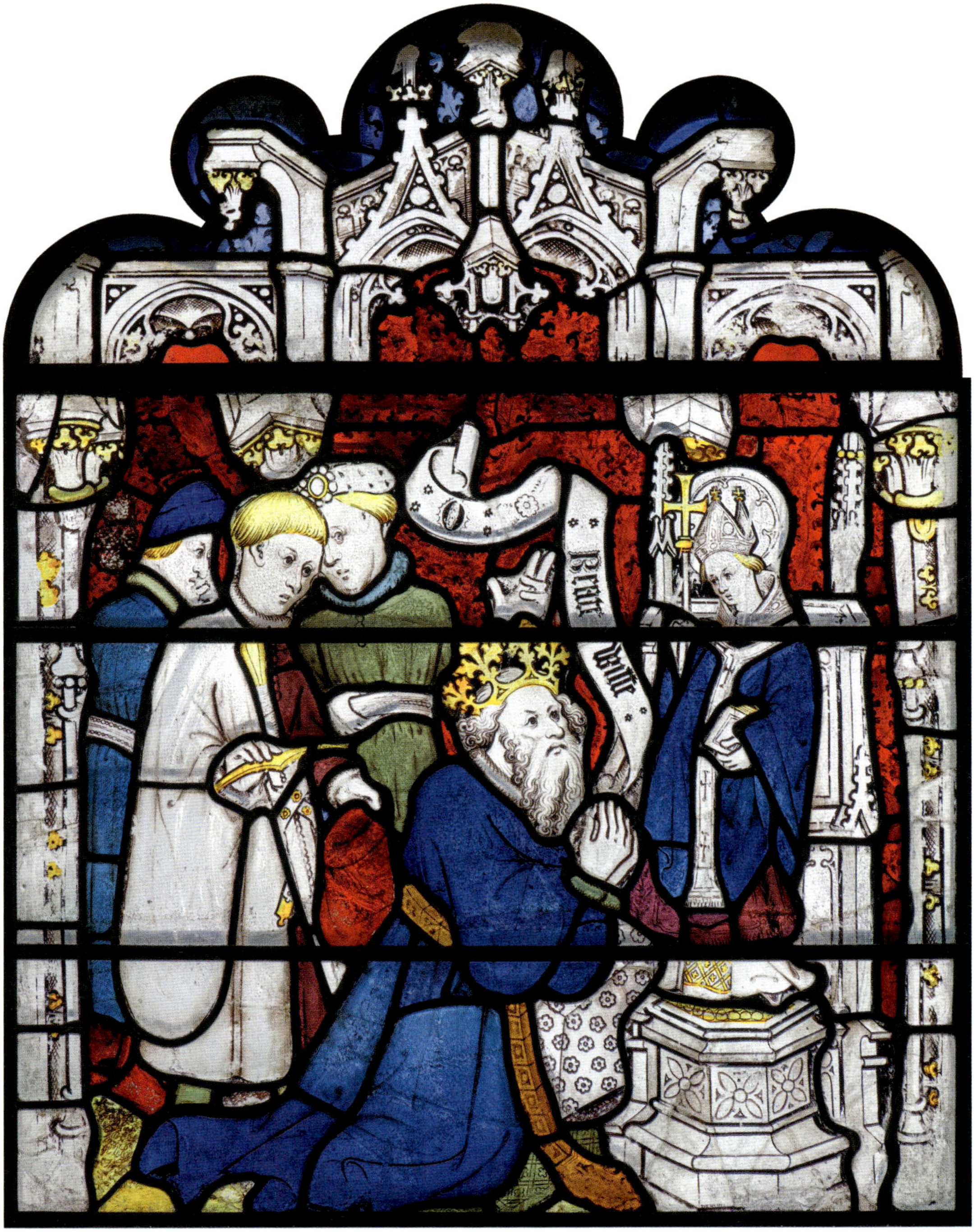

18d–19d King Edward gives thanks to St William for his deliverance

The king was unharmed, and immediately afterwards gave thanks to God and St William, ascribing his deliverance to the saint whom he had promised to honour. The king is shown kneeling before an image of St William, whom he addresses with the words *O Beate Willelme*. This is the only speech scroll in the window. The scene is observed by three courtiers. The man in front holds his red hat in his left hand and with his right supports the large sword of state, its point resting on the pavement, out of view behind the king, its hilt extending up as far as the man's shoulder.

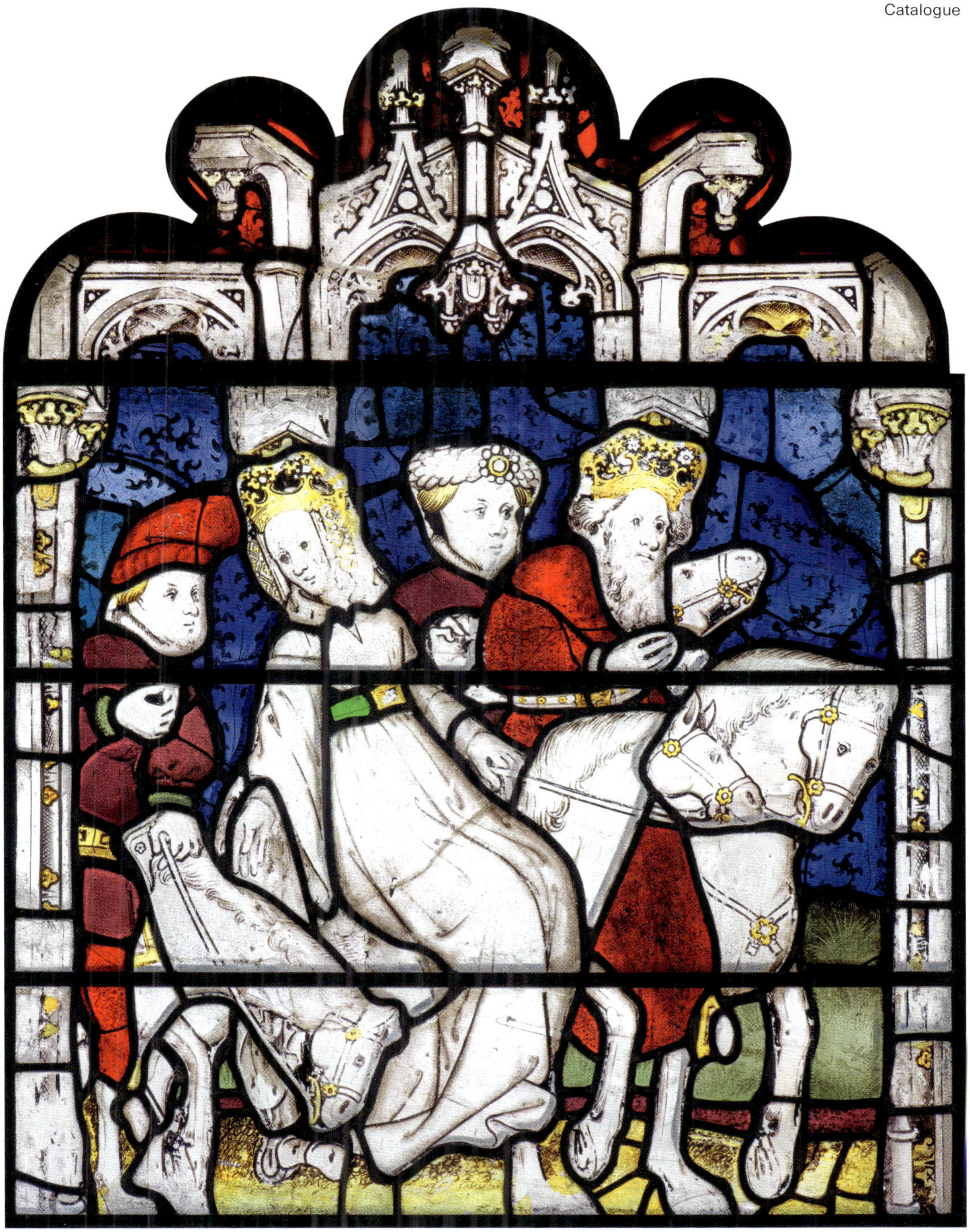

18e–19e King Edward and Queen Eleanor ride to York
The king and queen hasten to York, as the *Breviary* text emphasises. They are accompanied by two courtiers. All four are mounted on white horses. Queen Eleanor rides side-saddle.

Rows 20–25

The fourth section begins with the Translation of William's relics, which took place in January 1284. His bones were moved from the sarcophagus and placed in a portable reliquary (panels 20a–20b). The ceremony was presided over by Archbishop William Wickwane (20c). The sequence ends with the miracle of a man who was hit on the head by a falling stone but escaped unharmed (20d–20e).

Rows 21 and 22 contain miracles that took place after the Translation. There are five different stories, all of them quite distinctive, and all but one (panel 21e) are spread over two or more panels. Three of them involve the portable reliquary, which was processed around the Minster and the city from time to time (panels 21c–21d, 21e and 22e). The other two feature the tomb (panels 21a–21b and 22a–22b), which continued to be a focus for pilgrimage and a locus for healing miracles. The next eight panels (23a–24c) are very different in character. They are all individual scenes, and whereas 23c and 24c are new designs, the others are composed of figures and images of the tomb that are copied from some of the panels in rows 15, 16 and 17, and then combined in different ways. The narrative cycle concludes with a distinctive story of an aristocratic lady being trampled by a horse and then giving thanks for her deliverance at the tomb (panels 24d–24e). Her bright red dress recalls the heraldic colours of the Roos family, and it seems likely that the woman in question is Lady Beatrice de Roos, the principal donor of the window, who kneels directly below at the base of the window in panel 1e. Thus, the final episode at the top of the window refers the viewer back to the donor panel at the bottom.

The arrangement of frames in this section of the window differs slightly from sections two and three. In rows 20–22, lights a and b have Type B frames, while lights c–e have Type F frames, but with a variant design (Type F*) in panels 22c–22e. These have the typical Type F canopy across the top of the panel, but the side shafts are of a new design. Row 23 has Type B frames right across the row. This is the only row in the window (apart from the donor panels in the bottom row) that contains just a single frame design. In rows 24 and 25 at the top of this section, lights a–c have the same frames (Type G) as lights a–c in rows 12–13. Panels 24d–24e have a new design of side shafts (Type K) but they support canopies in panels 25d–25e that are the same design (Type H) as in panels 13d–13e.

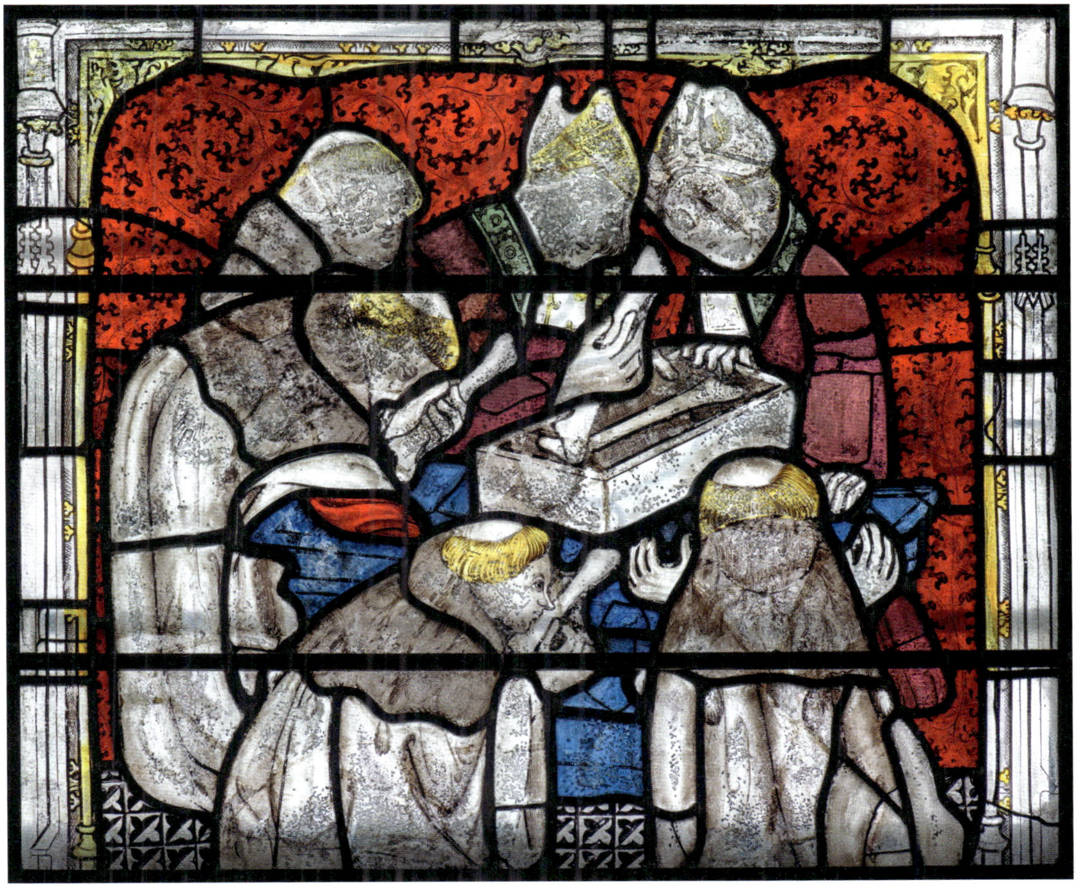

20a St William's tomb is opened

The tomb was opened during the night in the presence of Archbishop William Wickwane, the bishop of St David's, and the latter's brother, Antony Bek, the new bishop of Durham, accompanied by the dean and canons of the Minster. Taking the lid off the sarcophagus, they removed the bones of the saint and placed them in a reliquary chest. The panel shows four Minster canons and two episcopal figures around the open sarcophagus. The canon on the left leans over and reaches down into the sarcophagus with his right hand. In his left he holds one of St William's long bones, ready to pass it to the episcopal figure in the centre. The latter holds another bone in his right hand, and another long bone has been placed in the chest. In the foreground another canon kisses one of the bones, while the canon on the right raises his hands in prayer. The Translation of the relics took place on 8 January 1284.

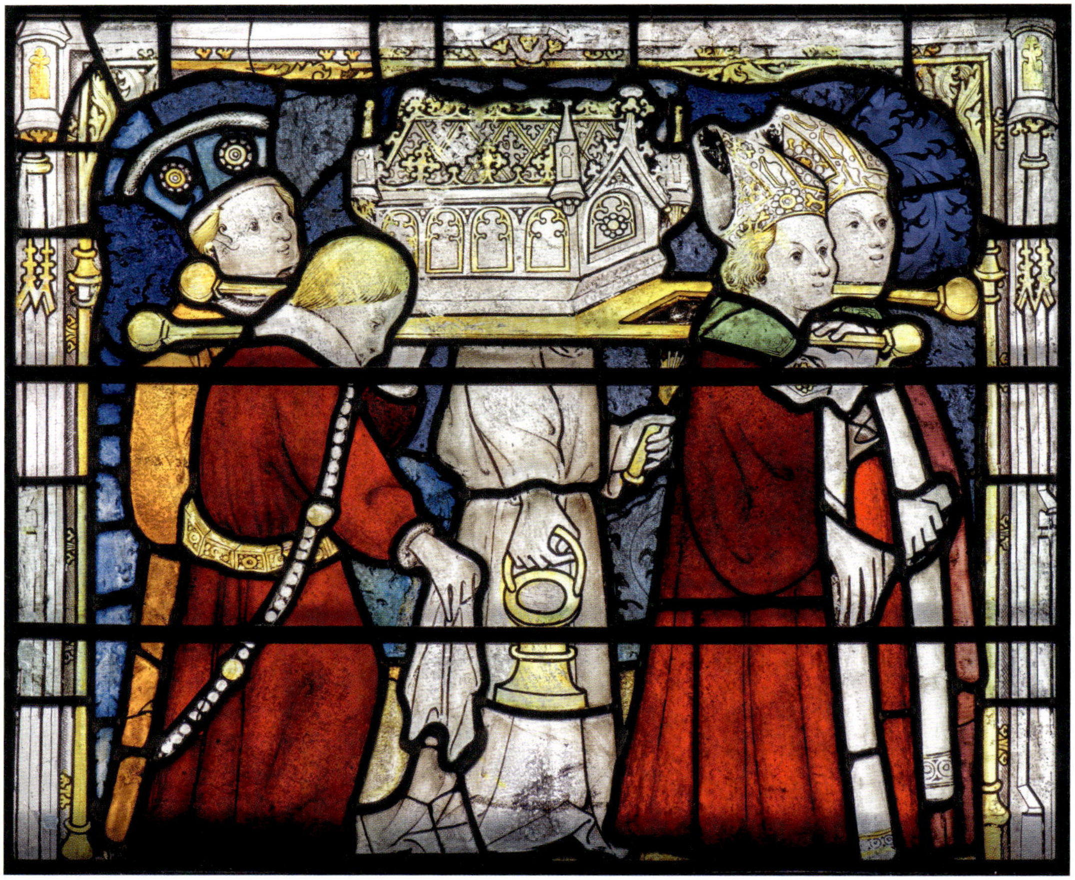

20b The relics of St William are carried in procession
The chest containing the bones has been placed in a precious-metal portable reliquary and is being processed around the Minster. Behind the two episcopal figures at the front, an acolyte holding the holy water vessel and aspergillum is partly hidden by the reliquary. At the rear is a layman dressed in orange wearing a large, ornate hat. According to the *Breviary*, the king himself helped to carry the reliquary on his shoulders, but he is not actually shown at the ceremony.

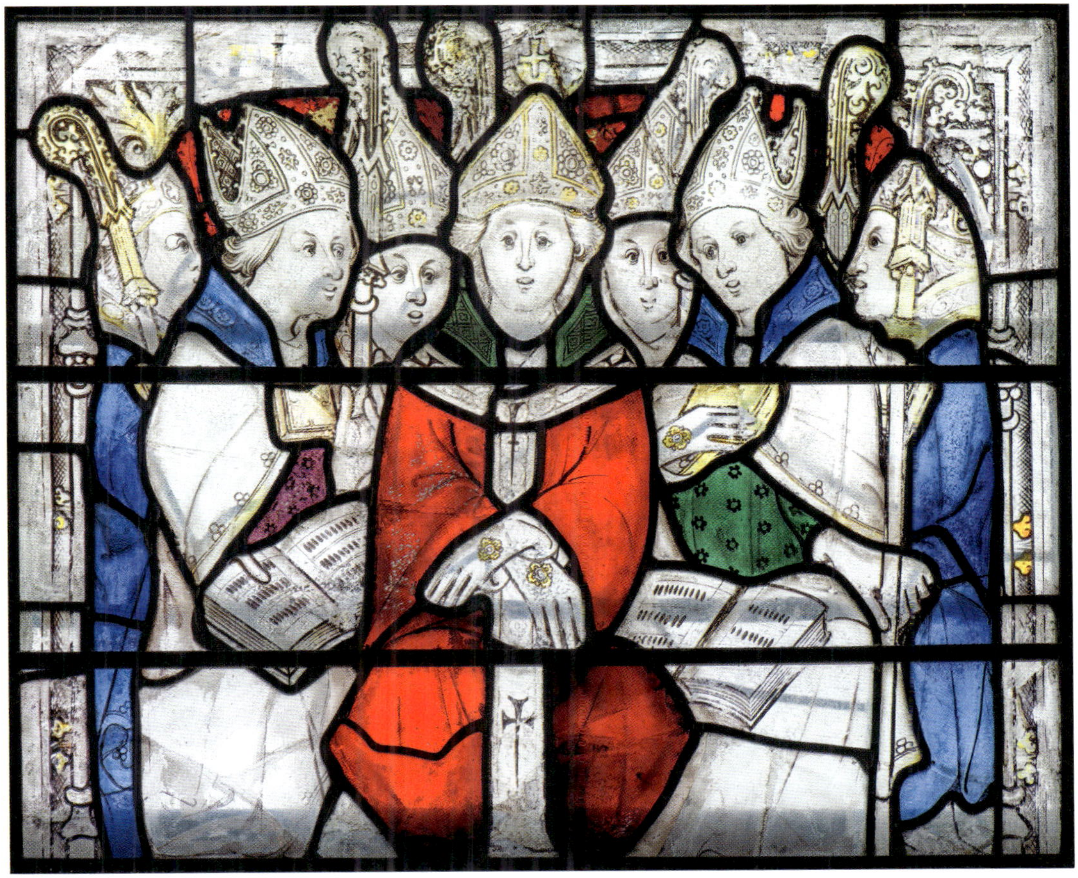

20c Archbishop Wickwane and six bishops
Archbishop Wickwane preached at the Translation ceremony. He is shown seated in the middle, wearing his pallium, accompanied by six bishops, each with mitre and crozier. Two of them have open books on their laps.

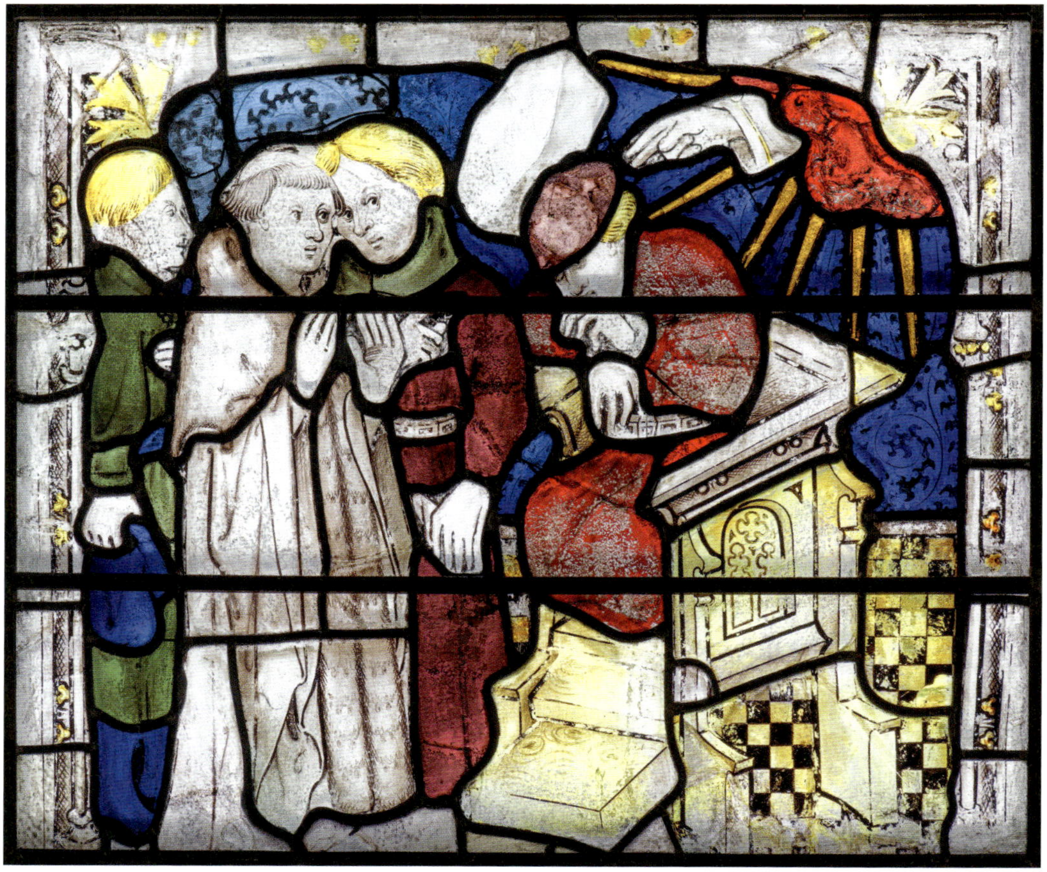

20d A servant is hit on the head by a stone

According to the *Breviary*, a servant of one of the canons fell asleep during matins with his head against the base of the pulpit from which the Gospel was read. During the third lesson, a stone column of some weight fell on his head. In the panel, the servant is hit on the head by a roughly shaped stone. The hand of God blesses him at the moment of impact, as the canon and two other men look on.

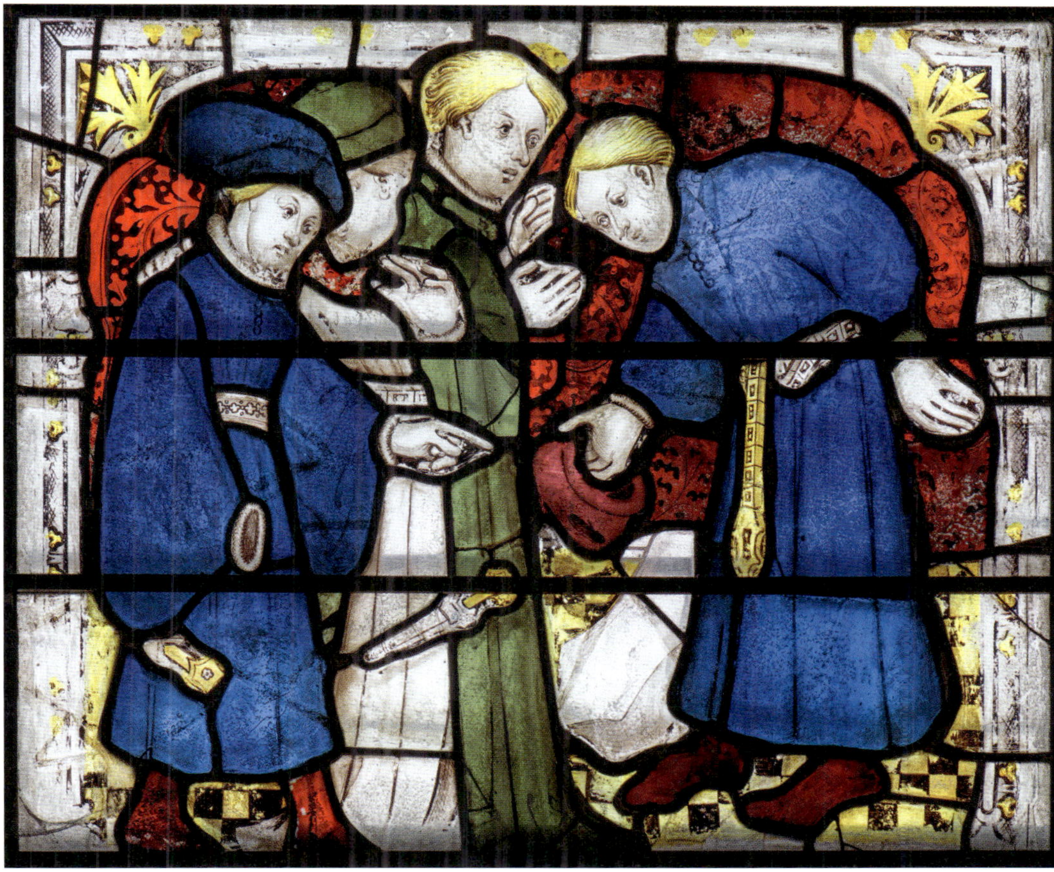

20e The servant escapes unharmed

The servant gets up unharmed and takes off the hat he had been wearing when hit by the stone, which lies on the floor. He gives thanks to God and St William for his escape. He bends forward to show that his head is unhurt and he also shows the damage to his hat, which the figure in blue points towards. This man, oddly, has withdrawn his right hand inside his sleeve. Two other onlookers express their astonishment.

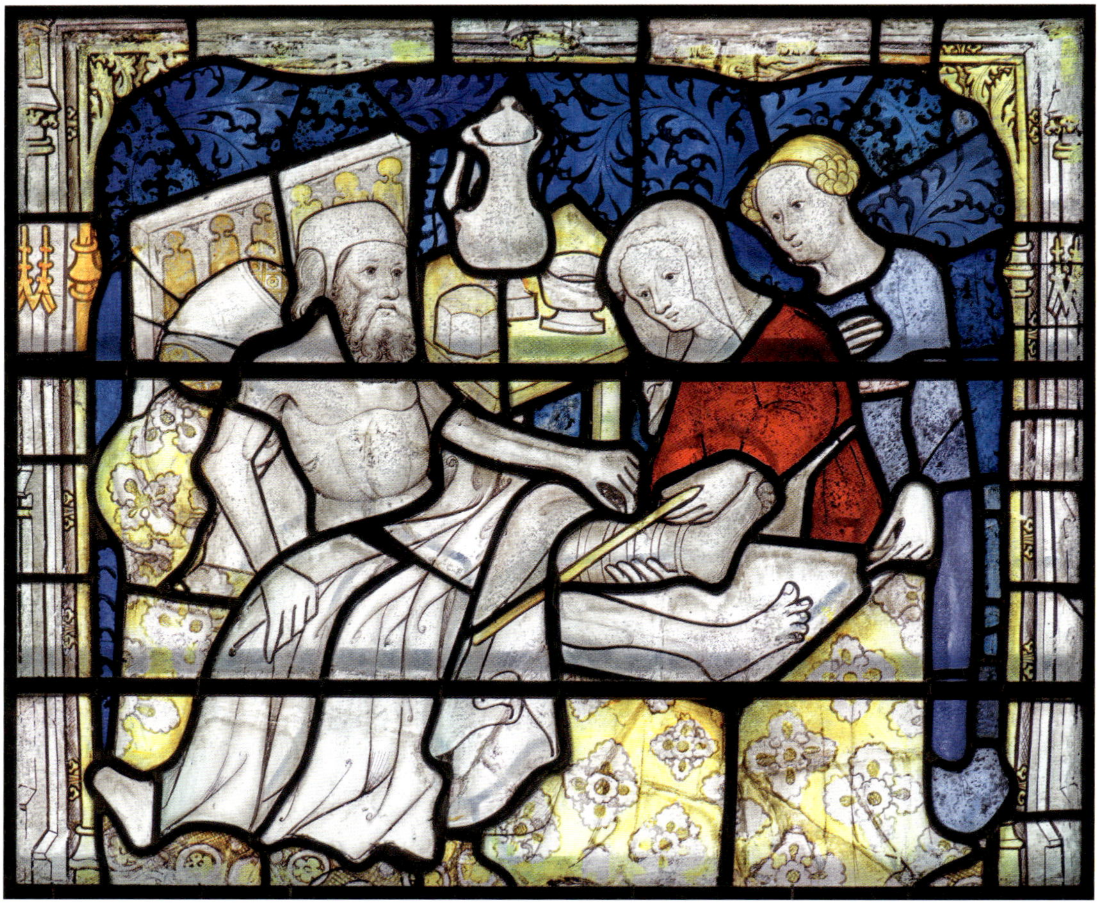

21a A man with a bandaged leg

This is the first of a pair of scenes depicting a miracle that took place shortly after the Translation. A man sits up in bed, naked except for a nightcap, and pulls back the bed-clothes to reveal his legs. His left leg is swollen and heavily bandaged. He watches as his wife or a servant measures his leg with a ruler in order to make a candle of the same dimensions in honour of St William. The maid, the elaborately decorated bed linen, the ornamental head-board and the well-appointed bedside table all indicate a wealthy household. In the *Breviary* text the man is identified as one of the Knights Templar. The Templars were suppressed in 1312 and in the window the man is represented as a layman.

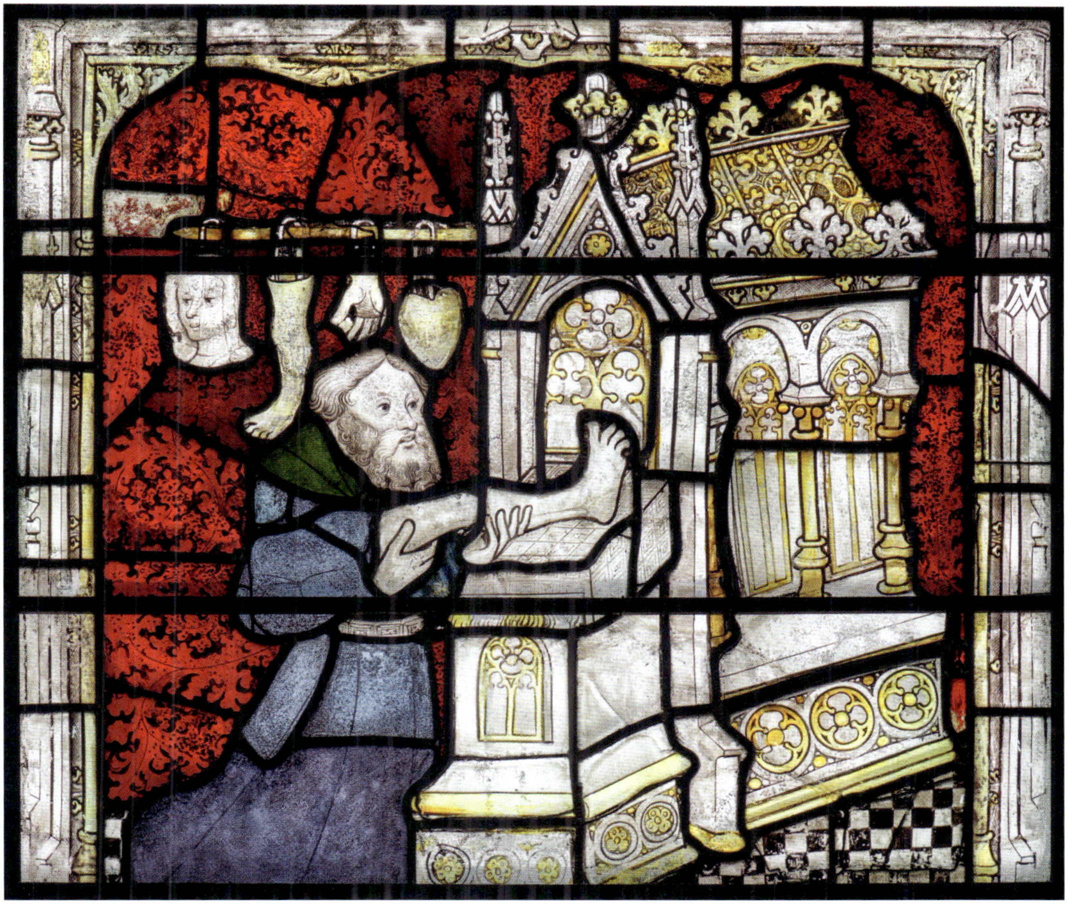

21b The man offers a model of his leg at the tomb

The sequel to panel 21a. The man kneels at the tomb offering a large model of his leg as a thank-offering for his recovery. Above his head, miniature models of a head, a leg, a hand and a heart hang from a rod. Later sources record many such *ex votos* in the Minster, the different body parts indicating the various afflictions from which the patients had recovered. A life-size, made-to-measure model of a leg would have stood out from all the rest. Some of these *ex votos* were made of precious metals, but many were made of wax.

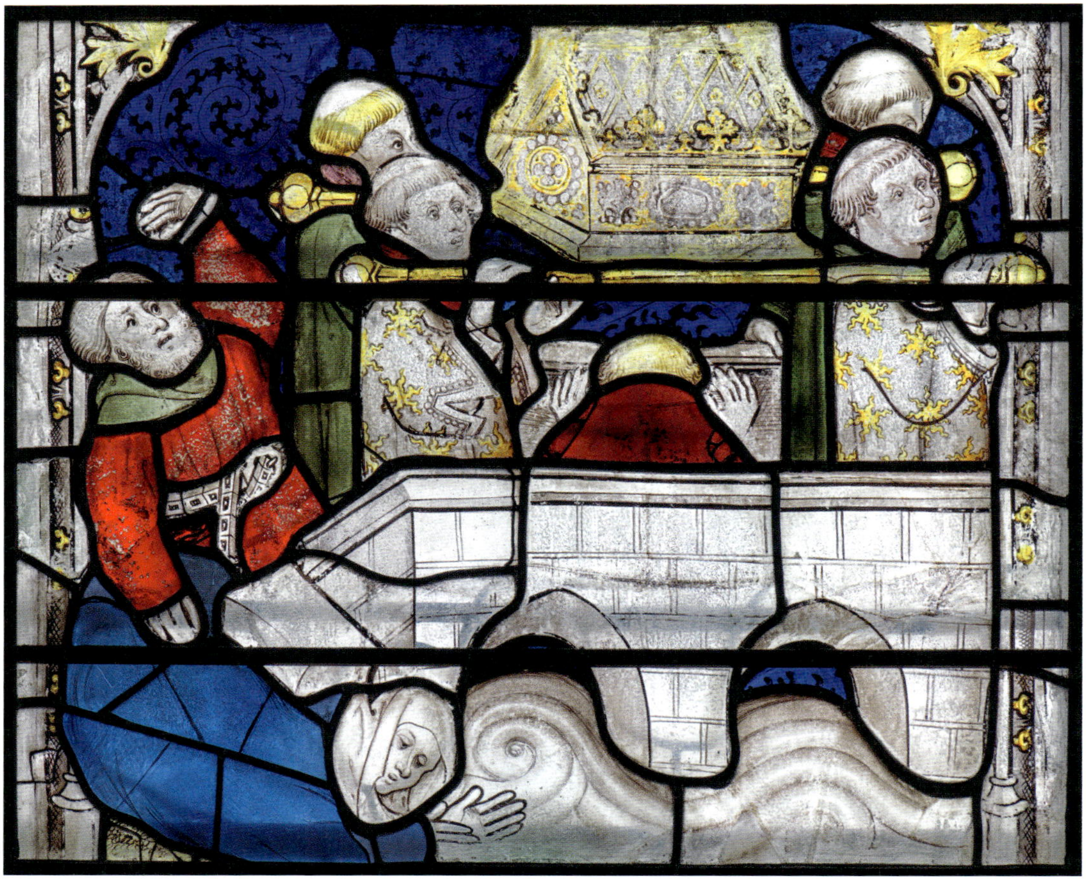

21c A woman falls into the river from Ouse Bridge

Panels 21c and 21d depict an incident similar to the miracle of Ouse Bridge in panel 9c. After the Translation of the relics in 1284, the portable reliquary would be processed around the city on special occasions. As it is being carried across Ouse Bridge by Minster clergy, a man in red (seen from behind) kneels in devotion. In the left foreground a woman falls into the river and is hit by a stone, much to the consternation of the man standing next to her. By this date a chapel dedicated to St William had been built on Ouse Bridge, but it is not represented, the focus being on the reliquary.

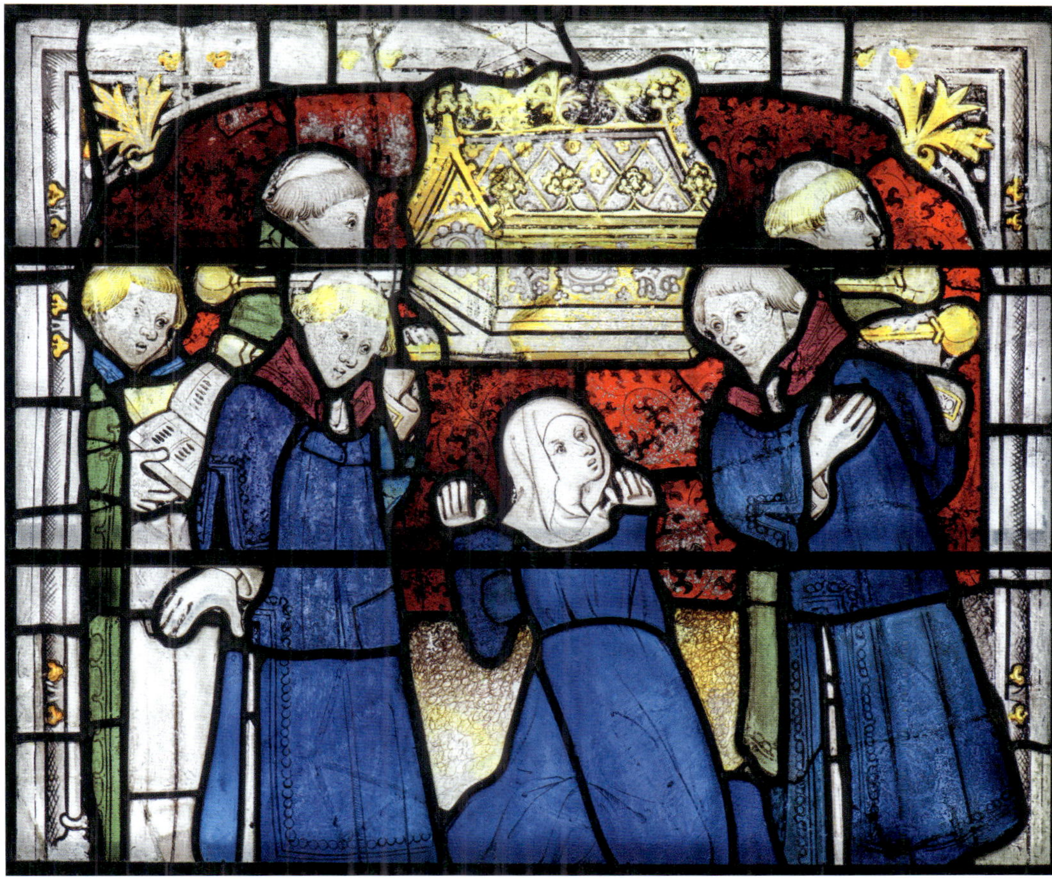

21d The woman is saved and gives thanks

The continuation of the story from panel 21c. The procession with the relics halts; the woman is saved, and she kneels beneath the reliquary in thanksgiving. There is no known written source for this miracle.

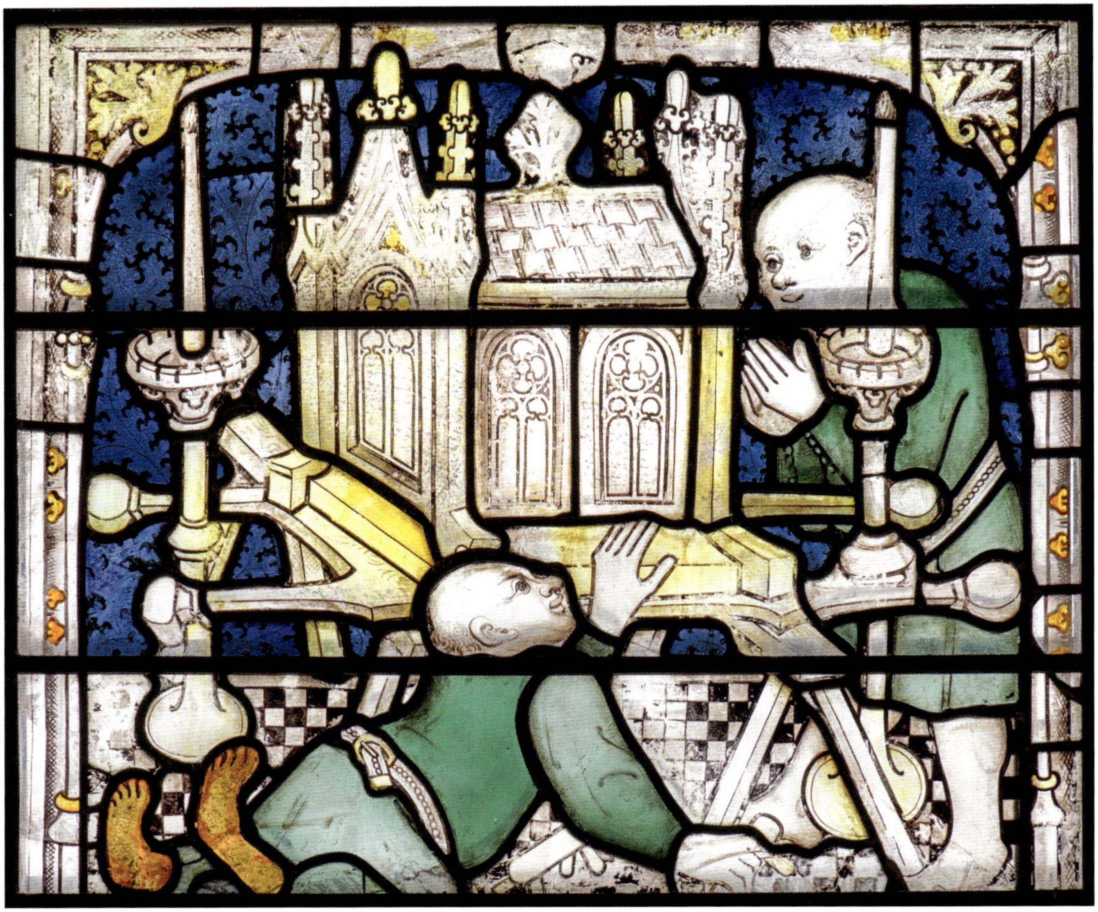

21e A disabled man is healed at the portable reliquary

On its return from being carried around the city in procession, the portable reliquary has been placed on trestles in the nave of the Minster, with a candlestick at either end. In the foreground, a man with legs contracted from birth, who had been asleep at the nearby tomb of the saint, crawls up to the reliquary using hand supports. On the right the man, identifiable by his bald, rounded head and the same distinctive pale green knee-length garment, stands upright and offers thanks. As in panel 17a, the same figure appears twice in the same scene.

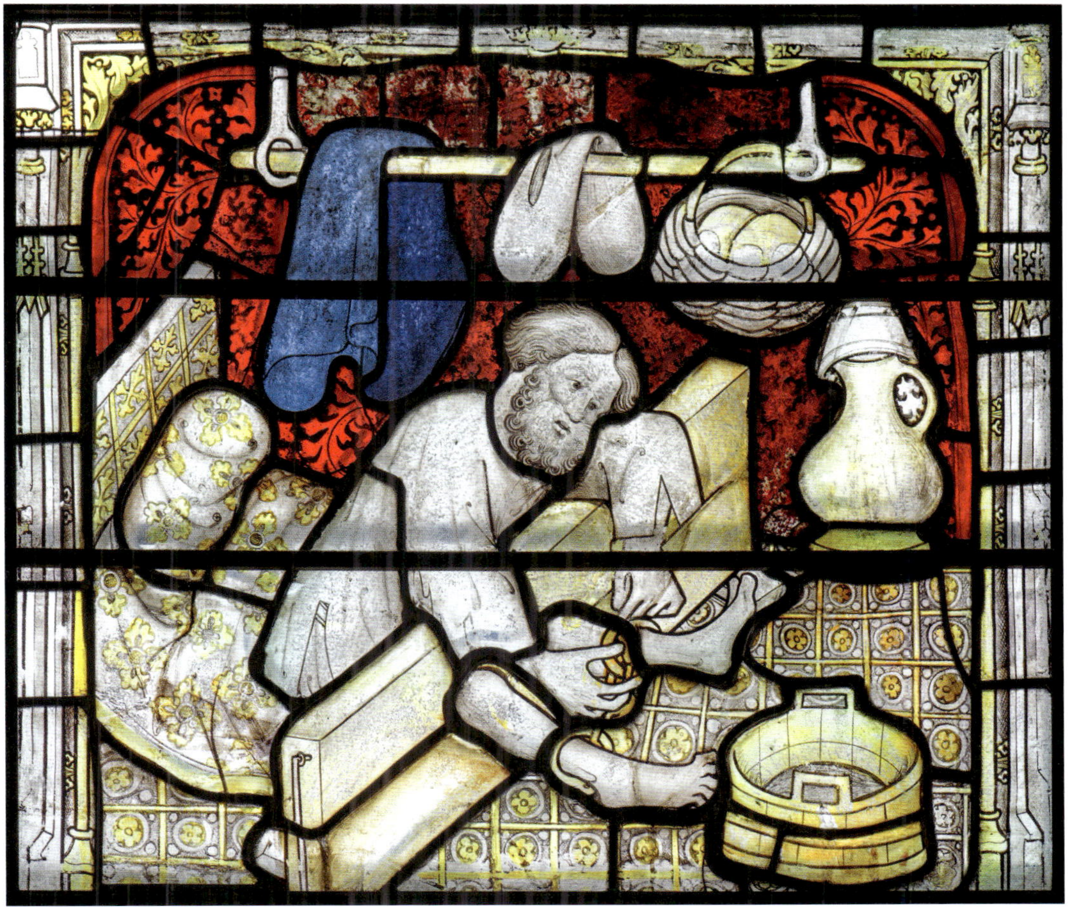

22a An imprisoned man seeks to be released

The first of a pair of scenes (panels 22a–22b) for which there is no known textual source. A man sits with his legs in some stocks and his ankles manacled together. He leans forward to try to release himself. He is being held in a room that looks surprisingly well appointed, with a floor of decorated tiles, a couch, and with clothes, provisions and a tub of water nearby. This suggests that the man may not be a criminal but a captive held to ransom.

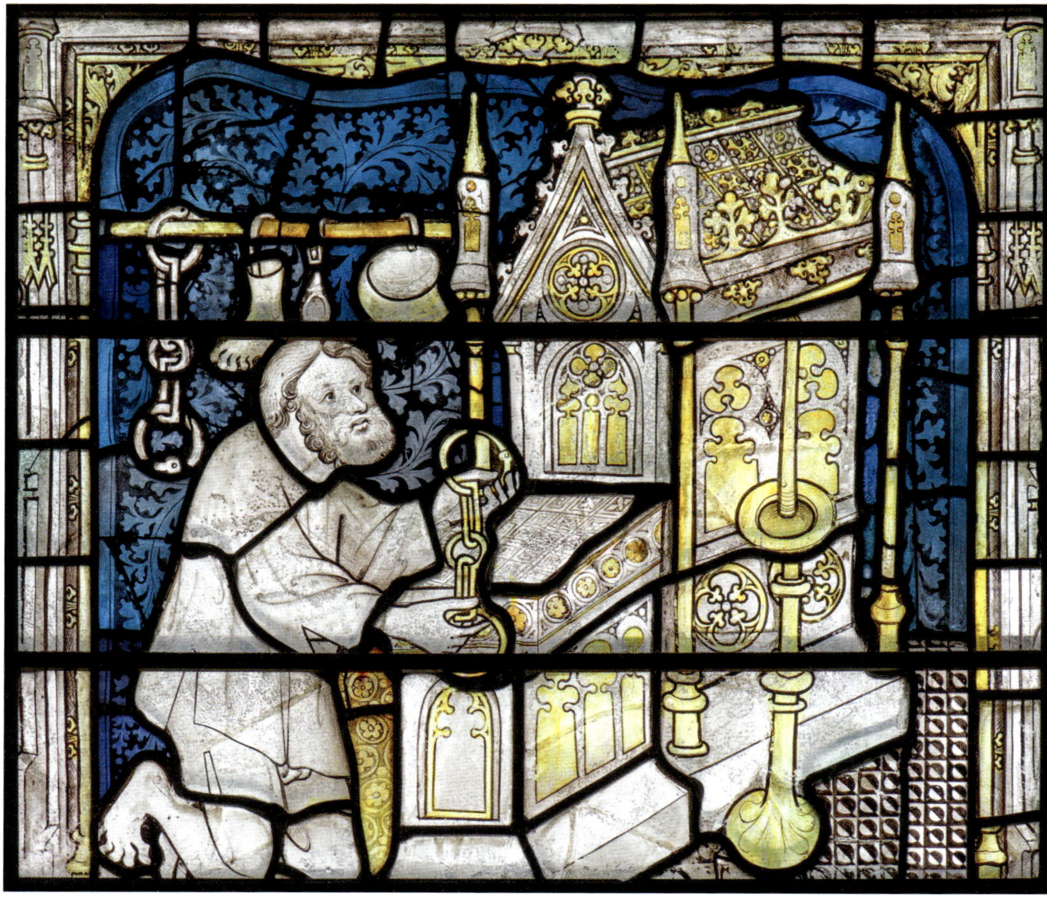

22b The freed prisoner offers his chains at the tomb

Following on from panel 22a, the man, barefoot and wearing the same bed-clothes, kneels at the tomb and offers his chains to St William in thanksgiving for his release. Other *ex votos* hang from a rod above his head, as in panel 21b, including another set of chains.

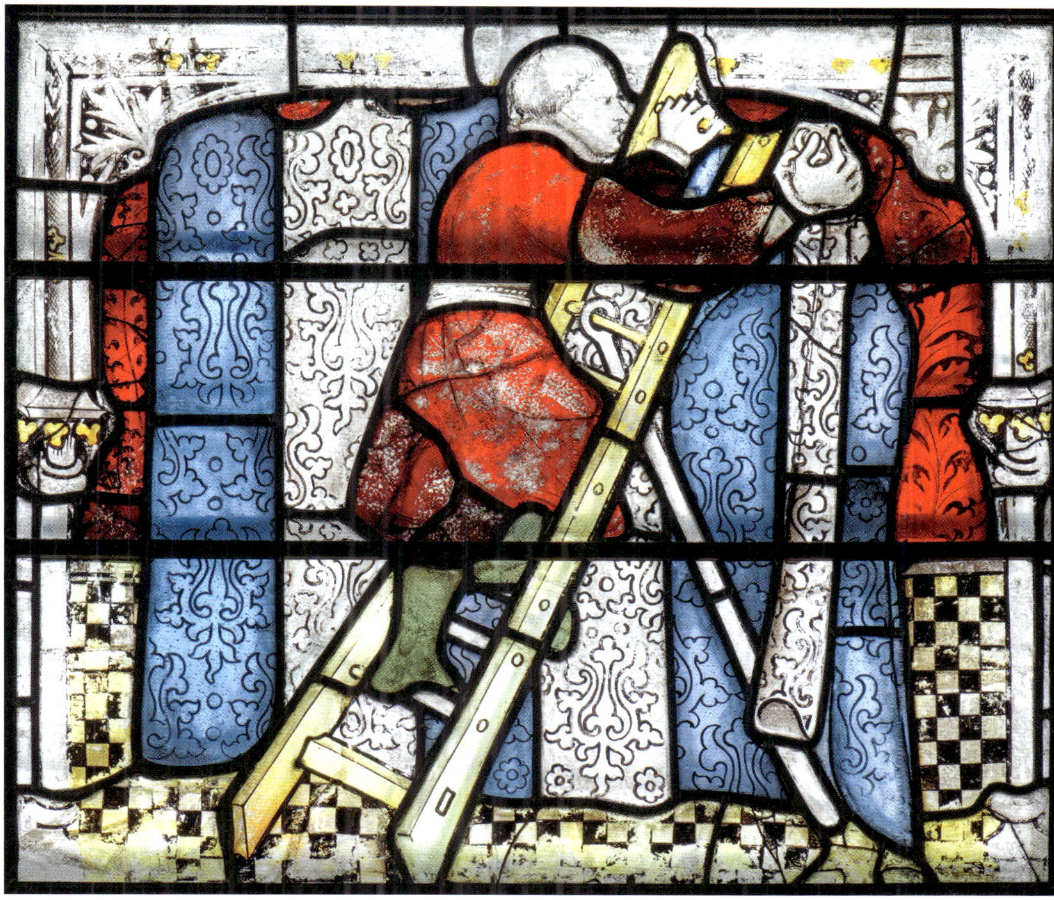

22c A man up a ladder hangs decorative textiles in a church

Panels 22c–22e form a sequence. It was common practice to mark major feast days by installing temporary decorative hangings in churches. A man is up a ladder, presumably in the Minster, hanging long strips of decorated textiles similar to those depicted in the donor panels (1a–1e).

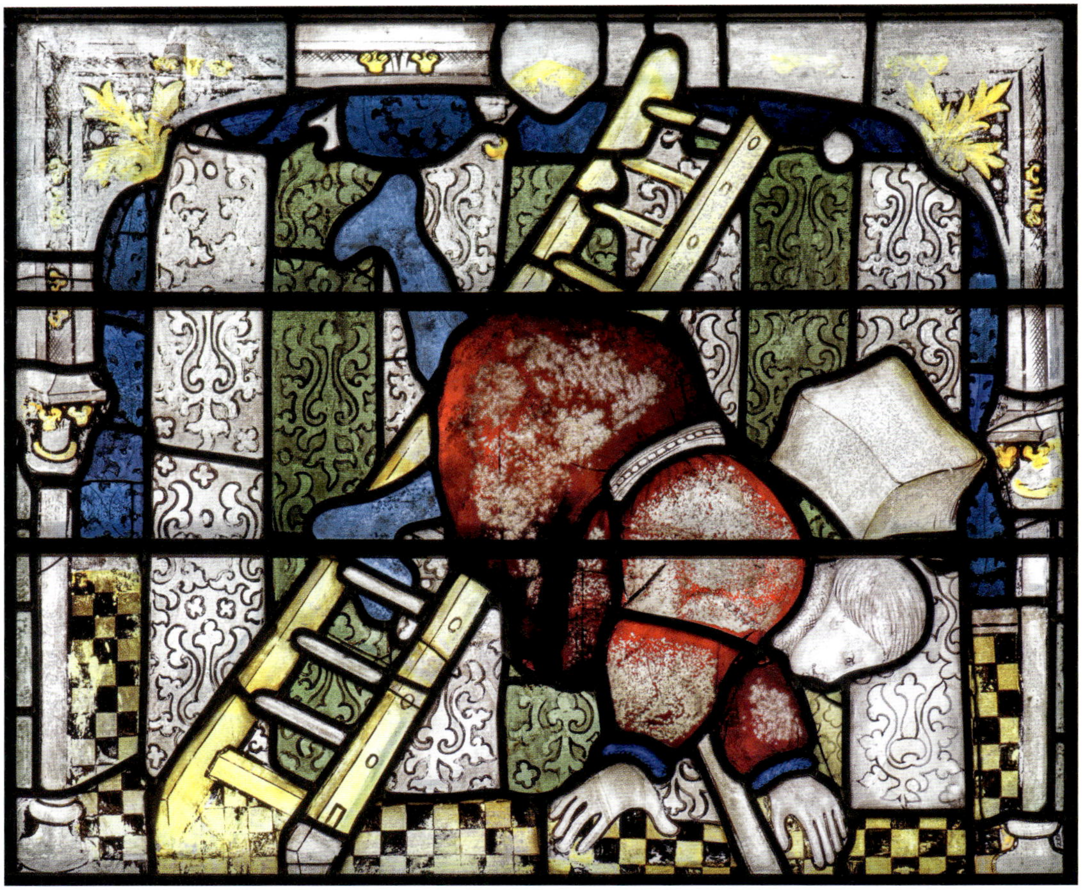

22d The man is hit on the head by a falling stone

This panel continues the story begun in 22c, and is very similar in design. While up the ladder installing the hangings, the man is hit on the head by a falling stone of considerable size and is cast to the ground.

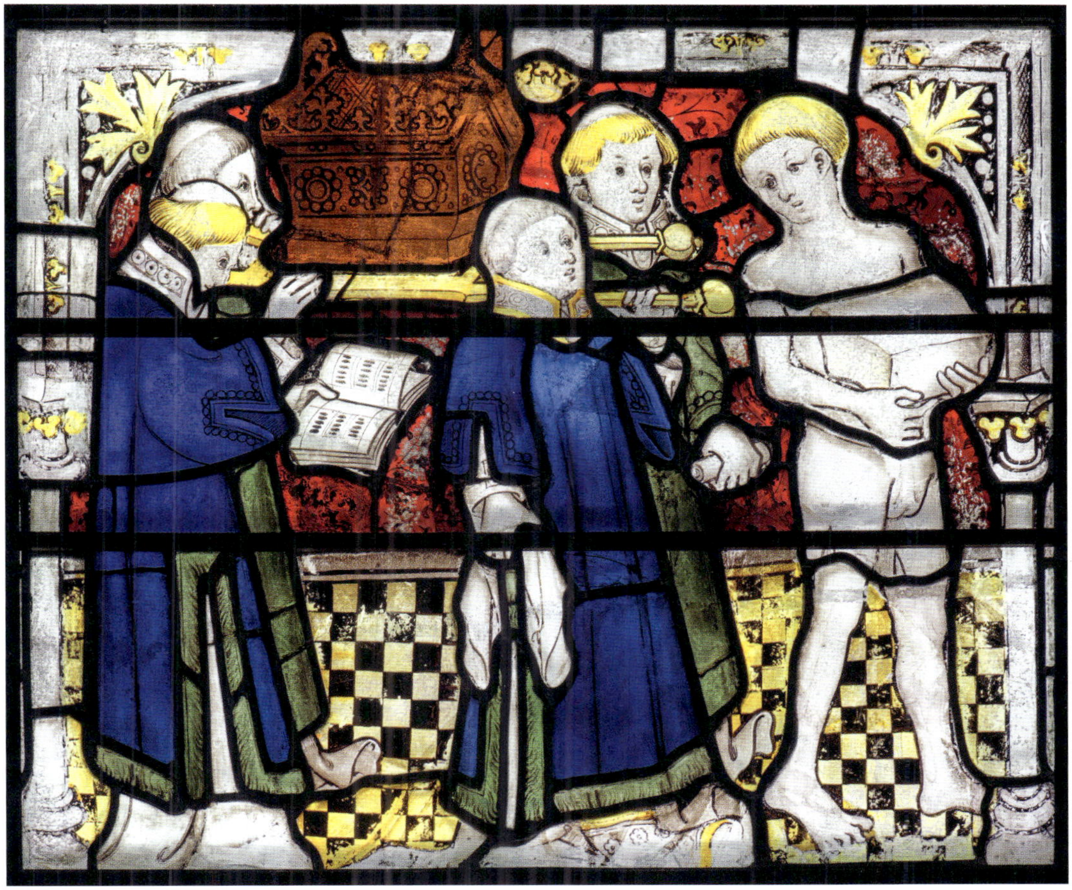

22e Carrying the stone, the man leads the portable reliquary in procession

Naked except for his underpants, the man carries the stone at the head of a procession with the portable reliquary. The reliquary has presumably been taken to the man's bedside, and now, cured, he returns to the Minster to give thanks and to present the stone at the tomb. The Minster possesses a block of stone bearing a medieval Latin inscription stating that it is the stone that fell on the head of Roger of Ripon.

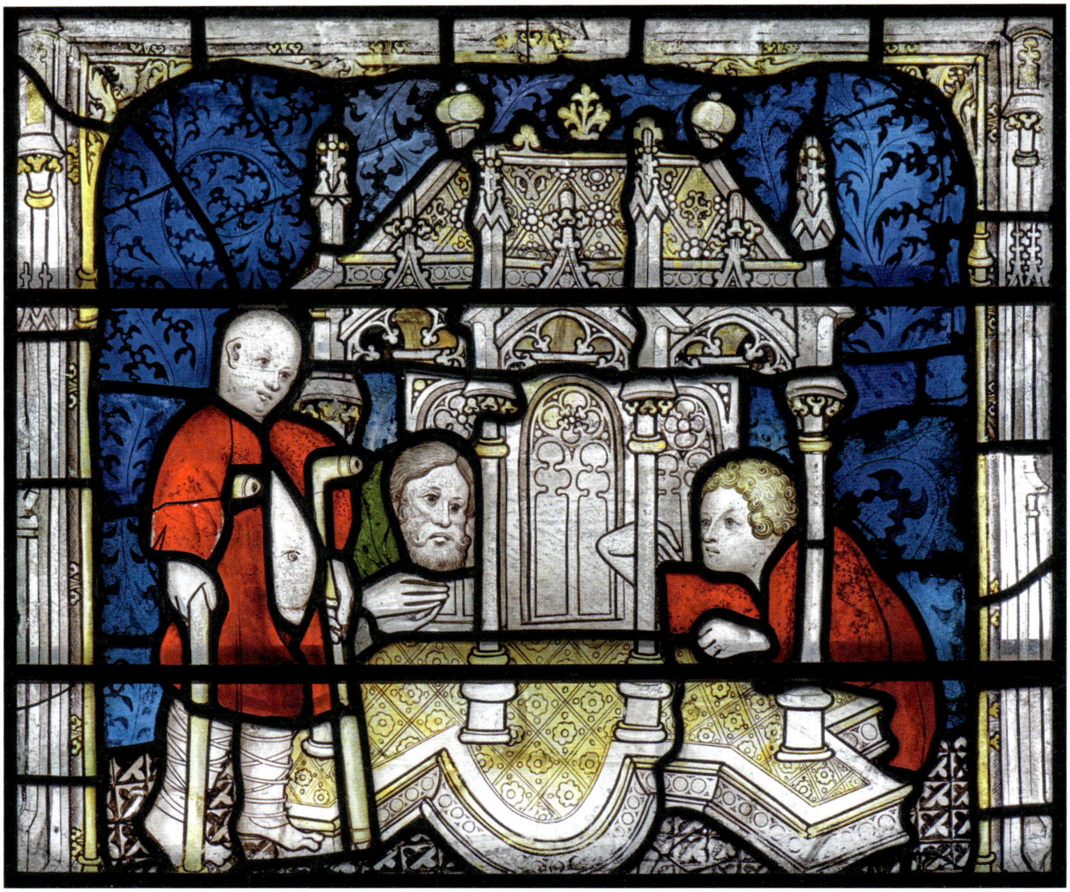

23a Three men at the tomb

This scene is based on panel 16a. The tomb is practically identical, as is the kneeling man in green on the left. The kneeling figure on the right is slightly adapted from the equivalent figure in panel 16a, while the standing figure on the left is taken from the same cartoon as a figure in panel 15b, with minor changes and the addition of a second crutch.

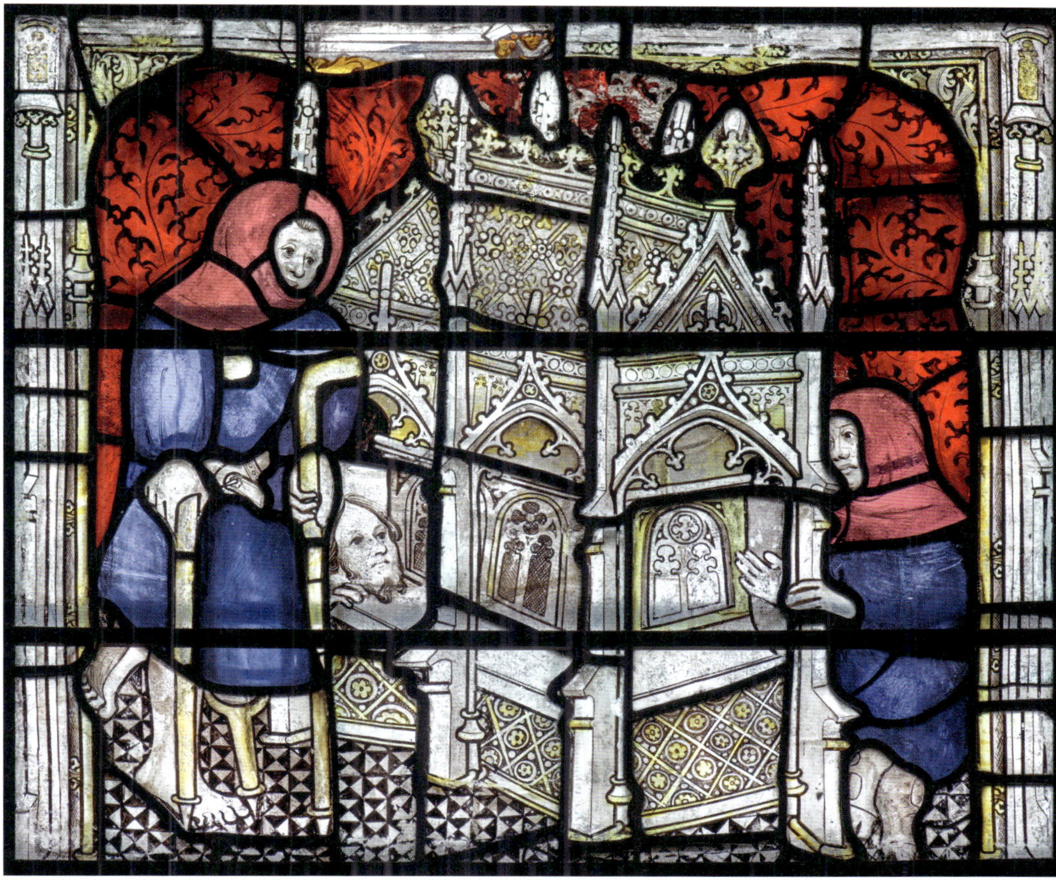

23b Three disabled men at the tomb

This panel is based on panel 15b. The tomb is taken from the same cartoon as the one in 15b, but with minor changes of details, notably the omission of the oil issuing from pipes. The largely replaced figure on the right and the head of the man up against the tomb are also taken from 15b, with minor changes. Two other figures in 15b have been omitted, while the man on crutches on the left is taken from the equivalent figure in panel 16a.

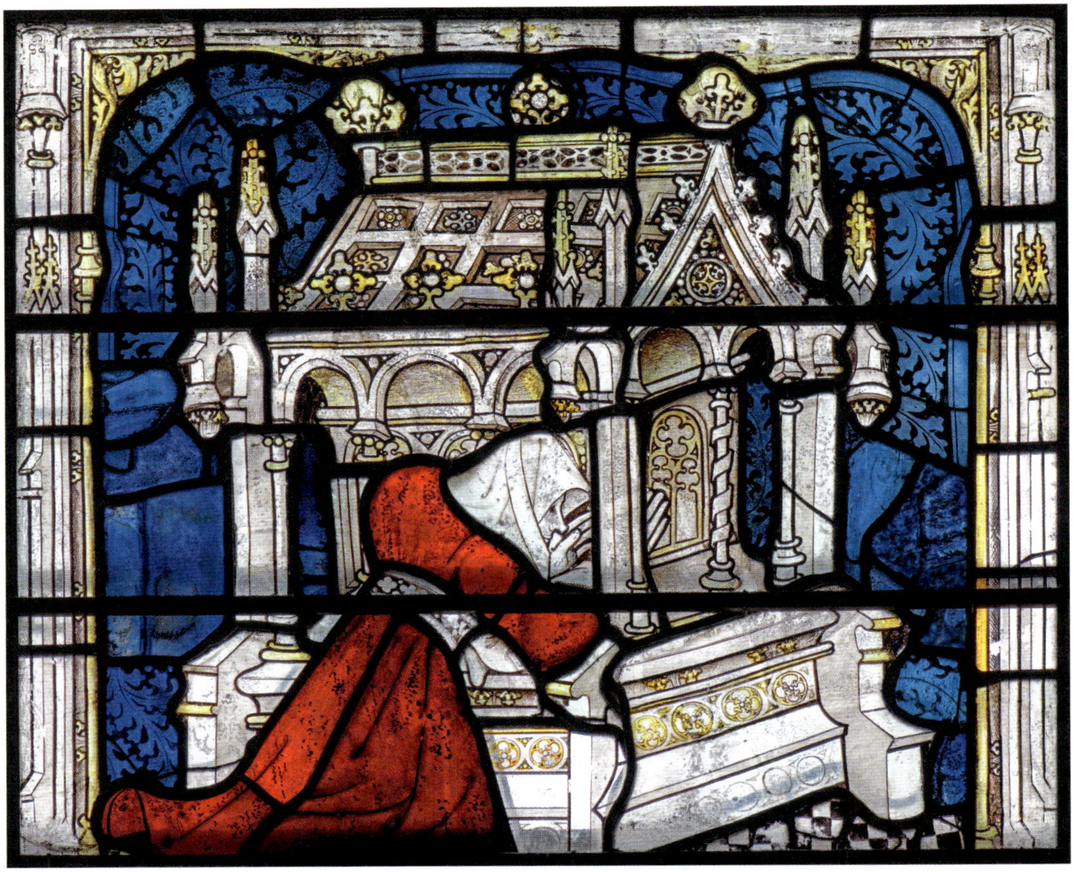

23c A woman kneels at the tomb

Unlike the other panels in row 23, this one is not copied from a previous panel. The tomb is depicted in great detail and occupies almost the whole panel. The woman, who appears to be hunchbacked, kneels right up against and partly inside the tomb structure. One of the early miracle stories describes a hunchbacked woman being healed at the tomb.

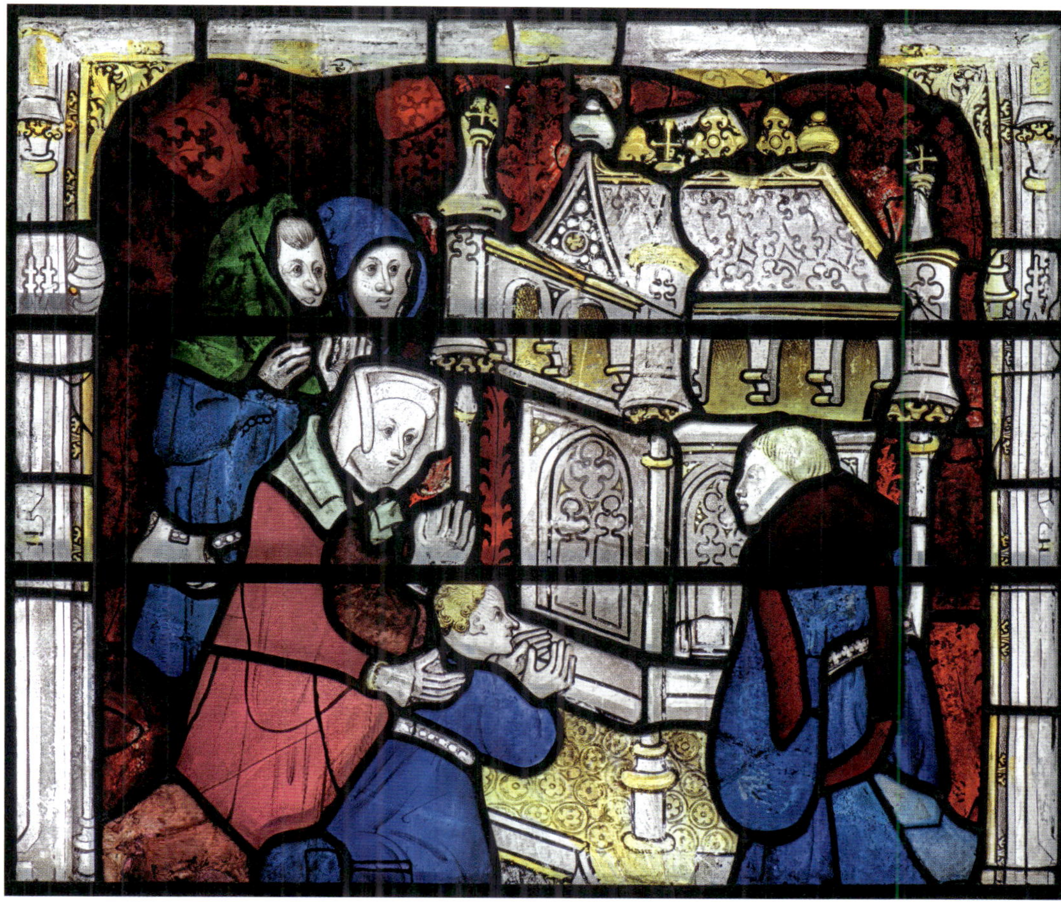

23d A group of people at the tomb

This scene is practically a copy of panel 17c. The tomb and the group of figures on the left are taken from the same designs, but with different colours and slight changes of detail, such as the head of the woman, which is taken from the woman in panel 16b. The only significant difference is the addition of the man on the right.

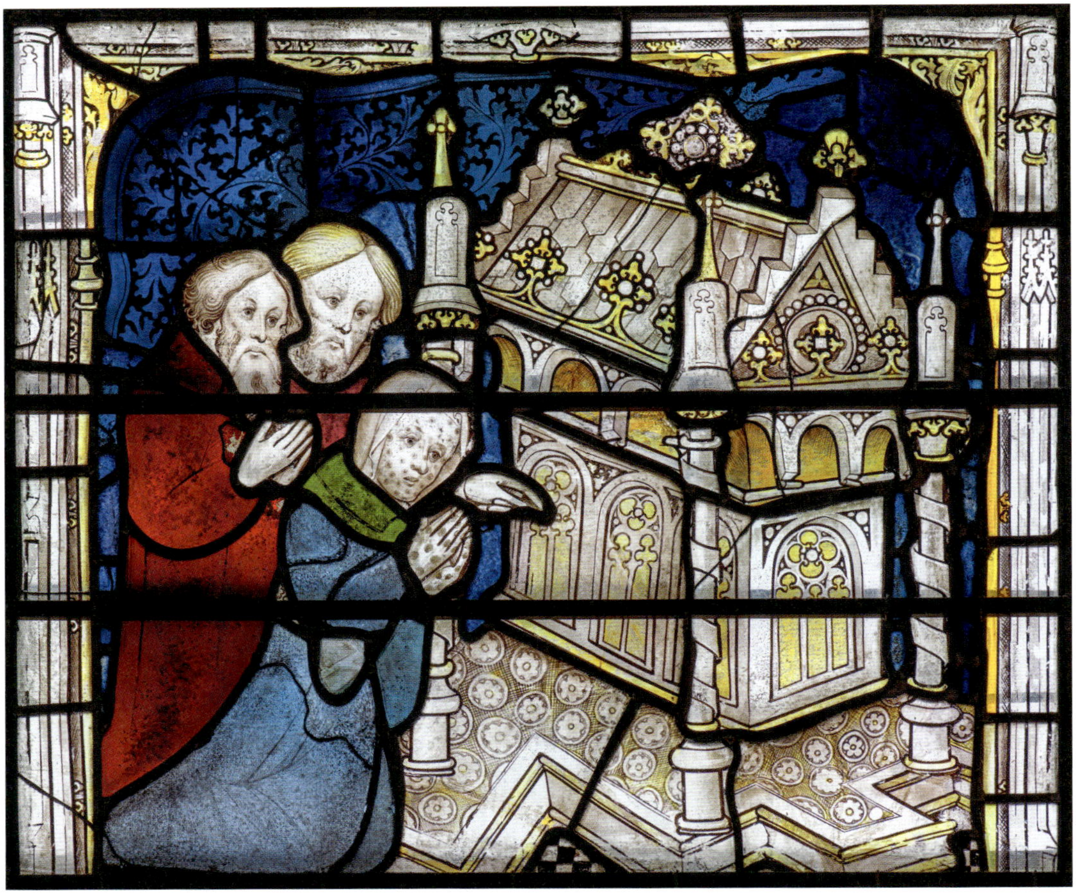

23e A leprous woman at the tomb

This scene is essentially a copy of panel 16c, but with the omission of the boy in the centre foreground. The tomb and the three figures are identical, apart from minor changes of detail. The most significant difference concerns the kneeling woman. In panel 16c she is praying for the boy to be healed, whereas here she is seeking healing for herself. The spots on the woman's face and hands would probably have been understood as leprosy. The absence of the boy renders the pointing hand of the man in the middle meaningless.

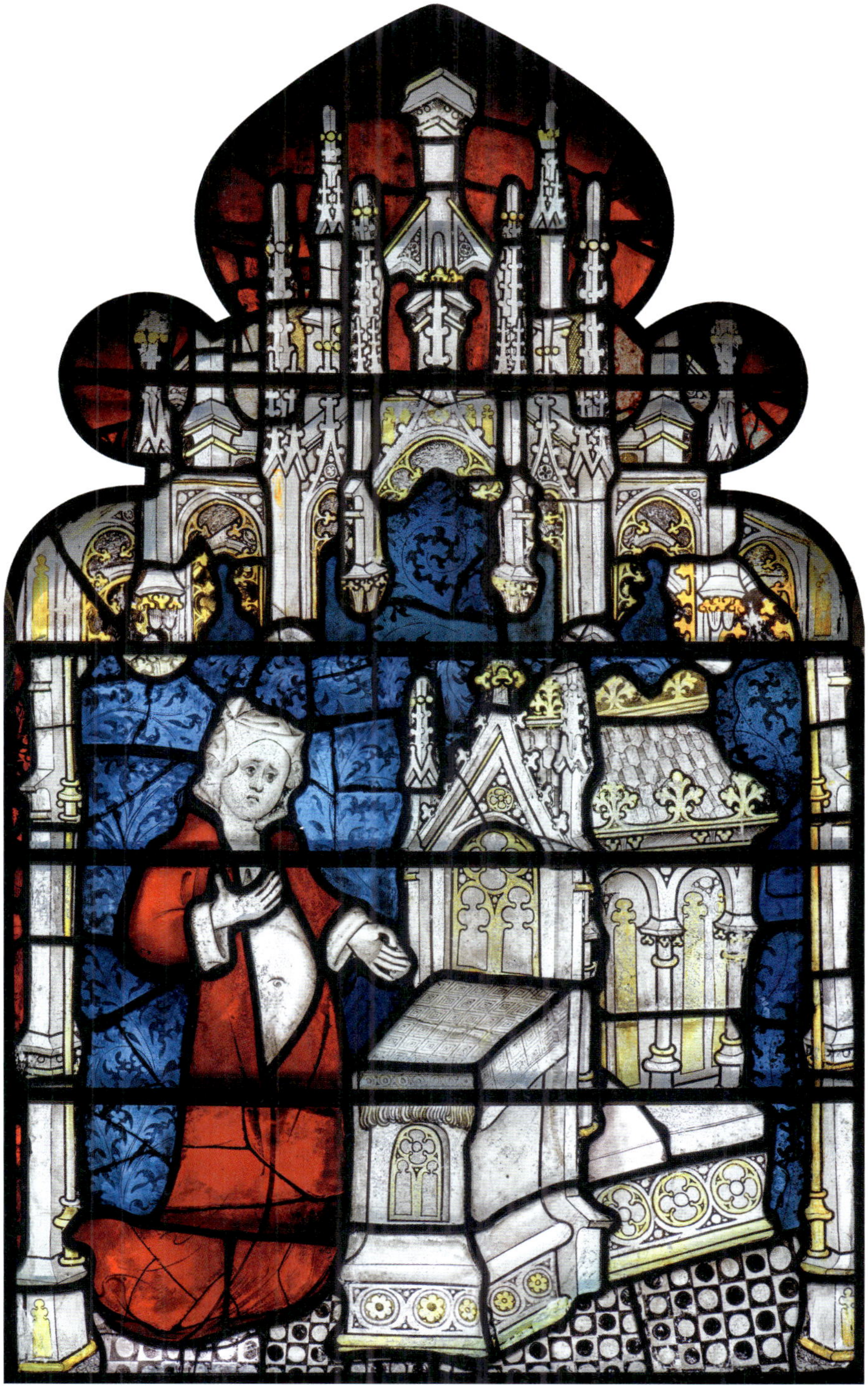

24a–25a A hydropsical woman at the tomb

This scene is a composite of elements from panels 17a and 21b. The tomb is taken from the same design as in 21b, but with minor differences in decoration. The woman is based on the woman who swallowed a frog, standing up, in panel 17a, but slightly adapted to show her with a swollen stomach. In 17a she holds a belt in her left hand, but here the belt is omitted. Instead she gestures vaguely towards the tomb, the thumb being particularly unconvincing.

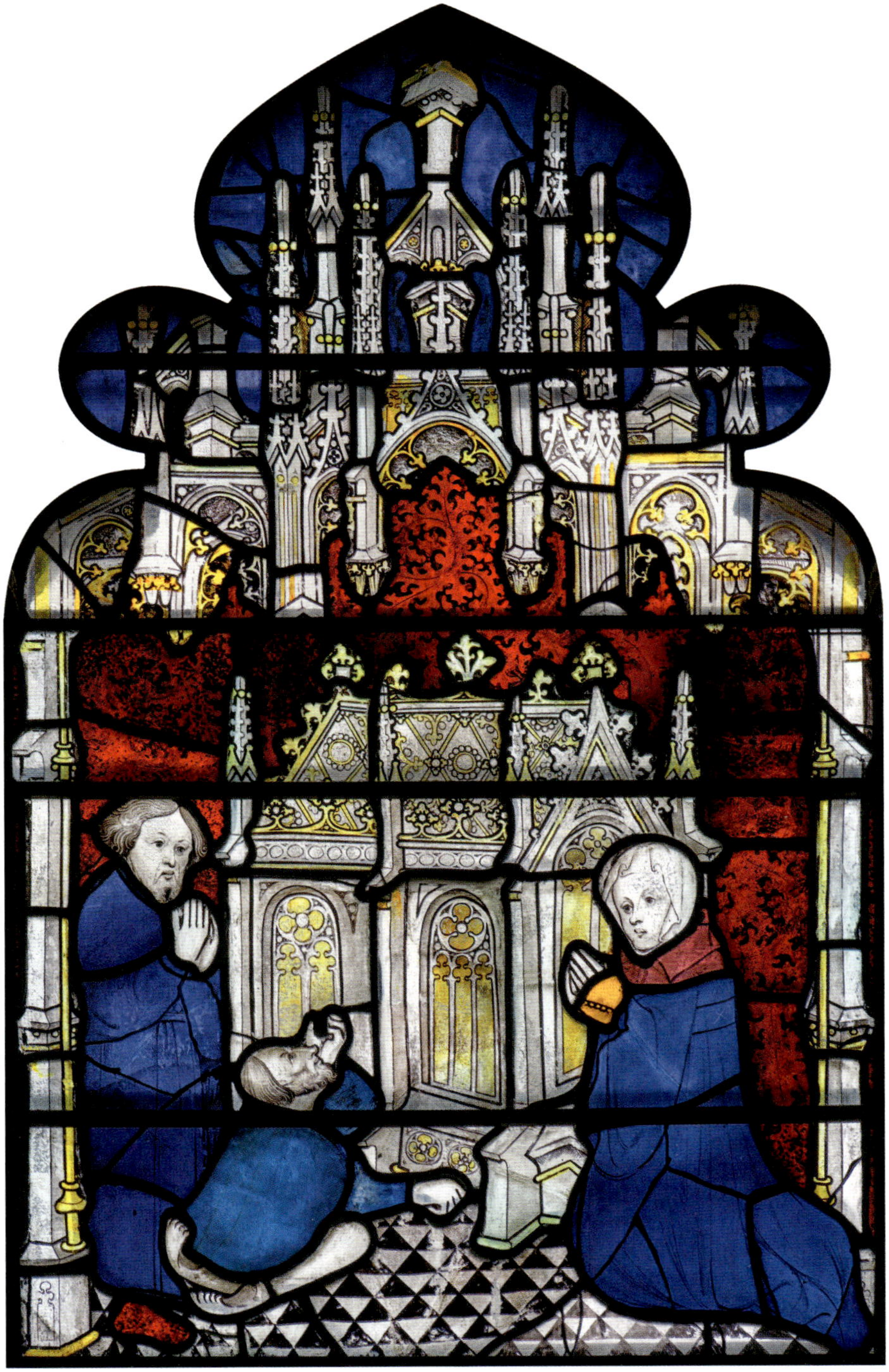

24b–25b Three supplicants at the tomb

This scene combines elements from three earlier panels. The tomb is from the same design as the one in panel 17b, but without the altar at the right-hand end. The man on the left is also taken from 17b, with changes of colour and detailing. The kneeling woman on the right is a reversed version of the woman in 16c. The man in the centre is adapted from the equivalent figure in 15b. In 15b his cupped left hand was raised to collect holy oil running from the tomb. Here, without the oil, the gesture loses its purpose.

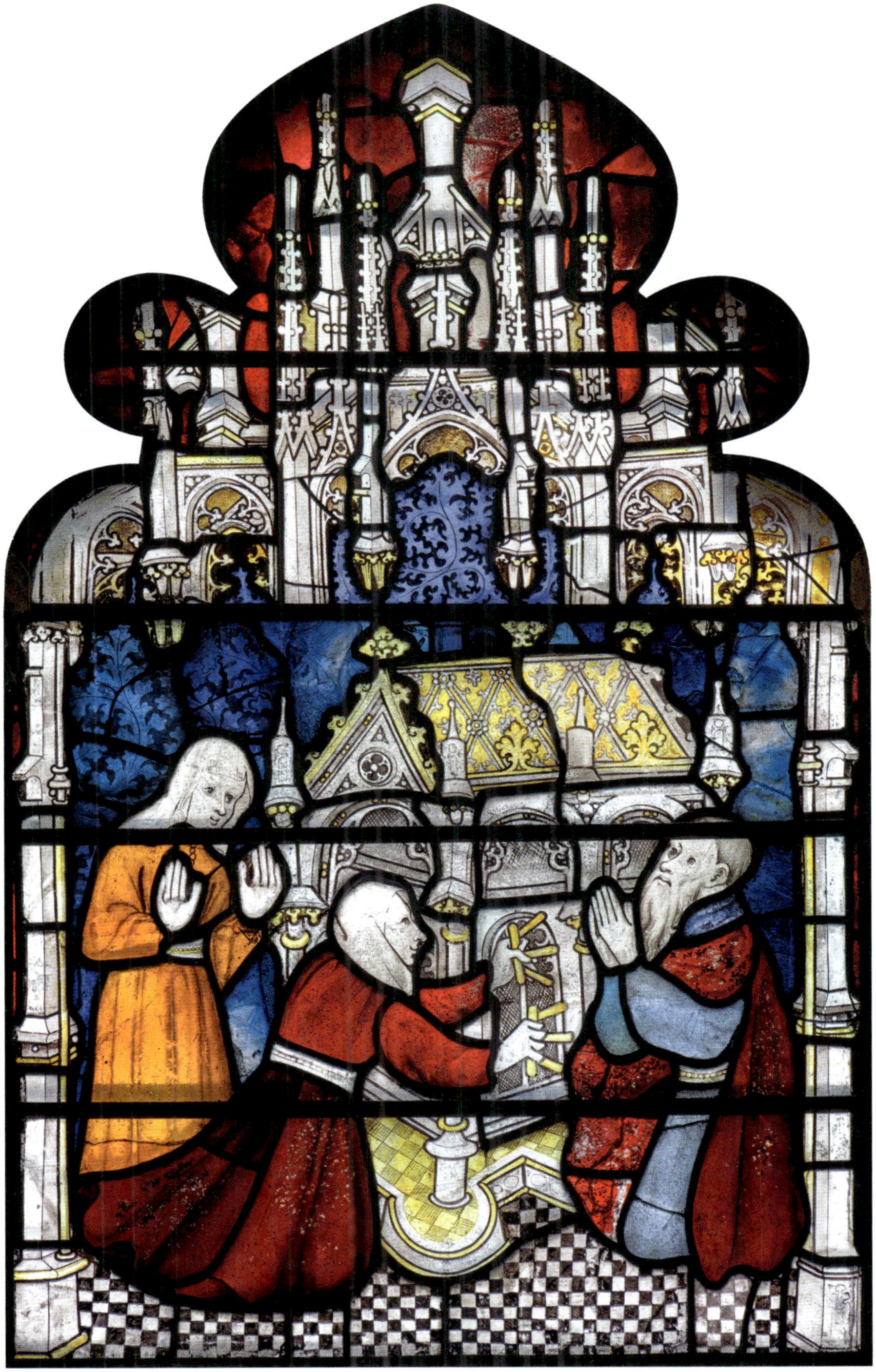

24c–25c A disabled woman is healed at the tomb

The woman in the centre holds up the hand supports that she had used to crawl to the tomb, like the man in panel 21e, but which she no longer needs. The man on the right kneels in prayer and the woman on the left raises her hands in amazement. Unlike the preceding panels, this is not a composite of pre-existing elements, but a completely new design, based perhaps on one of the early miracle stories.

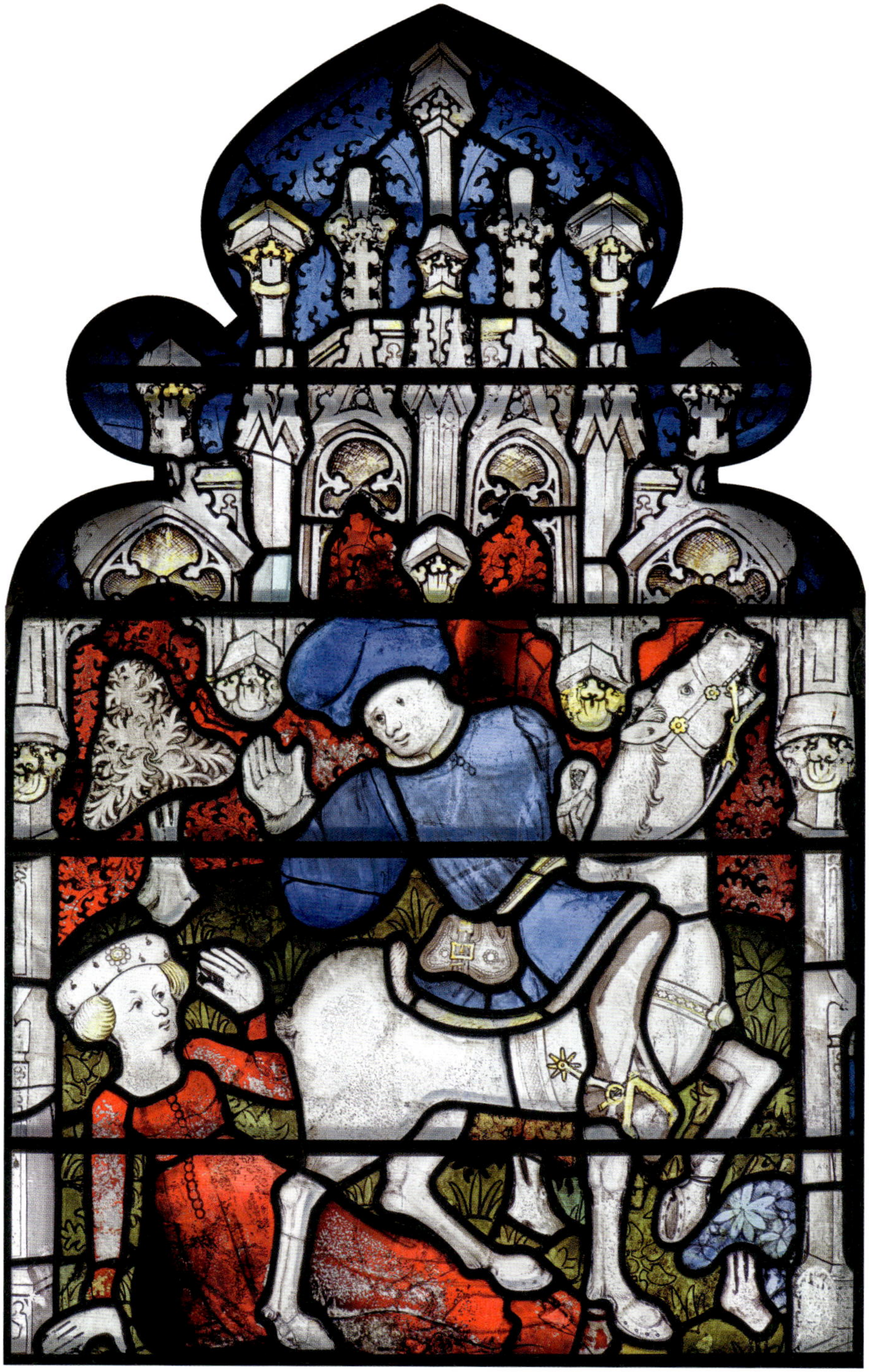

24d–25d A lady is trampled by a horse

The narrative ends in panels 24d and 24e with a pair of scenes. A young man on a white horse turns back to look at a woman lying on the ground beneath the rear legs of the horse. She is dressed all in red and wears an ermine-lined hat embellished with a circular brooch. Her hat and hairstyle are unlike those of the other women in the miracle scenes, but are similar to those of the courtiers attending King Edward and Queen Eleanor in row 18. They mark her out as an aristocratic lady. The figures are on a significantly larger scale than in many of the other miracle scenes.

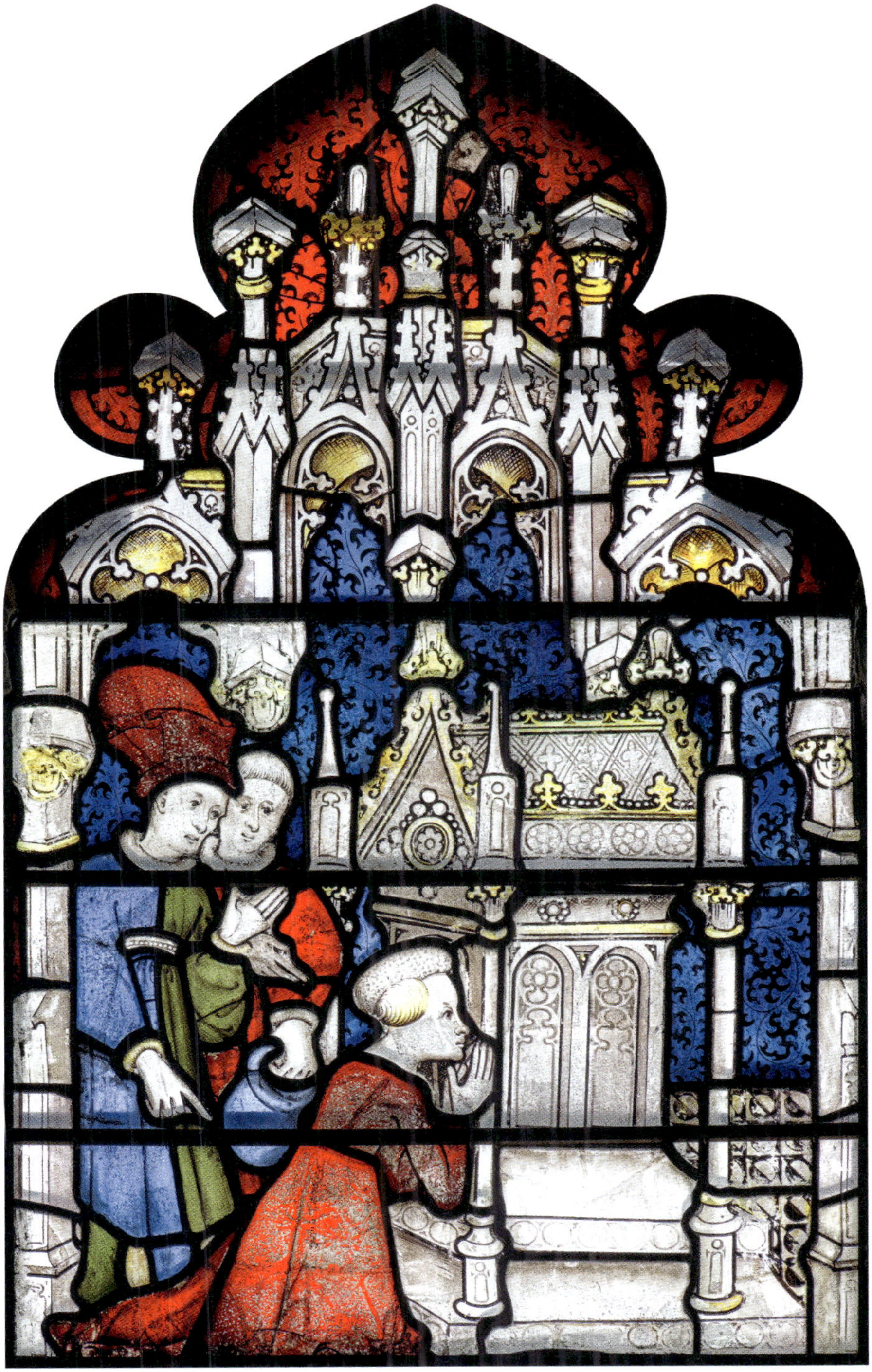

24e–25e The lady gives thanks at the tomb for her deliverance

This completes the episode begun in panel 24d. Accompanied by an attendant on the left wearing distinctive parti-coloured clothes and an elaborate red hat, and by another man who has doffed his hat, the lady, again dressed in red, kneels before the tomb to give thanks for surviving the accident. This, the last scene in the cycle, is directly above the figure of Lady Beatrice de Roos at the base of the window (panel 1e), and the lady dressed in red may be Lady Beatrice herself. The entire window may be a thank-offering to St William for her deliverance.

The Tracery Lights

The window culminates in the tracery with a vison of heaven. In the centre Christ is seated in majesty next to the Virgin Mary, who is crowned as queen of heaven (H2–H3). They are flanked by censing angels (H1 and H4) and accompanied by a heavenly host of figures standing in fictive architectural niches. These are all archbishops and kings, as befits a window dedicated to an archbishop saint with royal connections (A1–A4, A7–A10, B1–B2, C2–C3, C6–C7 and D1–D2). They are arranged in facing pairs, the archbishops (all with pallium and cross-staff) on the left, the kings (all with crown and sceptre) on the right. None of them have individual attributes or other means of identification. The figures are based on a limited number of cartoons, most of which are used more than once. The archbishops all

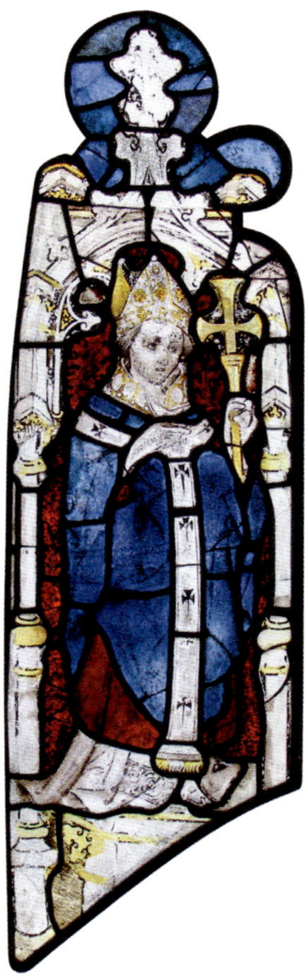

A1 An archbishop

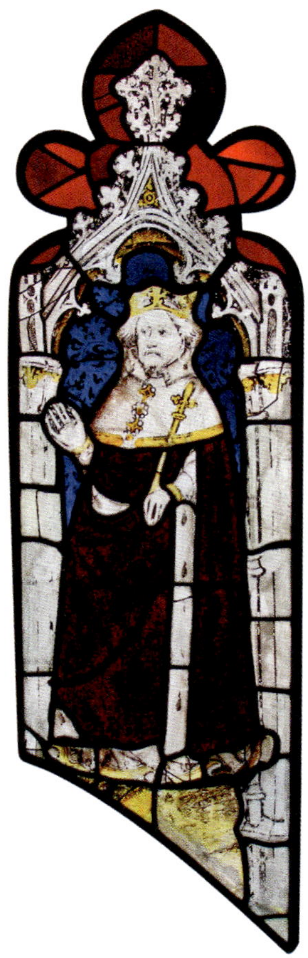

A2 A king
The king faces towards the archbishop in the adjacent light. The architecture is different from A1.

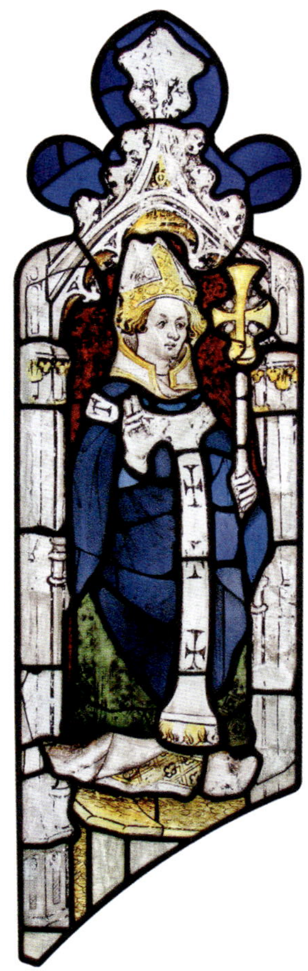

A3 An archbishop
The figure is similar to the archbishop in A1 but drawn from a different cartoon. The design of the niche is the same as in A2.

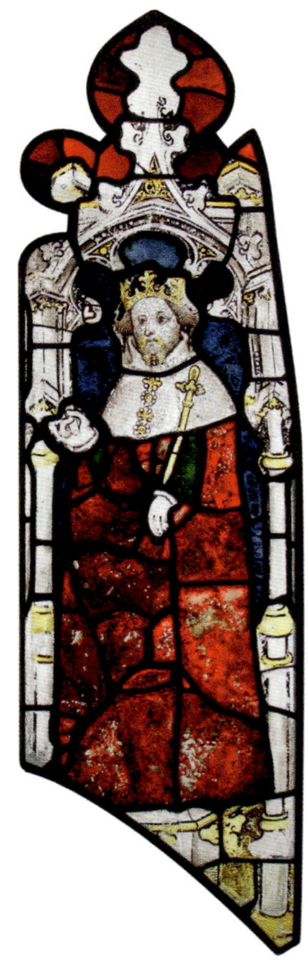

A4 A king
The king is similar to the one in A2, but holds a scroll in his right hand. The architecture of the niche is the same as in A1.

have blue chasubles contrasting with red backgrounds; the kings, who mostly have red robes and blue backgrounds, have a greater variety of poses and colours.

There is some variation in the designs of the architectural niches, and in all of the lights in row A the base of the niche is cut by the curve of the tracery. The panels in row A are interchangeable, as are those in row C, and some of the panels were moved around over the years. The present arrangement is probably the original one.

The small intermediary panels (A5–A6; C1, C4–C5 and C8; F1–F2; G2 and J1) contain plain glass and are not illustrated.

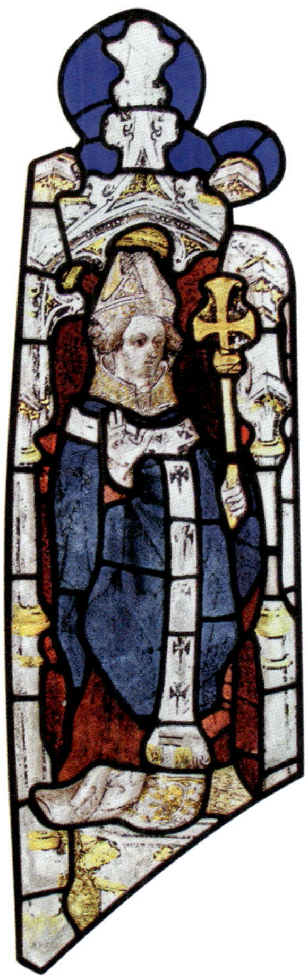

A7 An archbishop
The archbishop is taken from the same cartoon as the one in A3, but the niche design is the same as in A1.

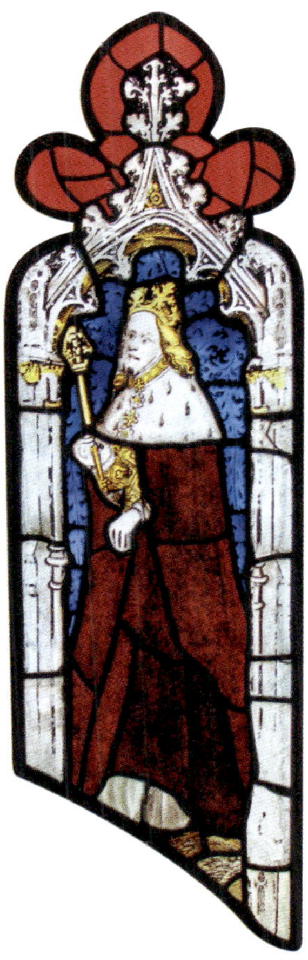

A8 A king
The king turns half-left towards the archbishop in A7 and holds his sceptre in his right hand. The niche design is the same as in A2.

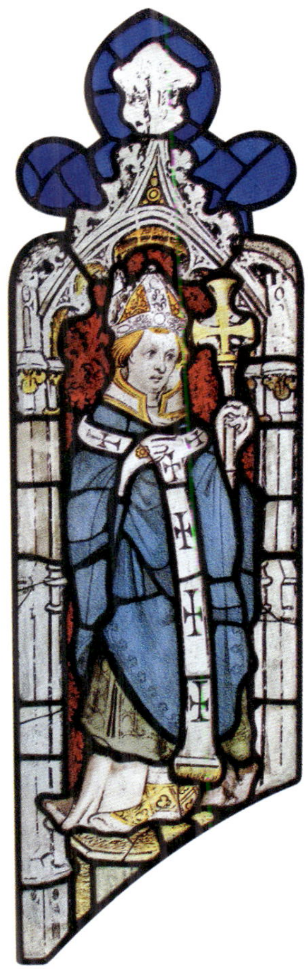

A9 An archbishop
The archbishop is based on the same cartoon as A1, but the niche is the same as A2.

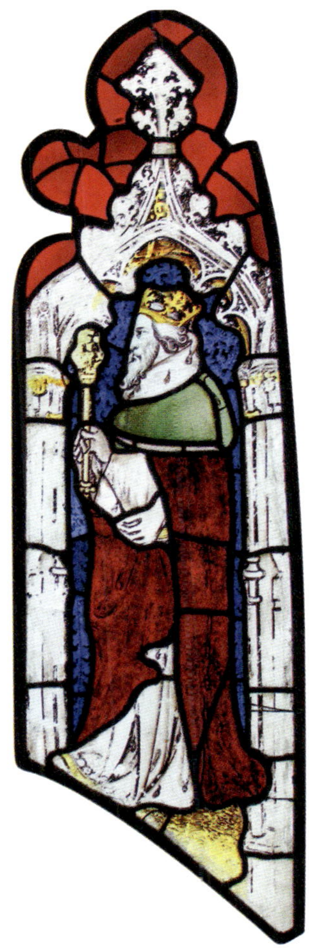

A10 A king
The niche design is the same as in A2.

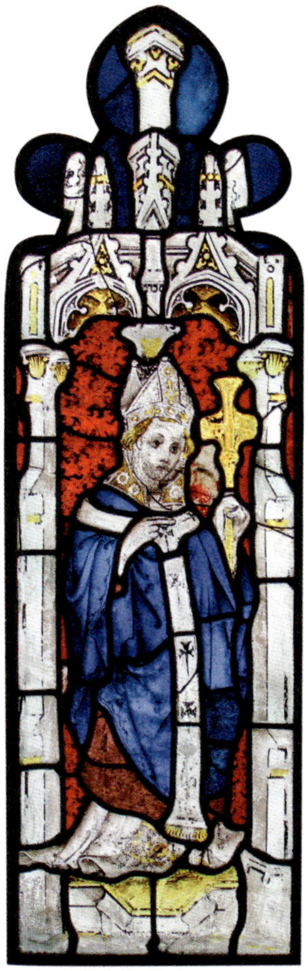

B1 An archbishop
The figure is taken from the same cartoon as A1, but the niche is different and is square at the bottom.

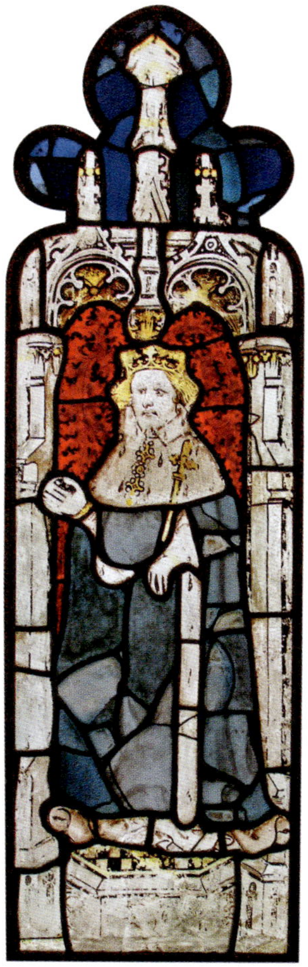

B2 A king
The king is taken from the same cartoon as A2. The niche is from the same cartoon as B1, but with a different base.

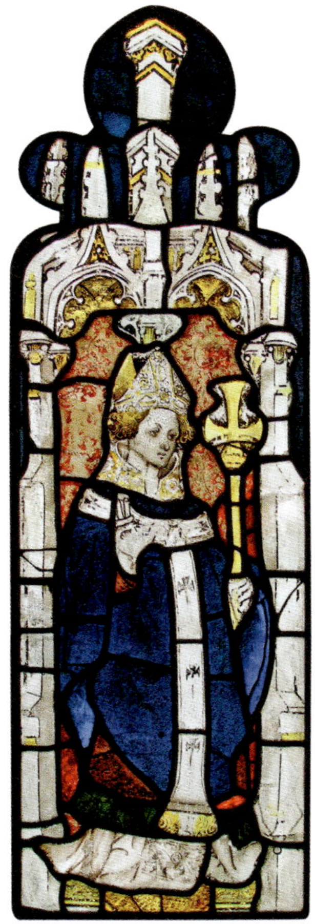

C2 An archbishop
The archbishop is taken from the same cartoon as A3. The doubled-arched niche is the same as B1, but with a shallower base and minor differences of detail.

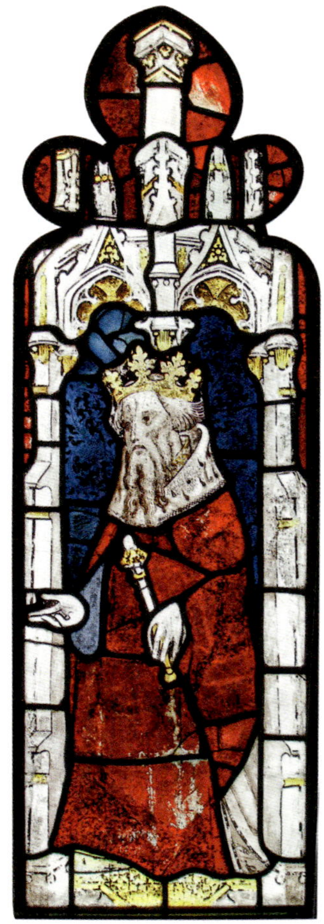

C3 A king
This king is different from all the others. The double-arched niche is taken from the same cartoon as B1.

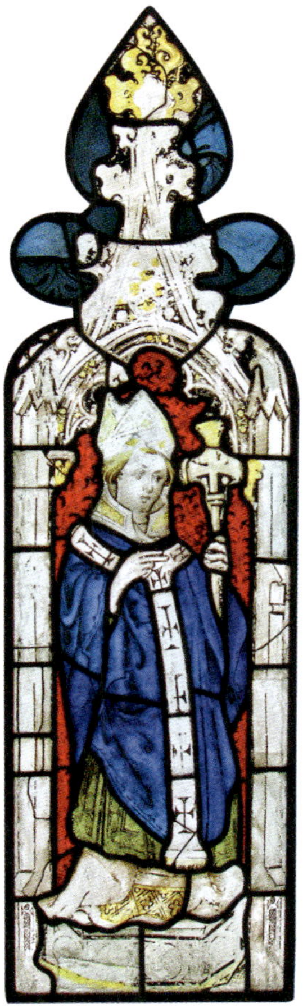

C6 An archbishop

Another archbishop taken from the same cartoon as A1. The design of the niche is found only here and in C7.

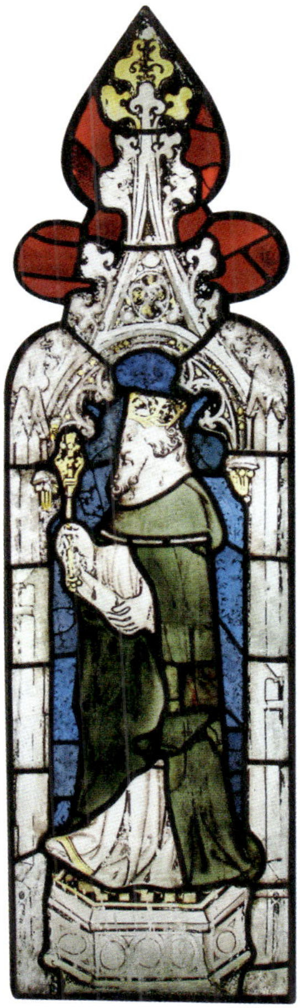

C7 A king

This king is almost identical to the one in A10. The design of the niche is the same as C6.

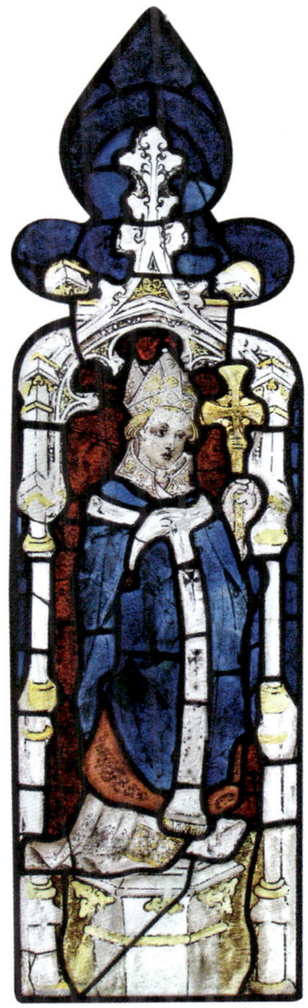

D1 An archbishop

This is very similar to A1, with the same cartoons and colours for the archbishop and the architectural niche.

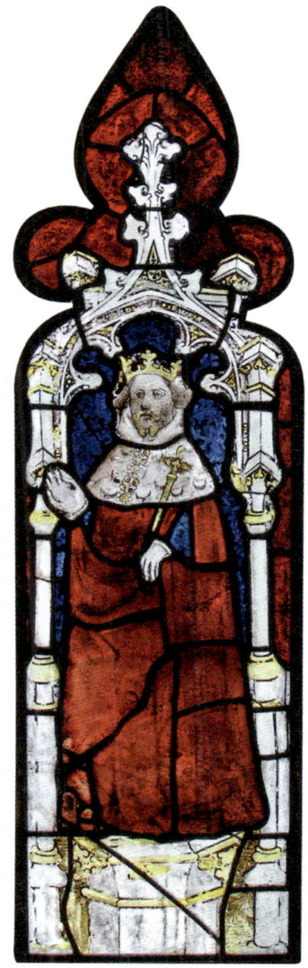

D2 A king

The king is from the same cartoon as A2, while the niche is from the same cartoon as A1.

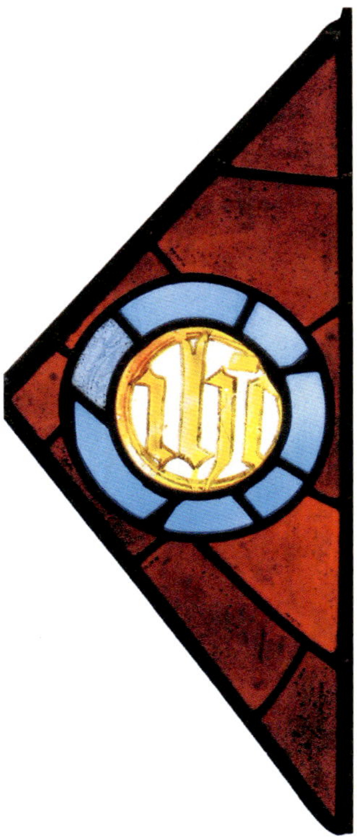

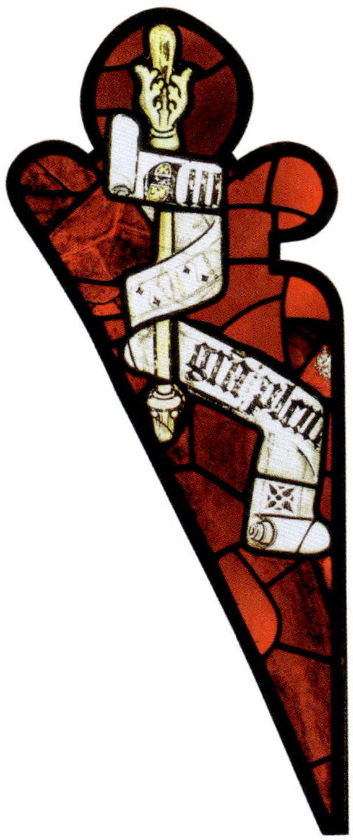

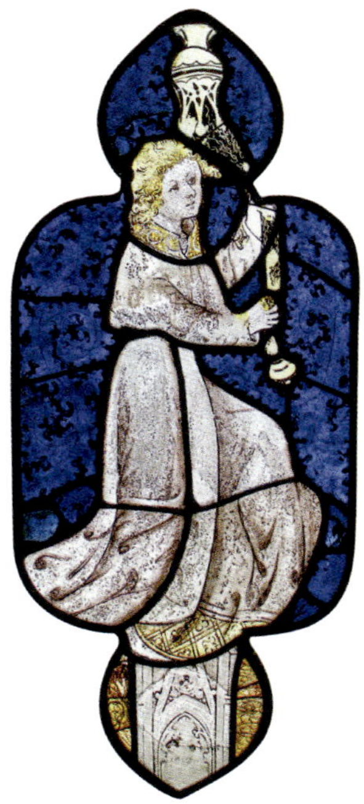

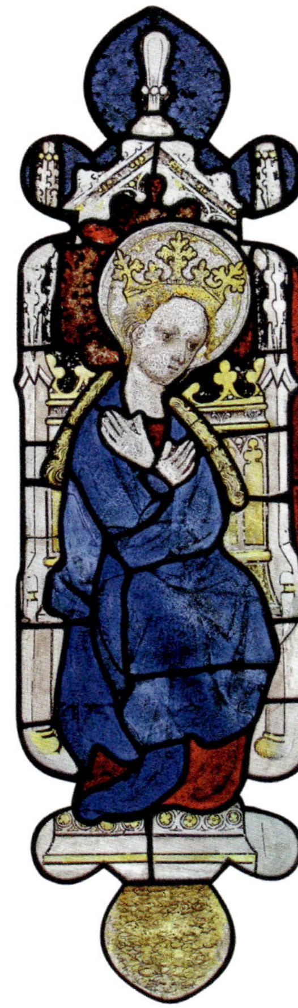

G1 Sacred monogram
The sacred monogram *ihc* in gold letters, paired with the monogram in G3.

E1 Inscription
A scroll wrapped around a sceptre bears the words of the angelic greeting to Mary at the Annunciation: *Ave gr[ati]a plena*, (Hail ... full of grace). Mary's name is in E2.

H1 Censing angel
A kneeling censing angel towards the figures of Mary and Christ in H2 and H3.

H2 The Virgin enthroned
The Virgin Mary sits enthroned as Queen of Heaven. She faces towards the seated Christ in H3.

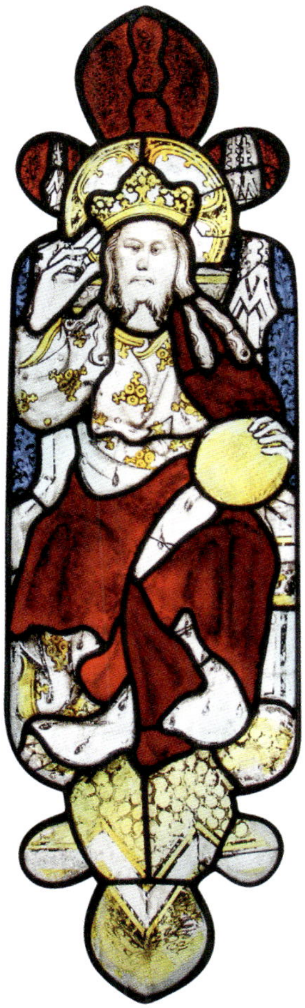

H3 Christ in majesty

Christ is seated on a throne in heaven, his left hand holding a golden orb, his right hand raised in blessing. His throne is set slightly higher than that of the Virgin Mary, emphasising his position as King of Heaven at the apex of the window.

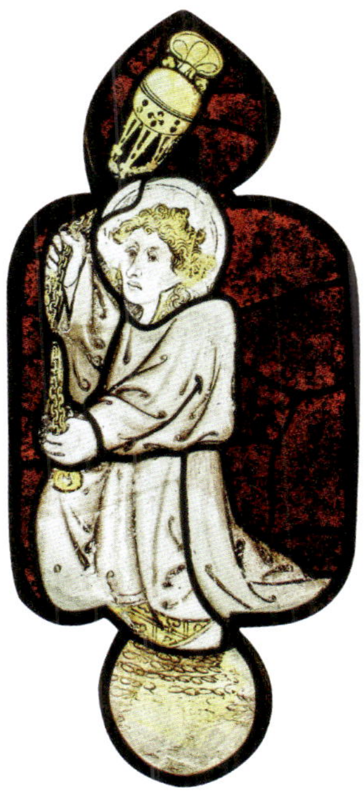

H4 Censing angel

This angel is the pair of the one in H1, facing left towards Christ and the Virgin.

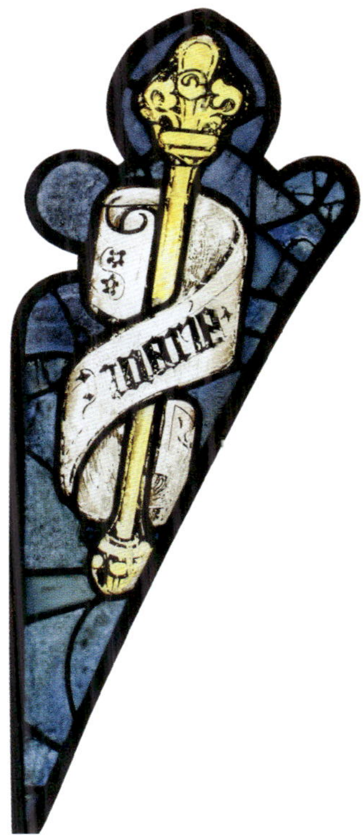

E2 Inscription

The pair to E1; a scroll wrapped round a large gold sceptre bears the name *Maria*.

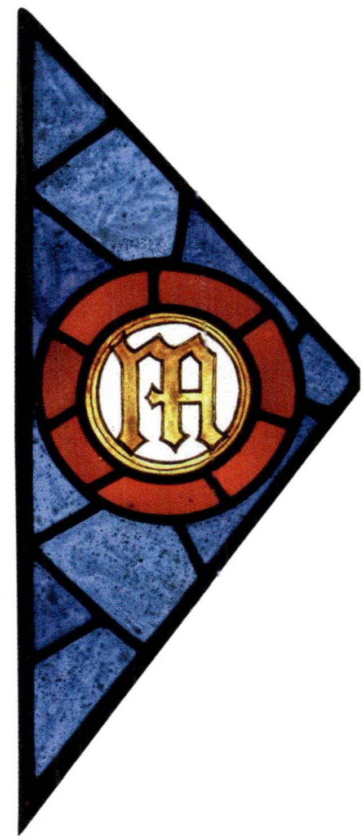

G3 Sacred monogram

The monogram *Maria* in gold letters, paired with the monogram in G1.

Appendix One

James Torre's Description of the St William Window

Transcription by Dr Katie Harrison

Torre's description of the St William Window (which he calls 'the Cross or Lanthorn window'), is to be found in volume 1 of his manuscript *Antiquities of York Minster* (Minster Library, YMA/ZC/L/1/7, ff. 35r–39r). The manuscript has recently been conserved and rebound, and high-resolution photographs can be viewed online at: https://yorkminster.contentdm.oclc.org/digital/collection/torremss/id/1010/rec/1

Torre listed the figurative panels in a continuous sequence numbered 1–120, starting at the apex of the window and concluding with the bottom row. He drew a diagram of the window (Fig. 5.1) showing the location of every panel, and he started each panel description by describing its position within the window, by row and by light, Within each section of the window, he numbered the rows from the top downwards, and within each row, he numbered the panels from left to right, 1–5. Thus, for instance, panel 4a is the first light of the second row down in the lowest section. Torre's marginal notes relating to the rows have been omitted.

In the table below, the panel descriptions have been tabulated in the order in which the panels are currently arranged and as illustrated in the Catalogue of the present book, that is to say, from the bottom upwards. The left-hand column gives the current panel number. The next column gives Torre's panel number; and in the case of those panels that were no longer in their original position when he recorded them, the position in which he saw them is given in brackets. The out-of-position panels are shaded in the diagram (Fig. 6.18).

His descriptions are formulaic , and he uses frequent abbreviations when identifying figures or recording colours, such as *abp* for archbishop and *B* for blue. The abbreviations have been silently expanded. Torre regularly uses heraldic terminology to describe colours and other details he noted, such as *gules* for red and *murry* for purple. Capitalisation and punctuation have been regularised.

Current Location	Torre's numbering	Description
1a	111 (2a)	In the 4th row and 1st light stands an image of our lady, robed *argent*, crowned *or*. And two knights in armour with swords by their sides kneel before it, bearing their arms upon their sur-coates thus, viz: 1. Ros [blazon drawing] 2. Ros [blazon drawing] 1st *gules,* a trefoil inter 3 water-budgetts *argent*. 2nd *gules,* a mullet of 6 poynts inter 3 water-budgetts *argent*.
1b	112 (2b)	In the 2nd light is another image of our lady, *argent*. And two other knights in armour with swords by their sides kneeling before it, their surcoates being charged with their arms thus, viz: 1. Ros of Hamlack [blazon drawing] 2. Ros of Hamlak [blazon drawing] 1. and 2. *gules,* 3 water-budgetts *argent*.
1c	113 (2c)	In the 3rd light kneel other 2 knights in armour with swords by their sides; the 1st with a prayer book open in his hand, the 2nd at prayers before an image of our lady in white rayment. Having on their surcoates *gules,* 3 water-budgetts *argent*, thus: Ros, Lord [blazon drawing], Ros, Lord [blazon drawing].
1d	114 (2d)	In the 4th light are kneeling at their devotions a lady, with a coronet on her head *or*, between 2 knights in armour with swords by their sides, on whose sur-coates is the Rosses arms, viz: *gules,* 3 water budgetts *argent*. And on her gown is barry of 6 *or* and *blue*. Lord Ros [blazon drawing], Constable [blazon drawing], Lord Ros [blazon drawing].
1e	115 (2e)	In the 5th light is a lady of the Rosses family kneeling before a crucifix *argent*; upon her gown *gules*, are 3 water-budgetts *argent*. Ros [blazon drawing].
2a	116 (1a)	In the bottom row and first light sitts a bishop inthroned, robed *blue* and *argent*, mytered *or*, his hands closed at his breast. On each side [of] him kneels a man habited *gules*. Behind the 1st man stand 2 women habited *blue*. Behind the 2nd stands the bishop's cross-bearer, habited *sanguine*.
2b	117 (1b)	In the 2nd light stands a bishop, robed and mytred argent, holding in his arms a child in white. On his right hand stands a woman habited *sanguine* and *or*. And 2 men by her, one of them being habited *blue*. On the other side stand 2 women, one of which is habited *sanguine*. And behind them stands a noble-man, habited *blue*.

2c	119 (1d)	In the 4th light sitts a monk habited *argent*, with a key in his hand *or*. Before whom stand and knell certain others, habited *argent* and *blue*.
2d (missing)	118 (1c)	In the 3rd light kneel 5 women, one habited *gules*, the rest *argent*.
2e	120 (1e)	In the 5th light lyes a man habited *vert* and a woman habited *argent*. And over them are 2 shin bones in saltire *argent*.
3a	106	In the next lower row and 1st light stand 2 monks and a nun, habited *blue* and respecting each other. One of the monks having a rockett down his back, *gules*. And about them stand 4 more monks and nuns diversly habited.
3b	103 (4c)	In the 3rd light sitts another archbishop, enthroned *or*, habited *gules*, pallium *argent*, myter *or*. And a monk (*argent*) kneels before him, holding a book open. And 2 other monks stand on each side [of] his throne, one habited *argent*, the other *gules*.
3c	108	In the 3rd light sitt severall monks and nuns about a counting table, selling *gold*; some habited *vert*, some *blue*, others *gules*.
3d	109	In the 4th light sitts a pope inthroned *or*, robed *gules*, with a monk and a nun, habited *blue*, lying prostrate and presenting him a charter *argent*. Behind them stand 3 other monks, habited *gules*.
3e	110	In the 5th light sitts another pope, enthroned *argent*, robed *blue*, tripple-crowned *or*. And before him kneel 2 monks presenting a charter; the one habited *blue*, the other *gules*. Behind them stand two other monks and a nun, habited *vert* and *blue*.
4a	101	In the 2nd row and 1st light sitts a king inthroned *argent*, robed *blue* and *gules*, crowned *or*. And another presenting him a book, closed *argent*, habited *blue*. Behind him stands a bishop, habited and mytred *argent*, crosyer *or*. And by him a woman stands in a *sanguine* and white habit and behind her a monk, habited blue with a crosyer (*or*) in his hand.
4b	107 (3b)	In the 2nd light kneel about an altar severall men and women habited *blue* and *argent*.
4c	102 (4b)	In the 2nd light sitts an archbishop inthroned, habited *gules*, pallium *argent*, myter *or*, elevating and expanding both his hands *argent*. A bishop, mytred *or*, stands on each side [of] his throne. And two others in white habits kneel before him, holding a book open *argent*.
4d	104	In the 4th light stand 2 monks (one habited *blue*, the other *or*) supporting a pall (*argent*) between them.
4e	105	In the 5th light rides a cardinall-bishop and 2 monks.
5a	96	In the upper row and 1st light a queen, crowned *or*, lyes in a *sanguine* bed, having a coronet (or myter) *gules*, held over her by 2 white hands.
5b	97	In the 2nd light sitts a pope inthroned, robed *gules*, pallium *argent*, tripple crowned *or*. On each side [of] him stand 2 cardinalls, habited *blue*, copes *gules*, touching the pope's crown with their hands.
5c	98	In the 3rd light sitts another pope enthroned *or*, robed *gules*, tripple-crowned *or*. And is adored by a monk lying prostrate at his feet, habited *argent*. Also 2 other monks kneel behind the last, one habited *blue* and *gules*, the other *vert* and *argent*.
5d	99	In the 4th light sitts another pope enthroned *argent*, robed *blue*, tripple-crowned *or*. With a cardinall sitting on one side, habited *sanguine*, cap *gules*. And a bishop on the other, habited *vert* and *gules*.
5e	100	In the 5th light sitts an archbishop enthroned, habited *blue*, pallium *argent*, myter *argent*. And a white monk sitts before him with a book open. Behind the archbishop sitt 2 other monks, one habited *blue*, the other *argent*.
7a	91	In the next under row and first light are two monks kneeling, supporting a golden cross-staff; the one habited *blue*, the other *gules*. And 3 other monks stand about them, whereof one is habited *gules*, the other 2 *gules* and *blue*.
7b	92	In the 2nd light is the representation of a church *argent* and a monk therein, habited *gules*, and severall persons riding to it.
7c	93	In the 3rd light there lyes a king in bed, covered *vert* and *blue*. And severall white monks and one nun stand about him; she being habited *sanguine*.
7d	94	In the 4th light a monk, habited blue, is kneeling at his devotions before an altar *argent* in a church *or* and *argent*.

7e	95	In the 5th light stands an abbot, habited *blue*, hooded *gules*, mytred *or*, delivering a bunch of keyes *or* to a monk standing by, habited *blue*. And 4 monks, habited *gules*, stand behind the said abbot.
8a	86	In the next lower row and in the first light rides a cardinal, habited *gules*, on a white horse. With his cross-bearer before him, mounted on another white horse, he being habited *blue*, his cross *or*.
8b	87	In the 2nd light sitts a king enthroned, robed *gules*, crowned *or*. And 2 others kneel before him, one habited *gules* and *blue*, the other *vert* and *gules*.
8c	88	In the 3rd light an archbishop habited *blue*, pallium *argent*, sitts at the helm of a ship with one mast *or* and *argent*. Also 2 sea-men sitt at the stern, habited *vert*, caps *or*.
8d	89	In the 4th light stands an archbishop, habited *gules*, pallium and myter *argent*, delivering a book to a monk standing by him, habited *blue*. Three other monks stand behind the last, whereof one is habited *sanguine*. Also another monk behind the archbishop, habited *blue*, mantled *vert*, holding a book in his hand, *argent*.
8e	90	In the 5th light stands an ancient king, robed *blue*, mantled ermine. And by his side a bishop, habited *vert*. Also a monk kneeles before the king, habited *gules*, mantle *or*, hood *blue*, presenting a book or charter to the king. Behind the king stand 2 noble-men, one habited *vert*, his cap checky. And behind the bishop stand 2 monks; 1st habited *argent* and *blue*, the other *gules*, cap *argent*.
9a	81	In the 4th row and 1st light is a cardinall riding on a white horse, habited *blue*, hooded *gules*, with his cross bearer before him, habited *blue*, cross *gold*. And 2 others accompanying him, habited *gules*.
9b	82	In the 2d light are severall persons on horse-back crossing the way, habited *gules* and *blue*.
9c	83	In the 3d light is a young lady abbess, habited *gules*, riding on a white horse before whom rides her cross-bearer, habited *vert* (cross *or*). And behind her stand 2 men, both capped *gules* and one habited *vert*.
9d	84	In the 4th light a monk, habited *blue*, kneeles before a reverend father, habited *argent*, standing over him with something in his hand. Also other men stand about them, one being an old man in a white cap, habited *vert*.
9e	85	In the 5th light kneeles an archbishop, habited *gules*, pallium *argent*, myter *or*. On each side [of] him stands another bishop, setting the myter on the archbishop's head; the one being habited *blue*, myter and crosyer *or*, the other habited *blue* and *vert*, myter and crosyer *or*. And behind them stands an attendant, habited *argent*, mantled *murry*.
10a	76	In the 3d row and 1st light kneels an archbishop at mass before an altar with a book open before him. And 3 monks kneeling behind him, the 1st habited *blue*, 2d *gules*, 3d *or*. Also another monk stands at the end of the altar habited *gules*.
10b	77	In the 2d light stands 9 monks about a table whereon is a banquet; two of them being habited *gules*, another *gules* and *blue*, the rest *blue*. Also a sanguine dogg sitts waiting for what may fall from it.
10c	78	In the 3d light lyes in a sanguine bed a sick lady, habited *gules*, holding her hand out for to receive the hoste (*argent*) from a monk yt stands at the bed's feet, habited *blue* and *gules*. Also 3 other women stand about the bed, habited *blue*.
10d (missing)	80 (10e)	In the 5th light lyes an archbishop sick in bed, covered *argent* and *gules*; on each side thereof sitts a woman weeping, habited *argent*.
10e	79 (10d)	In the 4th light a monk, habited *blue*, mantled *argent*, sitts upon the knee of a lady abbess, habited and mytred *argent*, to salute her. Behind him stands a young woman in a *green* habit. And behind her 2 monks, the one kneeling, habited *argent* and *blue*, the other standing, habited *argent*.
11a	71	In the 2d row and 1st light stands a Bishop habited *gules*, his crosyer and myter *or*. And several monks about him habited *gules* and *argent*.
11b	72	In the 2d light lyes a bishop, enshrined habited *gules* and *blue*, myter *argent* and *or*, about whom 4 men and 2 women kneel with hands elevated at prayer; the 1st and 2d being old men, habited *gules*, *blue* and *argent*, the other young men, 1st habited *blue* cap *vert*, 2d *sanguine* cap *blue*. The 2 women are both habited *blue*.
11c	63 (15c)	In the 3rd light stands an archbishop, habited *argent* and *argent*, pallium and myter *argent*, holding a golden cross-staff in his right and resting his other hand on the fore-head of a nun devoutly kneeling before him, habited *blue* and *argent*, vailed *argent*.
11d	74	In the 4th light are 2 white horses drawing a golden-spinnelled cart upon which sitts a man, habited *blue*. And the driver walking by it, habited *blue*, hood *murry*, with a whip in his hand *or*.

11e	75	In the 5th light is another pinacled-church *argent* and *or*. And 2 poor men sitting before the door thereof, whereof one is bare legged, habited *murry*, the other behind him habited *vert*, hood and cap *gules*.
12a	66	In the first row and 1st light are 2 monks habited *gules*, kneeling before an altar. And 3 others standing behind them, habited *blue*.
12b	67	In the 2nd light stand 2 monks bare-footed, habited *gules*. The one holding up a great stone *or*, the other stooping down to take up a broad stone that lyes at his feet. Behind the first sitts in a silver chair an old man, habited *gules* and *blue*, cap *vert*. And behind the other stands another man, with a naked sword in his hand, habited *gules*.
12c	68	In the 3rd light sitts in a white chair an old man, habited *blue*, mantled *murry*, with a blew cap on his head, tripple folded. Two monks lye at his feet, habited *gules*, the one lying upon the other with hands over his eyes. Over against them 6 monks stand upon a bridge, variously hooded and capped, viz *sanguine, blue, gules, vert* and *or*.
12d	69	In the 4th light is a monk habited *gules*, kneeling before an altar in a church *argent*, whereon stands the golden challice, covered. Also another monk stands behind him with hands conjoined at prayer, habited *sanguine*.
12e	70	In the 5th light is a church and altar *argent*, about which stand 2 monks, one habited *argent*, the other *gules*, holding a white patter [sic] in his hand. Behind the first stand 3 other men, 1st habited and capped *gules*, the 2nd *blue* and hooded *gules*, 3rd habited *vert*.
15a	61	In the lower row and first light is the picture of a fiery devill with a cloven foot, beasts tayl and horns and draggons wings, seizing a monk by the back, *blue*, as fleeing from him.
15b	73 (11c)	In 3d light is a pinacled church, *argent* and *or*, with a priest therein, habited *blue* and *gules*. And 2 monks standing one each side thereof, the one bare-headed, habited *gules* and *argent*, the other bare footed, habited *blue*, his good *murry* and *blue*.
15c	57 (16b)	In the 2nd light sitts a bishop habited *or*. And severall other standing about him variously habited, two whereof have golden keyes in their hands.
15d	64	In the 4th light is a church and altar, *argent* and *or*. Before which a nun kneels habited *blue*. Over against her stands a white monk with a book in his hand closed
15e	40 (21e)	In the 5th light is a church, pinacled *argent* and *or*, about which kneeles 2 monk[s], one habited *argent*, the other *blue*.
16a	56	In the 3rd row and 1st light is another pinacled church *argent* and *or*. And between 2 pillars of it are leaning an old man habited *gules*. And a monk with a spade in his hand, standing behind the old man, he being habited *gules*, hooded *argent*.
16b	62 (15b)	In the 1st light is another pinacled church *argent* and *or*. On the out side whereof stands a man, bare-legged, on which another man lyes his hand, habited *gules* and *argent*.
16c	58	In the 3rd light is another church, pillared and pinacled *argent* and *or*. Before which a woman kneels at prayer, habited *blue*, mantled *vert*. Behind her stand 2 old men, one being bare headed, habited *gules* and mantled *argent*. Before her leans a young man backwards, habited *gules*.
16d	59	In the 4th light is another pinacled church *argent* and *or*. Before which a monk kneeles, habited *blue*, and bends himself backwards with his fingers at his mouth.
16e	60	In the 5th light sitts a bishop, habited *blue*, mytred *argent*, holding a cross-staff in one hand and with the other taking hold on the mast of a ship *or*. Also 2 youths stand before him, habited *blue* and *or*.
17a	51	In the 1st light is a table with dishes thereon *blue* and *or*, where a monk sitts on one side and an holy man on the other, both habited *blue*.
17b	52	In the 2nd light is a curious church and altar, before which a woman kneels habited *blue*. And behind her 2 others, one whereof is habited *gules* and mantled *blue*. Also a monk stands against the woman, habited *argent*.
17c	53	In the 3rd light is another church and altar, before which kneels a priest, habited *blue* and *argent*. And behind him a nun, habited *sanguine*, hooded *vert*. Before her stand 2 other nuns, one habited *blue*, hooded *vert*, the other hooded *blue*.
17d	54	In the 4th light is St Paul's conversion, he being habited *gules* and *or*, falling backwards on a white horse, stricken to the ground by 4 rays of silver light issuing out of a cloud *blue*, hanging over them.

17e	55	In the 5th light is a ship with masts *or* and 2 monks therein, one habited *sanguine*, hooded *blue*, the other hooded *vert*. Also 3 men kneel by the ship side, the 1st habited *blue*, 2nd *vert*, 3rd headed *or*. And behind them stands a woman habited *blue*, elevating her hands at prayer.
18a	22 (24b)	In [the] 2nd light sitts a pope inthroned, robed *gules*, tripple-crowned *or*, giving a book (or charter) to two monks that submissively kneel before him; the one habited *blue*, hooded *gules*, the other hooded *blue*.
18b	47	In the 2nd light stands an old king in purple robes, and a young queen robed *blue* and *or*, both crowned and sceptred *or*. Before the king kneels 2 monks, one habited *blue*, hooded *gules*, the 2nd habited *gules*, hooded *blue*. And behind him stand 2 noble-men with coronets *or*, habited *blue*.
18c	48	In [the] 3rd light is an old king in *azure* robes fallen down to the ground. On one side stands a bishop, habited *gules*, mytred *or*, with both hands a little elevated and conjoyned. On the other hand stands a noble man in purple robes with hands elevated in the like manner.
18d	49	In the 4th light stands an archbishop by his throne *argent*, habited *blue*, pallium and myter *argent*, with a cross-staff in one hand and a book closed in the other. Before him kneels a king in *azure* robes praying to him in a form of words written upon an escrowle. Behind the king stand 3 men, one whereof is a noble man habited *vert*, furred *ermine* with a coronet *or*. The 2nd an officer habited *argent*, the 3rd habited *blue*.
18e	50	In the 5th light are a king and queen riding on white horses, he robed *gules*, she *argent* and *gules*. On his left hand rides a noble-man habited *gules*, behind the queen rides another, habit and cap *gules*.
20a	41	In the 1st light sitt 2 bishops, the one habited *gules*, the other sanguine, putting the bones of a saint into his shrine. On the other side kneel 2 monks habited *argent*.
20b	42	In the 2nd light is an Ark, *argent* and *or*, containing the Hoste, born upon the shoulders of 2 archbishops preceding, habited *gules*, palliums *argent*, mytred *argent* and *or*. And of a Cardinall (habited *or*, cap *sable*) and a monk, habited *gules*, having a string of beads about his shoulders, *or* and *argent*, who bear it up behind. Between them goes the cencer-bearer, habited *argent*, with the incence pot hanging by his side.
20c	43	In [the] 3rd light sitts an archbishop, habited *gules* and *blue*, cope *vert*, pallium and myter *argent*. And 2 other ~~monks~~ bishops sitt on besides him, habited *argent*, one of them having a book upon his knee, lying open.
20d	44	In the 4th light a monk, habited *gules*, sitts leaning forwards in a chair, *or*, with 5 golden rays issuing out of a cloud at his back. Before him stand 3 monks, the 1st habited *vert*, 2nd *argent*, 3rd *sanguine*.
20e	45	In the 5th light stands a woman, habited *argent* and *vert*, between 2 monks, habited *blue*.
21a	36	In the first light an old man sitting in a white habit, extending his hand to a woman, habited *gules*, holding a golden rod in her hand. And behind her stands another woman, habited *blue*.
21b	37	In the 2nd light is a curious church and altar, with an old monk kneeling at prayer before them, habited *blue*, hooded *vert*. Over whose head hangs upon a cross beam a woman's head, *argent*, with a legg, foot and heart, *or*.
21c	38	In [the] 3rd light is an Ark with the host therein, born on 4 men's shoulders, all kneeling. Two whereof on the fore side are bishops, coped *argent* and *or*. The other two on the far side being monks, habited *vert*. Under the Ark appears the host, *or*, elevated between 2 men's hands, nearly touching it with their fingers. Behind the two monks sitts a venerable old man, habited *blue* and *gules*, with right hand hanging down and left elevated. At his feet lyes a woman prostrate at prayer, habited *B*.
21d	39	In [the] 4th light is another Ark with the hoste in it, *argent* and *or*, born upon the shoulders of 4 monks, 2 habited *blue* and 2 *vert*. Between them kneels a woman, habited *blue*, with hands expanded. And behind them stands another monk, habited *vert* and *argent*, holding a book open in his hand.
21e	65 (15e)	In the 5th light is another pinacled church, *argent* and *or*. Before which is a pavement, checky *argent* and *sable*, on which lyes a monk, habited *vert*, extending one of [his] hands thereunto. Over against him stands another monk, bare-legged, habited *vert*, with hands conjoyned and elevated at prayer.
22a	32 (22b)	In the 2nd light sitts an old man on the ground, habited *argent*, leaning upon a long box, *or*, with a pitcher of one ear at his head and a well at his feet.
22b	31 (22a)	In the first light an old man, habited argent, kneeling before a church and altar. Over whose head a man's legg, couped, *argent*, hangs upon a cross beam.
22c	33	In the 3rd light is a man, habited *gules*, climbing upon a golden ladder reared against a great white pillar.
22d	34	In the 4th light is a man, habited *gules*, falling prostrate from a golden ladder reared against the far side of an altar, *paly* of 8 pieces *argent* and *vert*.
22e	35	In the 5th light are 4 monks carrying the Ark and hoste therein upon their shoulders. Those two on the farr side being habited *vert*. Also a man, habited *argent*, goes before them, bearing a box on his head.

23a	26	And in the first light is another church, *argent* and *or*, before which stands a monk habited *gules*, with another old man leaning his head towards him. Over against them a young man, habited *gules*, leans between two pillars of the said church.
23b	27	In the 2nd light is another church, curiously wrought *argent* and *or*, before which stands a nun, habited *blue*, hooded *sanguine*. And over against her, and behind a corner of the said church, kneels another of like habit.
23c	28	In [the] 3rd light is another church with a nun kneeling at her devotions, before the altar therein, habited *gules* and vayled *argent*.
23d	29	In the 4th light is another church, *argent* and *or*, with 2 nuns kneeling before it, one habited *blue*, the other *gules*. Also 2 other nuns standing over them, the one habited *sanguine*, vayled *blue*, the other vayled *blue* and *vert*.
23e	30	In the 5th light is another church, *argent* and *or*, before which kneels a woman, habited *blue*, hooded *gules*, and also 2 men, both habited *gules*.
24a	21	In the first light is the picture of a church and an altar with a bare-bellyed woman, habited *gules*, standing before them.
24b	46 (18a)	In the 1st row and the 1st light is a church curiously pinnacled, *argent* and *or*, with a checky pavement before it, checky *argent* and *sable*, upon which kneels a bishop, habited *blue*. Before him stands a grave man with hands conjoyned at prayer, habited *gules*. On the other side kneels a monk, habited *blue*, hooded *murry*, with hands a little elevated and conjoyned.
24c	23	In the 3rd light is another church and altar, *argent* and *or*, with a checky pavement before it, upon which kneels a nun habited *gules*, vayled *argent*, holding out a golden coronet (or wreath) to an old man who kneles over against her, with hands conjoyned at prayer. He being habited *gules* and *blue*.
24d	24	In [the] 4th light a man, habited blue, leans backwards upon a white horse, with hands spread and respecting a woman, habited *gules*, lying under the horse, as thrown from him.
24e	25	In the 5th light is another church, *argent* and *or*, before which kneels a lady at prayer, habited *gules*, and over whom stand two monks, one habited *vert*, the other blue with a high cap on his head *gules*.
A1	11	An archbishop, habited *blue* and *sanguine*, pallium *argent*, myter and cross-staff *or*.
A2	12	A king, robed *gules*, mantle *argent*, crown and scepter *or*.
A3	13	An archbishop, habited blue, pallium *argent*, myter and cross *or*.
A4	14	A king, robed *gules*, mantle *argent*, scepter and crown *or*.
A7	17	An archbishop, habited blue, pallium and myter *argent*, cross-staff *or*.
A8	18	A king, robed *gules*, mantle *ermine*, crown and scepter *or*.
A9	19	An archbishop, habited *gules*, pallium *argent*, cross-staff and myter *or*.
A10	20	A king, robed *gules* and *argent*, mantle *vert*, crown and scepter *or*.
B1	15	An archbishop, habited blue, pallium and myter *argent*, cross-staff *or*.
B2	16	A king, robed *blue* and *murry*, mantle *argent*, crown and scepter *or*.
C2	5	One is an archbishop, robed *blue*, pallium *argent*, myter and cross-staff *or*.
C3	6	A king, robed *gules*, mantle *ermine*, scepter and crown *or*.
C6	9	An archbishop habited *blue*, pallium and cross-staff *argent*, myter *or*.
C7	10	A king, robed *vert*, crowned *argent*, sceptred *or*.
D1	7	An archbishop, habited *blue*, pallium and myter *argent*, cross-staff *or*.
D2	8	A king, robed *sanguine*, mantle *ermine*, crowned *or*.
H1, H4	1, 2 [error, should be 4]	On each side [of] them [*viz.* H2–H3] kneels a man in a white rayment with a golden bird upon their heads.
H2	2	In the middle sitt enthroned: a queen, robed *blue*, crowned *or*, holding her hand[s] cross[ed] upon her breast and a little elevated.
H3	3	Also a king by her, robed *argent*, *or* and *gules*. Globe and crown *or*.

Appendix Two

Table of Latin Sources

Most of the narrative panels in the window relate to surviving York sources about St William. The table that follows lists the Latin texts that are relevant to each scene in the window, panel by panel.

The various texts overlap to some extent, and some of them exist in more than one version. The relationship between the different texts and the different versions has yet to be fully elucidated, but their connection to the panels in the window is generally clear. The texts were mostly printed in the late nineteenth century and translations of some extracts have been published, but full English translations are still awaited. The texts are as follows.

The *Vita Sancti Willelmi* or *Life of St William* (hereafter cited as the *Life*) is the single-most important source for the window. Written probably in the 1220s, around the time of William's papal canonisation (see Norton 2006, 180–201), the complete text survives in a single manuscript, which belonged to Thornton Abbey in Lincolnshire (Fig. 7.2) and was published by Raine 1879–94, II, 270–91. The text was obviously available at York in the Middle Ages, and extensive verbatim extracts or summaries were included in the York *Breviary* as readings for the Feast of St William on 8 June and its octave and for the weekly Commemoration of St William. These readings would have been very familiar to the York clergy. The *Breviary* is cited in the table from the two-volume edition by Lawley 1880–83. This was based on the version of the *Breviary* printed in Venice in 1493, though it may be noted that the extracts from the *Life* vary somewhat in different manuscripts of the *Breviary* (Figs. 3.23 and 7.3). The window includes scenes derived from passages in the *Life* that were not incorporated into the *Breviary*, so the full text of the *Life* must have been at hand when the window was designed.

The *Chronicle* of John of Hexham is one of the most important, near-contemporary chronicles for the reign of King Stephen. It is the best source for events at York and the dispute over the archbishopric between 1140 and 1153, and it is the principal source for the relevant section of the window. At York, a special abbreviated version of the *Chronicle* was produced that consists solely of extracts relating to York, copied in chronological order with minimal alterations and additions. In the fourteenth century, this *York Abbreviated Chronicle* of John of Hexham was incorporated into the Minster's *Registrum Magnum Album*, where it forms a continuation of Hugh the Chanter's *History of the Church of York*, which stops in 1127 (Fig. 7.4). The *York Abbreviated Chronicle* was presumably the version of John of Hexham consulted by John Thornton and his advisors. It was printed by Raine 1879–94, II, 220–27 and is cited in the table as *YAC*.

As well as existing as a separate text, the *York Abbreviated Chronicle* of John of Hexham was also used to make an extended version of the Minster's *Chronicle of the Archbishops*. This *Chronicle* is a composite text, which recounts the history of York's bishops and archbishops from Paulinus onwards. The section from 1140 to the later fourteenth century is attributed to the Dominican friar Thomas Stubbs, who obviously drew on earlier material. After the death of Archbishop Thurstan, the twenty-eighth archbishop, in 1140, the Stubbs *Chronicle* moves on to Henry Murdac, who is listed as the twenty-ninth archbishop. William's election, first archiepiscopate and deposition are covered in the entry on Henry Murdac. William then has his own entry as the thirtieth archbishop in 1153–4. The section on Henry Murdac, unusually, exists in two versions. The shorter version covers William's first archiepiscopate in a couple of paragraphs before a brief summary of Murdac's tenure of office. The wording about William echoes passages in the *Life* and gives an extremely abbreviated account of the election dispute. The second, much longer version combines the text of the shorter version with the text of the *York Abbreviated Chronicle* of John of Hexham. These two texts were copied almost verbatim and were integrated into a single, extended narrative with minimal alterations and adjustments. Thornton and his advisors would probably have had access to both those versions of the Stubbs *Chronicle*. At one point they demonstrably used the original version of the *York Abbreviated Chronicle* of John of Hexham, rather than the version incorporated into the longer version of the Stubbs *Chronicle*. Panel 7c, which shows the deaths of Pope Eugenius, Saint Bernard and Archbishop Murdac, is based on the *York Abbreviated Chronicle* of John of Hexham, which mentions the deaths of all three; whereas the longer version of the Stubbs *Chronicle* (and the *Life* likewise) mentions the deaths of the pope and the archbishop, but does not mention Bernard. But there is no doubt that Thornton and his advisors did consult the Stubbs *Chronicle*. Henry Murdac teaching his flock in panel 5e is based on a passage in the Stubbs *Chronicle*, and the entry on William in the Stubbs *Chronicle*, although largely covering the same ground (rather more succinctly) as the *Life*, also contains the episode of William's meeting with Roger of Pont l'Evêque at Canterbury in panel 8d, which is found nowhere else.

The two versions of the Stubbs *Chronicle* are printed in Raine, 1879–94, II, 388–97. In the table overleaf, the shorter version of the entry on Henry Murdac is cited as Stubbs (S), the longer version as Stubbs (L). The entry on William, for which there is only one version, is cited simply as Stubbs.

The *York Abbreviated Chronicle* of John of Hexham concludes with the death of Archbishop Henry Murdac in October 1153. The Stubbs *Chronicle* takes the story as far as William's death and burial in June 1154. Moving on to the posthumous scenes, most of the panels in rows 11–17 are based on miracle stories in the early-thirteenth-century *Life*. Many of these were incorporated into readings in the *Breviary*, often in abbreviated form, but some of the miracles in the *Life* do not appear in the *Breviary*, including the story of Ralph and Besing in row 12. Other sources were also available. A text known as the *Miracula* (miracles) is preserved in a seventeenth-century transcription from a now-lost wooden table, which was preserved in the Minster. This was probably similar in form and in date to the surviving fourteenth-century wooden tables known as the Tables of the Vicars Choral. The text, which was known to John Browne and Dr James Fowler, was published by Raine 1879–94, II, 531–43 and is discussed by Norton 2006, 150–80. It is a composite text. The main component is a list of thirty-three miracles recorded at the tomb in 1177. The accounts are mostly quite brief, and often include the name and/or place of origin of the individuals concerned. The text must have been written not long after, and a number of the miracles were incorporated into the early-thirteenth-century *Life*, which omits the personal details but generally develops the stories at greater length. The window includes a number of these early miracles recorded both in the *Life* and the *Miracula*. The *Miracula* also contains versions of the miracle at Ouse Bridge (panel 9c) and the Ralph and Besing story (panels 12a–12e). Although the *Miracula* has often been cited as a source for some of the early miracle stories in the window, all of them are also recounted (at greater length) in the *Life*, with the possible exception of the miracle in panel 17c. The *Miracula* also records other miracle stories of the late twelfth or early thirteenth century, which are not included in the *Life*, and three from the early fourteenth century, but none of these were used for the window. There is therefore some doubt as to whether the *Miracula* was a source for the window, even though the text was certainly available at the time.

However this may be, the existence of more than one version of some of the stories is a reminder that Thornton was probably able to draw on different versions of the stories when designing the window. There may have been other texts that have not survived, as well as oral traditions. Two of the miracles (panels 16d and 16e), which are not otherwise attested, seem to be alluded to in some liturgical verses cited by Fowler 1874, 279–80, and the distinctive scenes in panels 15a and 17d must derive from specific (but now lost) sources.

Rows 18 and 20 are based on a set of readings in the *Breviary* relating to the Translation of William's relics in 1284. The text in the edition by Lawley 1880–83, I, 180–85 is based on the edition of the York *Breviary* printed in Venice in 1493, which was also printed by Raine 1879–94, II, 547–50. Both editions are cited in the table. As is the case with the *Breviary* readings taken from the *Life* discussed above, the readings for the Feast of the Translation (8 January) differ in different manuscripts. Raine 1879–94, II, 544–46 printed another version from a manuscript that omits the scenes in panels 18c–18e, but includes some text that is not in the 1493 printed edition. This version is not cited in the table. A third version was printed in 1698 in the *Acta Sanctorum* for June (*Acta Sanctorum, Junii II*, 143–46, partly translated in Fowler 1874). This is a much longer version, though it lacks the opening sentences. It incorporates the material from the two previous versions just mentioned, but at much greater length. In addition, the *Acta Sanctorum* version includes accounts of four miracles that took place in the years immediately after the Translation. These are the basis for the scenes in panels 21a–21b and 21e. The *Acta Sanctorum* references are included in the table. These various *Breviary* readings evidently derive from an independent text describing the events connected with the Translation, which from internal evidence must have been written not long after the event. This text does not survive as such, but could be reconstructed more or less exactly by collating the various readings in the different versions of the *Breviary*, the *Acta Sanctorum* version being very close to the original.

There are no surviving written sources for panels 21c–21d and 22a–22e, except insofar as the Roger of Ripon stone (Fig. 7.5) relates to the incident in 22c–22e. Six of the panels in rows 23 and 24 are made up of elements taken from earlier miracle scenes, as described in the Catalogue, and therefore do not derive from specific texts, but panels 23c and 24c are new designs. Panels 24d and 24e were probably based on personal testimony if it is correct to identify the lady in the story as Beatrice de Roos, the principal donor of the window, as suggested in Chapter 4.

References

Acta Sanctorum, *21 (Junii II)*, (Antwerp 1698)

Breviarium ad Usum Insignis Ecclesie Eboracensis, 2 vols, ed. Mr Lawley, Surtees Society 71 and 75 (Durham 1880 and 1883)

Historians of the Church of York and its Archbishops, ed. James Raine, 3 vols, Rolls Series, 71 (London, 1879–94).

Fowler, James, 'On a Window Representing the Life and Miracles of St William of York at the North End of the Eastern Transept, York Minster', *Yorkshire Archaeological and Topographical Journal* III (1874), 198–348.

Norton, Christopher, *St William of York* (Woodbridge: York Medieval Press 2006)

Panel no.	Description	Latin Sources
1a	First donor panel	
1b	Second donor panel	
1c	Third donor panel	
1d	Fourth donor panel	
1e	Fifth donor panel	
2a	The marriage of William's parents	*Life*, 270; *Breviary*, II, 298 and 305; Stubbs (S) and (L), 389–90
2b	William's baptism	
2c	William's education	*Life*, 270–71; *Breviary*, II, 298 and 305
2d	[Replacement panel for William as treasurer of York Minster]	*Life*, 271; *Breviary*, II, 298 and 305
2e	The death of Archbishop Thurstan	*Life*, 271; *Breviary*, II, 298; Stubbs (S) and (L), 388–9; John of Hexham, *YAC*, 220–21
3a	The canons elect William as the next archbishop	*Life*, 271; *Breviary*, II, 298; Stubbs (S) and (L), 389; John of Hexham, *YAC*, 221
3b	William takes the oath of office	
3c	William's enemies conspire against him	*Life*, 271; *Breviary*, II, 298–9; Stubbs (S) and (L), 389–91; John of Hexham, *YAC*, 221
3d	William and his enemies petition the pope	*Life*, 271; *Breviary*, II, 299; Stubbs (S) and (L), 389–91; John of Hexham, *YAC*, 221–2
3e	The pope gives his judgement	John of Hexham, *YAC*, 221–2; Stubbs (L), 389–90
4a	The pope's letter is delivered to the dean of York	John of Hexham, *YAC*, 222; Stubbs (L), 390
4b	William prays before his consecration at Winchester	
4c	William is consecrated archbishop	John of Hexham, *YAC*, 222; Stubbs (L), 391
4d	The pope sends the pallium to William	John of Hexham, *YAC*, 223; Stubbs (L), 391
4e	Cardinal Hincmar carries the pallium to England	John of Hexham, *YAC*, 223; Stubbs (L), 391
5a–6a	The death of Pope Lucius	John of Hexham, *YAC*, 223; Stubbs (L), 391
5b–6b	The consecration of Pope Eugenius	John of Hexham, *YAC*, 223; Stubbs (L), 391
5c–6c	The Cistercians appeal to Pope Eugenius against William	John of Hexham, *YAC*, 223; Stubbs (L), 392
5d–6d	Pope Eugenius deposes William	John of Hexham, *YAC*, 224; Stubbs (L), 392–3; *Life*, 272
5e–6e	The new archbishop, Henry Murdac, teaches his flock	Stubbs (S) and (L), 393–4
7a	William retires to Winchester	*Life*, 272; *Breviary*, II, 300; John of Hexham, *YAC*, 224; Stubbs (L), 393
7b	William withdraws from the world	*Life*, 272–3; *Breviary*, II, 300
7c	The death of William's opponents	John of Hexham, *YAC*, 226–7
7d	The Holy Spirit reveals the news to William	*Life*, 274; *Breviary*, II, 300
7e	William is given spurs by Henry of Blois	*Life*, 274; *Breviary*, II, 300
8a	William travels to Rome again	*Life*, 274; *Breviary*, II, 301; Stubbs, 396
8b	William receives the pallium from the pope	Stubbs, 396; *Life*, 274; *Breviary*, II, 301
8c	William sails back to England	Stubbs, 396; *Life*, 274; *Breviary*, II, 301
8d	William meets Roger of Pont L'Evêque at Canterbury	Stubbs, 396
8e	William is greeted by King Stephen	
9a	William travels round his diocese	*Life*, 275; *Breviary*, II, 301
9b	William is greeted at the gates of York by the leading citizens	*Life*, 275; Stubbs, 396

9c	The miracle of Ouse Bridge	*Life*, 275–6; *Breviary*, II, 302; Stubbs, 396–7; *Miracula*, 539, no. 38
9d	William is greeted at the entrance to the Minster by the clergy	*Life*, 276
9e	William is enthroned in the Minster	
10a	William celebrates mass in the Minster on Trinity Sunday	*Life*, 277; *Breviary*, II, 302; Stubbs, 397
10b	William welcomes his guests to a feast	*Life*, 277; Stubbs, 397
10c	William takes to his bed and prophesies his death	*Life*, 277; *Breviary*, II, 303; Stubbs, 397
10d	[Replacement panel for William during his final illness]	*Life*, 277–8; *Breviary*, II, 303; Stubbs, 397
10e	William's death	*Life*, 278; *Breviary*, II, 303; Stubbs, 397
11a	William's burial	*Life* 278; *Breviary*, II, 303; Stubbs, 397
11b	William's body unharmed during a fire in the Minster	*Life*, 279–80; *Breviary*, I, 693–5
11c	The healing of a blind girl	*Life*, 281; *Breviary*, I, 695; *Miracula*, 531, no. 1
11d	A hydropsical woman is brought to the Minster	*Life*, 282–3, *Breviary*, I, 696–7
11e	The hydropsical woman is cured at the tomb	*Life*, 282–3, *Breviary*, I, 696–7
12a–13a	Ralph and Besing appear before a judge	*Life*, 289–90; *Miracula*, 539, no. 37
12b–13b	Ralph and Besing fight	*Life* 289–90; *Miracula*, 539, no. 37
12c–13c	Ralph is blinded by Besing	*Life*, 289–90; *Miracula*, 539, no. 37
12d–13d	Ralph prays at St William's tomb	*Life*, 289–90; *Miracula*, 539, no. 37
12e–13e	Ralph is given new eyes	*Life*, 289–90; *Miracula*, 539, no. 37
14a–14e	Plain glass	
15a	A man attacked by a devil	
15b	Disabled men collect holy oil seeping from the tomb	?*Life*, 278; ?*Breviary*, I, 180; ?Stubbs, 397
15c	A boy drowned in a well is revived by St William	*Life*, 290–91; *Breviary*, II, 313
15d	A woman with leprosy comes to the tomb to be healed	*Life*, 287–8; *Breviary*, II, 314–5
15e	Eight one-eyed men at the tomb	*Life*, 283; *Breviary*, II, 313
16a	Five disabled men come to the tomb to be healed	*Life*, 287; *Breviary*, II, 314; ?*Miracula*, 532, no. 3
16b	A paralysed man is brought to the tomb	*Life*, 288; *Breviary*, II, 314
16c	A boy with a deformed hand is cured at the tomb	*Life*, 286
16d	A hydropsical man at the tomb	Latin verses in Fowler 1874, 279
16e	St William saves a ship with a broken mast	Latin verses in Fowler 1874, 280
17a	A woman who swallowed a frog	*Life*, 284; *Breviary*, II, 215; *Miracula*, 535, no. 21
17b	The woman is cured at the tomb	*Life*, 284; *Breviary*, II, 215; *Miracula*, 535, no. 21
17c	A boy is cured at the tomb	?*Miracula*, 533, no. 12
17d	A man is thrown from his horse into a river	
17e	A child is saved from drowning in a river	*Life*, 291
18a–19a	William is canonised by the pope	*Breviary*, I, 180 = Raine 547; *Acta Sanctorum*, II, 143
18b–19b	King Edward I and Queen Eleanor of Castile are invited to the Translation of William's relics	*Breviary*, I, 181 = Raine, 548; *Acta Sanctorum*, II, 143
18c–19c	King Edward falls from a mountain in Wales	*Breviary*, I, 181 = Raine, 548; *Acta Sanctorum*, II,143
18d–19d	King Edward gives thanks to St William for his deliverance	*Breviary*, I, 181–2 = Raine, 548; *Acta Sanctorum*, II, 143
18e–19e	King Edward and Queen Eleanor ride to York	*Breviary*, I, 182 = Raine, 548; *Acta Sanctorum*, II,143
20a	St William's tomb is opened	*Breviary*, I, 182–3 = Raine, 548-9; *Acta Sanctorum*, II, 144

20b	The relics of St William are carried in procession	*Breviary*, I, 183–4 = Raine, 549–50; *Acta Sanctorum*, II, 144
20c	Archbishop Wickwane and six bishops	*Breviary*, I, 184 = Raine, 549; *Acta Sanctorum*, II,144
20d	A servant is hit on the head by a stone	*Breviary*, I, 183–4 = Raine, 549; *Acta Sanctorum*, II, 144
20e	The servant escapes unharmed	*Breviary*, I, 184 = Raine, 549; *Acta Sanctorum*, II, 144
21a	A man with a bandaged leg	*Acta Sanctorum*, II, 145
21b	The man offers a model of his leg at the tomb	*Acta Sanctorum*, II, 145
21c	A woman falls into the river from Ouse Bridge	
21d	The woman is saved and gives thanks	
21e	A disabled man is healed at the portable reliquary	*Acta Sanctorum*, II, 145
22a	An imprisoned man seeks to be released	
22b	The freed prisoner offers his chains at the tomb	
22c	A man up a ladder hangs decorative textiles in a church	
22d	The man is hit on the head by a falling stone	
22e	Carrying the stone, the man leads the portable reliquary in procession	
23a	Three men at the tomb	
23b	Three disabled men at the tomb	
23c	A woman kneels at the tomb	
23d	A group of people at the tomb	
23e	A leprous woman at the tomb	
24a–25a	A hydropsical woman at the tomb	
24b–25b	Three supplicants at the tomb	
24c–25c	A disabled woman is healed at the tomb	
24d–25d	A lady is trampled by a horse	
24e–25e	The lady gives thanks at the tomb for her deliverance	

Appendix Three

Concordance of Panel Numbers

Current Position	Previous Position
1a	1a
1b	1b
1c	1d
1d	1c
1e	1e
2a	7a
2b	2d
2c	2c
2d	2e
2e	10d
3a	3b
3b	4a
3c	2b
3d	3a
3e	4b
4a	2a
4b	3d
4c	3e
4d	4d
4e	4e
5a	4c
5b	5c
5c	5b
5d	5a
5e	5d

Current Position	Previous Position
6a	6b
6b	6a
6c	6e
6d	6c
6e	6d
7a	5e
7b	7d
7c	8a
7d	7c
7e	7e
8a	8b
8b	8c
8c	8d
8d	8e
8e	7b
9a	9a
9b	9b
9c	9c
9d	9d
9e	9e
10a	10b
10b	10a
10c	21d
10d	18a
10e	10c

Current Position	Previous Position
11a	11a
11b	10e
11c	15b
11d	11d
11e	11e
12a	12b
12b	12c
12c	12d
12d	12e
12e	12a
13a	13a
13b	13c
13c	13b
13d	13e
13e	13d
14a	Blank
14b	Blank
14c	Blank
14d	Blank
14e	Blank
15a	15a
15b	16a
15c	11b
15d	17e
15e	15e

Current Position	Previous Position
16a	15c
16b	17a
16c	21e
16d	15d
16e	11c
17a	16d
17b	16e
17c	16b
17d	16c
17e	21a
18a	3c
18b	18b
18c	18c
18d	18d
18e	18e
19a	19a
19b	19b
19c	19c
19d	19d
19e	19e
20a	20b
20b	20e
20c	20a
20d	20c
20e	20d

Current Position	Previous Position
21a	22a
21b	22b
21c	22c
21d	22d
21e	21c
22a	24d
22b	24e
22c	23b
22d	23c
22e	23d
23a	23a
23b	17d
23c	17c
23d	21b
23e	22e
24a	23e
24b	17b
24c	24a
24d	24b
24e	24c
25a	25b
25b	25a
25c	25c
25d	25d
25e	25e

In the table above, the left-hand column gives the current numbers of the panels in the main lights, as used in this book (Fig. 1.6). These are also the original positions of the panels in Thornton's window.

The right-hand column gives the position of the panels prior to the recent restoration. These are the same as the panel numbers in Tom French's 1999 CVMA monograph. Figure 6.20 shows the locations of the main light panels prior to the recent restoration, with those not in their original position highlighted in green.

Index

Principal coverage of a topic is entered in **bold**. For ease of reading Panel numbers and Row numbers are **also** entered in **bold**. Illustrations are entered in *italics*.

Further Reading

Benson, George
'The ancient painted glass windows in the Minster and city of York', *Annual Report of the Yorkshire Philosophical Society*, Leeds 1914

Boertjes, Katya
'Pilgrimage ampullae of York Minster and the healing oil from the shrine of St William' in S. Blick (ed.), *Beyond Pilgrim Souvenirs and Secular Badges – Essays in Honour of Brian Spencer*, Oxford: Oxbow 2007, 48–63

Brown, Sarah
'Our Magnificent Fabrick': An Architectural History of York Minster c.1220–1500, Swindon: English Heritage 2003

Apocalypse: The Great East Window of York Minster, London: Third Millennium 2014

The Great East Window, An English Masterpiece, London: Third Millennium, 2018

'Looking for John Thornton: The Great East Window of York Minster Revisited', in Sarah Brown, Sarah Rees Jones and Tim Ayers (eds), *York: Art, Architecture and Archaeology*, British Archaeological Association Conference Transactions XLII, Abingdon and New York: Routledge 2022, 133–56

'Beatrice de Roos (d.1415) and the Making of Art', *Journal of the British Archaeological Association* 176:1 (2023), 216–48

Browne, John
A Description of the Representations and Arms on the Glass in the Windows of York Minster, also the Arms on the Stone, Leeds 1915

Corpus Vitrearum International Guidelines for the Conservation and Restoration of Stained Glass (Corpus Vitrearum: Nuremberg 2004). Online at: https://cvi.cvma-freiburg.de/documents/CVConservationGuidelines.pdf

Drake, Francis
Eboracum, or the History and Antiquities of the City of York, York 1736

Fowler, James
'On a Window Representing the Life and Miracles of St William of York at the North End of the Eastern Transept, York Minster', *Yorkshire Archaeological and Topographical Journal* III (1874), 198–348

French, Thomas
'The Glazing of the St William Window in York Minster', *Journal of the British Archaeological Association* CXL (1987), 175–81

York Minster: The St William Window, Corpus Vitrearum Medii Aevi (Great Britain) Summary Catalogue V, Oxford: Oxford University Press, 1999

French, Tom and Winton, Penny
'St William Window: History and Conservation', *Friends of York Minster Annual Report* 71 (2000), 16–26

Gent, Thomas
The Ancient and Modern History of the Famous City of York, York, 1730

Harrison, Frederick
The Painted Glass of York, London: SPCK, 1927

Harrison, Stuart
'The shrines of St William of York reconstructed', Sarah Brown, Sarah Rees Jones and Tim Ayers (eds), *York: Art, Architecture and Archaeology*, British Archaeological Association Conference Transactions XLII, Abingdon and New York: Routledge 2021), 1–25

Harrison, Stuart and Norton, Christopher
York Minster: An Illustrated Architectural History 627–c.1500, York: The Chapter of York, 2015

Haselock, Jeremy and O'Connor, David
'The Stained and Painted Glass', G. E. Aylmer and R. Cant (eds), *A History of York Minster*, Oxford: Clarendon Press, 1977, 313–394

Knowles, J. <insert space>A.
'Additional Notes on the St William Window in York Minster', *Proceedings of the Yorkshire Architectural and the York Archaeological Society* I:2 (1934), 5–55

'Technical Notes on the St William Window', *Yorkshire Archaeological Journal* XXXVII (1951), 148–61

Milner-White, Eric
'The Return of the Windows: The Choir North Aisle, St William's Window', *Friends of York Minster Annual Report* 27 (1955), 25–29

Nilson, Ben
'A Reinterpretation of the St William Window in York Minster', *Yorkshire Archaeological Journal*, 68 (1996), 157–179

Norton, Christopher
'Sacred Space and Sacred History, the glazing of the eastern arm of York Minster' in R. Becksmann, (ed.), *Glasmalerei im Kontext-Bildprogramme und Raum Funktionen*, Nuremberg: Germanisches Nationalmuseum 2005, 167–81

St William of York, Woodbridge: York Medieval Press 2006

'The Saint William Window', *Friends of York Minster Annual Report* 77 (2006) 62–68

'Richard Scrope and York Minster', in P. J. P. Goldberg (ed.), *Richard Scrope, Archbishop, Rebel, Martyr*, Donington: Shaun Tyas 2007, 138–213

Raine, James (ed.)
Historians of the Church of York and its Archbishops, London: Rolls Series, 71.2 (1886), 270–91. 388–97, 531–43

Smith, Janice
'The St William Window: The Problem of Authorship', *The Journal of Stained Glass* XXIII (1999), 5–15.

'The St William Window, York Minster: Historiography and Restoration Histories', unpublished MPhil Thesis, University of York, 2002

Willmot, G. F.
'A Discovery at York', *Museums Journal* 57.2 (1957), 2pp.

Wilson, Christopher
The Shrines of St William of York, York: Yorkshire Museum 1977